PIMLICO

305

THE LONG AFFAIR

Scholar, statesman and writer, Conor Cruise O'Brien was born in Dublin in 1917 and graduated from Trinity College Dublin. He served as a senior member of the Irish Delegation to the United Nations from 1956 to 1960. In that capacity he attracted the attention of Secretary-General Dag Hammarskjöld, who appointed him as his Personal Representative in the breakaway Congo (now Zaire) Province of Katanga, then a major centre of international controversy. At the end of 1961 – after a short outbreak of military conflict and after the Katanga-related death of Dag Hammarskjöld – O'Brien resigned from UN service, and from the Irish Foreign Service, to regain his freedom of expression, which he applied to accusing the then Governments of Britain and France of having sabotaged the implementation of Security Council Resolutions for which they had voted. In the ensuing international controversy, O'Brien was supported by most Third World Governments, led by the Prime Minister of India, Jawaharlal Nehru.

O'Brien served as Vice-Chancellor of the University of Ghana and as Albert Schweitzer Professor of Humanities at New York University. In 1969, at the request of the Irish Labour Party, he returned to Ireland and was elected to the Dail in the Labour interest. In 1973 he became Minister for Communications in an Irish Coalition Government. In 1978, after the fall of the Government, he became Editor-in-chief of the *Observer* in London. He researched *The Long Affair* while Senior Research Fellow at the National Humanities Center, North Carolina in 1994 and 1995.

The most recent of Conor Cruise O'Brien's books are: *The Siege: The Story of Israel and Zionism* (1988); *The Great Melody: A Thematic Biography of Edmund Burke* (1992); *Ancestral Voices: Religion and Nationalism in Ireland* (1994); and *On the Eve of the Millennium* (1995). He also writes for leading newspapers and periodicals in Ireland, Britain and the United States.

THE LONG AFFAIR

Thomas Jefferson and the
French Revolution, 1785–1800

CONOR CRUISE O'BRIEN

PIMLICO

Published by Pimlico 1998

2 4 6 8 10 9 7 5 3 1

First published by Sinclair-Stevenson 1996
Pimlico edition 1998

Pimlico
Random House, 20 Vauxhall Bridge Road,
London SW1V 2SA

Random House Australia (Pty) Limited
20 Alfred Street, Milsons Point, Sydney,
New South Wales 2061, Australia

Random House New Zealand Limited
18 Poland Road, Glenfield,
Auckland 10, New Zealand

Random House South Africa (Pty) Limited
Endulini, 5A Jubilee Road, Parktown 2193, South Africa

Random House UK Limited Reg. No. 954009

A CIP catalogue record for this book
is available from the British Library

ISBN 0-7126-6683-4

Papers used by Random House UK Limited are natural,
recyclable products made from wood grown in sustainable forests.
The manufacturing processes conform to the environmental
regulations of the country of origin

Printed and bound in Great Britain by
Creative Print and Design (Wales), Ebbw Vale

CONTENTS

ILLUSTRATIONS

WHY THIS BOOK
IS SO LONG

Some who have read the manuscript think this book is too long. I don't agree, but the objection needs to be met, and that is the purpose of the present Foreword.

The basic reason why the book is so long is that I have consistently preferred direct quotation—even at length—to paraphrase and summary. The most important instance of this concerns Jefferson's own writings. Jefferson's biographers habitually paraphrase these, referring their readers to the appropriate places in Jefferson's published papers: references which few readers are likely to follow up.

I have found that the paraphrases, when compared with the originals, have a general tendency to distort. In each individual instance the distortion is usually slight, but the cumulative distortion—most conspicuous in the six volumes of Dumas Malone's biography—is great. It works by starting from a fixed perspective on Jefferson's character, and unconsciously inflecting the paraphrase to make it more compatible with the fixed view than the original is. The fixed view is derived from Jefferson's self-portrayals: as (among other things) an unusually, almost morbidly, sensitive person, shrinking from the hurly-burly of politics and especially from controversy. Paraphrase carried out in the fixed perspective tends to play down, and sometimes even simply edits out, material tending to suggest that there may be something wrong with the perspective.

In general, Jeffersonian paraphrase tends to distort, by blurring and softening the image of its hero. But the distortion is particularly marked in the area of my own primary concern: Jefferson and the French Revolution. Fixed-perspective Jeffersonians are in real trouble here, with that almost-morbidly-sensitive-hurly-burly-shrinking hero of theirs. Such a

Proustian character would have abhorred the excesses of the French Revolution, would he not? No doubt he would. But Thomas Jefferson did not. He approved of revolutionary violence in principle (*The Long Affair*, hereafter referred to as *TLA*, pp. 41–42). He admired the destructive determination of the French Revolutionaries (p. 60) and (as the Revolution entered its most sanguinary phase) he allowed for the existence of no such thing as French Revolutionary excesses. The French Revolutionaries could kill as many people as they chose to kill, whatever way they wanted, and it would be all to the good, since all was being done in the sacred cause of Liberty. Here in this Foreword, I am myself paraphrasing but the reader will find the original letter I am referring to reproduced in full on pages 145–47.

It is here, in the effort to muffle Jefferson's almost manic enthusiasm for the French Revolution (in 1792–93) that the fixed perspective begins to flicker. Even paraphrase can no longer serve. Omission is resorted to. The letter I have just referred to—the letter to William Short, of 3 January 1793—is the most important and revealing letter that is preserved from the period of Jefferson's maximum enthusiasm for the French Revolution (late 1789 to late 1793). But this apology for genocide is so grotesquely at variance with the morbidly sensitive Jefferson of the fixed perspective that Dumas Malone cannot afford to handle it at all, even with the sanitizing gloves of paraphrase. Having referred, nine pages earlier, to Jefferson's "personal distaste for disorder and violence" Malone has to glide quickly over the bloodthirsty effusion of 3 January 1793, and he does so with the following sentence: "This private letter contains as fervid comments as Jefferson ever made on the French Revolution and it has been widely quoted by later writers for just that reason" (references supplied in note 48 to chapter 4 of *TLA*). Malone refrains from quoting any part of the letter in question, and that single sentence is as near as his readers get to even a paraphrase. This is the most drastic example I know of the filtering out of "Jefferson on the French Revolution" by pious Jeffersonians. But the thing is going on all the time, in somewhat more subtle forms, whether muffled paraphrase or by omission. Hence the need to quote at whatever length is necessary what Jefferson actually says about the French Revolution.

The French Revolution was of central importance to the thought and emotions of Thomas Jefferson, and also to his far-reaching political calculations, throughout his period as Secretary of State (early 1790 to end 1793). From 1794 on, he was more cautious about it, but always attracted by it, and especially by his vision of a French Revolutionary occupation of England (*TLA*, pp. 218 and 244–45). Jefferson's interest in the French Revolution lasted from its beginning in July 1789—which he personally witnessed—up to the moment, on 15 December 1799, when Napoleon Bonaparte declared the French Revolution at an end (*TLA*, p. 250).

In *The Long Affair* I quote everything of significance (that has been preserved) that Jefferson wrote about the French Revolution during the decade of its existence. I have also quoted passages from his writings which have no ostensible connection with the French Revolution but nonetheless have a discernible and significant political relation to it. (See, for example, *TLA*, p. 132).

Those are my reasons for eschewing paraphrase, in the case of Jefferson's writings. But I have also preferred quotation to paraphrase in dealing with other writers, including writers about Jefferson. This is partly because I have come to have a lively apprehension—possibly an exaggerated one—of the distorting power of paraphrase. I am aware, for example, that if I were to paraphrase Dumas Malone, my subconscious mind might play tricks on me (and on Malone) similar, though with a different tendency, to those which I believe Malone's subconscious played on him, and on Jefferson, in his copious paraphrase of Jefferson's writings. So I quote Malone, and at length.

There is a positive purpose to this, in addition to the negative one of avoidance of paraphrase. Dumas Malone's biography is the most comprehensive statement that exists of what may be called the traditional, and near-hagiographical, assessment of Jefferson. Scholarly work on Jefferson has, at least in certain areas—notably slavery—been moving, during the last third of the twentieth century, somewhat away from that traditional picture. But the traditional picture has still great power over the public mind, even in high places. It is clear, for example, that it is the traditional picture that occupies the mind of President William Jefferson Clinton (*TLA*, pp. 301, 307). Many—and this may apply to the President—who revere the traditional picture, probably are a bit hazy about the details of any particular phase of Jefferson's career. *The Long Affair* deals with one particular phase, of a little more than a decade: Jefferson's relation to the French Revolution. It seems to me that that relation, which I have examined as closely as I could, is rather strikingly at variance with the traditional picture. That the distance between the traditional picture and the reality of a particular case may be appreciated, it is necessary that the traditional picture be represented, in parallel with the investigation of the particular case. And this is best done by quoting what Dumas Malone has to say—and sometimes noting what he fails to say—about each individual episode of the particular case.

There is also a special category in which quotation, as practiced in *TLA*, is vastly preferable to the usual summary—or paraphrase. This category consists of the dispatches of French diplomatic agents in the United States during the French Revolution and the instructions given to these agents by their revolutionary superiors. I have quoted these dispatches and instructions at length (in my own translation). The long quotations provide, as summary and paraphrase could never do, a panorama of relations between America and the French Revolution, as perceived by French Revolutionaries, during the different successive phases of that Revolution. And there is a bonus, from the reader's point of view. The dispatches etc. are not only historically informative, in a high degree. They are also often entertaining, though not intentionally so. They are a living part of that *mésentente cordiale* that prevailed in the relationship between America and the French Revolution throughout the 1790s (*TLA*, pp. 161–82, 221–41).

I also quote quite a lot from Jefferson's great editor, Julian P. Boyd. Boyd had his "Dumas Malone side," but that is not mainly why I quote him. I am deeply indebted to him (see Note on Sources) for several of his Editorial Notes, and especially for those on "The Politics of Mourning" and "*Rights of Man:* The Contest of Burke and Paine in America" (*TLA*, pp. 88–102 and 102–12). These are minute investigations into two episodes of great importance for the study of Thomas Jefferson and the French Revolution, and I have quoted at length from them primarily for that reason.

And I quote other scholars at length, when their writings are particularly pertinent to my subject: for example Frank L. Mott on *Jefferson and the Press* and the various scholars cited on Jefferson and slavery and race in chapter 7. In these cases I was calling (in effect) on expert witnesses, and it seemed important not to try to put words into their mouths.

In short, as I distrust paraphrase so much myself, I did not feel I could offer my readers a diet of paraphrase. And that is how this book got so long.

ACKNOWLEDGMENTS

Most of the work that went into *The Long Affair* was done during my two stints—1993–94 and 1994–95—as Senior Research Fellow at the National Humanities Center, Research Triangle Park, North Carolina. The Center provides its Fellows with a wonderfully propitious and congenial environment for research and with most stimulating and agreeable company, both at work and in times of relaxation. I owe a great intellectual debt to the Center collectively, and specifically to the following:

W. Robert Connor, Director, and Kent Mullikin, Deputy Director, of the Center.

Alan Tuttle, Librarian; Rita Vermillion, Associate Librarian; and Jean Anne Leuchtenburg, Director of Publications and Editor of the Center's organ *Ideas* (which published in its Winter 1994 number an early version of what has become the Prelude to *The Long Affair*).

Center staff members: Mary Donna Pond and Wayne Pond; Carlene Bechen; Dot Boatwright; Corbett Capps; Sandra Copeland (and Ron); Kit Flynn; Martha Goetz; Jean Houston; Carolyn Jackson; Teresa Lysinger; Sue Pares; Richard Schramm; Pat Schreiber; Robert E. Wright; Madeline Moyer, and especially Crystal and Darin Waters, parents of Jonathan, co-dedicatee of this book.

A very special word of thanks to Karen Carroll and Linda Morgan of Technical Services at the Center; Karen and Linda turned an unsightly mass of longhand into a handsome professional typescript, able to look two publishers in the eye.

Thanks also to the Fellows of the Center (1993–95) collectively and in particular to the following:

Evelyn Barish; Christopher Baswell; Judith Bennett; Edna G. Bay; Paula Giddings; Nicolas and Doina Harsanyi (and Anna); Claudia Koonz; Lawrence and Joanna Lipking; Joshua I. Miller; Professor Jin Di; Ankica Petrovic; Philip M. Richards; John Baldon Scott; Gary M. Shapiro; Katherine H. Tachau; Dorothy and John Thompson; Luise S. White; Vernon and Georganne Barton; Charles H. Capper; Denis Donohue; Francis V. O'Connor; David Constan, Toril Moi, and Nancy Scheper-Hughes.

I thank Lynde and Harry Bradley, Foundation of Milwaukee, Wisconsin, which generously supported my residence at the National Humanities Center; thanks particularly to Hillel Fradkin, the Foundation Vice President, for his personal interest in this project.

Thanks too to Andrew Schneider, who helped me, while in North Carolina, to research a book then provisionally entitled *The Founding Fathers and the French Revolution;* while working on this I took the decision to concentrate on Thomas Jefferson.

Thanks to the following friends in America: Deirdre Levinson Bergson and Alan Bergson of New York; David Bromwich of Yale University; Bill Chace, President of Emory University, Atlanta; Thomas and Jean Flanagan, State University of New York; James Olney, Louisiana State University (and Laura); David Grene and Emmet Larkin, University of Chicago; Xiaohuang Yin, San Francisco; Michael McDowell and Susan Flanigan of Washington and Ireland, parents of co-dedicatee and namesake Conor; Wilton Dillon, Smithsonian Fellow *emeritus,* Washington; Jean Haskell of Haskell Associates Philadelphia; Dr. James J. Lavelle, Bristol Township Commissioner; Helen Walton-Perros, State University of North Carolina; Mark Chello, Library of Congress, Washington; Helen Sotterer, Duke University.

I am glad to have the same publishers, in Britain and the United States, as I had for *The Great Melody: A Thematic Biography of Edmund Burke* in 1992—that worked very well, and so is this working: All my thanks to Christopher Sinclair Stevenson and Penelope Hoare in London and to Morris Philipson; Doug Mitchell; Jo Ann Kiser; Rina Ranalli; Julia Robling Griest; and Matt Howard in Chicago. Thanks also to Carol Heaton, my literary agent in London, for much wise advice and for all her help both to me and to the two publishers.

A special word of thanks to Jeffrey Young, of Emory University, who did a great deal of valuable work for me in the later stages of work on TLA, and came up with a number of new references. He also undertook a pilgrimage to Monticello on my behalf (see below). Jeff and Laurie Watell Young are the parents of Paris, third co-dedicatee.

I thank Doug Wilson for kindly inviting me to visit the International Center for Jefferson Studies at Monticello, and Doug Smith, the Director of that Center, for his kindness and hospitality to Jeff Young, when he visited it on my behalf. Thanks also to Ann Lucas, Lucia G. Stanton, Rebecca Bowman, and Erika Gentry, members of the Center's staff.

My already heavy intellectual debt to Owen Dudley Edwards, of the Department of History at Edinburgh University, has been greatly increased by his careful reading of the manuscript of *The Long Affair,* and by his many helpful suggestions, criticisms, and corrections; and especially for *enjoying* the book and sharing his enjoyment with me.

Thanks to friends in and of Ireland: My cousins David and Helen Sheehy, and their family; Kitty and Maurice Quinn; Patrick and Mary Lynch; Brian and Kate Garrett; Bob and Maureen McCartney; Tony Moriarty; Maurice and Frank Biggar; Jack and Doreen Brennan; Frank Callanan; Michael O'Leary; Eoghan Harris; Aengus Fanning; Willie Kealy; Gerry Mulligan; Anne Harris; Marianne Heron; Mary Kenny and Dick West; Father Michael O'Neill; Pat Cooney; Barry Desmond; Brendan Halligan; Garret and Joan FitzGerald; Gerry and Deirdre Gregg; Ruth Dudley Edwards; Tommy Murtagh and Simon.

Thanks to my children, their spouses, and my grandchildren: Donal, Rita and Sarah Cruise O'Brien; Fedelma, Nicholas, Mark, and Laurence Simms; Kate, Joe, and Alexander Kearney; Patrick and Margaret Cruise O'Brien—to all of these, for everything.

Finally, to Máire, for her lively interest in this project and encouragement for it from the beginning, for her enjoyment of the book and her company, both in North Carolina and Ireland.

FOUR AMERICANS IN PARIS,
CIRCA 1785
Benjamin Franklin, John and Abigail Adams,
Thomas Jefferson

Three of the Founding Fathers were in Paris on diplomatic missions for their country during the last years of the Ancien Régime. Benjamin Franklin was there for nine years, from 1776 to 1785, first as unofficial but influential envoy of Congress and then, after Saratoga, as Minister Plenipotentiary of the French Monarchy's new ally, the United States of America. Thomas Jefferson succeeded Franklin (as Jefferson stressed, no one could "replace" Franklin) as American Minister in Paris in 1785, and remained in that position into the new revolutionary dispensation. Jefferson left France in late September 1789, and in February 1790 became President Washington's Secretary of State. John Adams was in the French capital, on a variety of sometimes ill-defined diplomatic missions, several times between 1778 and 1785. His wife, Abigail, who was with him, was a notable personality in her own right, and had definite views on Parisian society, and especially on that part of it which consisted of the female admirers of Benjamin Franklin. Between them, the four remarkable Americans had a great deal of experience of pre-revolutionary France. They differed significantly, however, in their attitudes toward that experience.

How to view the French Enlightenment and the opening phases of the French Revolution was a matter that was to trouble all the Founding Fathers. At issue is not only the connection between the American and French Revolutions, but also the bearing of the Enlightenment on both revolutions as well as a fundamental inquiry about the Enlightenment itself: was it essentially a single phenomenon or was it divided into distinct Anglo-Saxon and French branches?

Jefferson appears as the embodiment of a link between the American Declaration of Independence and the French Revolutionary Declaration of the Rights of Man. Minister Plenipotentiary for the United States during the last crisis of the régime, he was there for the opening of the States-General (23 June 1789) and for the Fall of the Bastille on the fourteenth of the following month. Jefferson is believed to have played a part in formulating the Declaration of the Rights of Man and of the Citizen, adopted by the National Constituent Assembly, the revolutionary heir to the States-General, on 27 August 1789. He thus became the symbol of a proposition of which he came to be a fervent apologist: that the French Revolution was the continuation and fulfillment of the American one, both being manifestations of one and the same spirit of Liberty. Within a few years, that proposition was to become bitterly divisive, both among the American people and among the Founding Fathers themselves. The question of policy toward France was to range Jefferson and Madison, supported by James Monroe, against Hamilton and Adams. By that time, Franklin was dead. Washington first tried to hold the balance but ultimately threw his tremendous weight decisively against the Jeffersonian theory of the continuity and kinship of the two revolutions.

The four Americans were not in Paris as tourists, or even primarily as analysts of the French political scene, but as American diplomatic agents; formally so in three cases; informally but effectively in the case of Abigail. The primary business of the diplomatists was with the Court of the Sovereign to whom they were accredited: His Most Christian Majesty, Louis XVI. But they also had business, scarcely less important, with the court of public opinion, a much more significant factor than might be assumed from the highly misleading description of the France of Louis XVI as an absolute monarchy. The molding of public opinion was in the self-confident hands of a body of intellectuals, known to themselves and others as *les philosophes*. So it was the business of the diplomats to cultivate these philosophers as well as the Court. A mild, and quite tolerable, degree of tension was involved in this exercise. The Court was officially Christian—specifically Catholic—while the staple activity of *les philosophes* was ridiculing Catholicism, in the mode of their archetype and exemplar, Voltaire. Later it came to be believed, with justice, that the activities of the *philosophes* had undermined the whole of the Ancien Régime, by comprehensively discrediting its official ideology. But this was by no means apparent before 1789. The *philosophes* were comfortably part of the Ancien Régime, in all its secular aspects. They were highly influential, and uniformly well disposed towards the United States, partly because of its exemplary lack of a Church Establishment.

So it was the duty of these Americans, in their capacity as diplomatic agents, to cultivate the *philosophes,* whether or not they found them personally congenial or intellectually estimable. Only one of our four thoroughly enjoyed their company. This was not Thomas Jefferson—contrary to an impression that later became widespread—but Benjamin Franklin.

We all like to be liked, and the *philosophes,* to a man and woman, loved and almost adored Benjamin Franklin. As a class, these people delighted in paradoxes, and Franklin was the incarnation of a benign paradox. Thought to be a product of the Pennsylvania wilderness, Franklin had for these Parisians the charm of Rousseau's Noble Savage. But then he was a *scientific* savage, inventor of the lightning rod, which lent him great prestige in the eyes of the scientific popularizers of the *Encyclopédie.* This was a breathtaking, almost magical, combination, especially when Franklin was also credited, as by Mirabeau, with having carried out the American Revolution, virtually singlehandedly.

Franklin became a cult figure for the *philosophes* and their admirers: a sort of thaumaturge of the French Enlightenment. And it was altogether natural that Franklin should feel happy in the company of the *philosophes.* Among them, he was doing a supremely effective public relations job for his country. He also enjoyed the work and the company and was the more effective for that reason.

Franklin's colleague, John Adams, cast a cold and sardonic eye on the Pennsylvanian and his admirers. In his *Diary* on the occasion of one of Voltaire's last public appearances (Voltaire died the following month), Adams writes:

After dinner we went to the Academy of Sciences, and heard Dr. d'Alembert as Secretary perpetual, pronounce Eulogies on several of their Members lately deceased. Voltaire and Franklin were both present, and there presently arose a general Cry that Monsieur Voltaire and Monsieur Franklin should be introduced to each other. This was no Satisfaction. There must be something more. Neither of our Philosophers seemed to divine what was wished or expected. They however took each other by the hand. . . . But this was not enough. The Clamour continued, until the explanation came out *"Il faut s'embrasser, à la française!"* The two Aged Actors upon this great Theatre of Philosophy and frivolity then embraced each other by hugging one another in their Arms and kissing each other's cheeks, and then the tumult subsided. And the Cry immediately spread through the whole Kingdom and I suppose all over Europe *Qu'il était charmant! Ah il était enchantant, de voir Solon et Sophocle embrassans!* How charming it was! Oh it was enchanting to see Solon and Sophocles embracing![1]

The phrase "this great Theatre of Philosophy and frivolity" is apt. It tells us much about the level of intellectual and aesthetic standards—in this the most complacent decade of the French Enlightenment, on the eve of the French Revolution—that such an audience should place Voltaire, as a tragedian, on a level with Sophocles.

Voltaire and Franklin became tutelary deities of the French Revolution in its opening phases. Voltaire's remains were transferred to the Pantheon by order of the National Assembly on 10 July 1791. The Pantheon itself—formerly the Church of Sainte Geneviève, the patron saint of Paris—had not been available for occupation when the news of Franklin's death reached France in June 1790, but Franklin was immediately the subject of an outpouring of State, municipal, corporate, and private eulogies, known collectively as the "Apotheosis of Benjamin Franklin." When Mirabeau took the news to the National Assembly, he said, "Franklin is dead. . . . He has returned to the bosom of Divinity, this genius who freed America and poured over Europe torrents of light" (*lumière,* standing also for Enlightenment, specially identified with Paris, *la Ville Lumière*).

The twin phenomena of the revolutionary Apotheosis of Franklin and Pantheonization of Voltaire eloquently attest the strong sense which the French Revolutionaries of the first phase possessed of the continuity of their political activity with the intellectual activity of the *philosophes* of the Ancien Régime (including Franklin, who was the only person not French by language and culture who was admitted to that select company).

At a later period, from 1793 on, when the word "horrors" came in some quarters to be intimately associated with the French Revolution, the continuity of the bloody Revolution with the "Godless" French Enlightenment came to be a favorite theme of the Right, in France and America and elsewhere. It came to be mocked by the Left as a gross oversimplification, in such phrases as *"C'est la faute à Rousseau, c'est la faute à Voltaire."* But in the years 1789–91 the leaders of the French Revolution and their admirers at home and abroad took particular pride in the concept of the Revolution as the benign and glorious outcome of an Enlightenment that was supremely French, plus one American: Benjamin Franklin.

Franklin himself did not live long enough after the summer of 1789 for us to be quite sure whether he shared this notion of continuity, or if he did, how long he would have continued to do so. We have just three letters to go on, and they are partly contradictory. The first reference comes in a letter of 2 November 1789 to his friend Benjamin Vaughan, a valued propagandist for the American cause during the American Revolution. The letter seems to refer to the Fall of the Bastille, the news of which

The Apotheosis of Benjamin Franklin. *Au Génie de Franklin; Eripuit Coelo Fulmen, Sceptrumque Tirannis,* by Marguerite Gérard, 1778, after an etching by Jean Honoré Fragonard. Courtesy of the Philadelphia Museum of Art, given by Mrs. John D. Rockefeller. This was Franklin's first French apotheosis, on the occasion of the recognition of the United States by Louis XVI. A French Revolutionary apotheosis followed, on Franklin's death in 1790 (Prelude, p. 4; chapter 3, pp. 88–89).

would have reached Franklin in Philadelphia only recently: "The revolution in France is truly surprising. I sincerely wish it may end in establishing a good constitution for that country. The mischiefs and troubles it suffers in the operation, however, give me great concern."[2] ("Mischiefs and troubles" is probably an allusion to the lynching of Foulon and Berthier by the Paris mob.) This is quite similar to Edmund Burke's reaction to the news of the same events, which of course reached Burke earlier.

Franklin's next reference to the French Revolution is more negative. It comes in his letter of 13 November 1789 to a French friend, the *philosophe* Jean Baptiste Le Roy, a letter that was written possibly after learning of the massacre of members of the King's bodyguard and the abduction of the Royal Family from Versailles by the Paris mob (5–6 October 1789).

> It is now more than a year since I have heard from my dear friend Le Roy. What can be the reason? Are you still living? Or have the mob of Paris mistaken the head of a monopolizer of knowledge for a monopolizer of corn and paraded it about the streets upon a pole. . . . Great part of the news we have had from Paris, for near a year past, has been very afflicting. I sincerely wish it may all end well and happily, both for the King and the nation.[3]

Franklin's last word on the French Revolution is strikingly different, in tone and tendency, from the two preceding ones. Dated 4 December 1789, it is addressed to David Hartley:

> The Convulsions in France are attended with some disagreeable Circumstances; but if by the Struggle she obtains and secures for the Nation its future Liberty, and a good Constitution a few Years Enjoyment of those Blessings will amply repair all the Damages their Acquisition may have occasioned. God grant that not only the Love of Liberty, but a thorough Knowledge of the Rights of Man may pervade all the Nations of the Earth, so that a Philosopher may set his Foot anywhere on its Surface and say "This is my country."[4]

This is an interesting early example of a politically correct statement. It also anticipates the line which would be taken by Jefferson, Madison, Monroe, and the rest of the American Republicans, as long as three and four years later, at a time when the "disagreeable circumstances" to which Franklin here delicately alludes had become far bloodier than anyone (except Edmund Burke) could have dreamed of in 1789. But why the difference between Franklin's unwavering defense of the French Revolution, in this last letter, and the earlier letters, with their growing misgivings?

The answer lies, I believe, in the nationality and record of Franklin's three correspondents. The earlier letters were personal, addressed to trusted friends, neither of whom was English, and both of whom were pro-American. David Hartley was another matter altogether. He was an English politician who had been active as an intermediary between the British Government and the Americans at a time when George III, even after Yorktown, was hoping that the Americans might agree to terms, short of independence. John Adams regarded Hartley as a spy, and Franklin—whether he agreed with that or not—would never have confided in such a person. Franklin saw Hartley as trying—as he had tried earlier, in different circumstances—to drive a wedge between the Americans and the French, and Franklin was not to be drawn. He knew that, if he had written to Hartley in the same vein as to Vaughan and Le Roy, his words could have been used to damage relations between France and America, and damage Franklin's own image in both countries. These were the conditions that produced a degree of political correctitude otherwise rare in Franklin's correspondence.

In sum, I would classify Franklin as a person who was comfortable with the French Enlightenment, but not with the French Revolution. I think we can say with confidence that a person who found "great part of the news from Paris very afflicting," in the relatively mild conditions of 1789, could not have been other than revolted by the news from Paris in 1792–94. Another Founding Father was of sterner stuff, as we shall see.

John Adams held the most clear-cut and internally consistent position regarding the French Enlightenment and the French Revolution. He despised the French Enlightenment—as his comments on that encounter at the Academy of Sciences make sufficiently clear—and he detested the French Revolution from its inception and throughout its course. His earliest recorded reference to the French Revolution comes in a letter to the British radical churchman Dr. Richard Price (also a correspondent of Jefferson's). Price had sent Adams the pamphlet glorifying the French Revolution put out by the English Revolution Society in November 1789. This was the pamphlet that had kindled the rage of Edmund Burke against the French Revolution and driven him to write *Reflections on the Revolution in France*. Adams's spontaneous reaction was similar: "I know that encyclopedists and economists, Diderot and D'Alembert, Voltaire and Rousseau, have contributed more to this great event than Sidney, Locke or Hoadly, perhaps more than the American Revolution."[5]

Note the sharp distinction between the English and the French

John Adams, by John Singleton Copley, 1783. Oil on canvas, 238 x 147 cm. Courtesy of the Harvard University Portrait Collection, bequest of Ward Nicholas Boylston, 1828, to Harvard College. Adams and Jefferson were friends when this portrait was painted, but they quarrelled in 1791, over the French Revolution (chapter 3, pp. 107–9).

branches of the Enlightenment. Also the probably reluctant acknowledgment that the American Revolution had helped, in a significant degree, to prepare the way for the French one. Adams goes on: "I know not what to make of a republic of thirty million atheists. Too many Frenchmen, after the example of too many Americans, pant for equality of persons and property. The impracticability of this, God Almighty has decreed, and the advocates for liberty who attempt it will surely suffer for it."

Charles Francis Adams, in commenting on this passage, makes an interesting, but partly misleading, contrast between the attitudes of Adams and Jefferson towards the writers of the French Enlightenment. He notes:

> It would be difficult, in smaller compass, to point out the sources of the calamities that followed. The writer had never sympathized with the speculations of the class of French writers to which he refers. Mr Jefferson, on the contrary, naturally coincided with their views. Their want of a warm and yet restraining religious faith raised no ripple of distrust, for no image of the sort ever came reflected from his own mind, whilst Mr Adams's strong conviction of the impossibility of maintaining an equality of conditions in any civilized society, savored to him [Jefferson] of a backsliding into absolutism, which he [Jefferson] ever afterwards laid to his [Adams's] charge. But this suspicion of Mr Jefferson was really founded in a misconception of Mr Adams's whole cast of mind, which had been formed in the mould of the English writers, some of whom he names in his letter to Dr Price, and which never relished the vague and fanciful speculations of the French school.

Much of this is just, but part of it significantly exaggerates the intellectual divergence between Jefferson and Adams. *Both* these Founding Fathers, and not just one of them, were products of the English (or Anglo-Saxon or Anglo-Scottish) Enlightenment, and not of the French branch. Jefferson spent some years in France, and much time in the company of philosophers on the eve of the Revolution, to which the *philosophes* were deemed to have contributed, and since Jefferson, after his return to America, appeared for several years in the role of an enthusiast for that same Revolution, it became natural to assume that he had acquired his pro–French Revolutionary views from his friends and mentors, the *philosophes*. This view became current among Jefferson's enemies, the most implacable of whom, Alexander Hamilton, believed that he "drank freely of the French philosophy, in religion, in science, in politics."[6]

Thomas Jefferson himself, in appealing to the large pro-French component in American, and specially Virginian, politics in the first half of the 1790s, did nothing to dispel an impression consistent with his image as an enthusiast for French ideas. Jefferson was both a politician and an intellectual, and his politics were to become for a time more French than his intellect ever was.

It is not true to say, as C. F. Adams does, that Jefferson "naturally coincided" with the views of the *philosophes*. Like other great men, and especially great intellectuals, Jefferson naturally coincided with his own views, not those of others. And his views of what C. F. Adams calls "the vague and fanciful speculations of the French school" were not in fact any more respectful than those of John Adams.

In the Jefferson collection, now in the Library of Congress, there is a work by Condorcet, one of the most eminent of the *philosophes,* one of Franklin's chief posthumous eulogists and an acquaintance of Jefferson's. The work is entitled *Esquisse d'un tableau historique des progrès de l'esprit humain (Sketch of a Historic Tableau of the Progress of the Human Mind)*. Jefferson acquired the French edition, published posthumously in Paris in 1795, the author having perished in the previous year as a result of violent ill-treatment by partisans of the Revolution he had done so much to promote. Jefferson's copy carries a single annotation in his neat, legible hand. It appears on a passage in which Condorcet celebrates what he considers to be Descartes' immense contribution to the progress of the human mind. Jefferson comments:

> This account of Descartes is much too partial. His ingenious imagination led mankind astray and retarded science for an age or two. His fancies have yielded very slowly to the demonstrations of the experimental philosophers. To him was owing particularly that the French nation were so long and still are in the rear of others in physical sciences.

This negative assessment of the French intellectual tradition in the seventeenth and eighteenth centuries is confirmed and emphasized by another judgment of Jefferson's, this time arising from an essay by Voltaire, an entry on "Seashells" (*Coquilles*) in that pride and joy of the eighteenth-century French Enlightenment, the *Encyclopédie*.

(In the Library of Congress's Jefferson collection there is also a set of Voltaire's *Complete Works* in fifty-eight volumes, plus seven separate titles. Jefferson also possessed a second complete set of the *Works*. This interest in Voltaire became an object of Congressional concern in 1814 when, after the original collection of the Library of Congress had been destroyed by the British, Jefferson offered to sell his own library to Congress as the nucleus of a new collection. Some Congressmen thought that the morals of the legislature would be polluted by the acquisition of so many volumes of French immorality, even though all the immorality was still in the original French.

Eventually that particular objection was overcome, but suspicion still lingered about Jefferson's connection with French literature. Untutored minds, of whom there are always some, among parliamentarians as well as policemen, readily believe that if a person is the owner of a book, he is also a carrier of all the ideas which that book contains. This would be rather difficult, in the case of Jefferson, whose large library contains, for example, a great deal of Christian theology, together with many volumes of sermons, as well as Voltaire's blasphemies.)

Voltaire's essay on *Coquilles* in the *Encyclopédie* claimed, on the basis of research supposedly conducted in Touraine, that such shells could be produced by friction of earth and rocks, without animal participation. Jefferson made enquiries about this claim, in Touraine, and could find no confirmation of it. In his *Notes on the State of Virginia*, compiled in 1782, and published in London in 1785, Jefferson observed: "The establishment of the instance cited by M. de Voltaire, of the growth of shells unattached to animal bodies, would have been that of his theory. But he has not established it. He has not even left it on ground so respectable as to have rendered it an object of enquiry to the literati of his own country."

No one who penned that last devastating comment could have been a devotee of the French Enlightenment. And we know from Jefferson himself that his intellectual heroes all belonged to the English Enlightenment, not to the French branch. Alexander Hamilton, at an early stage in his foredoomed administrative partnership with Jefferson, asked him to identify the three worthies whose portraits hung on the walls of the study of the Secretary of State. Jefferson named them: "Bacon, Newton, Locke." Not a Frenchman in the lot. (Jefferson made a note of this conversation because Hamilton, in reply, imprudently said that Julius Caesar was the greatest man who ever lived. Jefferson took this down for possible later use in evidence against his great rival.)

Jefferson was not, I think, strongly influenced or impressed by the philosophers, at least collectively. The *Encyclopédie*—the greatest collective expression of *la philosophie*—was largely popular science and Jefferson clearly did not hold French scientific standards in high esteem. But there was one writer generally classed, I think wrongly, as a *philosophe* who may have influenced Jefferson, and perhaps profoundly so. This is Rousseau. If so, the debt was an unacknowledged one: I can find no significant explicit reference to Rousseau in Jefferson's writings, and only one significant implicit reference. This is Jefferson's use, in 1795, of the concept that people might be forced to be free. Jefferson was considering—and eagerly awaiting—a French Revolutionary occupation of England which would, from a Jeffersonian point of view, have been a liberation. "I do not indeed wish to see any nation have a form of government forced upon them; but if it is to be done, I should rejoice at its being a freer one." (For the context, see below, chapter 6, pp. 244–45). The basic concept here is taken from *Du contrat social* and is the most audacious of Rousseau's paradoxes: the notion that people may be "forced to be free" (*Social Contract:* first book, chapter 7, last paragraph). The intellectual inheritance here is quite clear, and it is a heritage of awesome import. For if the liberty which Jefferson preached so ardently throughout his career is something that can be forced on people who don't want it—as the French Revolutionaries were then doing throughout Europe—then his concept of liberty is radically different from what most people have taken it to be. Jefferson's use of this concept of Rousseau's implies (in my opinion) a general intellectual affinity between the two eighteenth-century thinkers. There is something in common also in the style of the two men, the frequent recourse to peremptory certitude and application, in a secular context, of concepts derived from dogmatic religion (see below, chapter 3, pp. 102–9). There is nothing comparable in Jefferson's relation to Voltaire or Diderot or the general run of the *philosophes*.

Jefferson was curious about the *philosophes;* indeed it would be hard to think of anything about which he was *not* curious. He frequented them as well as the courtiers, both because he was curious and because it was part of his job to cultivate them, for his country's sake. But he did not hold them in particularly high esteem, either intellectually or morally, and he did not find them particularly congenial company. It is clear from his letters that he was far more at home in the company of John and Abigail Adams, when all three were in Paris, than in the company of any Parisians whatever, whether these were *philosophes* or courtiers (or both, as was often the case).

In theory, we might take Jefferson's position to be closer to that of the *philosophes* than to that of the Adamses. Jefferson and the *philosophes* were all deists. The Adamses were devout Christians, in a New England tradition. But in reality any American gentleman who happened to be a deist had more in common with an American lady and gentleman who happened to be Christians than he had with deists *à la française*. French deists of the late eighteenth century were aggressively and contemptuously *anti*-religious. English-speaking deists were quieter and more respectful, and ill at ease with French militancy. Also there was a major (and related) difference, over sexual mores. French deists believed that chastity and monogamy were Christian vestiges, and therefore inherently ridiculous and the behavior of the *philosophes,* male and female, matched their beliefs. Jefferson and the Adamses strongly disapproved of this pattern of belief and behavior and this made them hold a little aloof from the society of these people, even while cultivating them, mainly for professional and patriotic reasons.

On these points, there was a significant difference between the Jefferson-Adams position, and that of the other great American who also resided in the neighborhood of Paris in those momentous years. Benjamin Franklin enjoyed the company of the *philosophes* without inhibition. He was not, to be sure, openly anti-religious. No representative of the United States could afford to be that, either then or later. But he allowed the *philosophes* to think that he privately shared their views. A French observer—probably a *bien-pensant* one—commented shortly after Franklin's arrival in Paris in November 1776:

> Doctor Franklin, arrived a little since from the English Colonies, is mightily run after, much fêted by the savants ... Our *esprits forts* have adroitly sounded him as regards his religion and they believe that they have discovered that he is a believer in their own—that is to say, that he has none at all.

Franklin allowed it to be understood that his lifestyle was as enlightened as his principles. Abigail Adams has pungently recorded her disapproval of Franklin's relationship with the widow of the eminent *philosophe* and financier Claude Adrien Helvétius (1715–71). Helvétius, being "an absolute-atheist," was one of the most advanced of the *philosophes.* His memory was held in high regard in Enlightenment circles in Paris on the eve of the Revolution. His bust was in a place of honor in the Jacobin Club in the early years of the Revolution, but was removed from there by order of Robespierre in 1792. His banishment signalled the rejection by the Revolution, under Robespierre, of the 1780s theatre of philosophy and folly, which Adams had scorned and which Franklin had quietly enjoyed. Madame Helvétius was very much part of that theatre. She was known as Notre Dame d'Auteuil, apparently because of the number of exceptionally enlightened abbés who used to congregate in her delectable villa in that semi-rural retreat, under the mild and magnificent eye of Benjamin Franklin.

Abigail Adams, in a letter to her niece, Lucy Cranch, on 5 September 1784, describes an encounter with Madame Helvétius, near the end of Franklin's time as American Minister Plenipotentiary to France:

> This lady [Madame Helvétius] I dined with at Dr. Franklin's. She entered the room with a careless, jaunty air; upon seeing ladies who were strangers

Abigail Smith Adams (Mrs. John Adams), by Gilbert Stuart, 1800/1815. Oil on canvas. © 1996 Board of Trustees, National Gallery of Art, Washington; gift of Mrs. Robert Homans. "A notable personality in her own right [with] definite views on Parisian society, and especially on that part of it which consisted of the female admirers of Benjamin Franklin" (Prelude, pp. 13–14).

to her, she bawled out, "Ah! mon Dieu, where is Franklin? Why did you not tell me there were ladies here?" You must suppose her speaking all this in French. "How I look!" said she, taking hold of a chemise made of tiffany, which she had on over a blue lute-string, and which looked as much upon the decay as her beauty, for she was once a handsome woman; her hair was frizzled; over it she had a small straw hat, with a dirty gauze half-handkerchief round it, and a bit of dirtier gauze, than ever my maids wore, was bowed on behind. She had a black gauze scarf thrown over her shoulders. She ran out of the room; when she returned, the Doctor entered at one door, she at the other; upon which she ran forward to him, caught him by the hand, "Helas! Franklin;" then gave him a double kiss, one upon each cheek, and another upon his forehead. When we went into the room to dine, she was placed between the Doctor and Mr. Adams. She carried on the chief of the conversation at dinner, frequently locking her hand into the Doctor's, and sometimes spreading her arms upon the backs of both the gentlemen's chairs, then throwing her arm carelessly upon the Doctor's neck.

Madame Helvétius, by A. M. Alfred Dutens. "This lady I dined with at Dr. Franklin's. She entered the room with a careless jaunty air; upon seeing ladies, who were strangers to her, she bawled out, 'Ah, mon Dieu, where is Franklin? Why did you not tell me there were ladies here?'" (Abigail Adams to Lucy Cranch, 5 September, 1784; Prelude, pp. 14–15).

I should have been greatly astonished at this conduct, if the good Doctor had not told me that in this lady I should see a genuine Frenchwoman, wholly free from affectation or stiffness of behaviour, and one of the best women in the world. For this I must take the Doctor's word; but I should have set her down for a very bad one, although sixty years of age, and a widow. I own I was highly disgusted, and never wish for an acquaintance with any ladies of this cast. After dinner she threw herself upon a settee, where she showed more than her feet. She had a little lap-dog, who was, next to the Doctor, her favorite. This she kissed, and when he wet the floor she wiped it up with her chemise. This is one of the Doctor's most intimate friends, with whom he dines once every week, and she with him. She is rich, and is my near neighbour; but I have not yet visited her. Thus you see, my dear, that manners differ exceedingly in different countries. I hope, however, to find amongst the French ladies manners more consistent with my ideas of decency, or I shall be a mere recluse.

As well as being rich, Madame Helvétius was descended from the *haute noblesse* of the European Ancien Régime. She belonged to one of the four great families of Lorraine, related to the imperial family of Austria, and hence to Marie-Antoinette.[7] What Abigail Adams was witnessing was a performance by a *grande dame* of the Ancien Régime, *épatant les bourgeois de Boston*. Abigail seems to have been unaware of this, and would not have liked Madame Helvétius any the better for knowing it.

The social gulf between the world of the Adamses and that of the Franklin circle in Paris is sufficiently evident in that description. Thomas Jefferson was too discreet to record criticisms of his illustrious predecessor or his friends but there can be no doubt that he greatly preferred, while in Paris, the company of John and Abigail Adams to that of Benjamin Franklin and Madame Helvétius.

ONE

A LONELY AMERICAN

Thomas Jefferson,
Minister Plenipotentiary at the Court of Louis XVI
1785–87

In this chapter we are looking at Jefferson's life in Paris at a time when most people, including Jefferson, were quite unaware that they were living in the last years of the Ancien Régime. In the next five chapters, we shall be looking quite closely at Jefferson's prolonged involvement with the French Revolution. Right now, we shall examine what is known of Jefferson, in relation to France and to America, in the period before the opening, in 1787, of what we retrospectively regard as the immediate pre-revolutionary process.

On 2 May 1785, Jefferson received notification of his election by Congress to succeed Franklin as the Minister to the French Court. During the same month the Adams family left for London, where John Adams had become Minister Plenipotentiary to the Court of Saint James.

This was a sad and lonely period in Jefferson's personal life. He was a widower—since 1782—with three young daughters. The eldest, Martha ("Patsy"), had come with him to Paris, where she was a boarder in a convent. She was thirteen years old at the time when her father entered on his duties as Minister Plenipotentiary in Paris. The relationship cannot have brought unalloyed comfort to either party, at this time. Jefferson was a most conscientious father, but hardly much fun. The earliest known letter from him to Patsy, dated from Aix, was written in March 1787, when Patsy was fifteen years old. Dumas Malone, Jefferson's most comprehensive biographer (and a highly sympathetic one) writes:

This was an era when the habit of parental moralizing was strong, but if Patsy had been less aware of her father's limitless kindness she might have

found some of his exhortations rather hard to bear. His standards of industry and resolution were no less appalling because he maintained them himself. In a single letter he said such things as these:

> Of all the cankers of human happiness none corrodes with so
> silent, yet so baneful an influence, as indolence. No laborious per-
> son was ever yet hysterical.
>
> It is while we are young that the habit of industry is formed. If
> not then, it never is afterwards. The fortune of our lives, therefore,
> depends on employing well the short period of youth.
>
> It is a part of the American character to consider nothing as
> desperate; to surmount every difficulty by resolution and contriv-
> ance. In Europe there are shops for every want; its inhabitants,
> therefore, have no idea that their wants can be supplied otherwise.
> Remote from all other aid, we are obliged to invent and to exe-
> cute; to find means within ourselves, and not to lean on others.
> Consider, therefore, the conquering your Livy as an exercise in the
> habit of surmounting difficulties . . .

Martha assured him that he might be at ease on the head of hysterics, for
she was not that lazy, and she solemnly promised to try to follow his advice
with the "most scrupulous exactitude." His later letters were less monitory.
He told her—somewhat self-consciously—about climbing the cliffs of the
Apennines, about listening to the feathered chorus at Vaucluse, about bliss-
fully sailing on the Canal of Languedoc under cloudless skies. In her woman's sphere, which he always sharply distinguished from that of man, he
wanted her to be industrious; he also wanted her to be aware of the incredible interest and richness of life as she went along.[1]

After Jefferson's wife died, his two younger children, Maria (Polly)
and Lucy, were cared for by his in-laws, Elizabeth and Francis Eppes, and
the children remained with the Eppeses at Eppington, Virginia, after Jefferson and Patsy had taken up residence in Paris. Later in 1784, Polly
and Lucy, and the Eppeses' daughter, also called Lucy, went down with
whooping cough, then an extremely dangerous malady. On 13 October
1784, Elizabeth Eppes wrote to Jefferson:

> Its impossible to paint the anguish of my heart on this melancholy occasion.
> A most unfortunate Hooping cough has deprived you, and us of two sweet
> Lucys, within a week. Ours was the first that fell a sacrifice. She was thrown
> into violent convulsions linger'd out a week and then expired. Your dear
> angel was confined a week to her bed, her sufferings were great though
> nothing like a fit. She retain'd her senses perfectly, called me a few moments

before she died, and asked distinctly for water. Dear Polly has had it most violent, though always kept about, and is now quite recovered. . . .

Be so good as to remember me most affectionately to my dear Patsy, and beg she will excuse my not writing until the gloomy scene is a little forgoten.[2]

Elizabeth Eppes's letter did not reach Jefferson until 6 May 1785, just four days after he learned of his appointment as Minister Plenipotentiary. The news of Lucy's death had, however, reached him several months before, through a weirdly casual passage in a prolix letter, conveyed to him by Lafayette, from the physician who attended the two Lucys in their last illness, Dr. James Currie. Dr. Currie wrote:

Where ever you may be I thank you Sir for your Synoptical View (given me in your letter) of the history of the Baloons, seemingly now forgotten here; and likewise for your friendly and genteel present of the Silver Casd. M. [Memorandum?] Book. Should any thing in the literary Way, which you think would be instructive or amazing to me Circumstanced as I am, your sending it me will be gratefully acknowledged and long remembered. The Politic business, &c. &c., in the publick way here, you'll have better information of by other channells than I could give, therefore, am silent on that head. I congratulate you on your quick passage to Europe. I hope it was a pleasant one, likewise, and that Miss Jefferson was not much disconcerted by her Nautical Journey. Mr. Eppes and family are now all Well. I am sincerely sorry my dear friend now to acquaint you of the demise of poor Miss L. Jefferson, . . .[3]

In these distressing family circumstances, both Thomas Jefferson and Patsy were naturally anxious that Polly, now aged seven, should join them in Paris. Polly herself wanted to stay where she was. Her fourteen-year-old cousin, John Wayles Eppes (who was later to marry Polly), included the following sentence in a letter he wrote to Jefferson on 22 May 1786, when Jefferson's tenure as Minister Plenipotentiary in Paris was just one year old:

I am affraid that notwithstanding your great desire to have cousin Polly with you it cannott be effected without forceing her, for she seems very much averse to it.[4]

On the same day as her cousin's letter, Polly herself wrote to her father a letter which ran in full as follows:

Dear Papa

I long to see you, and hope that you and sister Patsy are well; give my love
to her and tell her that I long to see her, and hope that you and she will
come very soon to see us. I hope you will send me a doll. I am very sorry
that you have sent for me. I don't want to go to France, I had rather stay
with Aunt Eppes. Aunt Carr, Aunt Nancy and Cousin Polly Carr are here.
Your most happy and dutiful daughter,

Polly Jefferson[5]

In the following year, Jefferson insisted that Polly must join him,
whether she wanted to do so or not. Dumas Malone writes:

Her aunt and uncle kept hoping her father would countermand his orders
since his promises to her seemed to be without effect. He was impelled to
explain further to the adults why he was so insistent. She would have advantages in France, undoubtedly, but he was thinking chiefly of something else.
He feared that, at her age, continued absence would weaken the tie between
her and her father and sister and make them strangers to her throughout
life. He was one who set great store by the family tie and his reasoning was
entirely sound, though it did not greatly appeal to a little girl who was much
more fearful of the weakening of her bond with the people she knew better
at Eppington.

Jefferson learned of the stratagems which were finally employed to get
his small daughter aboard a ship in a Virginia harbor. Her cousins visited
the vessel with her for a day or two, romping with her upon its decks and
in its cabins until she began to feel at home; once when she fell asleep the
others silently crept away, and when she awakened the voyage had begun.
This was in the month of May, 1787, and she was on the seas five weeks.[6]

A letter written by Jefferson during the month of Polly's enforced
return reflects the anxiety he felt on the subject: "I say nothing of my dear
Poll, hoping she is on her passage, yet fearing to think of it."[7]

Polly was not unaccompanied on her voyage. As Malone tells us: "As
an attendant she had, not an old nurse as had been expected, but a young
servant named Sally, sister of James whom Jefferson had brought to Paris,
and this girl proved to be of little help."[8]

Dumas Malone did not find it necessary to provide Sally and James
with a surname. A younger biographer fills in this detail. Polly Jefferson
was "attended by a servant, Sally Hemings, less than twice [Polly's] age."[9]
In reality the servant was one of Jefferson's house slaves. As Merrill D.
Peterson (but not Malone) also records, Jefferson's relations with Sally
Hemings later became the subject of gossip, and they afterward erupted

into public scandal, when they were used against President Jefferson in 1802 by a former political employee turned personal enemy, blackmailer, and Federalist pamphleteer, James T. Callender (below, chapter 3, pp. 111–12). Peterson writes:

> On September 1 there appeared in the *Recorder* a slanderous little piece, "The President Again," signed by Callender in the conviction that Jefferson would realize at least the heavy cost of his betrayal. "It is well known," the article began "that the man *whom it delighteth the people to honor,* keeps, and for many years past has kept, as his concubine, one of his own slaves. . . . By this wench, Sally, our President has had several children. . . . The African Venus is said to officiate as housekeeper at Monticello."
>
> Thus was launched the prolific public career of a tale that had tititlated Jefferson's enemies in the neighborhood of Monticello for years. The African Venus, Sally Hemings, was apparently the mulatto offspring of John Wayles and Elizabeth Hemings, his concubine, and hence the half-sister of Jefferson's departed wife. Sally it was who had accompanied Polly to Paris in 1787. After her return she had a number of children, all light skinned, whose paternity some wanton men ascribed to Jefferson. Like most legends, this one was not created out of the whole cloth. The evidence, highly circumstantial, is far from conclusive, however, and unless Jefferson was capable of slipping badly out of character in hidden moments at Monticello, it is difficult to imagine him caught up in a miscegenous relationship. Such a mixture of the races, such a ruthless exploitation of the master-slave relationship, revolted his whole being.[10]

One of the "wanton men" who ascribed the paternity of Sally's children to Jefferson was himself one of those children: Madison Hemings. Madison Hemings was born on 19 July 1805. He was emancipated—as were Sally's other surviving children (except two, who had already escaped from slavery and apparently passed for white)—under Thomas Jefferson's will, when he reached the age of twenty-one. Having been trained as a carpenter, he went to Ohio to earn his living. He gave an interview to an Ohio newspaper, when he was sixty-eight years old. In his account—presumably based on what his mother had told him—he tells of the arrival of Maria and Sally in Paris and of the sequel:

> Maria was left out here [United States] but was afterwards ordered to accompany him to France. She was three years or so younger than Martha. My mother accompanied her as her body servant. When Mr. Jefferson went to France, Martha was a young woman grown, my mother was about her age and Maria was just budding into womanhood. Their stay (my mother

and Maria's) was about eighteen months. But during that time my mother became Mr. Jefferson's concubine and when he was called home she was 'enceinte' by him. Soon after their arrival she gave birth to a child of whom Thomas Jefferson was the father. It lived but for a short time. She gave birth to four others, and Jefferson was the father of all of them. Their names were Beverley, Harriet, Madison (myself) and Ester.[11]

Madison Hemings's story is set out at length, and discussed, in the Appendix to this book. I happen to believe that story. But let us suppose that it is *not* true, and that the relationship between Jefferson and Sally Hemings was perfectly chaste, as we are told we must believe, if we are not to be classed with "wanton men" and—still worse—biographers in quest of "titillation."[12] If the relationship was in fact a chaste one, it was stranger than that set out in the plain narrative of Madison Hemings. Whatever else she may have been, Sally Hemings was certainly the half-sister of Jefferson's deceased wife. She had been the property of her father, John Wayles, Thomas Jefferson's father-in-law, who had bequeathed her to the Jeffersons, along with about 130 other slaves, including several other Wayles children. Even Virginius Dabney, the pious Jeffersonian author of *The Jefferson Scandals: A Rebuttal*, accepts that Jefferson (though not his wife) knew of the relationship.

Sally Hemings was a living reminder of that "mixture of the races . . . exploitation of the master-slave relationship" which we are told "revolted [Jefferson's] whole being." If it did, why did he keep this living reminder of what revolted his whole being in close (if chaste) attendance on him, for the next three years in Paris, and afterwards as a familiar house slave at Monticello for the rest of his life? Sally had arrived supposedly in "place of the old nurse who had been expected." So why did Jefferson not send this living reminder packing?

It is clear from the *known* part of the pattern of Jefferson's conduct towards Sally Hemings that he did *not* have the horror of miscegenous relations between master and slave that his biographers ascribe to him. He had indeed, like other white Southerners, a lively—and punitive—(see below, p. 266) horror of miscegenation between *black men and white women*. But from the fact that Sally Hemings was acceptable as a member of his household, we have to infer that he felt no horror at the idea of miscegenation between white masters and black female slaves. So if he felt comfortable with what John Wayles had done, with his female property, why should he not do the equivalent himself, and sleep with Sally Hemings?

As I said, I believe Madison Hemings's story, and I think the Jefferson of the biographers—for whom such behavior would be unthinkable—is a fictional construct. Exceptional in so many ways, Jefferson was a typical Virginia slaveowner in others (below, pp. 256–76) and there is no valid reason to suppose that he disdained the sexual perquisites available to his caste, any more than his father-in-law had disdained these.

The question of Jefferson's relationship to Sally Hemings is relevant to the general subject matter of this book. It is relevant because that relationship is an important part of Jefferson's relation to the institution of slavery, and because that, in turn, is relevant to Jefferson's relation to the French Revolution: a question examined at length in chapter 7.

Polly arrived in London en route to Paris in late June. Dumas Malone writes:

> Jefferson, recently back from his own trip [to the South of France] and facing an accumulation of three or four months' business, did not feel warranted in going to London for her, though events proved that this would have been the wisest course. . . . His solution of the problem was to send [Adrien] Petit, his trusted maître d'hôtel, but the child was afraid of a strange man who spoke an incomprehensible language.[13]

That "accumulation of business" is a Malone myth. Jefferson had taken a prolonged and leisurely holiday (below, p. 42) leaving his capable secretary, William Short, to run the Legation in his absence. Short could just as well have run it for another week or so, while Jefferson went to London to collect his daughter, as would have been natural. So why didn't he go to London? I believe that he was afraid to be in the same room with Sally and Abigail Adams.

Polly and Sally stayed with the Adamses in London. Abigail became fond of Polly (and Polly of her) but clearly did not quite know what to make of Sally (whom she does not name). In her first letter to Jefferson announcing Polly's arrival in London, Abigail writes: "The old Nurse whom you expected to have attended her, was sick and unable to come. She has a Girl about 15 or 16 with her, the Sister of the Servant you have with you." In a letter of the following day, Abigail again refers to "the Girl":

> The Girl who is with her is quite a child, and Captain Ramsey is of opinion will be of so little Service that he had better carry her back with him. But of this you will be a judge. She seems fond of the child and appears good naturd.[14]

Jefferson did not come to London, and Captain Ramsay was not allowed to bring Sally back with him to America. Instead, a white servant of Jefferson's collected Polly and Sally and took them back with him to the Hôtel de Langeac, Jefferson's splendid residence on the Champs Elysées.

The Adamses were clearly puzzled by these transactions.[15] They naturally expected their old friend to come in person, to meet and greet his daughter, after her very trying journey, and to renew their friendship. Indeed it was the obvious thing to do, professionally as well as personally: the American Minister in Paris and the American Minister in London had a lot to talk about. But the nature of the obstacle, in the way of Jefferson's travelling to London to collect his daughter, seems fairly obvious: Jefferson did not want to face questions from Abigail Adams about Sally Hemings.

The trouble, at this stage, was not about Jefferson's personal relations with Sally; if they became lovers at all, it was only at some time after Sally's arrival in Paris. The trouble, in June 1787, was with the Jefferson-Wayles-Hemings pattern of family relationships. Sally was a half-sister of Jefferson's wife. She was an aunt of Jefferson's daughter, Polly, whom she accompanied and attended as a slave. New Englanders were aware in general that such relations between families of masters and slaves were not uncommon in the South. And New Englanders disapproved. Abigail Adams, a strong-minded New England woman, detested such arrangements, as degrading to women in general, white as well as black. So it is understandable that Jefferson did not want to meet Abigail in the presence of his daughter, and of the young slave who was Polly's aunt.

To reiterate, I don't believe that Jefferson can have experienced anything like "horror" at the thought of master-slave miscegenous relationships. But I think that such relationships, both as a general feature of Virginian society and as affecting his own family, must have been, at the very least, a source of serious embarrassment to him, and probably also of shame and guilt.

Thomas Jefferson was a cultivated and travelled gentleman of his time. He mingled easily with the French nobility and cultural elite. Although he detested England, in the abstract, he had friendly relations with several members of the English radical elite. Although he was suspicious of the New England elite, his closest friends, during his Paris years, were John and Abigail Adams. Knowing all these people well, Jefferson had to know what they would think of the Jefferson-Wayles-Hemings pattern of family relations, if they knew of it.

In Paris—before the arrival of Polly and Sally—Jefferson had lived in close and friendly relations with John and Abigail Adams. But this could not have been so in Virginia; or even in Paris after the arrival of Sally and Polly. The patterns of Virginia and New England family relationships

Thomas Jefferson, by Mather Brown, 1786. Oil on canvas, 35¾ by 28½ in. Courtesy of Charles Francis Adams. This was painted in London when Jefferson was Minister Plenipotentiary for the United States in Paris. At that stage, Jefferson did not take the French or their politics particularly seriously. "Here we have singing, dancing, laugh [*sic*], and merriment. No assassinations, treasons, rebellions, or other dark deeds. When our king goes out, they fall down and kiss the earth where he has trodden; and then they go to kissing one another" (TJ to Abigail Adams, 9 August 1786; chapter 2, p. 39).

were simply too remote from one another to permit that. It was unthinkable that Abigail Adams could have had a half-sister who was her husband's slave or that—supposing the unthinkable to have happened—John Adams, after his wife's death, would have kept her half-sister in close and ambiguous attendance on him as a slave. Situated as he was, Jefferson had to be acutely aware of those New England unthinkabilities. And that awareness—and the emotions of shame and rage inseparable from it— had to affect his feelings about the relations between North and South, and also his feelings about how the French Revolution might change the balance of those relations to the benefit of the South (below, chapters 2 to 7).

The relation of New England to that Virginian family pattern was necessarily more important to Jefferson than the views of any non-Americans. But French and English views and potential views were also of some importance, if only because they were closer to those of New England than to those of Virginia.

The English would think of such a family pattern as akin to the phenomenon of "going native" among white men in the colonies: something that entailed a loss of caste, and therefore of social status, for the white participants. The French would regard the phenomenon itself with tolerant amusement, as something giving openings for spicy and exotic anecdotes. The systematic cover-up that such practices required, in American society of the time, would be a ripe and derisory example of Anglo-Saxon hypocrisy.

But New England in the person of the Adamses must have been by far the most embarrassing potential spectator of the Jefferson-Wayles-Hemings relationship, from Jefferson's point of view. The Adamses were well aware of the kind of relations between masters and female slaves that prevailed on many Southern plantations, but they thought of their cultivated and sensitive friend, Thomas Jefferson, as being above all that. The knowledge that he was not as much above it as they thought must have tormented Jefferson from time to time. We shall consider some of the wider implications of all that in chapter 7. For the moment, let us just note both the relevance to the French Revolution and the general points that the need to divert outside opinion from certain Virginian realities made Jefferson adept at laying smoke screens and that this aptitude stood him in good stead in his political career.

I

Polly arrived in Paris in the middle of July and her father then put her in the convent with Patsy. The children joined their father at weekends. Malone writes:

> Polly proceeded with her accomplishments at the convent, but when she was at the Hôtel de Langeac [Jefferson's Paris residence] it was Eppington that she most talked about. When she had been months in Paris her face kindled whenever she heard the name of her Aunt Eppes. That amiable lady proceeded to give birth to twins and her brother-in-law congratulated her on this double blessing and her obvious improvement in her trade [i.e. of wife and mother]. Continuing his letter, Jefferson said:

> > Polly is infinitely flattered to find a namesake [one of the twins] in one of them. She promises in return to teach them both French. This she begins to speak easily enough, and to read as well as English. She will begin Spanish in a few days, and has lately begun the harpsichord and drawing. She and her sister will be with me tomorrow. . . . I will propose to her, at the same time, to write to you. I know she will undertake it at once, as she has done a dozen times. She gets all the apparatus, places herself very formally with pen in hand, and it is not till after this and rummaging her head that she calls out, "Indeed, papa, I do not know what to say; you must help me," and, as I obstinately refuse this, her good resolutions have always proved abortive, and her letters ended before they were begun.

This is a rare and attractive glimpse of a Jefferson at home and at ease with his subject. We can almost see that little girl "rummaging her head." She will still not do what she's told, and her father accepts this, tenderly if ruefully. It might have been better if he could have brought himself to be less "obstinate" and give her the help she asked for, but his love for the child is altogether clear; and also, what is more rare, his respect for her individuality, even in rebellion.

Dumas Malone goes on:

> She did not inherit his fluency, and continued to be reluctant to write letters, even to those she loved. Though notably generous he was an exacting father and often a strongly possessive one, but he was never so foolish as to attempt to sever the tie between his little girl and the pleasant white house at Eppington. As things turned out this tie was renewed and strength-

ened in later years, and, although Polly became devoted to him, she was never her father's daughter in the sense that Patsy was.

The coming of Polly greatly relieved Jefferson's mind and increased his happiness but, like a letter from an old friend, it probably had the immediate effect of increasing his nostalgia. Both of his daughters were in Paris when he wrote Dr. George Gilmer that he wished he could eat some beef and mutton at Pen Park with him and his good old Albemarle neighbors. "I am as happy nowhere else and in no other society," he said, "and all my wishes end, where I hope my days will end, at Monticello. Too many scenes of happiness mingle themselves with all the recollections of my native woods and fields, to suffer them to be supplanted in my affection by any other. I consider myself here as a traveler only, and not a resident." [16]

It seems that about two years after the arrival of Polly, with Sally in Paris, Martha Jefferson attempted to enter a convent. Malone writes:

> Beginning in late April [1789], his daughters were regular members of his establishment, for he then removed them from the Abbaye de Panthémont. According to a family tradition the immediate occasion for this action was an impulsive letter to him from Martha, then in her seventeenth year, saying that she desired to become a nun. If his immature daughter did write such a letter it was just the sort of intimate personal record he would have wanted to keep from prying eyes and would have destroyed. The mere existence of the tradition is an argument that there is some degree of truthfulness in the story, but he might easily have withdrawn the girls from the convent at this time for other reasons. [17]

In her novel *Sally Hemings*, Barbara Chase-Riboud offers a plausible fictional interpretation of the "convent" episode. In her reconstruction, Chase-Riboud represents Maria's attempt to enter a convent as prompted by her discovery that Sally had become her father's mistress, an event that if we accept Madison Hemings's account must have taken place about this time: Sally, according to Madison, was pregnant when the Jeffersons returned to America at the end of 1789. The Chase-Riboud hypothesis is worth bearing in mind, but we need not linger on it here.

II

After Jefferson's return to America, late in 1789, he soon came to be regarded, by friend and foe alike, as America's most ardent Francophile. But in his recorded writings, from the time when he was actually living in France, there are few traces of sympathy with the French way of life, or even of any strong personal interest in French affairs. Much of this correspondence is, in the nature of the case, that of a conscientious working diplomatist, dealing with the Court and with French opinion-makers, especially those with a friendly interest in America. It is only in his letters to American friends that Jefferson allows his personal feelings about France and the French to show. These feelings are those of an extremely homesick American.

Jefferson's closest friends in Paris, and almost his only ones, had been John and Abigail Adams, and their departure from Paris, at the beginning of his own stint as Minister Plenipotentiary, was a severe blow to him. As he wrote to John Adams, shortly after the Adamses left: "The departure of your family has left me in the dumps. My afternoons hang heavily on me." [18] To another American friend, James Monroe, he wrote in the following month, in a more explicitly nostalgic vein:

> I sincerely wish you may find it convenient to come here. The pleasure of the trip will be less than you expect but the utility greater. It will make you adore your own country, it's soil, it's climate, it's equality, liberty, laws, people and manners. My god! How little do my countrymen know what precious blessings they are in possession of, and which no other people on earth enjoy. I confess I had no idea of it myself. [19]

In the opening of a letter to a non-political family friend, later in the same year, Jefferson seems to strike a much more positive note with regard to France and the French, but the promise of the opening is not sustained:

> I am much pleased with the people of this country. The roughnesses of the human mind are so thoroughly rubbed off with them that it seems as if one might glide thro' a whole life among them without a justle. Perhaps too their manners may be the best calculated for happiness to a people in their situation. But I am convinced they fall far short of effecting a happiness so temperate, so uniform and so lasting as is generally enjoyed with us. The domestic bonds here are absolutely done away. And where can their compensation be found? Perhaps they may catch some moments of transport above the level of the ordinary tranquil joy we experience, but they are separated by long intervals during which all the passions are at sea without rudder or compass. Yet fallacious as these pursuits of happiness are, they seem on the whole to furnish the most effectual abstraction from a contemplation of the hardness of their government. Indeed it is difficult to conceive how so good a people, with so good a king, so well disposed rulers in general, so genial a climate, so fertile a soil, should be rendered so ineffectual for producing human happiness by one single curse, that of a bad form of

government. But it is a fact. In spite of the mildness of their governors the people are ground to powder by the vices of the form of government. Of twenty millions of people supposed to be in France I am of opinion there are nineteen millions more wretched, more accursed in every circumstance of human existence, than the most conspicuously wretched individual of the whole United states.—I beg your pardon for getting into politics. I will add only one sentiment more of that character. That is, nourish peace with their persons, but war against their manners. Every step we take towards the adoption of their manners is a step towards perfect misery.[20]

The confusion of this passage is obvious. We may assume that Mrs. Trist, like almost all Americans in the aftermath of the American Revolution, had strong favorable presuppositions about France and the French, and that Jefferson was taking account of these, without really being able to share them. He liked to please those to whom he wrote, and was often less than candid. It's not probable that he really regarded "a bad form of government" as solely responsible for what he clearly disliked most about the French way of life, as it appeared to him: "The domestic bonds here are absolutely done away." This was no less true of the advanced thinkers and reformers with whom Jefferson was in frequent contact than it was of the Court. Nor did the French Revolution achieve a restoration of those domestic bonds.

Of course, if Jefferson's French contemporaries had known—as they did not—about his strictures on their immorality, they would have been furious about the hypocrisy of the Virginian slaveowner. Yet Jefferson's respect for those domestic bonds was quite real in its own way; he had been a loving husband, and was now a widower, and a loving father, which he always remained to his white children. To those of his children who were of mixed race, Jefferson was aloof, but not unkind, if we accept Madison Hemings's account. Jefferson probably thought of his relations with Sally Hemings—again if we accept M.H.'s account—as not interfering with "domestic bonds" which governed relations between white people exclusively. In any case, Sally Hemings did not join Jefferson in Paris until two years after this particular letter was written.

On the day following his letter to Eliza House Trist, Jefferson wrote to his nephew's tutor, Walker Maury, in a more robustly Americanist strain than he had used to Eliza "When I came here [to Paris]," he wrote,

I was not certain whether I might not find it better to send for him [TJ's nephew] hither. But I am now thoroughly cured of that Idea. Of all the errors which can possibly be committed in the education of youth, that of sending them to Europe is the most fatal. I see [clearly] that no American should come to Europe under 30 years of age: and [he who] does, will lose in science, in virtue, in health and in happiness, for which manners are a poor compensation, were we even to admit the hollow, unmeaning manners of Europe to be preferable to the simplicity and sincerity of our own country.[21]

Jefferson does not seem to have felt that he was contravening this principle in the cases of his own daughters. He was in fact conscientious—and perhaps even excessively so—about the education of his daughters, but when he talked at large about "the education of youth" he seems to have had boys exclusively in mind. Towards the close of the year that saw his appointment as Minister Plenipotentiary in Paris, Jefferson, in a letter to his brother-in-law Francis Eppes, condenses his feelings about America and Europe into a single sentence: "We all pant for America, as will every American who comes to Europe."

It is only in writing to Americans, especially Virginians, that Jefferson appears to "let himself go" during his Paris years, with regard to his personal opinions. In writing to French people, the tone is one of courteous formality. In part, but only in part, this can be ascribed to the reserve required of him by his diplomatic functions, in dealing with subjects of the Court to which he was accredited (even if some of these, like Lafayette, tended to regard themselves, even before the Revolution, as citizens of the French nation, in which Jefferson represented the American nation). But there is more to this than diplomatic discretion; it seems to me, as I read the correspondence, that he did not have any French friends, only well-disposed French acquaintances, who could be useful to his mission. And this is true even of Lafayette, whom Jefferson had known since the time of Lafayette's services during the American Revolution. It is not known exactly when Jefferson and Lafayette first met, but it was no later than May 1781, during the successful invasion of Virginia by British forces. Julian Boyd writes: "But there is no doubt that the two men met in Richmond at least as early as 8 May 1781. On that day Lafayette met with the Council [of the State of Virginia], TJ presiding [as Governor of the State]."[22] One might have thought that an acquaintance apparently so auspiciously begun would have ripened into friendship when Jefferson and Lafayette were working closely together in Paris three years later and afterward, as they did throughout Jefferson's period as Minister Plenipotentiary. Malone implies that such a ripening or, as he puts it, a blossoming, actually occurred. Writing of the opening period of Jefferson's Paris mission (1785–86) Malone says: "The mutual respect of Jefferson and Lafayette had now blossomed into enthusiastic mutual admiration."

Lafayette's enthusiastic admiration for Jefferson [though less than his veneration for Washington] is abundantly recorded, but it is hard to make out anything closely equivalent on Jefferson's side.

Most of Jefferson's letters to Lafayette are on the business of the Legation, in which Lafayette was always ready to assist. They deal with such matters as whale oil and tobacco, and other aspects of the commercial relations between America and France.[23]

Only once in the preserved correspondence between Jefferson and Lafayette during the period of Jefferson's Ministry in Paris is a personal note struck, and it is a disconcerting one. In November 1786, Lafayette wrote a letter to Jefferson, which has not been preserved. From the nature of Jefferson's reply, it seems that Lafayette had tried to tease Jefferson about some harness which Jefferson had just imported from England: a transaction which could be interpreted as a deviation from his well-known anti-English sentiments. Jefferson was not amused; his reply is freezing. It runs in full:

Dear Sir

I have received your favor of the second instant. The reason for my importing harness from England is a very obvious one. They are plated, and plated harness is not made at all in France as far as I have learnt. It is not from a love of the English but a love of myself that I sometimes find myself obliged to buy their manufactures. I must make one observation with respect to the use I made of my privilege. The minister of France in America has an unlimited privilege as to things *prohibited* as well as *dutied*. One third at least of the articles of consumption in his family must be foreign; not a twentieth part of those consumed in my family here are foreign; of course the loss of duties on that side the Atlantic is the triple of what it is on this. I have been moderate in my applications for passports hitherto and I shall certainly continue to be so.

I shall be happy to know of your arrival in town and am with sincerity your affectionate friend & servant,

TH: JEFFERSON[24]

If Lafayette replied to that snub, his reply has not been preserved. But about six months later, it seems that Lafayette must have indicated in some way that he was hurt by Jefferson's habitually cool and formal tone. Jefferson excuses himself, without greatly relenting from the courteous frigidity habitual in his correspondence with French men. At the close of an unusually long letter to Lafayette, in April 1787 Jefferson writes:

You will not wonder at the subjects of my letter: they are the only ones which have been present to my mind for some time past, and the waters must always be what are the fountain from which they flow. According to this indeed I should have intermixed from beginning to end warm expressions of friendship to you: but according to the ideas of our country we do not permit ourselves to speak even truths when they may have the air of flattery. I content myself therefore with saying once for all that I love you, your wife and children. Tell them so and Adieu. Your's affectionately,

TH: JEFFERSON[25]

This letter, containing an account of a tour of the South of France, is unprecedented in the Jefferson-Lafayette correspondence both for its length and general chattiness, as well as for the near-apology contained in its conclusion. I believe that Jefferson, as Minister Plenipotentiary of his country in France, now felt a need to mend his fences with an ally who, in April 1787, was playing a much more significant role in French politics than he had seemed to be playing in the previous November, when Jefferson had not hesitated to snub him. Between the two dates, a major political event had taken place. This was the opening of the Assembly of Notables (22 February 1787) summoned by Louis XVI in the first major attempt to resolve the increasingly desperate financial troubles of the Monarchy. The Assembly was in session during the time when Jefferson wrote that letter to Lafayette from the South of France, and Lafayette was cutting a big figure in the Assembly. Before the Assembly, he had been known in France mainly for his past deeds in America. Now for the first time he appeared as a rising actor in the now rapidly changing politics of France. The Jefferson letter that ends with the reference to "warm expressions of friendship" opens with the words: "Your head, my dear friend, is full of Notable things; and being better employed, therefore, I do not expect letters from you."

A competent diplomatist, such as Jefferson was (among so many other things), is bound to take note of, and respond to, changes in the status and influence of his correspondents, as Jefferson is doing in this letter of April 1787. Friendship is not a relevant category in correspondence of this kind. Jefferson's personal assessment of Lafayette, as expressed in a letter to Madison, written on the eve of the meeting of the Assembly of Notables, is distant, appraising, not unappreciative but with a note of condescension throughout, and something very like a flash of contempt at the end.

The *Marquis de Lafayette* is a most valuable *auxiliary to me*. His *zeal* is unbounded, and his *we[ight]* with those in *power great*. His *education* having been merely *military*, *commerce* was an unknown field to him. But his good sense enabling him to *comprehend* perfectly whatever is *explained to him, his agency* has been very *efficacious. He* has a great deal of *sound genius,* is well *remarked* by the *king* and rising in *popularity. He* has nothing against *him but* the *suspicion of republican principles.* I think he will one day *be of* the *ministry.* His *foible* is a *canine appetite for popularity and fame.* But he will get *above* this.[26]

Dumas Malone was shaken by Jefferson's adjective, hardly redolent of "enthusiastic admiration." Malone writes: "The word 'canine' was unpleasant, but Jefferson had correctly judged Lafayette's love for glory to be practically insatiable."[27]

Cool as it was, Jefferson's association with Lafayette was much closer, and of greater importance to him, than any other association that he had formed with any Frenchman during his Paris years. Those Frenchmen who are most often named in connection with him are the Abbé Mably, the Abbé Morellet, Condorcet, the Duc de La Rochefoucauld-Liancourt, and Brissot de Warville.

No correspondence between Mably and Jefferson has survived. Mably (and two other abbés of less note) had been part of Franklin's circle, and Jefferson dined with him occasionally (possibly to assert continuity with Franklin) and reported on his affability to Abigail Adams, who also knew him and the other abbés from Franklin's period as Minister Plenipotentiary. John Adams thought they might be spying on the Americans for the Court, but (characteristically) didn't much care whether they were or not. This association, on Jefferson's part, was of no intellectual or political significance (except for the possible connection with Franklin), but mainly social and superficial.

The Abbé Morellet was the French translator of Jefferson's *Notes on the State of Virginia,* and Jefferson's correspondence with Morellet is entirely about this translation.[28]

The most distinguished of the names which have been retrospectively associated with Jefferson, during his period as Minister Plenipotentiary in pre-Revolutionary Paris, are those of Condorcet and the Duc de La Rochefoucauld-Liancourt, both leaders of the intellectual (and, to some extent, the political) life of Paris in the 1780s, and later prominent in the early phases of the Revolution (and both massacred by Revolutionary mobs in 1792–93). Actually, if there was any serious intellectual contact between Jefferson and these personages, it has left no trace for the period during which Jefferson was in France. The Index to *The Papers of Thomas Jefferson* (edited by Boyd) that covers that period lists one letter from

Jefferson to Condorcet, and one from Jefferson to La Rochefoucauld. The reference in both cases is the same: "Volume 11, pp. 111–12." When consulted, the reference turns out to be to a circular letter officially transmitting to each of twenty-five persons (including Condorcet and La Rochefoucauld), a diploma attesting their membership in the American Philosophical Society.[29]

Thomas Jefferson could have had as much of the company of the Paris intellectuals of the period—the *philosophes* of the mid–1780s—as he chose to have. It later tended to be assumed, by friend and foe alike, that he chose to have a great deal. The record suggests otherwise. The French people with whom Jefferson communicated were those with whom his duties as Minister Plenipotentiary—and successor to Benjamin Franklin—required him to communicate, and no others. He was required to cultivate Lafayette, and he did so, though with some symptoms of distaste. He also corresponded with Brissot de Warville, later also prominent in the early stages of the French Revolution (and guillotined under the Terror). But his correspondence with Brissot was not about ideas, political or other, but about a study Brissot was then engaged in of the commerce between France and the United States, a subject requiring Jefferson's official interest.[30] When Brissot writes to Jefferson in a more philosophical vein, in the name of "*la cause de l'Humanité*" and appealing to Jefferson's "*Lumières*," he is politely rebuffed in a letter beginning: "I am very sensitive of the honor you propose to me of becoming a member of the society for the abolition of the slave trade."[31]

Judith Poss Pulley, in her unpublished dissertation on Jefferson's diplomatic mission, judiciously interprets the basic nature of Jefferson's relation to the *philosophes*:[32]

> Nearly all of Jefferson's French associates considered themselves followers of the *philosophes*, but this does not necessarily explain why he was attracted to them. Their sympathy for the American cause was a far more decisive factor. Certainly there were discussions of political philosophy, but for the most part these were instigated by the French who were eager to draw upon the knowledge and experience of the American minister. Jefferson was more interested in their talents as propagandists than in their philosophy. He had been sent to Europe, not to absorb its learning and culture, but to gain its respect and, more specifically, to secure the bonds of Franco-American friendship.

There was a linguistic barrier to spoken communication between Jefferson and his French contemporaries. Malone says that Jefferson never became fluent in the language, though eventually he made himself understood; he even claimed that he could not write it, though there is plenty of record that he did. His progress was naturally slow, since he was past forty and, his first associations being predominantly American, he rarely got beyond the sound of his native tongue. The Americans who happened to be this far from home sought each other out and constantly exchanged hospitalities; they comprised a close-knit group. Jefferson was one of the most honored members of this little band from the first, and after the departure of Adams and Franklin he became its acknowledged chief.[33]

When William Short arrived in Paris in 1784, at Jefferson's invitation (to become his private secretary), he was surprised by Jefferson's imperfect French.[34] Short took pains, while in Paris, to improve his own French, but Jefferson's remained imperfect. The fact that Thomas Jefferson could spend more than five years in France—August 1784 to October 1789—without learning to speak French is in itself not least of the oddities affecting his relationship with France. For Jefferson's capacity to learn, and his application in learning, when once his interest was aroused, were prodigious, and inspired awe both in his contemporaries and among their posterity. Julian P. Boyd justly writes:

> There was, next, the astonishing range of the man. His view swept an arc of the intellectual horizon wider even than that of Franklin. From architecture to zoology Jefferson probed, reflected, and adapted his findings to the society in which he lived. His insatiable inquiries fathered versatility. Even before he drafted the Declaration of Independence at thirty-three he could "calculate an eclipse, survey an estate, tie an artery, plan an edifice, try a cause, break a horse, dance a minuet, and play the violin," to say nothing of being an informed parliamentarian, a collector of manuscript laws, an author of a revolutionary tract, a craftsman in metal, a creative pioneer in archaeology, and an organizer of plans for improving the navigation of a river.[35]

If Thomas Jefferson had wanted to speak French, he would have learned to speak it. It might have taken him a little longer to learn it, at "past forty," than it would have earlier in his life, but it would not have taken him long. One has to conclude that he did not want to learn to speak French, or to become familiar with French people; he wanted to stay American. More precisely, he wanted to stay Virginian. He had made a little Virginia for himself in the Hôtel de Langeac on the Champs Elysées. He would stay in there (when not on his travels), avoiding the French as far as his Ministerial duties permitted, until the blessed day when he could return to Virginia with his children and his house slaves. He remained a Virginian planter and patriarch of the eighteenth century, with his recognized white family and his veiled and equivocal relationships with his partially white house slaves. America, with Virginia at its heart, was always the real world for Thomas Jefferson. Paris was a place of exile. It interested him, professionally and (to a lesser extent) intellectually, but his heart was in Virginia, among its peculiar institutions, which he occasionally deplored, but chose to live among as much as possible and to defend, while deprecating, in his own devious and effective way. (See chapter 7.)

TWO

A SOMEWHAT CLOUDED CRYSTAL BALL

*Jefferson as Witness of the
Last Years of the Ancien Régime*

1786–89

Jefferson's reports from Paris during the terminal crisis of the Ancien Régime often appear inconsistent, but there are some fairly consistent themes within them, sometimes in conflict with one another, and sometimes in harmony.

One theme is a wish to see France evolve in the direction of the American model, Liberty. As against that, there is the fear of anything that would undermine French military and naval strength, and so make Britain a far more formidable potential threat to the young United States. This fear makes Jefferson (in this period) wish to keep reform within limits, and to respect the Monarchy itself, seen as essential to the maintenance of French military strength. The third theme, tending to reinforce the second, is distrust of the capacity of the French to reform themselves without lapsing into anarchy.

This last theme comes out most clearly in a letter written to Abigail Adams (then in London) in August 1786. This letter was written at a time when the refusal of the *Parlements* to register royal edicts for new taxation was pushing the Monarchy into the financial crisis that would lead in early 1787 to the summoning of the Assemblée des Notables and then—after the failure of the Notables to resolve the financial and legal problems—to the summoning of the States-General for the summer of 1789. The attitude of the Parlements has been seen in retrospect as decisive in the breakdown of the French Monarchy: "In the absence of the Estates-General, the *parlements* had claimed to represent the nation and in the closing phase of their struggle with the crown had come, despite their innate conservatism, to use revolutionary language and to hold up for admiration the ideas of the American Revolution."[1]

Thomas Jefferson did not take the crisis at all seriously in this early phase. He wrote to Abigail Adams, on 9 August 1786:

Here we have singing, dauncing, laugh, and merriment. No assassinations, no treasons, rebellions nor other dark deeds. When our king goes out, they fall down and kiss the earth where he has trodden; and then they go to kissing one another. And this is the truest wisdom. They have as much happiness in one year as an Englishman in ten.—The presence of the queen's sister enlivens the court. Still more the birth of the princess. There are some little bickerings between the king and his parliament, but they end with a sic volo sic jubeo, thus I wish, thus I order.[2]

This letter should not be taken quite literally. Jefferson used to vary his tone, even more than most prolific letter writers do, in order to please the person he was writing to. In general, his letters to women are less solemn than his letters to men. With Abigail Adams he maintained at this time a kind of joking relationship, with a faintly flirtatious undertone, and a touch of nostalgia. In the Paris of a few years before, one of the things that had made the Adamses and Jefferson good company for one another was making gentle fun of French "philosophy and frivolity" as exemplified by Madame Helvétius and her circle.[3] He knows that Abigail will be amused and pleased by a letter in the tone of their former conversations. Even allowing for this factor, however, it is surprising that Jefferson could have referred to the conflict between king and parliament in the late summer of 1786 as "little bickerings" that could be ended by a Royal decree (sic volo, sic jubeo). That powerful mind seems, at this time, not to be fully engaged with what was going on before its eyes, for there was no secrecy about the gravity of the legal-financial crisis.

In a letter written to a Virginian Congressman, Edward Carrington, on the eve of the convening of the Assemblée des Notables, Jefferson appears to take the deepening crises rather more seriously, and with guarded optimism.

In my letter to Mr. Jay I have mentioned the meeting of the Notables appointed for the 29th. inst. It is now put off to the 7th. or 8th. of next month. This event, which will hardly excite any attention in America, is deemed here the most important one which has taken place in their civil life during the present century. Some promise their country great things from it, some nothing. Our friend de la fayette was placed on the list originally. Afterwards his name disappeared: but finally was reinstated. This shews that his character here is not considered as an indifferent one; and that it excites agitation. His education in our school has drawn on him a very jealous eye from a court whose principles are the most absolute despotism. But I hope he has nearly passed his crisis. The king, who is a good man, is favorably disposed towards him: and he is supported by powerful family connections, and by the public good will.[4]

In the following paragraph, Jefferson alludes to a factor which could affect French political and military power, and thereby the future of the United States: "The Count de Vergennes has within these ten days had a very severe attack of what is deemed an unfixed gout. He has been well enough however to do business to-day. But anxieties for him are not yet quieted. He is a great and good minister, and an accident to him might endanger the peace of Europe."[5]

Vergennes had fashioned the alliance between the French Monarchy and the American revolutionaries. The then Minister for Finance, Turgot, had opposed the alliance on the grounds that it would involve France in financial ruin and undermine the Monarchy. Turgot was right, but Vergennes was understandably very popular in America. Vergennes died less than a month after Jefferson's letter, on 13 February 1787.

On the day of the first meeting of the Assemblée des Notables, 12 February 1787, Jefferson wrote to Abigail Adams again. This is the letter that includes often-quoted words on rebellion in general: "The spirit of resistance to government is so valuable on certain occasions, that I wish it always to be kept alive. It will often be exercised when wrong, but better so than not to be exercised at all. I like a little rebellion now and then. It is like a storm in the Atmosphere."[6]

In their context, these general reflections do not contain a premonition or intimation of an impending revolution in France. Jefferson is referring to Shays's Rebellion in Massachusetts, the Adamses' home state. Jefferson, in an earlier letter, had intimated abstract approval of the spirit of the rebels, and Abigail had clearly shown that his attitude was repugnant to her. For him to return to the charge in this new letter, adding aesthetic or affective considerations to those of political theory, is a remarkable departure from his customary tactfulness, evident in almost all his letters, but especially so with Abigail Adams. This departure, combined with the language used—and especially the "storm" simile, which seems to be something more than a simile, suggests to me a significant degree of psychic disturbance induced by contemplating the idea of rebellion, or revolution.[7] I shall come back to that, with other instances.

The suggestion of psychic disturbance, triggered by the idea of rebellion in a Northern state, is strongly reinforced by another letter from Jef-

Declaration of Independence (detail), by John Trumbull, 1787–88. Here is Jefferson painted from life during the winter of 1787–88 at his Paris residence, the Hotel de Langeac (chapters 1 and 2).

ferson (to another correspondent), referring back to Shays's Rebellion near the end of the same year:

> The British ministry have so long hired their gazetteers to repeat and model into every form lies about our being in anarchy, that the world has at length believed them, the English nation has believed them, the ministers themselves have come to believe them, and what is more wonderful, we have believed them ourselves. Yet where does this anarchy exist? Where did it ever exist, except in the single instance of Massachusets? And can history produce an instance of a rebellion so honourably conducted? I say nothing of it's motives. They were founded in ignorance, not wickedness. God forbid we should ever be 20. years without such a rebellion. The people can not be all, and always, well informed. The part which is wrong will be discontented in proportion to the importance of the facts they misconceive. If they remain quiet under such misconceptions it is a lethargy, the forerunner of death to the public liberty. We have had 13. states independant 11.

years. There has been one rebellion. That comes to one rebellion in a century and a half for each state. What country before ever existed a century and half for each state. What country before ever existed a century and half without a rebellion? And what country can preserve it's liberties if their rulers are not warned from time to time that their people preserve the spirit of resistance? Let them take arms. The remedy is to set them right as to facts, pardon and pacify them. What signify a few lives lost in a century or two? The tree of liberty must be refreshed from time to time with the blood of patriots and tyrants. It is it's natural manure.[8]

Jefferson was to develop this line of thought, but much more radically, in his "Adam and Eve" letter of five years later (see chapter 4).

The part of Jefferson's letter to Abigail Adams of February 1787 that relates to French affairs is to the same effect as that of the previous August: the French may be so frivolous as to be incapable either of reform or of revolution.

Our Notables assembled to-day, and I hope before the departure of Mr. Cairnes I shall have heard something of their proceedings worth communicating to Mr. Adams. The most remarkeable effect of this convention as yet is the number of puns and bon mots it has generated. I think were they all collected it would make a more voluminous work than the Encyclopedie. This occasion, more than any thing I have seen, convinces me that this nation is incapable of any serious effort but under the word of command. The people at large view every object only as it may furnish puns and bon mots; and I pronounce that a good punster would disarm the whole nation were they ever so seriously disposed to revolt. Indeed, Madam, they are gone. When a measure so capable of doing good as the calling the Notables is treated with so much ridicule, we may conclude the nation desperate, and in charity pray that heaven may send them good kings.[9]

A week after the first meeting of the Assemblée Nationale, the Minister Plenipotentiary, rather strangely, left the scene of political action, Paris, for an extended tour of the South of France, Italy, and the French western seaports, from which he did not return until the end of June. So long an absence from the capital, at so critical a stage in the affairs of the country to which Jefferson was accredited, may be connected with the contempt for French politics and French politicians expressed in the letters to Abigail Adams.

On the eve of his departure from Paris, Jefferson wrote to Lafayette, advising restraint, as to the objectives to be aimed at in the Assemblée: "Keeping the good model of your neighboring country before your eyes you may get on step by step towards a good constitution. Tho' that model is not perfect, yet as it would unite more suffrages than any new one which could be proposed, it is better to make that the object."[10]

The advice to the French reformers of that period to aim no higher than the British Constitution may seem strange, especially if we compare it with Jefferson's apparently unbounded enthusiasm for the full-blown French Revolution (1789–93) and especially for its projected invasion of England (below, chapter 4). Yet Jefferson's advice to Lafayette fits the general pattern of his ideas about France in what we think of retrospectively as the pre-revolutionary period. He does not believe the French to be capable of anything so glorious as the American Revolution, and he fears that, were they to attempt anything of the kind, they would only succeed in weakening France as against England, and so imperiling the United States. Thus he advises the British Constitution as the most desirable model for a people who seem to be incapable of anything better.

Yet these particular themes, though often influencing Jefferson's thought during this period, are not the only ones. There is also the hope that, despite appearances, France may, after all, get more like America. Lafayette encourages this hope. Lafayette had played an important part in the Assemblée des Notables, while Jefferson was on tour. Jefferson who had advised Lafayette (in a slightly patronizing manner) about the policy he should follow in the Assemblée, begins to defer to Lafayette after the Assemblée has broken up. And the policy which Lafayette had followed, during the Assemblée, was quite different from what Jefferson had advised concerning the Assemblée's early days. Jefferson had advised moderation, which meant in practice cooperation with the king and specifically the granting of supply: "If every advance is to be purchased by filling the royal coffers with gold, it will be gold well employed. The king, who means so well, should be encouraged to repeat these assemblies."[11]

As regards the theory of the thing, Lafayette had accepted Jefferson's advice. He thought it would be a worthy aim to restore the old aristocratic constitution of France which was in his opinion "pretty much what it was in England before it had been fairly written down and minutely preserved."[12] In the more important matter of specifics, however, Lafayette's practice in the Assemblée ran counter to Jefferson's precept. Lafayette became the most vocal partisan of "redress of grievances before supply." The success of Lafayette and his friends led to the dismissal of the finance minister, Calonne, who had advised the convening of the Assemblée. After that, Lafayette went on to make the first genuinely revolutionary proposal to be formulated, since the start of the legal and financial crises. He concluded an address to the Assemblée, opposing the granting of new taxes, with the words "It seems to me that we have reached the point where we ought to beseech His Majesty once more to assume responsibility for all measures and to assure their happy outcome forever by convoking a national assembly."[13]

Louis Gottschalk comments:

> The effect of the phrase "national assembly" was electric. The boldest opponents of royal absolutism among parlementarians and *philosophes* had hitherto dared to suggest only the revival of the historic Estates General. In fact, a demand for the Estates General had already been made in the Second Bureau. But Lafayette now called for a "national assembly." The word "national" in his vocabulary meant "popular." A *national* assembly would be one controlled not by the upper two orders of society, as would the Estates General, but by the nation at large.
>
> The Comte d'Artois [the king's brother, a strong conservative] again lost his patience. Did Lafayette mean to ask for an estates general, he demanded. Lafayette was anxious not to be misunderstood. "Yes, Monseigneur," he answered, "and even better than that." Would Lafayette put his request in writing so that Artois might take it to the king? "Yes, Monseigneur." An awkward silence followed. No one indorsed Lafayette's request, and he was led to conclude that his colleagues thought that he had spoken without due regard for the seriousness of his proposal. One day he would be able to boast that he had had greater insight than they.[14]

Since it had become clear that the Notables were not about to grant supply without unacceptable conditions, the King dissolved the Assemblée. As it happened, the day on which the Assemblée was dissolved in Paris was also the day on which the American Constitutional Convention assembled for the first time in Philadelphia.

We do not know what Jefferson felt at the time about Lafayette's assumption of a political position so far in advance of what he himself had advised. One would expect him to have been concerned about the probable weakening in the military power of France as a result of the long financial crisis and the failure of the Assemblée des Notables to resolve it. One might have thought also that, having the probable military consequences in mind, he would have resented Lafayette's rejection of Jefferson's cautious advice, and especially Lafayette's leadership in the refusal of supply, and his evocation of the hazardous project of a National Assembly. But if Jefferson felt any such concerns, they have left no trace in his correspondence, as preserved, for most of the summer of 1787: there is a curious absence of political comment from the time of Jefferson's return to Paris (late May) to early August. By August, the royal finances had deteriorated further. Louis XVI after the collapse of the Assemblée was again, forlornly, trying to bully the Parlement into registering an edict for new taxation. Jefferson comments on the situation in two letters of 6 August. In both letters he envisages, for the first time, some kind of revolutionary development but one to be achieved almost mechanically, through the passage of time, and generational change. In the first, to a Franco-American correspondent, Michel-Guillaume Jean de Crèvecoeur, Jefferson writes,

> Great is the change in the dispositions of this country in the short time since you left it. A continuation of inconsiderate expence seems to have raised the nation to the highest pitch of discontent. The parliament refused to register the new taxes. After much and warm altercation a lit de justice has been held this day at Versailles; it was opened by the reading a severe remonstrance from the parliament, to which the king made a hard reply, and finished by ordering the stamp tax, and impot territorial to be registered.—Your nation is advancing to a change of constitution. The young desire it, the middle aged are not averse, the old alone are opposed to it. They will die; the provincial assemblies will chalk out the plan, and the nation ripening fast, will execute it.[15]

The second reference is contained in a long official dispatch to John Jay, then acting Secretary of State. Interestingly enough, most of the dispatch is devoted, not to the French internal crisis, but to European affairs in general. The reference to the French crisis comes towards the end of the long dispatch:

> The edict for the stamp tax has been the subject of reiterated orders and refusals to register. At length the king has summoned the Parliament to Versailles to hold a bed of justice, in which he will order them in person to register the edict. At the moment of my writing they are gone to Versailles for this purpose. There will yet remain to them to protest against the register as forced, and to issue orders against it's execution on pain of death. But as the king would have no peaceable mode of opposition left, it remains to be seen whether they will push the matter to this extremity. It is evident I think that the spirit of this country is advancing towards a revolution in their constitution. There are not wanting persons at the helm, friends to the progress of this spirit.[16]

Lafayette was at this time preeminent in this last category, and Jay would have understood this. So would Washington, if Jay showed him Jefferson's dispatch (as is probable). Jefferson accepted Lafayette's account of the proceedings of the Assemblées des Notables in the summer of

1787 and for the next two years Jefferson appears to see French political developments, almost entirely through the eyes of this one participant in them. R. R. Palmer writes:

> The truth seems to be that Jefferson's idea of what was happening was taken almost entirely from his good friend the Marquis de Lafayette, who played an active part in the Assembly of Notables, as in other later events. Professor Gottschalk, in his great work on Lafayette, allows that his hero in the troubled months of 1787 was somewhat naïve, that he only very slowly came to see the character of the aristocratic resistance to proposed reforms, and that in his patriotic and idealistic outburst he served as a cat's-paw for the privileged interests. At any rate, when Calonne announced that the monarchy was bankrupt, Lafayette and the Assembly refused to believe him. When he revealed the amount of the deficit, which was of old standing and greatly increased by the American war, they attributed it to his own maladministration, insisting that there had been no deficit in Necker's time a few years before. When Calonne desperately asserted that the govern-ment's income must be immediately raised, and that certain loopholes and privileges in the tax structure must be stopped, they retorted that econo-mies in expenditure would suffice. They accused Calonne of scandalous waste, graft and corruption, and denounced the monstrous prodigality of the royal court. Lafayette, in high-minded indignation, did as much as any man to draw this red herring of alleged personal dishonesty and courtly extravagance across the trail marked out by Calonne for structural reform. The trouble in this view was not in the legal and social organization of France, but in the misconduct of an overgrown and arrogant government.
>
> This was doctrine that a Virginia gentleman could readily understand. Powerful government was what Jefferson feared; monarchy was his buga-boo; it was resistance to tyrants that expressed the will of God. "You are afraid of the one—I, of the few. . . . You are apprehensive of Monarchy; I, of Aristocracy." So John Adams wrote to him, diagnosing the difference between them.[17]

This dependence on a single source, and that one a major participant, for interpretation of events over a period of years, at a time of rapid change, is so far from recommended diplomatic practice as to seem to call for some explanation. In the Jefferson-Lafayette case, the need for explanation is all the greater in that Jefferson, in the days before Lafayette rose to national prominence through his role in the Assemblée des Nota-bles, had not held Lafayette in particularly high esteem. It seems espe-cially odd that Jefferson should have taken for his chosen guide and mentor through this critical period, 1787–89, a person whom he had seen, only a short time before, as dominated by an "almost canine" desire for praise.

A part of the explanation is no doubt that Lafayette, who was in the thick of things throughout this period, was the most convenient and abundant source of information available to Jefferson. Lafayette was also very highly regarded in America—and in particular by George Washington—so that a fairly close association between him and the American Minister Plenipotentiary would be likely to be accepted as normal. Also, the fact that the leading French admirer of (and contributor to) the American Revolution was now beginning to play a leading role in the effort to reform French institutions was something of its nature congenial to the Americans concerned. Basically Lafayette was "our Frenchman" and therefore somebody to be backed up even though some, like Jefferson and Madison, privately did not consider "our Frenchman" quite all that he was cracked up to be.

Yet I think there is a more potent force than any of these behind Jefferson's excessive dependence on Lafayette in 1787–88. Jefferson in this period was almost desperately anxious to be done with Paris and get home. To his chronic homesickness, new and strong political motives had been added. A new Constitution for the United States had been enacted in his absence, and the nature of the future relations between the new Federal Government and his native Virginia is unclear and fraught. These matters, deeply affecting him as a Virginian and an American, and bound to shape his personal political future, have to be more important to him than anything, good or bad, that is happening to the French; as he then thinks. His mind as well as his heart are already away in America; his body will follow as soon as he can get it there. In October 1787, Congress had extended his period of duty for another three years. In November of the following year, however, Jefferson draws the attention of the Secretary of State, John Jay, to the unforeseen length of his service in France: five years, instead of the five months originally intended. Jefferson informs Jay that he will have to ask Congress for a short leave of absence: from the spring to the fall of 1789. Jefferson wrote:

> I must therefore ask of Congress a leave of short absence. Allowing three months on the sea, going and coming, and two months at my own house, which will suffice for my affairs, I need not be from Paris but between five and six months. I do not foresee any thing which can suffer during my absence. The Consular convention is finished except as to the exchange of

ratifications, which will be the affair of a day only. The difference with Schweighauser & Dobree relative to our arms will be finished. That of Denmark, if ever finished will probably be long spun out. The ransom of the Algerine captives is the only matter likely to be on hand. That cannot be set on foot till the money is raised in Holland, and an order received for it's application. Probably these will take place, so that I may set it into motion before my departure. If not, I can still leave it on such a footing as to be put into motion the moment the money can be paid. And even, when the leave of Congress shall be received, I will not make use of it, if there is any thing of consequence which may suffer; but would postpone my departure till circumstances will admit it.[18]

With his mind on America, from 1787 on, Jefferson is content to follow Lafayette's estimate of the direction in which French affairs are moving: a peaceful, or mostly peaceful, evolution into a stable constitutional monarchy. Jefferson wrote to John Adams in the late summer of 1787: "I think that in the course of three months the royal authority has lost, and the rights of the nation gained, as much ground, by a revolution of public opinion only, as England gained in all her civil wars under the Stuarts. I rather believe too they will retain the ground gained, because it is defended by the young and the middle aged, in opposition to the old only. The first party increases, and the latter diminishes daily from the course of nature."[19]

In general, Jefferson's tone in discussing French affairs in 1787–88 is calm, rational, and somewhat detached, even a little bored. But there is one *apparent* exception. Jefferson in late 1787 is suddenly getting very excited about *kings*. In a letter written shortly before the philosophical "course of nature" letter to John Adams, Jefferson discusses some military moves then being carried out by various European powers. He then concludes his letter as follows:

So much for the blessings of having kings, and magistrates who would be kings. From these events our young republics may learn many useful lessons, never to call on foreign powers to settle their differences, to guard against hereditary magistrates, to prevent their citizens from becoming so established in wealth and power as to be thought worthy of alliance by marriage with the neices, sisters &c. of kings, and in short to besiege the throne of heaven with eternal prayers to extirpate from creation this class of human lions, tygers and mammouts called kings; from whom, let him perish, who does not say 'good lord deliver us,' and that so we may say, one and all, or perish is the fervent prayer of him who has the honor to mix with it sincere wishes for your health and happiness, and to be with real attachment and respect dear Sir your affectionate friend & humble servant,

TH: JEFFERSON[20]

When Jefferson's normally stately style turns strident, it is well to wonder what is going on; especially when, as in this case, the stridency doesn't seem to be related to the general context and pattern of what Jefferson had been saying. True, Jefferson had long been a strong opponent of monarchy as an institution. But he had not at any time shown hostility to the particular Monarch to whose Court he was accredited. He believed in the good intentions of Louis XVI, and hoped (at this time) that Louis was about to become the central pillar of an emerging constitutional monarchy. So why now—with this benign process, as he believed, well under way, in the "course of nature"—does Thomas Jefferson suddenly start ranting about "prayers to extirpate from creation this class of human lions, tygers and mammouts called kings"—dehumanizing language which appears to anticipate that of Louis's executioners, Robespierre and St. Just, six years later?

Could Thomas Jefferson have ever seen poor well-meaning Louis as a "lion," a "tyger" or a "mammout"? I don't believe he ever did. I believe that when Jefferson wrote those words he was thinking about George Washington, then soon about to become first President of the United States, under the country's new Constitution.

Before any readers dismiss this hypothesis as wildly extravagant, I suggest they consider two other letters written by Jefferson, also in late 1787. The more explicit of these is one to John Adams, in November 1787:

> How do you like our new constitution? I confess there are things in it which stagger all my dispositions to subscribe to what such an assembly has proposed. The house of federal representatives will not be adequate to the management of affairs either foreign or federal. Their President seems a bad edition of a Polish king. He may be reelected from 4. years to 4. years for life. Reason and experience prove to us that a chief magistrate, so continuable, is an officer for life. When one or two generations shall have proved that this is an office for life, it becomes on every succession worthy of intrigue, of bribery, of force, and even of foreign interference. It will be of great consequence to France and England to have America governed by a Galloman or Angloman. Once in office, and possessing the military force of the union, without either the aid or check of a council, he would not be easily dethroned, even if the people could be induced to withdraw their

votes from him. I wish that at the end of the 4. years they had made him for ever ineligible a second time. Indeed I think all the good of this new constitution might have been couched in three or four new articles to be added to the good, old, and venerable fabrick, which should have been preserved even as a religious relique.[21]

One wonders where "a bad edition of a Polish king" might figure in the monarchical-zoomorphic procession conjured up by Jefferson's imagination in the letter to David Humphreys? Perhaps a hyena might meet the case.

The second relevant reference is contained in a letter from Jefferson to George Washington himself, written on the same day as the letter to David Humphreys. At this time, the Constitutional Convention was still in progress and Jefferson expresses his hopes for its outcome. The hopes also imply misgivings. Jefferson writes: "I remain in hopes of great and good effects from the decisions of the assembly over which you are presiding. To make our states one as to all foreign concerns, preserve them several as to all merely domestic, to give to the federal head some peaceable mode of enforcing their just authority, to organize that head into Legislative, Executive, and Judiciary departments are great desiderata in our federal constitution."[22]

The Constitution, when completed, provided for a much stronger Executive than Jefferson had hoped for, and his November letter to Adams reflects his chagrin at this outcome. But it is clear that he already, even while the Convention is still sitting, fears movement in that direction.[23] After surveying military developments in Europe, in a similar but more restrained vein to that of the same day's letter to David Humphreys, Jefferson concludes in a letter to Washington:

Upon the whole I think peace advantageous to us, necessary for Europe, and desireable for humanity. A few days will decide probably whether all these considerations are to give way to the bad passions of kings and those who would be kings. I have the honour to be with very sincere esteem and respect dear Sir Your most obedient & most humble servant,

TH: JEFFERSON[24]

". . . and those who would be kings." Could that be aimed at Washington himself? Perhaps not consciously, but I think Jefferson did have Washington in mind, as well as others, notably Adams himself and perhaps, already Hamilton. After Jefferson returned to the United States, the Republican press, under Jefferson's patronage, was to make monarchical tendencies in the Federal Government a constant theme. Hamilton and

Adams were the main targets of explicit attacks, but Washington himself was not spared. He was attacked in the Republican press, occasionally and obliquely from 1791 to 1794, and directly, viciously, and copiously from 1795 until the end of his Presidency in 1796.[25]).

It is at least clear that, in this fateful historical interlude, of less than two years, between the conclusion of the American Constitutional Convention and the outbreak of the French Revolution, the Minister Plenipotentiary in Paris was more preoccupied, intellectually and emotionally, with the trend of American affairs than with what was happening in France. Might not liberty be waning in America while it was waxing in France? Some time later, but not during this interlude, Jefferson was to put the question: Might not the flame of liberty in France rekindle the liberty of America?

During 1788, these questions remain, as it seems, on the back burner. Jefferson, during this period, realizes that, however he may feel about some aspects of the Federal Constitution, he is going to have to live within it. He writes to Madison about it in a respectful vein in November 1788:

Mr. Carrington was so kind as to send me the 2d. vol. of the Amer. phil. transactions, the federalist, and some other interesting pamphlets; and I am to thank you for another copy of the federalist and the report of the instructions to the ministers for negotiating peace. The latter unluckily omitted exactly the passage I wanted, which was what related to the navigation of the Missisipi. With respect to the Federalist, the three authors had been named to me. I read it with care, pleasure and improvement, and was satisfied there was nothing in it by one of those hands [John Jay], and not a great deal by a second [Alexander Hamilton]. It does the highest honor to the third [James Madison], as being, in my opinion, the best commentary on the principles of government which ever was written. In some parts it is discoverable that the author means only to say what may be best said in defence of opinions in which he did not concur. But in general it establishes firmly the plan of government. I confess it has rectified me in several points. As to the bill of rights however I still think it should be added, and I am glad to see that three states have at length considered the perpetual re-eligibility of the president as an article which should be amended. I should deprecate with you indeed the meeting of a new convention. I hope they will adopt the mode of amendment by Congress and the Assemblies, in which case I should not fear any dangerous innovation in the plan. But the minorities are too respectable not to be entitled to some sacrifice of opinion in the majority. Especially when a great proportion of them would be contented with a bill of rights.[26]

No doubt this is partly politic; Jefferson knew how large a part Madison had played in the drafting of the Constitution and he knows also that he is going to need Madison as a political ally (below, chapter 3). It's significant I believe that when Jefferson calms down (for the moment) about American politics, he also gets calmer about France. The passion for extirpating kings, so inflamed in late 1787, seems to have left him altogether by the summer of 1788, when he writes:

> As to the opposition which the English expect from the personal character of the king, it proves they do not know what his personal character is. He is the honestest man in his kingdom, and the most regular and oeconomical. He has no foible which will enlist him against the good of his people; and whatever constitution will promote this, he will befriend. But he will not befriend it obstinately. He has given repeated proofs of a readiness to sacrifice his opinion to the wish of the nation. I believe he will consider the opinion of the States general as the best evidence of what will please and profit the nation and will conform to it. All the characters at court may not be of this disposition, and from thence may possibly arise representations capable of leading the king astray. But upon a full view of all circumstances, I have sanguine hopes that such a constitution will be established here as will regenerate the energy of the nation, cover it's friends and make it's enemies tremble. I am, with very great esteem Dear Sir your friend & servt.,
>
> TH: JEFFERSON[27]

Privately, Jefferson's hopes, in relation to the future of France, seem not to have been quite so sanguine, or so Lafayettean, in late 1788, as they are made to appear in the letter to Cutting. Jefferson was always more inclined to open his mind to James Madison than to any other correspondent, and what he tells Madison, in November 1788, is significantly different from what he had told Cutting in August. To Madison, Jefferson wrote: "Here things internally are going on well. The Notables, now in session, have indeed past one vote which augurs ill to the rights of the people. But if they [the people] do not obtain now so much as they have a right to, they will in the long run. The misfortune is that they are not yet ripe for receiving the blessings to which they are entitled."[28]

But what will happen when people receive blessings to which they are entitled, but unfortunately are not yet ripe for receiving? Thomas Jefferson, on the eve of 1789, does not choose to examine the disquieting implications of his message to Madison. Nor did he ever examine them.

Early in the month after that in which he sent that basically pessimistic message to Madison, Jefferson wrote to Washington one of the most curious letters in the curious collection of Jefferson's prognostications on the eve of the French Revolution. The passage begins with a ringing declaration of revolutionary faith and conviction, and later tails off with a lament about how the bright prospects are about to be dashed by French morals and the influence of women:

> In every event, I think the present disquiet will end well. The nation has been awaked by our revolution, they feel their strength, they are enlightened, their lights are spreading, and they will not retrograde. The first states general may establish 3. important points without opposition from the court. 1. their own periodical convocation. 2. their exclusive right of taxation (which has been confessed by the king.) 3. The right of registering laws and of previously proposing amendments to them, as the parliaments have by usurpation been in the habit of doing. The court will consent to this from it's hatred to the parliaments, and from the desire of having to do with one rather than many legislatures. If the states are prudent they will not aim at more than this at first, lest they should shock the dispositions of the court, and even alarm the public mind, which must be left to open itself by degrees to successive improvements. These will follow from the nature of things. How far they can proceed, in the end, towards a thorough reformation of abuse, cannot be foreseen. In my opinion a kind of influence, which none of their plans of reform take into account, will elude them all; I mean the influence of women in the government. The manners of the nation allow them to visit, alone, all persons in office, to sollicit the affairs of the husband, family, or friends, and their sollicitations bid defiance to laws and regulations. This obstacle may seem less to those who, like our countrymen, are in the precious habit of considering Right, as a barrier against all sollicitation. Nor can such an one, without the evidence of his own eyes, believe in the desperate state to which things are reduced in this country from the omnipotence of an influence which, fortunately for the happiness of the sex itself, does not endeavor to extend itself in our country beyond the domestic line.[29]

Concerning such references by Jefferson to the behavior of French women, Bernard Bailyn comments: "This theme of sexual promiscuity as the ultimate corruption had a general meaning to this typically Puritan revolutionary and recent widower."[30]

To one who, like myself, is disposed to accept Madison Hemings's account of his parentage (chapter 1) the description of Thomas Jefferson as "typically Puritan" sounds strange. Yet it may well be accurate in a way. Jefferson's horror of promiscuity was probably quite genuine. What Jefferson objected to about French morals was the absence of stable "domestic bonds." The relationship described by Madison Hemings can be regarded as a domestic bond, and a stable one since it produced children over the period of 1789 to 1806. (The possible bearings of all this on Jefferson's feelings with regard to liberty, slavery, and the French Revolution are considered in chapter 7.)

The Virginian patriarch's views on French forms of immorality were well established by this time, but there is something new in the prominence attributed to these, in negative relation to the possibility of any desirable change in French political arrangements. The assertions about the power of French women may be seen as a specific example of the claim in the letter to Madison about the French not being ripe to receive the blessings of liberty.

This passage in the letter to Washington is a notable example of a central weakness in Jefferson's political thought in the period of the French Revolution. This is the tendency to separate a hypostatized abstraction—"the nation"—from the actual living people who make up the nation. "The nation" is all that it ought to be; it is "awaked" (by America), "enlightened"; its "lights are spreading" and it "will not retrograde." But unfortunately this marvellous nation suffers from a mysterious and fatal disability. While beyond reproach itself, it is hindered by a set of "manners" which are so depraved as to render the sublime qualities existentially inherent in "the nation" altogether inoperative as a result of its "manners": that is, the actual patterns of behavior of the people who make up the nation. For "the nation" to be redeemed, you would need to get rid of the people who made it up. And we shall see later (below, pp. 145–47) with what rigor this logical razor is applied in the case of the greatest of all the Jeffersonian hypostatized abstractions: Liberty.[31]

Writing to two English-speaking radicals—Richard Price and Thomas Paine—at the beginning of 1789, Jefferson suppresses the reservations made in his letters to Madison and Jefferson, about unripeness and the manners of the nation, concentrating on the "never retrograde" principle, but suggesting moderate objectives. He writes:

> Upon the whole it has appeared to me that the basis of the present struggle is an illumination of the public mind as to the rights of the nation, aided by fortunate incidents; that they can never retrograde, but from the natural progress of things must press forward to the establishment of a constitution which shall assure to them a good degree of liberty. They flatter themselves they shall form a better constitution than the English. I think it will be better in some points, worse in others. It will be better in the article of representation which will be more equal. It will be worse, as their situation obliges them to keep up the dangerous machine of a standing army. I doubt

too whether they will obtain the trial by jury, because they are not sensible of it's value.[32]

To John Jay (11 January) Jefferson writes in a similar strain. In March, he is still generally confident, but also a little apprehensive about what will actually happen when the States-General meet:

> The difficulties which now appear threatening to my mind are those which will result from the size of the assembly. 1200. persons, of any rank, and of any nation, assembled together would with difficulty be prevented from tumult, and confusion. But when they are to compose an assembly for which no rules of debate or proceeding have been yet formed, in whom no habits of order have been yet established, and to consist moreover of Frenchmen among whom there are always more speakers than listners, I confess to you I apprehend some danger. However I still hope that the good sense of the body, and the coolness and collectedness of some of their leaders will keep them in the right way, and that this great assembly will end happily.[33]

In March also, Jefferson made a significant and propitiatory move in relation to American politics. He wrote to David Humphreys to convey his overall acceptance of the Constitution, and his loyalty to George Washington:

> The operations which have taken place in America lately, fill me with pleasure. In the first place they realize the confidence I had that whenever our affairs get obviously wrong, the good sense of the people will interpose and set them to rights. The example of changing a constitution by assembling the wise men of the state, instead of assembling armies, will be worth as much to the world as the former examples we had given them. The constitution too which was the result of our deliberations, is unquestionably the wisest ever yet presented to men, and some of the accomodations of interest which it has adopted are greatly pleasing to me who have before had occasions of seeing how difficult those interests were to accomodate. A general concurrence of opinion seems to authorize us to say it has some defects. I am one of those who think it a defect that the important rights, not placed in security by the frame of the constitution itself, were not explicitly secured by a supplementary declaration. There are rights which it is useless to surrender to the government, and which yet, governments have always been fond to invade. These are the rights of thinking, and publishing our thoughts by speaking or writing: the right of free commerce: the right of personal freedom. There are instruments for administering the government, so peculiarly trust-worthy, that we should never leave the legislature

at liberty to change them. The new constitution has secured these in the executive and legislative departments; but not in the judiciary. It should have established trials by the people themselves, that is to say by jury. There are instruments so dangerous to the rights of the nation, and which place them so totally at the mercy of their governors, that those governors, whether legislative or executive, should be restrained from keeping such instruments on foot but in well defined cases. Such an instrument is a standing army. We are now allowed to say such a declaration of rights, as a supplement to the constitution where that is silent, is wanting to secure us in these points. The general voice has legitimated this objection. It has not however authorized me to consider as a real defect, what I thought and still think one, the perpetual re-eligibility of the president. But three states out of 11. having declared against this, we must suppose we are wrong according to the fundamental law of every society, the lex majoris partis, to which we are bound to submit. And should the majority change their opinion, and become sensible that this trait in their constitution is wrong, I would wish it to remain uncorrected as long as we can avail ourselves of the services of our great leader, whose talents and whose weight of character I consider as peculiarly necessary to get the government so under way as that it may afterwards be carried on by subordinate characters.[34]

So no more "bad edition of a Polish king." But Jefferson's reservations about Washington's power had not altogether disappeared; only gone underground. (See below, chapter 3.)

In early May, on the eve of the meeting of the States-General, the first serious violence broke out in Paris. In his report to Jay, Jefferson plays down the violence and dissociates it from the Revolution:

The revolution of this country has advanced thus far without encountering any thing which deserves to be called a difficulty. There have been riots in a few instances in three or four different places, in which there may have been a dozen or twenty lives lost. The exact truth is not to be got at. A few days ago a much more serious riot took place in this city, in which it became necessary for the troops to engage in regular action with the mob, and probably about 100 of the latter were killed. Accounts vary from 20. to 200. They were the most abandoned banditti of Paris, and never was a riot more unprovoked and unpitied. They began under a pretence that a paper manufacturer had proposed in an assembly to reduce their wages to 15. sous a day. They rifled his house, destroyed every thing in his magazines and shops, and were only stopped in their career of micheif by the carnage above mentioned. Neither this nor any other of the riots have had a professed connection with the great national reformation going on. They are

L. ACCOMPLISSEMENT DU VŒU DE LA NATION

Procession of the States-General at Versailles, 4 May 1789. *L'Accomplissement du Voeu de la Nation,* anonymous engraving, Bibliothèque nationale, Paris. Courtesy of Giraudon/Art Resource, New York. Thomas Jefferson, as Minister Plenipotentiary of the United States, was present at the opening of the States-General in the Hotel des Menus Plaisirs. Jefferson wrote to Madison: "The States General were opened the day before yesterday. Viewing it as an Opera it was imposing" (TJ to JM, 11 May 1789; chapter 2, p. 58).

such as have happened every year since I have been here, and as will continue to be produced by common incidents.[35]

The contrast between this assessment and what Jefferson had had to say earlier about Shays's Rebellion is remarkable. Shays's rebels, after all, had also material motives for what they did. No less striking is the contrast between Jefferson's response to the events of May and his response to later acts of mob violence in Revolutionary Paris. But Jefferson had an unshakable confidence in his own ability to discern, whatever the circumstances, where exactly the tree of Liberty was situated, which mobs were pure-souled patriots "manuring the tree with their blood" and which were just "abandoned banditti," having no "connection with the great national reformation."

On 6 May 1789, the States-General opened. Jefferson has a little difficulty in taking this event altogether seriously. This was the sort of occasion on which "the manners of the nation" obscure the view of "the nation" itself:

> The States general were opened the day before yesterday. Viewing it as an Opera it was imposing; as a scene of business the king's speech was exactly what it should have been and very well delivered, not a word of the Chancellor's was heard by any body, so that as yet I have never heard a single guess at what it was about. Mr. Neckar's was as good as such a number of details would permit it to be. The picture of their resources was consoling and generally plausible. I could have wished him to have dwelt more on those great constitutional reformations which his "Rapport au roy" had prepared us to expect. But they observe that these points were proper for the speech of the Chancellor. We are in hopes therefore they were in that speech, which, like the Revelations of St. John, were no revelations at all.[36]

That May, Jefferson had even more difficulty than usual in concentrating on the affairs of France. A letter to James Madison, five days after the opening of the States-General, begins as follows: "My last to you was of the 15th. of March. I am now in hourly expectation of recieving my leave of absence. The delay of it a little longer will endanger the throwing my return into the winter, the very idea of which is horror itself to me. I am in hopes this is the last letter I shall have the pleasure of writing you before my departure."[37]

Jefferson's report to Madison, in the same letter, on the progress of the revolution in France is optimistic, still separating the accompanying violence from the abstract revolution:

> The revolution of France has gone on with the most unexampled success hitherto. There have been some mobs occasioned by the want of bread in different parts of the kingdom, in which there may have been some lives lost, perhaps a dozen or twenty. These had no professed connection *generally* with the constitutional revolution. A more serious riot happened lately in Paris in which about 100 of the mob were killed. This execution has been universally approved, as they seemed to have no view but mischief and plunder. But the meeting of the states general presents serious difficulties which it had been hoped the progress of reason would have enabled them to get over.

The most pressing question of the hour was whether the States-General would sit "by Order"—Nobility, Clergy, Third Estate—or together, in which case the Third Estate, equal now in number to the other two Orders taken together, would dominate the proceedings. Jefferson, influenced by his personal contacts in Paris—which were almost exclusively with the "advanced" section of the Nobility—had believed that the Nobility would voluntarily accept merger with the other Orders. In fact, the Nobility resisted the merger and even Lafayette—to Jefferson's dismay and against his advice—felt constrained by his instructions from the local *noblesse* in Auvergne, to resist it.[38]

In reality, it was the lower clergy who made the decisive break with their own superiors and decided to merge with the Third Estate. Jefferson had not foreseen this development, and at the time of his letter to Madison is still underestimating "the sons of the peasantry" with whom he had no personal contact.[39] He writes, in the same letter to Madison, "Five sixths of that representation consists of the lower clergy, who being the sons of the peasantry are very well with the tiers etat. But the bishops are intrigueing and drawing them over daily."

On 19 June 1789, the majority of the clergy decided to join with the Third Estate. In his dispatches of 24 June and 29 June (*JP*, Boyd, Vol. 15, pp. 205–9 and 221–23). Jefferson gave Jay a detailed account of the development and outcome of the crisis. The dispatch of 29 June ends with the words: "This great crisis being now over, I shall not have matter interesting enough to trouble you with as often as I have done lately. There has nothing remarkeable taken place in any other part of Europe."

The dispatches to Jay were confided by Jefferson (for transmission to Jay), to his friend John Trumbull, the painter of the American Revolution, then about to return to the United States. Jefferson had already sent Trumbull the dispatch of 24 June, and he sent that of 29 June with a covering note:

> I took the liberty on the 26th. inst. of troubling you with a packet for Mr. Jay giving him an account of the crisis into which the seance royale of the 23d. had thrown this country. I now trouble you with the inclosed, which will inform him that all is settled by a reunion of the three orders in one chamber in consequence of a letter from the king: so that all danger of civil commotion here is at an end, and it is probable they will proceed to settle to themselves a good constitution, and meet no difficulty in doing it.—No congê yet. I am with great esteem and attachment Dear Sir Your friend & servt.,
>
> TH: JEFFERSON[40]

The *congé* awaited is that of the U.S. Congress for Jefferson's home leave; the French Senate had already agreed that William Short, the Secretary of the Legation, should act as Chargé d'Affaires. Jefferson's certitude that "this great crisis" is "now over" and "all danger of civil commotion

... at an end" may be connected with his anxiety to get home. Leaving the French Revolution behind him, safely wrapped up.

On 11 July, Jefferson writes to Thomas Paine a more glowing account of the triumph of the French Revolution:

> The *National assembly* then (for that is the name they take) having shewn thro' every stage of these transactions a coolness, wisdom, and resolution to set fire to the four corners of the kingdom and to perish with it themselves rather than to relinquish an iota from their plan of a total change of government, are now in complete and undisputed possession of the sovereignty. The executive and the aristocracy are now at their feet: the mass of the nation, the mass of the clergy, and the army are with them. They have prostrated the old government, and are now beginning to build one from the foundation.[41]

Tom Paine liked the bit about setting "fire to the four corners of the kingdom" etc. so much that he incorporated it in a letter which he wrote to Edmund Burke (of all people) on 17 January 1790. Paine assumed that Burke, since he liked the American revolution, must love the French one (a proposition that seemed self-evident to Paine and Jefferson and many others). Actually, when he received Paine's letter, Burke was already at work on *Reflections on the Revolution in France* (published 1 November 1790). A distinguished French historian of the eighteenth century, Patrick Thierry, believes that this passage in Paine's letter "made no small contribution to the fury" with which Burke reacted against the French Revolution.[42] This is the only example I know of a Jeffersonian influence—or rather impact—on Edmund Burke. The case is of considerable interest in view of Jefferson's later reactions to Burke's *Reflections,* on whose composition Jefferson had unwittingly impinged (below, pp. 102–3). The idea that it is admirable on the part of a representative assembly to resolve "to set fire to the four corners of the kingdom and to perish with it themselves rather than to relinquish an iota from their plan" is a product of the wilder shores of Thomas Jefferson, along with "the tree of liberty" and "Adam and Eve" (see below, pp. 145–48).

Jefferson adds a summary of the National Assembly's agenda, together with an assurance that the Assembly will complete it successfully:

Recapitulation.
Declaration of the rights of man.
Principles of the monarchy.
Rights of the nation.
Rights of the king

Rights of the citizens.

Organisation and rights of the national assembly.

Forms necessary for the enaction of laws.

Organisation and functions of the provincial and municipal assemblies.

Duties and limits of the judiciary power.

Functions and duties of the military power.

You see that these are the materials of a superb edifice, and the hands which have prepared them, are perfectly capable of putting them together, and of filling up the work of which these are only the outlines.

Two days later, Jefferson had an addition to make to his letter to Paine:

Mr. Necker was dismissed from office the evening of the 11th. and set out for Geneva. This was not generally known in Paris till yesterday afternoon. The mobs immediately shut up all the playhouses. The foreign troops were advanced into the city. Engagements took place between some of them and the people. The first was in the place Louis XV. where a body of German cavalry being drawn up, the people posted themselves upon and behind the piles of stones collected there for the bridge, attacked and drove off the cavalry with stones. I suspect the cavalry rallied and returned, as I heard shortly after in the same spot a considerable firing. This was a little before dusk, and it is now early in the morning: so I have not ascertained any particulars. Monsr. de Montmorin has resigned. It is said the Baron de Breteuil is taken into the ministry but I cannot affirm this. The progress of things here will be subject to checks from time to time of course. Whether they will be great or small will depend on the army. But they will be only checks.[43]

Jefferson's third letter to Tom Paine that month was his first written (to anyone) after the Fall of the Bastille. As such, it merits being quoted in full, as follows:

I wrote you by post on the 13th. That day all the rest of the ministry was dismissed except Villedeuil and Barentin. The new ministers were Breteuil, Broglio, Vauguyon, de la Porte, de la Galaisiere, and Foulon. The people of Paris forced the prisons of St. Lazare, where they got some arms. On the 14th. they took the Invalids, and Bastille, and beheaded the Governor and Lt. Governor of the latter and the Prevost des marchands. The city committee is determined to embody 48,000 Bourgeois and named the Marquis de la Fayette commander in chief. The king hereupon went to the States general, and surrendered as it were at discretion and this day he and they have come in solemn procession to satisfy the city. He has sent to Brussels to recall Mr. Necker; he has accepted the resignations of Villedeuil, Barentin and Broglio and to-day or to-morrow will receive those of Breteuil and the rest. I imagine that from 60. to 80,000 armed Bourgeois lined the streets through which he passed to day. A more dangerous scene of war I never saw in America, than what Paris has presented for 5. days past. *This places the power of the States general absolutely out of the reach of attack, and they may be considered as having a carte blanche.*[44]

I have italicized the last sentence in the above letter because of the assured and unwarranted assumption it contains. This is that the victory of the armed sections of the populace in the streets of Paris leaves "the States general" (by now the National Assembly) firmly in charge of the situation ("having a carte blanche"). Subsequent events were amply to demonstrate the fallacy in that assumption.

On the same day, Jefferson wrote a letter to another radical English acquaintance, Richard Price. For the most part, the letter to Price necessarily covers much the same ground as the one to Paine. But there is one new note, implying Jefferson's recognition of the political efficacy of decapitation:

The people without then forced the place, took and beheaded the Governor and Lt. Governor, and here compleated arming themselves. The same day they beheaded the Prevost des marchands, discovered in a treacherous correspondence against them [*sic*]. The Marquis de la Fayette was made commander in chief of the men raised. Repeated addresses from the States, met repeated refusals from the king, instigated by his new ministers and others. But after the decapitations before mentioned, and the taking of the Bastille, he determined (of his own motion as some say) to comply with the desires of the states.[45]

In his official report to John Jay, two days later, Jefferson struck the same note, but this time explicitly and definitively. Having told Jay of the seven revolutionary killings (and, as in the previous letters, without any hint of disapprobation) Jefferson goes on:

These events carried imperfectly to Versailles were the subject of two successive deputations from the States to the King, to both of which he gave dry and hard answers, for it has transpired that it had been proposed and agitated in Council to seize on the principal members of the States general, to march the whole army down upon Paris and to suppress it's tumults by the sword. But at night the Duke de Liancourt forced his way into the king's bedchamber, and obliged him to hear a full and animated detail of the disasters of the day in Paris. He went to bed deeply impressed. The decapita-

tion of de Launai worked powerfully thro' the night on the whole Aristocratical party, insomuch that in the morning those of the greatest influence
on the Count d'Artois represented to him the absolute necessity that the
king should give up every thing to the states.[46]

Jefferson goes on, with an inflection of revolutionary sarcasm, to describe the conciliatory demeanor of the "Aristocratical party" in the
States General after they had had time to meditate upon de Launai's fate:
"The Aristocrats of the Nobles and Clergy in the States general vied with
each other in declaring how sincerely they were converted to the justice
of voting by persons, and how determined to go with the nation all it's
lengths."

In a letter to Madison three days later—again covering the same general topics—Jefferson again notes the pivotal efficacy, in these transactions, of decapitation: "But the decapitations being once known there and
that there were 50, or 60,000 men in arms, the king went to the States,
referred every thing to them, and ordered away the troops."[47]

Jefferson was quite right, of course, in observing the efficacy of terror
in history, and especially revolutionary history. Where he was mistaken
was in assuming that the politicians who were benefitting from its exercise, in a particular conjuncture, would themselves be immune from its
operations in all future conjunctures. Others besides the American diplomatist were taking note of the efficacy of terror during this period. Dan-
ton, Marat, St. Just, and Robespierre were among those who could observe it, and draw lessons from it. The lessons were fatal to many of those
from whom Jefferson had imbibed his understanding of the Revolution.
Brissot de Warville, Condorcet, and Rochefoucauld all perished in the
Terror in 1792–93. Lafayette escaped the guillotine only by defecting
from the Revolution into the cold and grudging, but to him more merci-
ful, arms of the Counter-revolution.

In August and September 1789, Jefferson was busy preparing for his
return to the United States, with his daughters and house slaves. On 13
September he wrote his last letter from Paris to Thomas Paine. In this
letter Jefferson is just as confident as he was immediately before the Fall
of the Bastille that the French Revolution is over, and that nothing remains but to embody it in constitutional form: "Tranquillity is well established in Paris, and tolerably so thro' the whole kingdom; and I think
there is no possibility now of any thing's hindering their final establishment of a good constitution, which will in it's principles and merit be
about a middle term between that of England and the United States."[48] It
is instructive to compare this letter, of 13 September 1789, with one writ-

ten by Edmund Burke later in the same month. Burke was replying to a letter from his friend William Windham, written two days later than Jefferson's to Paine, and in exactly the same mood of confident optimism. Windham had written: "What is said of the disorder and irregularity of the national assembly has, I think, a great deal of exaggeration: at least, if a due consideration be had of all the circumstances. My prediction was, (and accounts which I heard since my being there, have contributed to confirm it) that they would very soon become perfectly orderly."[49]

Burke replied, on 27 September:

> That they should settle their constitution, without much struggle, on paper, I can easily believe; because at present the Interests of the Crown have no party, certainly no armed party, to support them; But I have great doubts whether any form of Government which they can establish will procure obedience; especially obedience in the article of Taxations. In the destruction of the old Revenue constitution they find no difficulties—but with what to supply them is the Opus. You are undoubtedly better able to judge; but it does not appear to me, that the National assembly have one Jot more power than the King; whilst they lead or follow the popular voice, in the subversion of all orders, distinctions, priveleges impositions, Tythes, and rents, they appear omnipotent; but I very much question, whether they are in a condition to exercise any function of decided authority—or even whether they are possessed of any real deliberate capacity, or the exercise of free Judgement in any point whatsoever; as there is a Mob of their constituents ready to Hang them if They should deviate into moderation, or in the least depart from the Spirit of those they represent.[50]

Eight days later, events occurred in Paris which demonstrated that Burke, not Windham or Jefferson, had got it right:

> On 5 and 6 October a crowd of 30,000 Parisians, men and women, marched to Versailles and forced their way into the palace shouting "A Paris! A Paris!". Louis XVI, prompted by Lafayette, gave way, with the words: "My friends, I shall go to Paris, with my wife and my children: it is to the love of my good and faithful subjects that I entrust my most precious possessions." The royal family then made their way from Versailles to the Tuileries, in the midst of the crowd, which included women carrying pikes. The significance of the *journées* of 5th and 6th October is assessed by a modern French historian as follows: "The sun had ceased to set at Versailles in the splendid isolation determined by Louis XIV. The October rain brought back the King to the Tuileries, which he was not to leave, except for prison, and then the scaffold."[51]

I know that some of my readers will feel that I have been paying far too much attention to these clouds in the Jeffersonian crystal ball. And certainly I have paid far more attention to what Jefferson actually wrote about the French Revolution—by quoting from the relevant writings and commenting on them—than previous writers on him (other than the editors of his collected papers) have done. A waste of time? I don't see how it can be. Most people will concede that the French Revolution is important and that Thomas Jefferson is important. So how can Thomas Jefferson's day-by-day comments as a witness of the French Revolution not be important? It is true that a reader who has had the opportunity to consider the body of these comments may well not agree with Dumas Malone's assessment of them. Malone, who quotes only a tiny proportion of this material, writes,"He was in a highly favorable position to see history in the making at a time when supremely important history was being made, and he accompanied his informal but careful account of events with thoughtful comments. These reflected his personal philosophy and point of view, and are of special interest now for just that reason, but they were generally penetrating and judicious." [52]

In fact, these letters and dispatches are less important for what they have to tell us about the French Revolution than for what they may tell us about Thomas Jefferson. Yet they do tell us quite a lot about the early stages of the French Revolution. Basically, they reflect the assumptions, hopes, prognostics, and interpretations of the particular section of French society with which alone Jefferson was in regular contact during his Paris years.

This section consisted of the intellectuals who made up the reformist element of the French nobility in the Paris region in the late 1780s. Jefferson shared their assumptions and hopes; in so far, that is, as he could make those of *any* foreigners his own: these people were still foreigners, with many of the undesirable moral characteristics of foreigners—but foreigners of a relatively estimable description and worthy of encouragement, up to a certain point. These things being so, Jefferson also went along with their prognostics and interpretations, which were almost uniformly optimistic. This factor, I believe, accounts for the frequency and confidence of Jefferson's erroneous predictions during this period (mainly 1787–89) and for the dauntless persistence with which, despite so many unforeseen developments, he returns to erroneous predictions, always of the same type.

The value of these letters and dispatches to students of the French Revolution is that they give us a kind of collective portrait of the *Weltanschauung* of the intellectuals who made the first breakthrough into the

French Revolution, without having even a glimmering of an idea of what that which they were breaking through into was going to be like.

What do these letters and dispatches have to tell us about Thomas Jefferson? That is a large matter, to which we shall have to return, when we shall be in a position to compare Jefferson's writings about these early phases of the French Revolution with the positions he will take in America, concerning the later phases. But the collection of letters we have been considering does form a whole in itself, and we can now offer some preliminary observations about it.

Jefferson is a prophet, but not in the predictive sense of that term. He is a prophet in the spiritual sense, a being whose imagination is ablaze with a vision. Specifically, he is the prophet of the American Revolution, the author of the American Holy Book, the Declaration of Independence. He sees his own life as dedicated to what the Declaration calls "the holy cause of freedom." In France, he sees people like Lafayette as anxious to dedicate their own country to that holy cause. He wants to help them, without being quite convinced that the French are morally worthy of the American example. But he reports their exertions in that direction with as much optimism as he can muster; for France to get even a little bit like America would strengthen the cause of America, and of freedom. He sees that cause as threatened by monarchical tendencies in America itself, and tendencies in France in the opposite direction could help the friends of freedom in America.

The prophet in Jefferson becomes explicit only in rare utterances in his correspondence: the "tree of liberty" passage being the most noteworthy in his letters of the period we have been considering.[53] Six years after Jefferson used that metaphor in a letter, it became part of the French Revolutionary vocabulary. The terrorist Bertrand Barère used a variant of it in the peroration of his speech calling for the execution of Louis XVI: "The tree of liberty, as an ancient author remarks, flourishes when it is watered with the blood of all varieties of tyrants." Commenting on this statement of Barère, Macaulay, reviewing Barère's Memoirs (Edinburgh Review, April 1844), observes, "We wish that a note had been added to inform us from what ancient author Barère quoted. In the course of our own small reading among the Greek and Latin writers, we have not happened to fall in with trees of liberty and watering-pots full of blood; nor can we, such is our ignorance of classical antiquity, even imagine an Attic or Roman orator employing imagery of that sort."[54] We know, however, (as Macaulay probably did not) that Jefferson, while living in France, had "employed imagery of that sort." Barère, of course, could not possibly have known of Jefferson's letter of 13 November 1787 to William Stephens Smith. But it is possible that Jefferson, in conversation with his French revolutionary acquaintances, may have used this metaphor (in some form) so that it then passed into currency. For example if, say, Condorcet or Rochefoucauld, in July—August of 1789, expressed misgivings about the manner in which Foulon and Berthier met their deaths, the metaphor about the tree would have been quite likely to spring from Jefferson's lips. Repeated, it could easily have reached Barère. There is no way of knowing, but I don't think Barère's use of that Jeffersonian metaphor can be purely coincidental. In any case, the image of the bloodthirsty tree became part of the revolutionary imagination lasting into the twentieth century. In "The Rose Tree"—the most "revolutionary" of the four poems which W. B. Yeats wrote about the Easter Rising of 1916—the last stanza runs:

> "But where can we draw water",
> Said Pearse to Connolly,
> "When all the wells are parched away?
> O plain as plain can be
> There's nothing but our own red blood
> Can make a right rose tree".

As I said, the prophet in Jefferson does not often find utterance. But the fact that the prophet is mostly silent does not mean that he is not always *there*. He is a brooding presence, possessor of the standard of Liberty, by which all things are to be measured. And the prophet in Jefferson, as in so many others of his kind, is a ruthless prophet.

It is noteworthy that it is only with the advent of revolutionary bloodshed, on and immediately after 14 July 1789, that Jefferson begins to show himself as first excited and then enthusiastic about the French Revolution. The Revolution is bloody; therefore it is a real, and not just a metaphorical, revolution. The French are, after all, worthy of the Americans.

From Cowes, on his return journey to America from Revolutionary France, Jefferson wrote his last "Old World" letter to Tom Paine. Word had just reached Jefferson of the second wave of French Revolutionary violence, in the events that accompanied the abduction of the Royal Family from Versailles to Paris, on 4–5 October 1789, with Lafayette and the National Assembly trailing in the wake of the triumphant Paris mob, Jefferson writes to Paine: "I have no news but what is given under that name in the English papers. You know how much of these I believe. So far I collect from them that the king, queen, and national assembly are removed to Paris. The mobs and murders under which they dress this fact are like the rags in which religion robes the true god."[55]

The "true god" . . . For Jefferson, on his way back to America, the French Revolution and the American are now integrated as inseparable parts of the same "holy cause of freedom," and will remain so for at least the next four years.

THREE

BRINGING THE TRUE GOD HOME

The French Revolution in American Politics
after Jefferson's Return

1789–91

When Jefferson, returning from France, disembarked at Norfolk, Virginia, on 23 November 1789, he learned from the newspapers that he had been appointed Secretary of State in the new Federal administration. Washington's letter and commission nominating him to the post reached him nearly a month later, at Eppington. Jefferson was reluctant to accept. In his letter to Washington he wrote:

> But when I contemplate the extent of that office, embracing as it does the principal mass of domestic administration, together with the foreign, I cannot be insensible of my inequality to it: and I should enter on it with gloomy forebodings from the criticisms and censures of a public just indeed in their intentions, but sometimes misinformed and misled, and always too respectable to be neglected. I cannot but foresee the possibility that this may end disagreeably for one, who, having no motive to public service but the public satisfaction, would certainly retire the moment that satisfaction should appear to languish.[1]

According to Merrill Peterson's version of this letter: "So far as the question depended on himself, Jefferson wrote he much preferred his post in Paris."[2] But this is not what "Jefferson wrote." What Jefferson wrote was: "On the other hand I feel a degree of familiarity with the duties of my present office, as far at least as I am capable of understanding it's duties." Jefferson is contrasting the familiar with the unfamiliar; not expressing a personal preference for Paris. His correspondence from Paris amply demonstrates that his personal preference was for being in America, in comparison with anywhere else, including Paris, e.g. "I pant for America." Peterson's version is a good example of a tendency among

Jefferson's biographers to blur the outlines of their subject, by their de-cided preference for paraphrase as against quotation, and by introducing into their paraphrases sentimental and otherwise misleading assumptions of their own. Jefferson is much more interesting, if less holy and more fallible, than his biographers would allow him to appear.

In his letter, Jefferson, having expressed reluctance, leaves the deci-sion to Washington:

> But it is not for an individual to chuse his post. You are to marshall us as may best be for the public good: and it is only in the case of it's being indifferent to you that I would avail myself of the option you have so kindly offered in your letter. If you think it better to transfer me to another post, my inclination must be no obstacle: nor shall it be, if there is any desire to suppress the office I now hold, or to reduce it's grade. In either of these cases, be so good only as to signify to me by another line your ultimate wish, and I shall conform to it cordially.[3]

Washington's reply (21 January 1790) is courteous, and its uncharac-teristic length—emphasizing the importance of the post—is evidence of a strong wish to have Jefferson in the Cabinet. But Washington will not make the decision for Jefferson: ". . . it must be at your option to deter-mine relative to your acceptance of it, or your continuance in your Of-fice abroad."[4]

Jefferson replied from Monticello, accepting, on 14 February 1790, and he took up his new duties in New York, at that time the Federal capital, at the end of March.

Both Jefferson's initial reluctance to accept the post of Secretary of State and his final decision to accept have to do with the fraught relation-ship which existed, in the early years of the new Constitution of the United States, between the Commonwealth of Virginia and the new Fed-eral Government. This relationship was also to be of crucial importance for the development of the French Revolution *as an issue in American internal politics* in the early 1790s, and especially for the central role of Thomas Jefferson in the handling of that issue in the same period. This seems an appropriate point, in the present narrative, to consider this rela-tionship.

I. VIRGINIAN POLITICS

The politics of Virginia, in relation to the Federal Government, circa 1790, were highly complex, and have been the subject of a number of scholarly studies. For the limited purposes of the present inquiry, I have used five relevant monographs. In chronological order of their original completion, these are: C. H. Ambler, *Sectionalism in Virginia from 1776 to 1861* (first published, 1910; reissued in New York, 1964); David K. McCarrell, *The Formation of the Jeffersonian Party in Virginia* (unpublished Ph.D. thesis, Duke University, 1937); Harry Ammon, *The Republican Party in Virginia, 1789 to 1824* (unpublished Ph.D. thesis, University of Virginia, 1948); Noble E. Cunningham, Jr., *The Jeffersonian Republicans: The Format of Party Organization 1789–1801* (Chapel Hill, N.C., 1957); and Norman K. Risjord, *Chesapeake Politics, 1781–1800* (New York, 1978). The following outline of the general relationship between Virginia and the Federal Government and of Jefferson's position within that relationship, around 1790, is mainly based on these studies as well as on the papers of Jefferson and Madison.

The ratification of the Constitution by Virginia had been obtained only with difficulty, and would probably not have been obtained at all had it not been for Washington, who threw his immense personal prestige and popularity onto the scales for ratification. Among the regions of Virginia which held out against ratification was the Piedmont, the region in which Jefferson's native Albemarle County was situated. Patrick Henry devoted all his famous oratorical power to the defeat of ratification. McCarrell summarizes the principal themes of Henry and his supporters: "the dangers to liberty, the threat to Virginia's position in the union, the possible loss of political independency, the probable effect of a national Executive and Judiciary, standing armies and federal Marshalls as coercive agencies, the nationalizing tendencies inherent in the Constitution and the need for prior amendments."[5]

There was also another theme in the ratification debates, a theme not mentioned by McCarrell, or by any of the other writers I have been using here, but nonetheless a matter of record. This was the theme of slavery. *The Documentary History of the Ratification of the Constitution* records utterances of anti-Federalist and Federalist speakers on this subject. The speakers on slavery included the leading anti-Federalist speaker, Patrick Henry, and two Federalists, George Nicholas and Edmund Randolph. (Madison's intervention on the reclamation of escaped slaves is considered later.)

On June 24, 1788, Patrick Henry wrote,

They [the new Congress] will not take the opinion of this Committee [in Virginia] concerning its operation. They will construe it as they please. If you place it subsequently, let me ask the consequences? Among ten thousand implied powers which they may assume, they may, if we be engaged in war, liberate every one of your slaves if they please. And this must and will be done by men, a majority of whom have not a common interest with you. . . . In this State there are 236,000 blacks, and there are many in several other States. But there are few or none in the Northern States, and yet if the Northern States shall be of opinion, that our numbers are numberless, they may call forth every national resource. May Congress not say, that every black man must fight?—Did we not see a little of this last war?—We were not so hard pushed, as to make emancipation general. But acts of Assembly passed, that every slave who would go to the army should be free. Another thing will contribute to bring this event about—slavery is detested—we feel its fatal effects—we deplore it with all the pity of humanity. Let all these considerations, at some future period, press with full force on the minds of Congress. Let that urbanity, which I trust will distinguish America, and the necessity of national defence:—Let all these things operate in their minds. They will search that paper, and see if they have power of manumission.—And have they not, Sir?—Have they not power to provide for the general defence and welfare?—May they not pronounce all slaves free, and will they not be warranted by that power? There is no ambiguous implication, or logical deduction—The paper speaks to the point. They have the power in clear unequivocal terms; and will clearly and certainly exercise it. As much as I deplore slavery, I see that prudence forbids its abolition. I deny that the General Government ought to set them free, because a decided majority of the States have not the ties of sympathy and fellow-feeling for those whose interest would be affected by their emancipation. . . . I repeat it again, that it would rejoice my very soul, that every one of my fellow beings was emancipated. As we ought with gratitude to admire that decree of Heaven, which has numbered us among the free, we ought to lament and deplore the necessity of holding our fellow-men in bondage. But is it practicable by any human means, to liberate them, without producing the most dreadful and ruinous consequences? We ought to possess them in the manner we have inherited them from our ancestors, as their manumission is incompatible with the felicity of the country. But we ought to soften, as much as possible, the rigour of their unhappy fate. . . . This is a local matter, and I can see no propriety in subjecting it to Congress.[6]

On 16 February 1788, George Nicholas had this to say: "The next objection is that if this [Federalist] government is adopted the property that we have in slaves may be lost or injured [by ratification]. So far is this from being true that we can venture to say that the new government will be the best security that we can have for retaining that property."

Edmund Randolph in Virginian Convention Debates, 24 June 1788, said:

> That Honorable Gentleman, and some others, have insisted that the abolition of slavery will result from it [ratification] and at the same time have complained that it encourages its continuation. The inconsistency proves, in some degree, the futility of their arguments. But if it be not conclusive, to satisfy the Committee that there is no danger of enfranchisement taking place, I beg leave to refer then to the paper itself. . . . I ask, and will ask again and again, till I be answered (not by declamation) where is the part that has a tendency to the abolition of slavery?[7]

The above statements are clearly carefully weighed, and appear to reflect the importance given to the subject in the minds of delegates to the Convention. And even where the word "slavery" was not specifically mentioned, the fact of slavery must have been subliminally pervasive in the whole debate over ratification. When the renowed champion of liberty, Patrick Henry, inveighed against the dangers posed by ratification to the liberty of Virginia all his hearers knew that that liberty included the liberty to own slaves. The threat to the liberty of Virginia was also a threat to slavery, in Virginia.

Randolph's reference to what he saw as inconsistency in the anti-Federalist arguments on slavery probably has to do with the anti-Federalist "libertarian" argument (found in drafts of the Declaration of Independence) hostile to the slave trade (as distinct from slavery) and directed in the ratification debates against the clause allowing the importation of slaves for twenty years. When George Mason raised this objection in the Virginian debates of June 1788, Madison, having dealt with that point, without directly entering into the question of whether the Constitution might or might not eventually threaten the institution of slavery, went on to refer to the substantial advantages which slaveowners would derive from ratification:

> Another clause secures us that property which we now possess. At present, if any slave elopes to any of those States where slaves are free, he becomes emancipated by their laws. For the laws of the States are uncharitable to one another in this respect. But in this Constitution, "No person held to service, or labor, in one State, under the laws thereof, escaping into another, shall in consequence of any law or regulation therein, be discharged from

such service or labor; but shall be delivered up on claim of the party to whom such service or labour may be due." — This clause was expressly inserted to enable owners of slaves to reclaim them. This is a better security than any that now exists.[8]

This argument of Madison's may well have swung the vote in the Virginian Convention in favor of ratification.

In the event, Virginia ratified the Constitution by a narrow margin: eighty-nine to seventy-nine. Significantly for Jefferson's political context, the Piedmont's delegates were "almost unanimous in opposition to the Constitution."[9] After the ratification the anti-Federalist opposition accepted their defeat to the extent of abandoning direct frontal attacks on the Constitution as a whole. Instead, the anti-Federalists concentrated on amendments, and won considerable support for these even among those who had supported ratification. On 30 October 1788, the Virginian House of Delegates voted by eighty-four to thirty-nine in favor of a series of resolutions by Patrick Henry declaring that amendments to the Constitution were necessary and urging Congress to call a second Convention immediately.[10] Norman Risjord, who has used multivariable analysis to determine the deciding factors behind Federalist and anti-Federalist loyalties in Virginia, concludes that:

> federalists in general were men with some sort of out-of-state contact, interest or allegiance. . . . They tended to be well-to-do and educated, were often born or educated outside the State, had entrepreneurial interests instead of or in addition to agriculture, and held positions of high rank in the Continental service during the Revolution. Antifederalists, with some exceptions, of course, were more typical of the society that elected them. They were "middling" planters, born locally and of English stock, and possessed little formal education or other broadening experiences. At the same time it should be remembered that the biggest single factor in political affiliation was residence. Voting, in short, followed regional patterns.[11]

Jefferson's position is interesting in relation to the Virginian patterns described by Risjord. He had almost all the "qualifications" of a proper Federalist and was on excellent terms with the most eminent Virginian Federalist (after Washington), James Madison. On the other hand, his home territory, the Piedmont, and his home county, Albemarle, were anti-Federalist. This political context required careful handling. As Risjord notes, Jefferson, while in Paris, had "received an enormous amount of political intelligence on the Virginian scene but remained reluctant to make his own position generally known."[12] It should also be noted that the Virginian anti-Federalists, as described by Risjord, were precisely the sorts of Americans who were most attracted to the cause of the French Revolution.

Virginia had ratified the Constitution, but the Constitution, and especially the Federal Government, remained unpopular in Virginia. Some of that unpopularity rubbed off on those Virginians who were identified with the Constitution in the public mind. Chief among these was James Madison, both because of his large known share in the shaping of the Constitution itself, and for the leading part he had played in securing ratification by the Virginian Convention in 1788. As a Virginian correspondent wrote from Richmond late in 1788 to Jefferson, then still in Paris: "You will no doubt be informed that Richard Henry Lee and McGrayson are elected the Senators [for Virginia] in the New Constitution. Mr. Madison was too federal to be chosen." [13] When (under the Constitutional arrangements then in force) U.S. Senators came to be elected by the Virginia House of Delegates, on 6 November 1788, Madison ran third out of three nominees and was consequently not elected to the Senate. Madison subsequently ran for election to the House of Representatives. James Monroe (later a friend and ally of Madison and Jefferson, and an enthusiast for the French Revolution) ran against Madison. Madison won, but only after committing himself to the early amendment of the Constitution he had helped to draft. He issued a statement on the eve of the elections stating that "while the Constitution was pending he had opposed alterations, believing that some plan of unity was necessary. The situation had now changed and amendments of the right kind, pursued in the right spirit, might not only reconcile many honest opponents but might also be a real safeguard of personal liberty." Therefore it was now his opinion that it was the duty of the first Congress to revise the Constitution by proposing such amendments as would secure all essential rights, particularly "those of liberty of conscience in the fullest extent." [14] After that, Madison defeated Monroe by a margin of 336 in a total vote of 2,480. One commentator (McCarrell) calls this "a scant margin"; another (Ammon) calls it "a substantive majority." [15] However one classifies it, it must have been narrow enough to keep Madison, as a Congressman, mindful of the fact that his electoral base in Virginia was not altogether secure, and that he would do well to keep a certain distance from the Federal Government, whose large authority he had earlier done so much to establish.

Circumstances attending the actual setting up of the new Federal structures, in 1789, tended to increase Virginian fears—propagated in Jefferson's correspondence—of monarchical possibilities lurking in the new Constitution: On 23 May 1789 Madison had reported to Jefferson—then still in Paris—on the addresses of the Senate and the House of Representatives to Washington on the occasion of his inauguration:

> My last inclosed copies of the President's inauguration Speech and the answer of the House of the Representatives. I now add the answer of the Senate. It will not have escaped you that the former was addressed with a truly republican simplicity to G. W. Presidt. of the U.S. The latter follows the example, with the omission of the personal name, but without any other than the constitutional title. The proceeding on this point was in the House of Representatives spontaneous. The imitation by the Senate was extorted. The question became a serious one between the two houses. J. Adams espoused the cause of titles with great earnestness. His friend R. H. Lee altho elected as a republican enemy to an aristocratic constitution was a most zealous second. The projected title was—His Highness the President of the U.S. and protector of their liberties. Had the project succeeded it would have subjected the President to a severe dilemma and given a deep wound to our infant government.[16]

Jefferson replied on 29 July:

The president's title as proposed by the senate was the most superlatively ridiculous thing I ever heard of. It is a proof the more of the justice of the character given by Doctr. Franklin of my friend [John Adams]: "Always an honest man, often a great one, but sometimes absolutely mad." I wish he could have been here [in Paris] during the late scenes. If he could then have had one fibre of aristocracy left in his frame he would have been a proper subject for bedlam. The tranquility of this place has not been disturbed since the death [by decapitation] of Foulon and Bertier.[17]

The friendship between Adams and Jefferson, formed in Paris five years before, is beginning to crumble under the pressures of politics. In the Presidential election, under the system then in force, John Adams had become Vice President, by having received the greatest number of votes for the Presidency next to Washington. Adams was now not only Washington's designated successor, should Washington die in office; he was also Washington's most likely successor by electoral process (as he duly became in 1796). For Virginians, the prospect of a Yankee President was inherently unpalatable. Virginians saw Adams's move over the Presidential title as an attempt to magnify the office for his own personal future benefit. Madison's language implies, it seems to me, an inclination towards that hypothesis. In calling the move "ridiculous" and ascribing it to a fit of madness, Jefferson is here being relatively charitable, owing no doubt to that old friendship. In any case, for most Virginians suspicious of monarchical, urban, commercial, and authoritarian tendencies, John Adams as top Yankee, and presumptive next President, is necessarily prime suspect. These considerations have to be taken into account in relation to the controversy over the French Revolution, involving Jefferson and Adams, which broke out in 1791 (below, pp. 107–9).

Thomas Jefferson, on his return to his native Virginia at the end of 1789, found himself in an extraordinarily favorable position, in relation to Virginian politics. His fame was unclouded because he had had the good fortune, politically speaking, to be away from America when the great controversy had raged over the ratification of the Constitution. He had not had to range himself publicly on either side; he had not had to make speeches, he had not had to vote. His views were known, in somewhat diverse forms, through his letters. He was known not to be opposed to the Constitution as a whole, but to be in favor of amending it. Most especially, he was known to be vigilant against any "monarchical" tendencies that might declare themselves within and around the new Federal Government.

In the circumstances, Washington's offer of the post of Secretary of State was one that had to be pondered carefully, as Jefferson did ponder it. On the one hand, it offered a route into the national politics of the new Federation. On the other hand, the Federal Government was already unpopular with Virginians—and likely to grow more unpopular as Virginians experienced Federal power. As it happened, the growth in unpopularity was becoming palpable at the very time when Jefferson was considering Washington's offer. Harry Ammon writes:

> The immediate cause for the revival of political animosities was Hamilton's Report on Finances of January, 1790. Until the submission of this report the measures of the federal government had met with increasing approval in the Old Dominion. Now, as Hamilton's proposals were translated into law by Congress, there was a growing discontent. The plan as a whole was not condemned, but only those portions relating to the assumption of the state debts and the establishment of a national bank.[18]

Might not participation in the Federal Government undermine Jefferson's position in Virginia and—as a necessary consequence of that—rule him out as a future President of the United States?

Proper Jeffersonians will find this whole train of thought distasteful since it depicts their hero as thinking like a politician and harboring a high ambition. We are to think of Thomas Jefferson as having a soul above such things. We are to take seriously, and without reservation of any kind, his frequent assurances of his desire to retire into private life, and of his abhorrence of the hurly-burly of controversy. This interpretation seems to me hard to reconcile with the realities of Jefferson's career. A person did not, even then, become President of the United States by means of a desire to retire into private life and by shrinking from controversy. The ambition has to be there, however unavowed—even disavowed—and also the capacity to attain the object of your ambition, by the political arts necessary for that attainment.[19]

I do not mean by this that Jefferson was driven by ambition in any ignoble sense, or in any sense incompatible with his known political convictions. I accept Jefferson's claim, in his letter to Washington of 15 December 1789, of "having no motive to public service but the public satisfaction." But that motive is by no means incompatible with a discreetly unavowed ambition to serve the public, to the public satisfaction, in the highest office in the nation.

Thomas Jefferson was a conviction politician. He saw himself as the prophet and champion of Liberty. And how could the prophet and champion of Liberty allow the Presidency of the United States to fall into the hands of a person who could not be trusted to uphold the Liberty of the people? A person like John Adams.

Jefferson's principles were not at all at variance with his ambition. On the contrary, it was his principles that made it his duty to be ambitious, behind what Edmund Burke would call "a politick, well-wrought veil."

Madison was extremely anxious that Jefferson would accept the post of Secretary of State and it was also Madison who made it possible for Jefferson to solve his principal problem in that connection: how to be a member of the Federal Government, without losing the confidence of Virginians? Madison himself had had a problem with the confidence of Virginians, but he had done much to recover that confidence, by pressing for Constitutional amendments, by successfully opposing John Adams's "monarchical" proposals in relation to the President's title, and then by emerging as an informal leader of the opposition, in the House of Representatives, to Washington's administration. Jefferson, from within that administration, maintained an informal partnership with Madison throughout Jefferson's period as Secretary of State. Through this partnership, the leader of the opposition gained an unrivalled insight into the internal working of the administration which he opposed. Jefferson, for his part ensured—mainly but not exclusively through Madison—that Virginians would see him consistently as he saw himself: as the great defender of Liberty within an administration which was otherwise some-what suspect, in relation to that holy cause.

Those who depict Thomas Jefferson as an unworldly person, discon-nected from the sordid expedients of practical politics, should try to ex-plain how that picture can be reconciled with the partnership between Jefferson, as a member of Washington's first administration, and the leader of the opposition to that administration, James Madison. The rec-onciliation has never been attempted, although the biographers and edi-tors have to acknowledge the existence and the nature of that partnership.

II. JEFFERSON, THE PRESS, AND THE FRENCH REVOLUTION

One of the first concerns of the new Secretary of State was to get a better press in America for the French Revolution. This was a major interest of Jefferson's throughout his period as Secretary of State. He began by work-ing on John Fenno, the publisher of the *Gazette of the United States*. The *Gazette* was a quasi-official journal founded "for the purpose of dissemi-nating favorable sentiments of the federal constitution and its administra-tion."[20] Jefferson was determined that the *Gazette* should also be used for "disseminating favorable sentiments"[21] about the French Revolution. Actually, favorable sentiments of that kind were already widely and strongly prevalent throughout the United States in 1789–90. In the cir-cumstances, the priority given by the new Secretary of State to improving what would now be called "the image" of the French Revolution might seem somewhat excessive. But Jefferson had two reasons for acting as he did. The first reason was a general one. Most of the news reports on the French Revolution that appeared in the American press came from British sources and were therefore, in Jefferson's view, tainted. The second reason was specific, and partly personal: and it was this reason in my opinion that lent such urgency to this project of Jefferson's. The *Gazette of the United States* was at this time serializing the *Discourses on Davila*. The *Discourses* were published anonymously, but Jefferson had been in-formed that they were by John Adams. They were, and they were critical of the French Revolution—"We are told," Adams had written, "that our friends, the National Assembly of France, have abolished all distinctions. But be not deceived, my dear countrymen. Impossibilities cannot be per-formed. Have they levelled all fortunes, and equally divided all property? Have they made all men and women equally wise, elegant and beautiful?"

The unfinished *Discourses on Davila* were included long afterwards in the *Collected Works of John Adams*. Adams wrote a characteristic pref-atory note:

This dull, heavy volume still excites the wonder of the author—first that he could find, amidst the constant scenes of business and dissipations [distractions] in which he was enveloped, time to write it; secondly that he had the courage to oppose his opinions to the universal opinion of America, and indeed of all mankind. Not one man in America then believed him. He knew not one and has not heard of any since who then believed him. The work, however, powerfully operated to destroy his popularity. It was urged as full proof that he was an advocate for monarchy, of laboring to introduce a hereditary president in America.[22]

Actually, the *Discourses on Davila* can have had very few readers, and no significant impact, by themselves, on American public opinion. They consist for the most part of general philosophical ruminations, oddly intertwined with great gobbets of French sixteenth-century history, whose relevance to modern times was visible to the learned author, but must have been exceedingly obscure to such readers of the *Gazette of the United States* as may have tried to tackle the *Discourses*. But the ineffectiveness of the *Discourses* as propaganda was beside the point. The real significance of the *Discourses* lay in what they revealed of the mind of their author to the mind of Thomas Jefferson. The publication of the *Discourses,* following so shortly on John Adams's proposal of a "monarchical" style for the President of the United States, seems to have convinced Jefferson that the Vice President was a person of dangerous dispositions and would be a dangerous Vice President. And also that he was a vulnerable candidate for the Presidency.

Jefferson induced Fenno to "balance" anti–French Revolution excerpts from the *Discourses* with pro–French Revolution material supplied by Jefferson from other sources, and also to supplement the British reports with reports from a pro–French Revolution, French-language publication, the *Gazette de Leide.* Jefferson had by this time succeeded in imbuing Washington (though not for long) with something of his own conviction that the British were spreading malicious lies against the great and good Revolution in France. In the summer of 1790 Washington told the Comte de Rochambeau that Americans had learned to discard English reports of events in France. "Happily for you," he wrote, "we remembered how our own armies, after having been all slain to a man in the English News Papers, came to life again and even performed prodigies of valour against that very Nation whose News-papers had so unmercifully destroyed them. Mr. Jefferson, Mr. Trumbull and some others have taught us to believe more cautiously and more correctly on these points."[23]

There was a fallacy there. The British press had had strong motives for maligning the American Revolutionaries with whom they were at war, just as the British press was later to have strong motives for maligning the French Revolutionaries when they were at war with *them,* from February 1793 on. But in 1790, Britain and France were at peace, and many Britons—including all the Whigs, except one—took as favorable a view of the French Revolution as most Americans did. Where Americans saw the French Revolution as imitating the American one, British admirers of the French Revolution saw it as imitating *their* Glorious Revolution of 1688, and as ending (as they thought) like the British one, in constitutional monarchy.

British passions were not engaged against the French Revolution in 1790, and there was therefore no adequate reason why British reports should be suspect. Thus the British reports of the *journées* of 5 and 6 October 1789 were substantially correct; the mobs and violence had really been there. But Jefferson had been able to write them off as British fabrications.

From the moment of Jefferson's departure from France, he automatically categorized all reports reflecting adversely on the French Revolution in the same way: "British lies." This was an effective way of defending the French Revolution before the American public in this period (as Washington's reaction showed).

But the defense was all the more effective, coming from Jefferson, because Jefferson passionately needed to believe it himself. For Jefferson, from late 1789 to 1793, the French Revolution was inherently impeccable. It was not a changing set of processes within terrestrial politics. It belonged, along with the Declaration of Independence, in the domain of the sacred and immutable. The French Revolution had become an aspect of "the true god," inseparably and eternally part of "the holy cause of freedom" proclaimed in the Declaration. To question the French Revolution was "heresy"; to attack it was "blasphemy." These religious terms, so applied, had by now become standard parts of the political vocabulary of the two secular thinkers Jefferson and Madison. (Madison had become Jefferson's unquestioning disciple, in all that pertained to the French Revolution, from the time of Jefferson's return to America at the end of 1789.)

Jefferson was a passionate devotee of the French Revolution, but he was also a calculating and subtle propagandist in its favor. This showed in his selection, for publication in Fenno's *Gazette,* of Edmund Burke's first public statement *against* the French Revolution. This was Burke's speech on the Army Estimates, delivered on the Commons in 9 February 1790. Burke's purpose in this speech was to warn his Party leader, Charles

James Fox, that if he publicly took up the cause of the French Revolution (which he did, not long afterward) he would have serious trouble within his Party, coming from Edmund Burke. To make this threat credible, Burke uses large, sweeping assertions. There is nothing here that resembles the long analytical parts of the later *Reflections on the Revolution in France* (November 1790) or even the persuasively worded parts of Burke's argument with Fox on the floor of the House of Commons (April—May 1791). The speech of 9 February 1790 is like a prelude to a declaration of war. This is Burke at his most aggressive. The speech opened with the words:

> The french have proved themselves the ablest architects of ruin that ever existed in the world. In one summer they have done their business for us as rivals in a way more destructive than twenty Ramillies or Blenheims. In this very short space of time they have completely pulled down to the ground their monarchy; their church; their nobility; their law; their revenue; their army; their navy; their commerce; their arts; and their manufactures. They now are lying in a sort of trance—an epileptic fit—exposed to the pity or derision of mankind, in wild ridiculous convulsive movements, impotent to every purpose but that of dashing out their brains against the pavement. Yet they are so very unwise as to glory in a revolution which is a shame and disgrace to them. They have made their way to the very worst constitution in the world by the destruction of their country.[24]

Jefferson rightly calculated that this speech, when reproduced in an American newspaper, would be helpful rather than harmful to the cause of the French Revolution. The year 1790 was outwardly the calmest in the history of the Revolution. The French Revolution seemed in that year, to almost all observers, to be settling down in the reassuring guise of a constitutional monarchy. Burke knew that the apparent stability was deceptive, and the constitutional monarchy a fraud, since the Monarch was in reality a prisoner, and the National Assembly itself was deliberating under the threatening eyes of the Paris mob. But it took later events—beginning with the flight and recapture of the unfortunate "constitutional monarch" in June 1791—to vindicate Burke's insights. In 1790 the mere possession of those insights, quite unshared by anyone else, made Burke sound almost crazy, to many both in Britain and in America. For Jefferson the publication by Fenno of this "extreme" polemic against the French Revolution served to discredit the more "moderate" expression of similar sentiments in the *Discourses on Davila*.

By the early part of 1790, Jefferson's view of the French Revolution seemed on the way to establishing itself as an aspect of the policy of the

U.S. administration. Washington seemed broadly sympathetic, and Jefferson seemed to be gaining control of American coverage of the French Revolution. As Secretary of State, Jefferson had the power to designate three newspapers as authorized to "print the federal statutes." This power could be used to inflect editorial policy, as Jefferson was now inflecting Fenno's. But Alexander Hamilton, as Secretary of the Treasury, had even greater power in this kind—through the placing of Treasury advertisements—and in the late summer of 1790, Hamilton used this power to turn the *Gazette of the United States* round into downright and implacable hostility towards the French Revolution. On 28 July 1790 the *Gazette* published the last of the extracts it ever ran from the *Gazette de Leide*, Jefferson's recommended source for coverage of the French Revolution. On 21 August, the *Gazette* gave a thoroughly Burkean account of the decision-making process in Revolutionary Paris: "At the time of passing the decree of the National Assembly, by which the King is deprived of the prerogatives of making peace and war, Fifty thousand persons surrounded the place of meeting. Had the decision been different—bloodshed and carnage would probably have been the consequences." [25]

Julian P. Boyd comments: "The voice of the *Gazette of the United States* had undergone a remarkable change, and it can scarcely be a matter of mere coincidence that the last issue of Fenno's *Gazette* in which any possible connection between Jefferson and its editor can be shown was the issue that appeared on the very day that Washington gave his approval to the assumption bill." [26]

The assumption bill—the first major initiative of Alexander Hamilton as Secretary of the Treasury—committed the Federal Government to assume the debts of the States. The connection between such a measure and the question of the coverage of the French Revolution in the *Gazette of the United States* is far from obvious, yet the connection is real. It was not that Jefferson and Madison were now opposed, specifically, to the assumption bill. Hamilton had done a deal with them whereby they would not oppose his bill and he would not oppose the situation of the Federal capital on the Potomac: a matter of even greater moment to the Virginians than a financial measure which they distrusted.

Hamilton's disapproval of pro–French Revolution propaganda in the *Gazette of the United States* was not specifically linked with the assumption bill, but it was strongly linked with the general financial policy of which the assumption bill was the first fruit. Hamilton's financial policy was firmly based on sound money and free trade: policies popular in the Northern cities, and especially in commercial and financial circles there, but unpopular in most of the South, with its debt-ridden landowners and comparatively uninfluential trade (except in and around certain seaports, notably Charleston, South Carolina). This is the general context which gives the debate in the United States over the French Revolution its importance even as early as 1790. It was important for American reasons, not for French ones.

Throughout America, in this period, Revolutionary France was popular, and Britain was unpopular. But the popularity of France and unpopularity of Britain were not evenly distributed, either regionally speaking or in terms of class. Broadly, most of the South could be uninhibited in its Gallomania and Anglophobia, because it had relatively little to lose. The Northern merchants and associated classes needed to be no more Anglophobe than was compatible with their most vital interest: the continuing development of trade with Britain, by far their largest market, and principal source of supply. Some Southerners, like Jefferson and Madison, argued for the replacement of Britain by France as the principal trading partner of the United States. But no one actually engaged in trade was buying that one in the 1790s.

The weighty considerations inhibiting Anglophobia among well-off people in the North tended to keep enthusiasm for the French Revolution also within bounds. Britain and the French Revolution were not then in conflict, but the rhetoric of the pro–French Revolution people (encouraged, though not publicly indulged in by Jefferson at this time) was violently Anglophobe. All bad news concerning the French Revolution was "British lies." Many Americans found that very easy to believe. In the North, those who found it easiest to believe were those who (rightly or wrongly) did not believe that they had anything to lose by an interruption or diminution of trade with Britain. In the North, therefore, the French Revolution was a potentially divisive subject, along class lines. The South was much less divided than the North, because of the lesser importance, in most of the region, of trade with Britain. Charleston and the rest of the coastal region of South Carolina seem to have constituted a partial exception, more similar to the North than the rest of the South was. Rachel N. Klein, who has made a special study of attitudes to the French Revolution in South Carolina in the 1790s, writes: "Together with Charleston artisans and a small group of coastal speculators, backcountrymen were the most enthusiastic proponents not only of the French Revolution but of French expansionist schemes into Canada and the Southwest. [See below, chapter 5, pp. 154–55]. At the same time, many leading lights of the coastal elite saw the French Revolution as a warning signal against reapportionment in the State Government."[27] Yet even in Charleston, there was a great deal of enthusiasm for the French Revolution, as was to be attested by the great welcome given there to Citizen Genet in the early summer of 1793 (below, pp. 153–54). Concerning the aftermath of Genet's arrival, Klein writes: "During the summer of 1793, residents of the city organized the Republican Society of South Carolina which was dedicated to the support of France and to the suppression of lurking aristocracy at home. At least forty-four of the seventy-seven identifiable members were city craftsmen or artisans or mechanics, and at least twelve were native merchants." [28]

Virginia, led in this matter by Jefferson, backed by Madison and Monroe (and by George Mason and others), appears as more solid, in support of the French Revolution, than South Carolina was. But there was a general perception, shared by the French themselves, that the South as a whole, was more pro–French Revolution than the North was, although in the early nineties the French Revolution had wide and firm support in every region, though not in every class. All the above refers to white people, only. Black people in the Southern states were not regarded either as a class or as part of a class. They were "that species of property" (a definition used by James Madison among others).

For the interests which Alexander Hamilton represented—and which he identified, not unreasonably, with the long-term interests and prosperity of the United States—Jefferson's effort to capture the *Gazette of the United States* for the cult of the French Revolution was a matter of serious concern, principally because of the character and reputation of the *Gazette* as an organ of the administration. That cult, if it appeared to be sanctioned by the administration, could do serious damage to the relations between the United States and Britain and thereby to the American economy. So Hamilton moved efficiently to extricate the *Gazette* from the tightening grasp of Jefferson and the American cult of the French Revolution. The lever of the Secretary of the Treasury was control of most governmental advertising. Writing of the autumn of 1790—just after the *Gazette*'s defection from the French Revolution—Julian P. Boyd notes, "About this time the *Gazette of the United States* began to receive treasury department advertisements (over three columns being in the issue of 2 October 1790), whereas in the spring of that year it had very little advertising of any sort." [29] Hamilton had made Fenno an offer Fenno could not refuse. From August 1790 on, the *Gazette of the United States* never again had a good word to say about the French Revolution.

Jefferson was learning something about the relative strengths of a Secretary of State and a Secretary of the Treasury in the new Federal Government.

In a serious modern study of the period, *The Age of Federalism*, [30] the name of Alexander Hamilton is included in a list of "early enthusiasts" for the French Revolution. In *The Papers of Alexander Hamilton*[31] I can find no trace of Hamiltonian enthusiasm for the Revolution, at any stage. The earliest statement on the subject recorded in the *Papers* comes in a letter to Lafayette dated 6 October 1789. The letter runs:

> I have seen with a mixture of Pleasure and apprehension the Progress of the events which have lately taken Place in your Country. As a friend to mankind and to liberty I rejoice much in the effort you are making to establish it while I fear much for the final success of the attempt and for the danger in case of success of innovations greater than will consist with the real felicity of your Nation. . . . And I dread the reveries of your Philosophic politicians who appear in the moment to have great influence and who being mere speculatists may aim at more refinement than suits either with human nature or the composition of your Nation.[32]

The dominant note is clearly that of apprehension, somewhat muted, out of courtesy to Lafayette. The letter is in fact quite similar to Edmund Burke's first reaction to the news of the French Revolution:

> As to us here our thoughts of every thing at home are suspended, by our astonishment at the wonderful Spectacle which is exhibited in a Neighbouring and rival Country—what Spectators, and what actors! England gazing with astonishment at a French struggle for Liberty and not knowing whether to blame or to applaud! The thing indeed, though I thought I saw something like it in progress for several years, has still something in it paradoxical and Mysterious. The spirit it is impossible not to admire; but the old Parisian ferocity has broken out in a shocking manner. It is true, that this may be no more than a sudden explosion: If so no indication can be taken from it. But if it should be character rather than accident, then that people are not fit for Liberty, and must have a Strong hand like that of their former masters to coerce them. Men must have a certain fund of natural moderation to qualify them for Freedom, else it become noxious to themselves and a perfect Nuisance to everybody else. What will be the Event it is hard I think still to say. To form a solid constitution requires Wisdom as well as spirit, and whether the French have wise heads among them, or if they possess such whether they have authority equal to their wisdom, is to be seen.[33]

Edmund Burke was not an "early enthusiast" for the French Revolution. Neither was Alexander Hamilton.

In the immediate aftermath of the coup over the *Gazette,* Hamilton wrote a letter to George Washington containing what looks like an effort to offset Jeffersonian influence over Washington in relation to the French Revolution. Hamilton is writing about rumors of a possible Anglo-Spanish war, and he cautiously assesses the possible role that revolutionary France might play in relation to such a conflict. The following is the conclusion of his assessment.

> It is possible indeed that the enthusiasm [which the transition] from Slavery to Liberty may inspire, may be a substitute for the energy of a good administration and the spring of great exertions. But the ebullitions of enthusiasm must ever be a precarious reliance. And it is quite as possible that the greatness, and perhaps immaturity, of that transition may prolong licentiousness and disorder. Calculations of what may happen in France must be unusually fallible, not merely from the yet unsettled state of things in that kingdom, but from the violence of the change, which has been wrought in the situation of the people.[34]

After the loss of the *Gazette,* Jefferson continued his efforts to influence the American press in favor of the French Revolution. He worked first with Benjamin Franklin Bache and his *General Advertiser* and later with Philip Freneau and his *National Gazette* (see below, pp. 119–26). But these outlets could not fully compensate for the loss of the *Gazette of the United States.* In the spring and early summer of 1790, Jefferson had been able to get his totally favorable interpretation of the French Revolution accredited, to a significant extent, in what was accepted as the organ of the Federal administration. From August 1790 not only was that organ closed to him, it was totally dominated by a Hamiltonian interpretation diametrically opposed to the Jeffersonian one. Granted the crucial importance of the issue, both for Jefferson and Hamilton, Hamilton's ideological annexation of the *Gazette* marked a sharp decline in Jefferson's authority, relative to that of Hamilton.

What made the matter still worse, from Jefferson's point of view, was that his need to influence unofficial publications, in a direction opposed to that of the official one, put him in the dangerously equivocal position of appearing to oppose an administration of which he remained a part. Thus, Jefferson's concern with the presentation of the French Revolution in the American press, combined with his continuing political partnership with the opposition leader, James Madison, put him on a course which would eventually cost him the confidence and esteem of George Washington himself (see below, pp. 92–106).

Yet in 1790–91 there were powerful political considerations working in Jefferson's favor. The presence in the administration of a Virginian who possessed the confidence of so many discontented Virginians was important for the minimizing of the sectional differences which threatened the young United States. So it looks as if Washington was prepared to overlook, by reason of that factor, the rather peculiar means by which his Secretary of State managed to retain the confidence of those Virginians, who already were beginning to detest Jefferson's Cabinet colleague Alexander Hamilton. In the management of sectional differences, a certain amount of duplicity has to be tolerated. That there were certain limits to that toleration appears from two episodes of 1790–91 considered below (pp. 92–100 and 105–8).

By late 1790, the French Revolution is moving to the Left, and Lafayette's influence is waning, as is clear from the dispatches of the American Chargé d'Affaires in Paris, William Short, Jefferson's friend and former secretary. If the French Revolution was getting beyond Lafayette, it was getting beyond anything that Washington—as distinct from Jefferson, Madison, and Monroe—could approve. The author of *George Washington and the French Revolution* concludes his survey of the year 1790 with the words: "Thus with the close of 1790, it should have been clear to informed circles in the United States, to George Washington most of all, that the French Revolution was entering upon a new and dangerous phase which might burst the bubble of inflated reputations and which might undo besides much of the good that already was accomplished."[35]

III. THE POLITICS OF MOURNING

From the spring of 1790 to the spring of 1791 a complicated, prolonged, and at times somewhat farcical episode occurred which—ambiguous though it is in some ways—sheds more light on the relations between America and the French Revolution than anything else that happened before the even more instructive arrival and exploits of Citizen Charles-Edmond Genet as Minister Plenipotentiary of the French Republic, a little more than three years later (see below, chapter 5).

The episode of 1790–91 unfurls around the disputed question of how to commemorate—and above all how *not* to commemorate—the life and death of Benjamin Franklin. There are varying interpretations, but let us begin by setting out the facts and relationships that are not in dispute.

News of the death of Benjamin Franklin reached New York on 22 April 1790. On the same day, James Madison in the House of Representatives moved that the members wear badges of mourning for Franklin for a month. The motion was adopted by the House, apparently without debate. On the following day in the Senate, Charles Carroll, a Maryland Senator, urged that the Senate make a similar gesture. The motion was opposed before it could be seconded, and as it found no seconder it had to be withdrawn. Jefferson wrote succinctly to William Short in Paris: "The house of representatives resolved to wear mourning, and does it. The Senate neither resolved it nor do it."[36] Jefferson also, as he later recalled, proposed to Washington, but in vain, that the Executive should follow the example of the House and not that of the Senate in this matter: "I proposed to General Washington that the Executive department should wear mourning. He declined it, because he said he would not know where to draw the line, if he once began that ceremony."[37]

At this stage, it does not appear that the topic of the French Revolution had been overtly introduced into the American discussion of how, or whether, to honor the memory of Benjamin Franklin. But, as subsequent developments were to make amply clear, it was conflicting feelings about the French Revolution that shaped the whole Franklin episode. Franklin, representative of the United States in France throughout the American Revolution, had become the symbolic figure, for both French and Americans, of Franco-American friendship. And by 1790 Franco-American friendship meant specifically *friendship with the French Revolution*.[38] Jefferson and his friends argued that gratitude to France for her past support for the American Revolution required that Americans should now support the French Revolution. Jefferson's opponents over this basic issue— of whom the most conspicuous was John Adams and the most determined was Alexander Hamilton—firmly rejected that proposition. But they also recognized the great emotional power which it exercised over many Americans. They were correspondingly suspicious of appeals to friendship with France, and of gestures in line with such appeals. Madison's proposal in the House was certainly intended as such a gesture, and was perceived as such in the Senate. Hence the Senate's adamant refusal to follow suit.

There is a certain irony in the Senate's spurning of the Madisonian gesture. For the Senate was here fulfilling precisely the role that Madison (in harmony with Hamilton, during the Constitution-making phase) had designed for it within the Constitution. It was designed and structured to be capable of resisting waves of popular opinion, such as were the pro-French waves of the early 1790s. It was there to stand for stability and property rights. Gestures perceived as encouraging to American sympathizers with the French Revolution, who were also enemies to American commercial dealings with Britain, represented everything the Senate was created to restrain. So, in rejecting the Madisonian gesture, the Senate was doing what Madison, in his capacity as Constitution-maker, had set it up to do.

As well as the "class" component in the Franklin episode, so clearly signalled by the clash between the Senate reaction to the "mourning" proposal and that of the more popular and populist House of Representatives, there was also a clear sectional component. As Julian Boyd points out: "In both houses the act of homage had been proposed by southerners. In the Senate all who are known to have spoken in opposition were, like Franklin himself, natives of New England."[39]

The news of the proceedings in Congress reached Paris in June, in a garbled manner. American sympathizers with the French Revolution hastened to tell their friends in France about the decision of the House, but said nothing about what had happened in the Senate.[40] Mirabeau, in his address of 11 June 1790, told the National Assembly that "the American Congress" had "decreed" a period of mourning "for two months" for Benjamin Franklin. Most members of the National Assembly probably did not know that the American legislature, unlike their own, was bicameral. French revolutionaries were enthusiastic but extremely vague about America, and the rhetorical tendency of the time was to assume that the American Constitution and the Constitution which the National Assembly was then engaged in framing (with a unicameral legislature) were virtually identical. Mirabeau "proposed that the members of the National Assembly wear mourning [for Franklin] for three days and that 'the President [of the National Assembly] write to the American Congress' informing them of these proceedings." Mirabeau's motion was carried by acclamation.

The mantle of Benjamin Franklin, as a symbol of revolutionary virtue, was now contested between rival factions of the French Revolutionaries: a sinking faction and a rising one. The sinking one—including Mirabeau, Lafayette, Sieyès, and La Rochefoucauld—was still dominant in the National Assembly, but was already suspect in the eyes of advanced revolutionaries, especially in Paris. It was the Paris Commune, not the National Assembly, which had the confidence of those revolutionaries, for the good reason that Paris was more revolutionary than the rest of the country, and had been setting the pace since the July and October days of 1789. The Commune was not going to let the National Assembly keep the mantle of Franklin all to itself. On the same evening as the National Assembly decided to mourn for Franklin, the members of the Commune met and authorized a public eulogy of Franklin, to be delivered by an approved revolutionary of the advanced description, the Abbé Fauchet. Like most persons particularly admired by French Revolutionaries in 1790–91, Fauchet fell into terminal disfavor in 1792–93. He was expelled from the Jacobin Club on 19 September 1792 and was guillotined shortly afterwards. His prominent role in the Apotheosis of Benjamin Franklin had given poor Fauchet his finest hour. Fauchet's eulogy was delivered in the Halle-aux-blés on 21st July "before some three thousand persons, including Lafayette, Mirabeau, Sieyès, and others of the National Assembly." The leaders of the Assembly were no more willing than their rivals to let go of the mantle of Benjamin Franklin. It was essentially the rivalry between these factions which had led to the extraordinary series of Parisian celebrations called by Gilbert Chinard *"l'Apothéose de Benjamin Franklin"* (referred to in the Prelude to this book).

Not to be outdone by the National Assembly, the Commune also directed its President, Abbé Benière, to write "to the American Government," in this case transmitting Fauchet's eulogy.

Reports of the Franklin proceedings in the National Assembly appeared generally throughout the American press during August 1790. Perhaps significantly, only Bache's *General Advertiser,* then under Jeffersonian influence and patronage, appears to have noticed the proceedings of the Commune. The *General Advertiser* described Fauchet's eulogy as "abounding with all that energy of sentiment, elegance of style, and animation of utterance peculiar to the Nation that almost idolizes whatever is American."[41]

Early in December 1790, the two sets of French communications on the subject of Franklin reached Philadelphia. One was a letter addressed by "The President of the National Assembly of France to the President of Congress." The other was the message from the Commune. This consisted of a letter accompanied by a bulky packet. The letter was addressed to "the President and Members of the American Congress." Both letters were of course incorrectly addressed, in terms of the American Constitution. Their arrival therefore—and also for other reasons—presented the President with a dilemma. His handling of the dilemma has been variously interpreted, but we shall leave questions of interpretation until later. The actual sequence of events, bizarre as it may appear, has to be set out.

For the moment, Washington did nothing about the letter from the National Assembly. But he sent the other letter, and the accompanying packet, both unopened, to John Adams, as President of the Senate. On the following day, John Adams sent the letter and packet back, still unopened, to the President, but with an intimation on behalf of the Senate that they "might be opened with propriety by the President." Washington still refused to open the letter and packet, and did not at this stage even know who exactly they were from. He told his private secretary, Tobias Lear, to send to the Secretary of State the "Letter and packet from the President of the National Assembly of France" with the request that the

Secretary of State report what, if anything, should be communicated to Congress. Jefferson's reply follows in full:

> I have now the honour to return you the letter from the President of the Assembly of representatives for the community of Paris to the President and members of Congress, which you had recieved from the President of the Senate with the opinion of that house that it should be opened by you, and their request that you would communicate to Congress such parts of it as in your opinion might be proper to be laid before the legislature.
>
> The subject of it is the death of the late Dr. Franklin. It conveys expressions from that respectable city to the legislature of the United States, of the part they take in that loss, and information that they had ordered a solemn and public Oration for the transmission of his virtues and talents to posterity; copies of which for the members of Congress accompany their letter: and it is on the whole an evidence of their marked respect and friendship towards these United States.
>
> I am of opinion their letter should be communicated to Congress, who will take such notice of this friendly advance as their wisdom shall conceive to be proper. I have the honour to be with the most profound respect, Sir, Your most obedient & most humble servant,
>
> TH: JEFFERSON[42]

As Boyd disapprovingly observes, "Washington chose, however, to disregard the opinion of the Senate, the recommendation of Jefferson, and indeed the intent of the communication itself. He sent Benière's letter and the copies of Fauchet's eulogy not to the Congress but to the Senate only, perhaps because only the Senate shared with the President a constitutional role in foreign affairs."[43]

Senator Maclay of Pennsylvania described in his diary the reception accorded by Vice President Adams and the Senate to the communications of the Paris Commune regarding Benjamin Franklin: "Our President [Adams] looked over the letter some time and then began reading the additions that followed the President's name [Benière, President of the Paris Commune]. He was Doctor of the Sorbonne, &ca. &ca. to the number of 15 (as our President said). These appelatives of Office, he chose to call titles, and then said some sarcastic things against the National Assembly for abolishing Titles."

Adams knew the use that Jefferson and his friends had been making of his proposed title for the President and he is teasing them here at the expense of the French Revolutionary institution for which they professed such admiration. (The actual message before the Senate was from the

Paris Commune, not from the National Assembly, but Senators may well have been hazy about this.) Maclay's account goes on:

> I could not help remarking that this whole Matter was received and transacted with a coldness and apathy that astonished me, and the letter and all the Pamphlets were *sent down* to the Representatives, as if unworthy the attention of our body. I deliberated with myself whether I should not rise and claim one of the copies in right of my being a Member. I would however only have got into a wrangle by so doing, without working any change on my fellow-Members. There might be others who indulged the same sentiments. But 'twas silence all![44]

On 10 December 1790, the House received Benière's letter and the twenty-six copies of Fauchet's eulogy. On the following day John Beckley, Clerk of the House (and confidant of Thomas Jefferson) wrote to Tobias Lear, Secretary to the President: "I am desired by the Speaker of the House of Representatives, to enclose to you, two Copies of the Civil Eulogy of Doctor Franklin pronounced by [sic] the Commonality of Paris, with a request that you will hand them to the President for his own use."[45] (This looks like an implicit rebuke from the House to the President for having sent the documents to the Senate only, contrary to the advice of the Secretary of State.)

On 13 December, on the motion of Representative Smith from South Carolina, "the House directed the Speaker to express its appreciation for this 'tribute to the distinguished merit of Benjamin Franklin, a citizen of the United States.'" The French chargé incorrectly reported that the Senate had taken similar action, which it never did. In the long Editorial Note headed "Death of Franklin: The Politics of Mourning in France and the United States," Julian P. Boyd offers the following comment on the peculiarity of these transactions:

> It can scarcely be supposed that Jefferson was unaware of this second and more glaring display of coldness on the part of the Senate, still less so that he was indifferent to the question of what response, if any, would be made to the similar communication from a body representing the whole of France. Abbé Sieyès' eloquent tribute to Franklin as a man of universal humanity and his hope that this solemn act of homage would strengthen the bonds between the two nations, thus laying the foundation for the enjoyment of liberty in "an indisoluble chain of connexion among all the people of the earth," could not have left him as unconcerned as Johnson, Ellsworth, King, Paterson, Schuyler, and others of the Senate majority obviously had been. But, so far as the records reveal, Washington had not asked

Jefferson to draft an acknowledgment of these friendly sentiments. All that is known with certainty is that Sieyès' letter was transmitted by the President's secretary merely for the "perusal" of the Secretary of State. If in fact Washington did not discuss it with Jefferson, his action in this instance stands in stark contrast to the kind of close consultation on drafts of dispatches, letters, messages, and proclamations that had prevailed ever since Jefferson entered office. Such collaboration between the President and the Secretary of State had never been more intimate than at this particular moment, as the documents on the French representation, on the British impressments, on the mission of Gouverneur Morris, and on the fixing of the seat of government clearly indicate.

Yet the draft reply to Sieyès' letter was not prepared by the Secretary of State, who happened to possess a personal knowledge of the leaders of the National Assembly and who was highly respected by the moderates among them. For that duty the President turned instead to the Secretary of the Treasury, who had no first-hand knowledge or experience of the revolutionary movement in France and who, of course, had no responsibility for the conduct of foreign affairs. This remarkable procedure was not only a striking departure from customary practice: it was also a violation of Washington's own declared principles of administration. Jefferson had drafted the President's response to a letter from the French monarch some months earlier. He would do the same a year later. Why, then, was the Secretary of State apparently disregarded in a matter involving the legislature of France? Why indeed should this departure from administrative principle and practice have been compounded by another obvious impropriety in diplomacy? For, as head of state making an official response to a communication from the parliamentary body of another nation, Washington by this act not only flouted time-honored diplomatic tradition: he also committed his own office to the risk of affronting the monarch of France and, more important, his ministers. The tradition had not arisen out of an exaggerated concern for mere diplomatic protocol. It had developed over the centuries out of the need of sovereign states in their relations with each other to observe recognized rules of comity. Washington, as prudent and just as he was courteous, was not likely to disregard either his own accustomed administrative procedures or the necessary rules of diplomatic discourse without good and sufficient reason. Why did he do so in this instance?[46]

A good question. We are now into matters of interpretation. Boyd rightly dismisses the previously traditional explanation with reference to Washington's supposedly inordinate sensitivity to matters of protocol (which were in fact treated with scant ceremony by almost everybody involved in these particular transactions). "The most plausible explanation," Boyd goes on, "is to be found not in the trivial question of protocol concerning forms of address but rather in the deep political cleavages within the country, within the administration, and within the Congress." This is surely correct. What follows is less convincing.

The anomaly that perplexes Boyd most, and appears to distress him, is that Washington asked the Secretary of the Treasury, not the Secretary of State, to prepare the answer to the President of the National Assembly. Boyd's answer is that Washington did so on the advice of Jefferson himself, on the ground that Hamilton's authorship would win the letter acceptance in the conservative Senate. Having stressed that Senatorial conservatism—which no one questions—Boyd goes on:

> Facing these realities, Washington may well have hesitated to subject the condolences of the National Assembly to the chilling kind of response that the Senate had accorded Carroll's original motion to follow the House in paying homage to Franklin. To have done so would have been to invite an almost certain affront to a friendly ally. Such a gratuitous rejection of a significant expression of friendship would have been especially damaging at this moment, when France was formally protesting American legislation that Washington himself had regarded as being contrary to justice as well as policy. It is therefore quite plausible to suppose that Washington deliberately chose the unopened letter from the commune of Paris—perhaps in full knowledge of its precise character, certainly in awareness that it did not speak for the whole of France—as a means of testing the temper of the Senate. If so, the answer was immediate and unequivocal. The Senate coldly dismissed the friendly gesture as of no concern to itself, even though it did request the President to lay before it such of the substance of Benière's letter as might be deemed worthy of consideration.

> These two well-concealed tests, if such they were, provided as exact a gauge as could be desired for estimating what action the Senate would take on the letter from Sieyès. To avoid the risk of an affront to the National Assembly that could not be concealed and to insure a decent reciprocation of friendly sentiments by the government of the United States, only one course seemed open—that is, for the President himself to make the response. Yet Sieyès' letter would still have to be laid before Congress. What if the Senate should persist in its intransigent attitude? Again only a single unexceptionable course seemed likely to insure at least the outward appearance of friendliness. The response would have to be drafted by that member of the cabinet whose leadership the Senate accepted virtually without question—the Secretary of the Treasury.

Such, at any rate, was the course that Washington adopted, thereby seeming to ignore the member of the cabinet in whose province these matters fell and at the same time violating both administrative practice and diplomatic tradition. But for these very reasons it becomes implausible if not incredible to suppose that Washington, then in habits of close and intimate consultation with his Secretary of State, did not consult him at every stage of this delicate episode. All that preceded and all that followed the adoption of this strategy to circumvent the Senate majority—particularly the choice of a quiet, adroit, and effective means of achieving a desired end—points convincingly to the source of Washington's invitation to Hamilton to draft the response. Such finesse seems easily attributable to the hand of the Secretary of State.[47]

But it is not at all plausible to suppose "that Washington deliberately chose the unopened letter from the commune in Paris . . . as a means of testing the temper of the Senate." Washington *knew* the temper of the Senate, as he also knew the very different temper of the House. The two tempers were already evident, in what related to Franklin and France, from the different responses of the two Houses to the proposal to go into mourning for Franklin. And Washington's own response had been the same as that of the Senate, not that of the House. The Executive did not go into mourning any more than the Senate did. The House was left alone to mourn for Benjamin Franklin. As we know from Jefferson's own later recollection, Washington turned down Jefferson's suggestion for Executive mourning for Franklin. In view of the close correlation between that notion and pro–French Revolution sentiment, it does not appear that Washington at this time was anxious to encourage such sentiment.

The idea that it was *Jefferson* who suggested to Washington that Hamilton should draft a letter that was clearly appropriate to Jefferson's own department is so improbable, humanly, politically, and administratively, that it would require some pretty solid evidence in its support, before it could be even seriously entertained. And there is no such evidence. As Boyd himself says, "So far as the records reveal" Washington did not ask Jefferson to draft an acknowledgment to Sieyès's letter, which would have been the normal course. Instead Sieyès's letter was transmitted merely for the "perusal" of the Secretary of State.[48] When the reply to Sieyès was drafted, by Hamilton, Boyd himself says, "As to it, [Tobias] Lear [Washington's secretary] offered no explanation but gave an order: it was a communication from the President 'which the Secretary of State will transmit accordingly.' Presumably the letter—in Washington's holograph—was signed, sealed, addressed, and ready to be dispatched. Jefferson carried out the directive in silence."[49]

On the one occasion during this episode when Washington is known to have asked Jefferson for advice, he then rejected the advice, as Boyd acknowledges. Jefferson recommended that Benière's letter and packet be laid before Congress. Instead, the President sent the letter and packet to the Senate only (where Washington must have known they would get a most chilly reception). Yet we are also told (p. 90) that it is "implausible if not incredible to suppose that Washington, then in habits of close and intimate consultation with his Secretary of State, did not consult Jefferson at every stage of this delicate episode." All, according to Boyd, was part of a "strategy" dictated by the "finesse" of the Secretary of State.

It's very hard to accept this interpretation. Are we to suppose, for example, that Washington "consulted" Jefferson before referring Benière's letter and documents to the Senate alone, after Jefferson had advised him in writing to send these to Congress?

The central fact in this episode that has to be explained is Washington's decision to cut across what appeared to be normal administrative lines and entrust to the Secretary of the Treasury, and not to the Secretary of State, the drafting of the reply to the President of the French National Assembly. The simplest and most parsimonious explanation is that Washington felt at this time that he could trust Alexander Hamilton, and could not trust Thomas Jefferson, with the handling of this particular matter.

If we make the straightforward assumption that Hamilton, not Jefferson, was advising Washington on how to handle the communications from France, in such a way as to deaden repercussions of sympathy with the French Revolution, the other aspects of the handling begin to make a kind of sense they otherwise would not. Washington's long delay in posting the more weighty document of the two—that from the National Assembly—can be understood as a way of gaining time, for the lowering of emotion. In "the politics of mourning," mourning has a sell-by date; by the time the National Assembly's letter reached Congress, people had more or less forgotten what it was about. In the meantime the bizarre communication from a municipal authority had been to the fore and had been laughed out of court in the Senate. "Strategy" of some kind, there, but definitely not Jefferson's.

In resisting the obvious explanation—without explicitly referring to it—Boyd relies on just two arguments. The first consists of what he calls Washington's "habits of close and intimate consultation with his Secretary of State." The relevant correspondence, while hardly as cordial as that language would suggest, shows that Washington was indeed in the habit of relying on his Secretary of State for advice, drafts, etc., in all that concerned the relations between the United States and foreign governments. But the Franklin transaction does not fall into that category at all. No foreign government is involved here. The Government of France, recognized by the United States, was still that of Louis XVI, and would still be that of Louis XVI when the Constitution on which the National Assembly was then working came into force (September 1791) and as long as that Constitution remained in force (which was less than a year). The foreign bodies seeking to address the President and the Congress were bodies which had no diplomatic functions or status whatever: the French legislature and the municipality of Paris (which by this time was overshadowing the French legislature, which it would later purge). This was not a diplomatic transaction, belonging administratively in the sole sphere of the Secretary of State. This was a revolutionary transaction. The French Revolution was reaching out, through its two principal organs at this time, to its sympathizers in America. Thomas Jefferson was known to be one of these sympathizers. Alexander Hamilton was known not to be one. That is why Washington entrusted the task of replying to the President of the National Assembly to Alexander Hamilton and not to Thomas Jefferson.

The communications from Paris were neither diplomatic nor altogether foreign. They represented the internal politics of the French Revolution seeking to blend with the internal politics of the United States. And in all that concerned the internal politics of the United States, it was on his Secretary of the Treasury that Washington placed his reliance, officially as well as personally.

Boyd's second argument, in his attempt to resist the obvious, is equally baseless. Boyd theorizes that Jefferson advised Washington to get Hamilton to draft the reply to the National Assembly in order to insure that the Senate would not reject Washington's reply. This is more in the realm of fantasy than of reasonable speculation. Washington was not a weak President needing to thread his way through a hostile Senate on the coattails of a powerful Secretary of the Treasury. Washington's prestige and influence were immense. No Senator, at this time, would have challenged whatever civility it might be that Washington might choose to address to the President of the National Assembly by way of reply to his message. Whether Jefferson or Hamilton drafted the message would have made no difference to the Senate. On such a document, George Washington's signature was all that mattered.

Washington needed no "strategy" to get a message through the Senate. But he did have a clear well-reasoned strategy *for the United States* in this period. Alexander Hamilton was his chief-of-staff for the execution of this strategy. The strategy was about the laying of solid foundations for the future security and greatness of the United States. National unity, social stability, sound money, and flourishing commerce were vital to the strategy. Kindling enthusiasm for the French Revolution was not only no part of the strategy but represented a real threat to it, on several fronts. The cause of the French Revolution was divisive in American society, both class-wise and sectionally, as the sharpness of the division between the two Houses of Congress starkly illustrated. Enthusiasts for the French Revolution were invariably also enemies of Hamilton's sound-money policies. They were also violent Anglophobes, hostile to those who were enriching both themselves and America through trade with Britain, America's principal trading partner by far, during this period. Enthusiasts for the French Revolution wanted trade redirected to France which—if feasible at all—would have involved massive interference with freedom of commerce.

The strategy of Washington and Hamilton was strongly supported by the Senate. So all in all the cool response of both the Senate and the Executive to those cordial overtures on behalf of the French Revolution is fully understandable.

The choice of Hamilton for the actual drafting of that message, and the sending of it to Jefferson with an order merely to transmit it, are remarkable also in another way. *Pace* Julian Boyd, this was a severe snub by Washington to Jefferson. And it was a snub which was easily avoidable. Had he wished to do so, Washington could have consulted Hamilton privately, and then asked Jefferson to draft the message, while giving him instructions about what he wanted in the draft. Jefferson would certainly have complied with the instructions, and that would have taken care of the message to the President of the National Assembly. But it looks as if another kind of message is also involved: a message from Washington to Thomas Jefferson. By the pointed gesture of getting Hamilton to do the actual drafting of a message which Jefferson will simply transmit, Washington is putting Jefferson under notice that his flirtation with the French Revolution has attracted unfavorable attention. By this time, Madison—not long before described as "Washington's right hand man"—was assuming the role of leader of the opposition in the House of Representatives to Washington's administration, especially with regard to financial policies. Washington must have been aware of the very close relationship between his own Secretary of State and the leader of the opposition in the House. It was Madison who had started the whole troublesome "Franklin" affair, by inducing the members of the House to pledge themselves to wear mourning for a month for Benjamin Franklin. And it was Jefferson who had then suggested to Washington that he should follow the example of Madison and the House. And also Jefferson who had advised Washington to send the message of the National Assembly not only to the Senate, but also to the House, where it was certain of a favorable reception.

All in all, I think that Washington's handling of the Franklin episode shows that, before the end of 1790, Washington had lost confidence in Jefferson over the wide range of matters that pertained to the French Revolution *as an issue in the internal politics of the United States*. Washington still wanted Jefferson as his Secretary of State and relied on him for advice on the matters strictly pertaining to the office of Secretary of State: primarily, relations with foreign governments. But over matters where the French Revolution impinged on the emotions of Americans, and thereby on the internal politics of the United States, Washington now knew that the man he could rely on was his Secretary of the Treasury.[50]

Before leaving this episode behind, I should like to say a final word—by way of a kind of reparation—about Julian P. Boyd and that Editorial Note of his. As indicated, I find Boyd's theory, about the whole episode's having been governed by a Jeffersonian "strategy," to belong in the domain of fantasy. But—if we can leave the theory to one side for a moment—I find that Editorial Note extraordinarily impressive and moving. Even when this scholar, under pressure of strong emotion, is about to yield to fantasy, his scholarship is so scrupulous that he himself supplies his readers with the details that will demolish his own theory. Boyd deserves great credit for discerning the importance of this peculiar, and occasionally farcical, episode and for examining it so closely. Other writers on the period, in related fields, have either missed it altogether or paid it scant attention. In, for example, Louis Martin Sears's (chronologically arranged) *George Washington and the French Revolution* (Detroit, 1960), chapter 4 ("1790"), there is not a word about the Franklin episode. In a much more recent work, already mentioned, Stanley Elkins and Eric McKitrick, *The Age of Federalism,* the long and often useful chapter (8) devoted to "The French Revolution in America" has nothing about the Franklin episode either. Nothing either in the chapter (4) "The French Revolution and the Awakening of the Democratic Spirit," in James Roger Sharp's *American Politics in the Early Republic: The New Nation in Cri-*

sis (Yale, 1993). Nor does the episode rate a mention in the relevant section (chapters 12 and 13 of volume 6) of Douglas Southall Freeman's *George Washington: A Biography* (New York, 1954) or in the relevant chapter (22) of volume 3 of James Thomas Flexner's *George Washington* (Boston, 1969, 1970).

Presumably these writers dismissed this episode as merely bizarre. But Boyd clearly saw that the episode had something of importance to tell him about a matter of deep concern to him: the relationship between George Washington and Thomas Jefferson. Boyd obviously does not like what the episode seems to be telling him. Agitation, even anguish, are apparent in his account, as he wrestles against the obvious. In the end, as is not uncommon with Jeffersonian scholarship, piety prevails over common sense. Still "Death of Franklin: The Politics of Mourning in France and the United States" remains a most remarkable essay, and has more to tell us about the subject of the present study than is to be found in the biographies. In concluding the discussion of this episode, I should like to quote the eloquent passage in which Boyd summarizes the general theme. The passage is a kind of epitome of the essay itself, in that most of it is sound, but that it ends on a note of Jeffersonian orthodoxy, unwarranted by the data. The passage runs:

In both houses the act of homage had been proposed by southerners. In the Senate all who are known to have spoken in opposition were, like Franklin himself, natives of New England. But the differing attitudes of the two houses and of the representatives of the two sections on this purely formal matter reflected far deeper political cleavages than those arising from mere personal animosities. The flawed gesture, presaging storms to come, assumed quite another aspect in Europe. When news of it arrived there, Madison's simple tribute to a venerated citizen lost every trace of ambiguity attached to it by the Senate's failure to act. It appeared instead as another clear trumpet call out of the West, shattering monarchical tradition and rallying the forces of reason, virtue, and liberty. Thus transformed, it resounded back across the Atlantic as an echo wholly changed in meaning and multiplied many times in power. In this altered form it again entered American politics, grating with even harsher intensity on the nerves of those who, like Senator Paterson of New Jersey, thought republicanism fine in theory but something else in practice. It thereby exacerbated deep divisions in the nation that were nowhere more sharply discernible than behind the closed doors of the Senate. The episode, perfectly symbolizing the revolutionary tides that had flowed eastward from America to Europe and were now beginning to return with redoubled force, illumines the nature of the breach between those who welcomed the new day and those who resisted it.[51]

"Those who welcomed the new day" are clearly Jefferson and Madison and their supporters. But how about "those who resisted" the new day? Are we to understand that the forces of darkness and old night are arrayed behind Alexander Hamilton and John Adams? If so, they are arrayed behind George Washington as well, though Boyd doesn't want to see that.

IV. BURKE, PAINE, AND JEFFERSON

In the next episode that involved an interaction between the French Revolution and the politics of the United States, the political controversy was precipitated by Thomas Jefferson himself.

Edmund Burke's *Reflections on the Revolution in France* had been published in London on 1 November 1790. On 22 February 1791 Paine's reply, *Rights of Man*, was published in London, dedicated to the President of the United States (whose permission for the dedication had not been asked). About four weeks later, the first copies of *Rights of Man* arrived in Philadelphia. After (apparently) having read both *Reflections* and *Rights*, Jefferson wrote to a sympathetic English correspondent, Benjamin Vaughan:

> The Revolution of France does not astonish me as much as the Revolution of Mr. Burke. I wish I could believe the latter proceeded from as pure motives as the former. But what demonstration could scarcely have established before, less than the hints of Dr. Priestley [Dr. Joseph Priestley, leading English radical, and a friendly correspondent of Jefferson's] and Mr. Paine establish firmly now [sic]. How mortifying that this evidence of the rottenness of his mind must oblige us now to ascribe to wicked motives those actions of his life which wore the mask of virtue and patriotism.[52]

The mode of reasoning here is curious. The "rottenness" of Burke's mind is deemed to be "firmly established," beyond the need for argument, by the "evidence" of his book in its totality (combined with unspecified hints by Priestley and Paine). Then this imputation of "rottenness," now claimed to be established fact, must "oblige us" to ascribe everything in Burke's whole life to wicked motives. This is a clear case of the old *Odium theologicum* transferred to a new and nominally secular sphere. The heretic and blasphemer who opposes the French Revolution represents the forces of evil in the universe and is himself totally evil and all the worse for having formerly worn the mask of virtue and patriotism (over the American Revolution). Fortunately, *Rights of Man* is there as a heavenly antidote. Jefferson goes on, "We have some names of note here who have apostatized from the true faith: but they are few indeed, and the body of our citizens are pure and unsusceptible of taint in that republicanism. Mr. Paine's answer to Burke will be a refreshing shower to their minds."

The manner in which the "refreshing shower" should first fall on American soil was a matter of considerable concern to Jefferson and his friends. Merrill D. Peterson writes:

> In the spring [Jefferson] was unwillingly thrust on the stage as a political gladiator against his old friend John Adams. The controversy between Edmund Burke and Thomas Paine on the French Revolution supplied the background. American opinion of the Revolution, favorable at the outset, had already begun to divide when the English polemics reverberated across the Atlantic in the early months of 1791. Burke's *Reflections on the Revolution in France* captured conservative feelings for the cause of order, tradition, church, privilege, and royalty in France. No sooner was Paine's vigorous democratic reply, the first part of the *Rights of Man,* received on this side of the water than arrangements were made to publish it. John Beckley, Clerk of the House of Representatives and political accomplice of his fellow Virginians, had this purpose in hand, but before sending the pamphlet to the printer, he lent it to Madison, who then passed it on to Jefferson with instructions to return it to Beckley. But that gentleman called before Jefferson had finished. He promised to hurry Burke to his grave and then sent the murderous tract to Jonathan B. Smith, whose brother was to print it.[53]

Jefferson sent the book to S. H. Smith's father, Jonathan Bayard Smith, with the following note:

Apr. 26, 1791.

Th: Jefferson presents his compliments to Mr. Jonathan B. Smith, and in consequence of the inclosed note and of Mr. Beckley's desire he sends him Mr. Paine's pamphlet. He is extremely pleased to find it will be re-printed here, and that something is at length to be publicly said against the political heresies which have sprung up among us. He has no doubt our citizens will rally a second time round the standard of Common sense.

He begs leave to engage three or four copies of the republication.[54]

Of Jonathan Bayard Smith, Julian Boyd writes:

Jefferson later explained to Washington that he was "an utter stranger to J. B. Smith, both by sight and character." There is no reason to doubt the statement, but it is remarkable that he did not know the man to whom his note was addressed. Smith was a prominent Philadelphia merchant. He had been a zealous supporter of the Revolution from the beginning and was active in civic and political affairs. He was a man of varied cultural interests, being a trustee of the University of Pennsylvania and of the College of New Jersey, of which he was a graduate. Both he and Jefferson were active members of the American Philosophical Society. The minutes of the Society are not clear as to whether both were present at the smaller meetings where they could scarcely have avoided becoming acquainted. But certainly both had been present a few weeks earlier at the large gathering of members who assembled in the Hall and marched to the German Lutheran Church for the memorial tribute to Franklin. Under these circumstances Jefferson's certainty that he was addressing a stranger is surprising, though perhaps his assurance arose from the nature of Beckley's directions or from his own undeniable haste. But that he wrote under the conviction that he was addressing a stranger is confirmed by his error in presuming Jonathan Bayard Smith to be the brother instead of the father of the printer.[55]

The American edition of *Rights of Man* received some advance publicity in the *General Advertiser,* edited by Benjamin Franklin Bache, then a channel for Jeffersonian views of the French Revolution, and a friend and ally of John Beckley's. The American edition of *Rights of Man* appeared on 3 May 1791, with a publisher's preface, preceding even the dedication to the President. The preface said:

> The following Extract from a note accompanying a copy of this Pamphlet for republication, is so respectable a testimony of its value, that the Printer hopes the distinguished writer will excuse its present appearance. It proceeds from a character, equally eminent in the councils of America, and conversant in the affairs of France, from a long and recent residence at the Court of Versailles in the Diplomatic department; and, at the same time that it does justice to the writings of Mr. Paine, it reflects honor on the source from which it flows, by directing the mind to a contemplation of that Republican firmness and Democratic simplicity which endear their possessor to every friend of the "Rights of Man."
>
> After some prefatory remarks, the Secretary of State observes:[56]

The extract that followed consisted of Jefferson's note to J. B. Smith, minus the opening sentence.

As Boyd says, "Thus introduced, Paine's *Rights of Man* fell like a thunderclap on the quiet capital. The expressions of the Secretary of State more than the pamphlet itself, we may be sure, took precedence in the political gossip of the boardinghouses, the taverns, and the Philadelphia dinner tables."[57]

In a letter to Washington, five days after the publication of the American edition of *Rights of Man,* Jefferson wrote:

The last week does not furnish one single public event worthy communicating to you: so that I have only to say "all is well." Paine's answer to Burke's pamphlet begins to produce some squibs in our public papers. In Fenno's paper they are Burkites, in the others Painites. One of Fenno's was evidently from the author of the discourses on Davila. I am afraid the indiscretion of a printer has committed me with my friend Mr. Adams, for whom, as one of the most honest and disinterested men alive, I have a cordial esteem, increased by long habits of concurrence in opinion in the days of his republicanism: and even since his apostacy to hereditary monarchy and nobility, tho' we differ, we differ as friends should do.—Beckley had the only copy of Paine's pamphlet, and lent it to me, desiring when I should have read it, that I would send it to a Mr. J. B. Smith, who had asked it for his brother to reprint it. Being an utter stranger to J. B. Smith, both by sight and character, I wrote a note to explain to him why I (a stranger to him) sent him a pamphlet, to wit, that Mr. Beckley had desired it; and to take off a little of the dryness of the note, I added that I was glad to find it was to be reprinted, that something would at length be publicly said against the political heresies which had lately sprung up among us, and that I did not doubt our citizens would rally again round the standard of Common sense [the title of Paine's American Revolutionary pamphlet of 1776]. That I had in my view the Discourses on Davila, which have filled Fenno's papers for a twelve-month, without contradiction, is certain. But nothing was ever further from my thoughts than to become myself the contradictor before the public. To my great astonishment however, when the pamphlet came out, the printer had prefixed my note to it, without having given me the most distant hint of it. Mr. Adams will unquestionably take to himself the charge of political heresy, as conscious of his own views of drawing the present government to the form of the English constitution, and I fear will consider me as meaning to injure him in the public eye.—I learn that some Anglomen have censured it in another point of view, as a sanction of Paine's principles tends to give offence to the British government. Their real fear however is that this popular and republican pamphlet, taking wonderfully, is likely at a single stroke to wipe out all the unconstitutional doctrines which their bell-weather Davila has been preaching for a twelvemonth. I certainly never made a secret of my being anti-monarchical, and anti-aristocratical: but I am sincerely mortified to be thus brought forward on the public stage, where to remain, to advance or to retire, will be equally against my love of silence and quiet, and my abhorrence of dispute.[58]

On the day before the letter to Washington was written, the Attorney General, Edmund Randolph, had visited Jefferson to put the question "Had he, as Secretary of State, authorized publication of his note to [John Bayard] Smith?" Jefferson denied it and on the following day—the day on which Jefferson's letter to Washington is dated—Washington's secretary, Tobias Lear, reported to the President that the Secretary of State had given the Attorney General this assurance:

> Mr. Jefferson said that so far from having authorized ["publication of the extract from his note which appeared prefixed to . . . Paine's Pamphlet"], he was exceedingly sorry to see it there; not from a disavowal of the appro-bation which it gave the work; but because it had been sent to the Printer, with the pamphlet for re-publication, without the most distant idea that he would think of publishing any part of it. And Mr. Jefferson further added, that he wished it might be understood that he did not authorize the publica-tion of any part of his note.[59]

It is clear from the dates that Jefferson wrote the letter of 8 May only after he knew, from his conversation with the Attorney General, that he was in trouble with Washington. If Washington accepted what Jefferson said, he didn't write to tell him so. As Boyd notes sadly: "To Jefferson's prompt and candid explanation of his note to Smith, Washington re-turned only an icy silence." Jefferson's explanation was prompt indeed—right on the heels of that visit from the Attorney General—but Washing-ton doesn't seem to have agreed that it was "candid." Over the "Franklin" episode Boyd had fought hard against the evidence, as we have seen, to convince himself and his readers that Jefferson retained Washington's full confidence. With the "Paine" episode, Boyd gives up, on this point. He writes:

> The evidence is largely hidden in Washington's silence, but, viewing the relationship of the two men during the remainder of Jefferson's tenure as Secretary of State and over the ensuing years . . . it is difficult to escape the conclusion that the deterioration of the bonds of friendship, trust, and affection that once existed between the central figure of the Revolution and the pre-eminent spokesman for its moral and philosophical propositions had its origin in the unauthorized publication of Jefferson's letter to Jona-than Bayard Smith.[60]

In reality, the "Paine" episode must have confirmed the distrust which Washington *already* entertained of his Secretary of State at the time of the "Franklin" episode. And if Washington really believed that the "Paine" publication was "unauthorized" he would no doubt have reassured Jefferson on that point. Instead, there is that "icy silence."

John Adams's son, John Quincy Adams, wrote a reply to Paine under the pen name "Publicola" and took up a key point in Jefferson's preface: "I am somewhat at a loss to determine," he wrote, "what this very respectable gentleman means by *political heresies*. Does he consider this pamphlet of Mr. Payne's as the canonical book of political scripture? As containing the true doctrine of popular infallibility, from which it would be heretical to depart in one single point? . . . I have always understood, Sir, that the citizens of these States were possessed of a full and entire freedom of opinion upon all subjects civil as well as religious; they have not yet established any infallible criterion of *orthodoxy*, either in church or state: . . . and the only political tenet which they would stigmatize with the name of heresy, would be that which should attempt to impose an opinion upon their understandings, upon the single principle of authority." The people, *Publicola* declared, were not disposed to rally around the standard of any man. But if Paine were to be adopted as the holy father of their political faith and *Rights of Man* be taken as "his Papal Bull of infallible virtue," then this testament of orthodoxy should be examined and if found to contain many spurious texts, false in their principles and delusive in their inferences, the apocryphal doctrines should be expunged.[61]

Many writers answered "Publicola" and, as American public opinion at this time was overwhelmingly on the side of Paine and the French Revolution, the controversy was extremely damaging to Adams, and proportionately beneficial to Jefferson. On 17 July, while this controversy was in full swing, Jefferson wrote to John Adams for the first time since the American publication of *Rights of Man*, two-and-a-half months before. Having said his little piece about trying "to take off a little of the dryness of the note," etc., Jefferson goes on:

> I thought so little of this note that I did not even keep a copy of it: nor ever heard a tittle more of it till, the week following, I was thunderstruck with seeing it come out at the head of the pamphlet. I hoped however it would not attract notice. But I found on my return from a journey of a month that a writer came forward under the signature of Publicola, attacking not only the author and principles of the pamphlet, but myself as it's sponsor, by name. Soon after came hosts of other writers defending the pamphlet and

attacking you by name as the writer of Publicola. Thus were our names thrown on the public stage as public antagonists. That you and I differ in our ideas of the best form of government is well known to us both: but we have differed as friends should do, respecting the purity of each other's motives, and confining our difference of opinion to private conversation. And I can declare with truth in the presence of the almighty that nothing was further from my intention or expectation than to have had either my own or your name brought before the public on this occasion.[62]

In his reply, Adams is magnanimous, in his acceptance of Jefferson's story, but cannot conceal his deep resentment:

Yesterday, at Boston, I received your friendly Letter of July 17th. with great pleasure. I give full credit to your relation of the manner, in which your note was written and prefixed to the Philadelphia edition of Mr. Paines pamphlet on the rights of Man: but the misconduct of the person, who committed this breach of your confidence, by making it publick, whatever were his intentions, has Sown the Seeds of more evils, than he can ever attone for. The Pamphlet, with your name, to So Striking a recommendation of it, was not only industriously propagated in New York and Boston; but, that the recommendation might be known to every one, was reprinted with great care in the Newspapers, and was generally considered as a direct and open personal attack upon me, by countenancing the false interpretation of my Writings as favouring the Introduction of hereditary Monarchy and Aristocracy into this Country.[63]

In his reply to Adams's letter, Jefferson improves on his previous claim that he did not intend *publication* of his comments. He now says that he did not have Adams in mind at all, when he *wrote* the comment:

Indeed it was impossible that my note should occasion your name to be brought into question; for so far from naming you, I had not even in view any writing which I might suppose to be yours, and the opinions I alluded to were principally those I had heard in common conversation from a sect aiming at the subversion of the present government to bring in their favorite form of a King, lords, and commons.[64]

Believers in Jeffersonian candor should contrast this assurance to Adams in August, with what Jefferson had told Washington in May:

That I had in my view the Discourses on Davila . . . is certain. But nothing was ever further from my thoughts than to become myself the contradictor *before the public* [emphasis added]. To my great astonishment however, when the pamphlet came out, the printer had prefixed my note to it, with-

out having given me the most distant hint of it. Mr Adams will unquestionably take to himself the charge of political heresy, as conscious of his own
views of drawing the present government to the form of the English constitution, and I fear will consider me as meaning to injure him in the public
eye.

Adams was incensed by Jefferson's denial that in attacking political
heresies he had had Adams in view. Merrill D. Peterson writes: "This little
piece of mendacity, while meant to close the wound, had the opposite
effect. Adams made no reply, nor would the two correspond again for
several years."[65]

During the period of his correspondence with Adams, Jefferson was
writing to Tom Paine in a rather different vein:

> Your favor of Sep. 28. 1790. did not come to my hands till Feb. 11. and
> I have not answered it sooner because it said you would be here in the
> Spring. That expectation being past, I now acknolege the reciept. Indeed I
> am glad you did not come away till you had written your "Rights of man."
> That has been much read here, with avidity and pleasure. A writer under the
> signature of Publicola attacked it. A host of champions entered the arena
> immediately in your defence. The discussion excited the public attention,
> recalled it to the "Defence of the American constitutions" [by John Adams]
> and the "Discourses on Davila," [also by John Adams] which it had kindly
> passed over without censure in the moment, and very general expressions
> of their sense have been now drawn forth; and I thank god that they appear
> firm in their republicanism, notwithstanding the contrary hopes and asser-
> tions of a sect here, high in names, but small in numbers. These had flat-
> tered themselves that the silence of the people under the "Defence" and
> "Davila" was a symptom of their conversion to the doctrine of king, lords,
> and commons. They are checked at least by your pamphlet, and the people
> confirmed in their good old faith.[66]

Jefferson did not tell *Paine* that the publication of that excerpt had
been unauthorized, nor did he tell the American public that. Paine and
the American public took the excerpt at face value and thought all the
better of Jefferson for it. *Much* better. The publication and its consequences were a popular political bonanza for Jefferson as Boyd acknowledges: "The national debate between *Publicola* and his adversaries thus
fixed John Adams in the public mind, however unjustly, as an advocate
of a monarchical form of government for the United States. In consequence, as James Monroe saw immediately, Jefferson's stature as a champion of the republican cause had been vastly magnified."[67]

James Monroe—a strong supporter of Jefferson and the French Revolution—had written to Jefferson:

> The contest of Burke and Paine, as reviv'd in America with the different publications on either side is much the subject of discussion in all parts of this state. Adams is universally believ'd to be the author of Publicola and the principles he avows, as well as those of Mr. B. as universally reprobated. The character of the publick officers is likewise pretty well known. At first it was doubted whether you would not be compell'd to give your sentiments fully to the publick, whether a respect for yourself and the publick opinion would not require it of you. Whilst the fever was at the height the opinion preponderated in favor of it. At present it appears unsettled, especially as Adams is not the avow'd author of Publicola, and so many writers have taken up the subject in your favor. Your other engagements which employ so much of your time necessarily, are certainly to be taken into the calculation and must have great weight. The publick opinion however will before long fully disclose itself on the subject of government, and as an opportunity has and is in some measure offer'd you to give the aid of your talents and character to the republican scale, I am aware you must have experienc'd some pain in repressing your inclinations on the subject. Your sentiments indeed, if they had been previously question'd, are made known as well by the short note prefixt to Paines pamphlet, as a volume could do it.[68]

Reading over those lines, I would not rate James Monroe as a firm believer in the "unauthorized publication" theory. Not that it was *altogether* theoretical. In the literal sense, but only in the literal sense, the publication of that excerpt *was* unauthorized. Nobody will ever find a smoking gun in the shape of a letter from Jefferson, telling Jonathan Bayard Smith he could publish. But Jefferson was a man of the world, who also knew the world of books. He was not the kind of innocent who would "dash off" (Boyd's expression) a few lines to a publisher, which would make a marvellous blurb for the book he is about to publish, and then be "thunderstruck," as Jefferson affected to be, when the publisher actually published the blurb. Jefferson was a politician who made assiduous well-calculated use of the press. He knew the world of Benjamin Franklin Bache and Philip Freneau and he fed them stuff. The idea of the deniable deal was not something to which he was a total stranger. This was a hot one and had to be denied, so Jefferson supplied stout denials to the appropriate people, but not to the general public, who never learned of the denials.

As to the technique of the operation, what I imagine happened is as follows. An intermediary lets the publisher know that it's all right to use the message, provided an "excuse" is included (as it was) in order to make it clear that Jefferson had *not* authorized it. I suspect the hand of John Beckley, who often seems to be around when something fishy in the Jeffersonian line is cooking.[69] Beckley was, for example, chief organizer of the prolonged Jeffersonian undercover efforts to dig up dirt on Alexander Hamilton, the most successful result of which was the detection and disclosure of Hamilton's liaison with Mrs. Reynolds. A glimpse of Beckley's *modus operandi* can be found in a letter from him of June–July 1793, quoted in an editorial note in *The Papers of Alexander Hamilton*. Beckley is reporting on a conversation with an informant, Jacob Clingman, who has been telling him about people who might help in discrediting Hamilton:

> Clingman also says, that Fraunces told him, he could, if he pleased, hang Hamilton. And altho' he considers Fraunces as a man of no principle, yet he is sure that he is privy to the whole connection with Duer, and is the agent between them, for supplying the latter with money, and that he saw him when last in New York, pay money to Duer's Clerk (who brought a note to him for it) and took his receipt. He tells me too, that Fraunces is fond of drink and very avaricious, and that a judicious appeal to either of those passions, would induce him to deliver up Hamilton's and Duer's letters and tell all he knows.
>
> Clingman further informs me, that Mrs. Reynolds has obtained a divorce from her husband, in consequence of his intrigue with Hamilton to her prejudice, and that Colonel Burr obtained it for her: he adds too, that she is thoroughly disposed to attest all she knows of the connection between Hamilton and Reynolds: This, if true, is important.[70]

Syrett identifies this as "a letter to an un-named addressee." It is not hard to guess the name.

The biographical problem of how to reconcile the Jefferson-Beckley relationship with Jefferson's reputation for sanctity is handled with some dexterity by Merrill D. Peterson in relation to the publicizing, in 1797, of Hamilton's liaison with Mrs. Reynolds. (The "Callender" referred to by Peterson was a scurrilous journalist who was, at the material time being paid by Jefferson for abusing Hamilton.) Peterson writes:

> Callender later turned against Jefferson, and publicized his liaison with Sally Hemings.
>
> The notorious Reynolds affair, for five years a well-kept secret among half a dozen Republicans, including Jefferson, blew up in the summer months. Beckley fed the scandal to Callender, and he published it in a tract

Jefferson neither approved nor disapproved. Although his scrupulous respect for privacy in affairs of personal honor would never permit him to indulge his own pen on this tawdry episode in Hamilton's career, he could not forbid it to hacks like Callender.[71]

Jefferson-Beckley operations were carefully planned and well concealed, and it seems to me that the affair of Jefferson's "unwitting" contribution to the American edition of *Rights of Man* bears the marks of such an operation.

Rational people are generally assumed to intend the consequences of their acts, especially when these consequences are beneficial to themselves, and the consequences of this particular act were hugely beneficial to Thomas Jefferson. By this adroit economical stroke Jefferson was casting himself as the good guy, and his main rival, John Adams, as the bad guy, in the eyes of the American public, on a subject about which most Americans felt strongly at this time.

Not that that was all there was to it, by any means. For Jefferson—and indeed also for John Beckley, who was a Jeffersonian zealot, not a mercenary—this was not just a political stroke but a blow struck in the holy cause of freedom, of which the French Revolution was as much part as the American Revolution had been. Heretics—like Adams and Hamilton—had to be punished. Washington—perhaps not himself a heretic, but arch-protector of the heresiarch Hamilton—was in need of a warning. The huge popularity of the French Revolution among the American people had to be mobilized by the holy, to save the heritage of the American Revolution from the heretics and the corrupt. That mobilization was contrary to the grand strategy being pursued by Washington and Hamilton for the future benefit of the United States, and their distrust of Jefferson must have been profound in proportion to the magnitude of his adverse enterprise.

Deviousness is permitted to the holy, in a holy cause. The wisdom of the serpent is commended to the faithful. The Jeffersonian scholars—biographers and editors in particular—deny the deviousness whenever possible, and they all deny it in the case of the letter to Jonathan Bayard Smith. The same scholars exalt the wisdom of their hero. But they fail to notice that the same wisdom, when manifest in action, is often of the serpentine kind.

FOUR

APPROACH AND ADVENT
OF THE FRENCH REPUBLIC,
ONE AND INDIVISIBLE

1791–92

Early in January 1791, George Mason wrote to Thomas Jefferson: "As I well know Your Attachment to the sacred Cause of Liberty must interest You in the Success of the French Revolution, it is with great pleasure I can inform You, that it is still going on prosperously."[1]

In the following month, Jefferson replied, relating "the Success of the French Revolution" and "the sacred Cause of Liberty" specifically to the internal politics of the United States, with the Federalists cast in the role of a heretical sect:

> I consider the establishment and success of their [French Revolutionary] government as necessary to stay up our own and to prevent it from falling back to that kind of Half-way-house, the English constitution. It cannot be denied that we have among us a sect who believe that to contain whatever is perfect in human institutions; that the members of this sect have, many of them, names and offices which stand high in the estimation of our countrymen. I still rely that the great mass of our community is untainted with these heresies, as is it's head.[2]

The last four words have a rather hollow ring in the context. George Washington may be "untainted" personally but if he is, he is ineffective, since his government needs to be "stay[ed] up" by the "Success" of the French Revolution from "falling back" into that "Half-way-house." And George Mason may well have wondered how it comes about that this untainted President keeps Alexander Hamilton, the heresiarch of the tainted sect, in his Cabinet and acquiesces in his Anglophile and otherwise suspect policies.

The exchange between Jefferson and Mason is illuminating with regard to the power of the French Revolution in American politics generally, and in Virginian politics in particular, in the early 1790s. Only a few years before, George Mason had been the intellectual leader of the anti-federal side in the debates in Virginia over the Constitution and had thus been the adversary of the great Federalist James Madison, now Jefferson's chief ally. But over the French Revolution, these three Virginians are now allies. The sacred cause of Liberty, identified with the success of the French Revolution, closes some past Virginian divisions (while threatening to open others, notably between Washington and the Jeffersonians) and opens up the attractive possibility of mobilizing "the great mass" of their "untainted" community against the heresies of a sect which happens to be most strongly established among the commercial and political classes of the Northeastern region of the United States.

Jefferson's biographers and editors often refer to such letters as this one to George Mason as "private letters." Yet there is nothing private about them. These are what were called in the eighteenth century "ostensible" letters: letters meant to be shown to sympathizers. Through such letters, Jefferson was sending two simple, closely related messages to influential Virginians. The first message confirms Virginian suspicions of the Federal Government. The second shows that Thomas Jefferson, though a member of that government, is not corrupted by it, but still pure in heart and always vigilant in the cause of Liberty, Virginia, and the French Revolution.

I

As Secretary of State, Thomas Jefferson was putting out essentially the same message, during the same period, to the diplomatic representatives of revolutionary France. The French Chargé d'Affaires Louis-Guillaume Otto reported to his Foreign Minister in July 1791:

> Above all it is M. Jefferson who takes the greatest interest in the success of our great revolution. He has often told me that the work of our National Assembly will serve to regenerate not only France but also the United States, whose principles were beginning to become corrupted. Almost all the Whigs or the genuine Republicans of this country are of the same opinion.[3]

Otto also knew that sympathies with the French Revolution were not evenly distributed regionally in the United States in the early 1790s: "M. Jefferson, like all southerners, is a republican at heart."[4]

The stress on the word "republican," as early as 1790–91, is interesting. France, in this period, was not a republic, nor was the National Assembly majority republican. The constitution which the Assembly was shaping was for a constitutional monarchy and it was on this constitution that foreign admirers of the French Revolution—like Jefferson and Madison in the United States and Charles James Fox and Richard Brinsley Sheridan in Britain—appeared to hang their hopes at this point. Yet some in the National Assembly, and many in and around the Paris Commune, were already dreaming of a full-blown republic. It would seem that this tendency was represented in the French Foreign Ministry, and that Jefferson was felt to be in sympathy with it. On the American side, "Republican" was just coming into use at this time to refer to the emerging party of Jeffersonian inspiration, opposed to the Federalists under Alexander Hamilton. The choice of the name "Republican" reflects Jefferson's adroitness as a propagandist. If you were not a republican, then you must be a monarchist; which is precisely the label Jefferson and his friends were trying to pin on the Federalists, for their undoing.

France was not yet a republic, but the French Revolution was already heading in that direction by the spring of 1791. The National Assembly was again feeling the overt pressure of the streets of Paris. William Short, Jefferson's protégé, now Chargé d'Affaires in Paris, reported to the Secretary of State early in March "scenes of disorder and riot . . . of the most alarming kind" for which the departure from Paris of the King's aunts had provided "one of the pretexts." Short commented: "Such scenes must be expected so long as the present anarchy continues."[5] Near the end of the following month Short reported again: "Paris has been for eight days past and still is in a degree of fermentation of which there is no example." Short sees a threat of "a new revolution."[6]

On this letter, Julian P. Boyd comments: "Separated from TJ and looking upon the revolutionary scenes from a different geographical and philosophical perspective, Short at this time exhibited an increasing departure from the views of his mentor concerning the direction in which the revolutionists were moving."[7]

Whatever we may think of the merits of "the direction in which the revolutionists were moving," there can be no doubt that William Short was right about what that direction actually *was*: that of "a new revolution," which came about in the late summer of the following year, when the constitutional monarchy was overthrown, the constitution (then less than a year old) was scrapped, and those who had shaped it were massacred, guillotined, or driven into exile by the masters of the new French Republic. Short's dispatches of this period possess both an acuteness and a degree of prescience which had been largely lacking in Jefferson's own dispatches of 1787–89. But then Short was a diplomatist, and nothing but a diplomatist. Jefferson was also an American politician, thinking about American politics, and the bearing of the holy cause of the French Revolution on American politics and ethics.

The conditions Short is describing in the spring of 1791 are basically the same as those which Edmund Burke had discerned below an apparently calm surface of French politics in September 1789. The National Assembly, in its constitution-making activities, had been "deviating into moderation" in 1790 to 1791, and for this "a Mob of their constituents" was threatening "to Hang them": a threat that was to be made good in 1792–93.

I don't think Jefferson's ideas about "the direction in which the revolutionists were moving" in the spring of 1791 *necessarily* diverged from those of Short. The sequel indeed would suggest that they did not. Jefferson's enthusiasm for the French Republic was to be even greater (or at least more fervently expressed) than what he had felt for the National Assembly when it was shaping the constitutional monarchy (see chapter 2). The deposition of the King, the September Massacres, the execution of the King, did not in the least shake Jefferson's identification of the French Revolution with the holy cause of freedom (see below, pp. 137–51). So there is no need to assume that he would have differed from Short's *analysis*. But as we know from the sequel (below, pp. 144–47) Jefferson detested the tone and manner in which Short described the revolutionary events. Short's dispatches, which Washington would have to see, were of a kind to play into the hands of the Federalists. Jefferson had now—especially after the *Rights of Man* affair—a large political capital locked up in the French Revolution, as perceived by masses of untainted Americans: to put it no higher, though Jefferson himself sincerely put it far higher. In the doctrinal contests there was far more at stake than appeared. This was a spiritual conflict under political appearances. The champions of the holy cause of Freedom, symbolized most vividly by the French Revolution, were arrayed against the forces of "rottenness," symbolized by Burke's satanic *Reflections*.

II

The month of June 1791 is the watershed of the French Revolution. From this month on, those who had led the Revolution in 1789–90 are entering a period of terminal discredit, while their most vociferous critics are competing among themselves for the succession.

The pivotal events consisted of the attempted escape of the royal family from Paris (20 June) and their recapture at Varennes five days later. The mere attempt at escape shattered beyond repair what had been the official myth of the French Revolution since 1789. According to the myth, the King had been cooperating voluntarily with the leaders of the National Assembly in working out a Constitution in which the King would be Chief Executive: a constitutional monarchy, on the British model, just as Jefferson had proposed to Lafayette (above, chapter 2). Foreign admirers of the French Revolution took this constitution-making seriously, and felt assured of its success. Jefferson believed that the constitution makers had not only "the materials of a superb edifice" but were also "perfectly capable of putting them together" (see chapter 2). Charles James Fox, for his part, applied the "edifice" metaphor, in even more glowing style. On 15 April 1791—little more than two months, as it happened, before the flight to Varennes—Fox told the House of Commons that he for one admired "the new constitution of France, taken together, as the most glorious and stupendous edifice of liberty, which had been erected on the foundation of human liberty in any time or century."[8]

Edmund Burke—who publicly broke with Fox over the "stupendous edifice" speech—had seen the edifice in question for the fraud it was, more than a year before Fox delivered this rhapsody in its honor. Burke had declared that the supposed Chief Executive, the constitutional monarch, was in fact no more than a political prisoner. On 20 June 1791 the prisoner himself dramatically demonstrated that Burke had been right, by escaping from his captors, leaving behind him a document acknowledging that he had been acting under duress. Five days later the royal family were captured at Varennes and brought back to Paris through streets thronged with huge silent crowds.

William Short reported the escape of the Royal family in a dispatch dated 22 June 1791, adding an undated postscript ending with the sentence: "The crisis is really tremendous and may have a disastrous issue."[9] Four days later, Short reported: "You will easily conceive that the post of M. de la fayette becomes the most disagreeable and dangerous that can be imagined. . . . The people of Paris headed by some popular ambitious persons declare loudly in favor [of] a republican government. They have much influence on the deliberations of the assembly."[10]

On June 29, Short added a shrewd assessment of the political situation in the aftermath of Varennes: "It seems clear to me that a great opposition is forming in the spirit of the people without, to that of the members within, the assembly. The latter, as I have said, wish to support the form of a monarchy. The former are becoming every day under the influence of their clubs, leaders and journals, more and more averse both to the substance and form."[11]

On 29 August, Jefferson, as Secretary of State, acknowledged receipt of these three dispatches of Short's. Jefferson made no comment on their content. In general he did not comment on Short's dispatches from Paris in 1791 and most of 1792. I suspect that the reason for this rather strange silence is that the Secretary of State knew by this time that his own views on the French Revolution were not shared by his President (but see below, pp. 143–44).

On 14 September 1791, Short announced that on that day the French constitution was completed, by the King's acceptance of it. Ten days before, Short had analyzed the political context of this transaction with his usual acumen:

> He will probably pronounce his acceptation in a few days. But as it is evident that he is not freer in this acceptation than in the sanction of the laws against which he protested, it is much to be feared that the nation at large will have no confidence in this adhesion. Such a government without confidence, which is its essence, is nothing more than a state of anarchy and will be productive I fear of much misfortune.[12]

Jefferson refused to take in the message of Short's dispatches, or to acknowledge that anything had changed in the French Revolution with the flight and recapture of the "constitutional monarch." On 30 August—the day he acknowledged receipt of Short's three post-Varennes dispatches—he wrote to Condorcet regarding the imminent "completion" of the French constitution: "I am looking ardently to the completion of the glorious work in which your country is engaged."[13]

The Secretary of State's lack of attention to what was actually happening in France in 1791, and was being faithfully reported to him, is remarkable. He writes exactly as if the date was still 1789. It is clear that for him (at this time) the French Revolution is not a series of human and terrestrial events and transactions in a foreign country. It is a sacred and static abstraction, an angelic auxiliary for the cause of freedom in America, and for the discomfiture of Alexander Hamilton and John Adams (but see below, pp. 145–48).

As for Madison, all of whose ideas about the French Revolution were based on Jeffersonian illusions or fictions, he managed to see the "acceptance" of the Constitution by the recaptured King—three months after his enforced return to Paris—as a free act from which the happiest inferences for the future could be confidently drawn: "The French Revolution seems to have succeeded beyond the most sanguine hopes. The King, by freely accepting [*sic*] the constitution, has baffled the external machinations against it, and the peaceful election of a legislative assembly of the same complexion with their predecessors, and the regular commencement of their functions have equally suppressed the danger of internal confusions."[14]

As everyone knows, James Madison was one of the wisest constitutional thinkers who have ever lived. That he should fall for the impudent and short-lived fraud of the French Constitution of 1791–92 might seem strange. But then neither Madison nor Jefferson ever thought about the French Revolution in itself. They thought about it *as an issue in American politics*. And they fantasized its relation to the abstract idea of Liberty.

III

In the second half of 1791, Jefferson and Madison were greatly preoccupied with the foundation of a paper which would be a vehicle for Republican propaganda, an unusual combined operation for a member of a government and an opposition leader. The vehicle proved to be the *National Gazette,* edited by Philip Freneau. The *National Gazette* began to appear on 31 October 1791. In August, Jefferson had supplied Freneau with a sinecure appointment as clerk-translator in the Department of State: The characteristics that made Freneau the ideal editor for the *National Gazette* are listed by Boyd (vol. 20, p. 737) as: ". . . his own deep antipathy to the British people and their government, his uncritical acceptance of all propaganda favorable to the progress of the revolution in France, his hatred of monarchy and all its manifestations, and his devotion to the principles of the American Revolution as he understood them."[15]

Jefferson also kept Freneau supplied with a flow of confidential material (from the files of the Department of State) and other forms of patronage. As Samuel Forman wrote,"Jefferson could not have been more interested in [the *National Gazette*] if his political life had depended on its success. He was always writing about it to his friends, calling attention to its merits and drumming up subscribers and subscriptions. . . . The chief business of the Gazette was to destroy Hamilton, the one man in whom the hopes of the Federalists lay."[16] In its early months, the *National Gazette* was fairly discreet in its criticisms of the administration which was subsidizing it (through Jefferson). But by the summer of 1792 the *Gazette* was mounting a full-scale attack on Alexander Hamilton and the financial policies of Washington's administration (of which of course Jefferson was still a member). Hamilton (using the initials "TL" in the *Gazette of the United States*) asked some pertinent questions:

> Is it possible that Mr. Jefferson, the head of a principal department of the Government can be the Patron of a Paper, the evident object of which is to decry the Government and its measures? If he disapproves of the Government itself and thinks it deserving of opposition, could he reconcile to his own personal dignity and the principles of probity to hold an office under it and employ the means of official influence in that opposition? If he disapproves of the leading measures . . . could he reconcile it with the principles of delicacy and propriety to continue to hold a place in that administration, and at the same time to be instrumental in vilifying measures which have been adopted by majorities of both branches of the Legislature and *sanctioned by the Chief Magistrate of the Union?*[17]

To Washington, Jefferson issued one of those portentous disclaimers of which he had the knack. He admitted that he had supplied Freneau with copies of the (pro–French Revolution) *Gazette de Leide,* in order to provide the President and the public with "juster views of the affairs of Europe than are available from any other public source." Jefferson went on:

> But as to any other direction or indication of my wish how his press should be conducted, what sort of intelligence he should give, what essays encourage, I can protest in the presence of heaven, that I never did by myself, or any other, directly or indirectly, say a syllable, nor attempt any kind of influence. I can further protest, in the same awful presence, that I never did by myself or any other, directly or indirectly, write, dictate or procure any one sentence or sentiment to be inserted *in his, or any other gazette,* to which my name was not affixed, or that of my office.[18]

As the foremost historian of American journalism comments: "It's clear that Jefferson's explanation to Washington was a fairly transparent 'alibi'."[19]

Julian P. Boyd ends the section of his Editorial Note that deals with the foundation of the *National Gazette* with the words:

> The unavoidable conclusion is that the offer of official patronage and the founding of the *National Gazette,* despite disclaimers by Jefferson, Madison, and Freneau, were unquestionably interconnected. It is not likely that the appointment to the clerkship tipped the scales with so independent a person as Freneau, sensitive as he always was to the suspicion of being

influenced in his actions by another. The arrangement with Childs and Swaine which freed him of financial responsibility was probably the most decisive factor. But this is irrelevant to the question of improper conduct raised by Hamilton. In seeking—and unquestionably receiving—Jefferson's prior counsel on the planning of the newspaper, Freneau contradicted his sworn testimony that the Secretary of State had at no time "urged, advised, or influenced" his coming to Philadelphia as editor. By the same token, the impression Jefferson sought to give the President—and his defenders to convince the public—that the appointment and the founding of the paper were unrelated is not persuasive. Considering the nominal duties given to the translating clerk and the highly disproportionate compensation he received, it can scarcely be denied that Jefferson had in fact offered and Freneau had accepted what can only be described as a political sinecure.

The pain in the words "unavoidable conclusion" and "what can only be described" is evident. Throughout the previous nineteen volumes of his great edition of the Jefferson Papers, Julian P. Boyd had repeatedly taken Jefferson at his word, even where the context cast doubt on Jefferson's version. By the end of volume 20, Boyd can no longer do this. The passage quoted above is not an isolated one. Having described Madison's extensive contributions to the *National Gazette,* Boyd goes on: "The contributions made by Jefferson to the *National Gazette,* despite the solemn assurance given to the President that he had never written or procured a single sentence for it, were more varied and more extensive than those of Madison."

It wasn't just a question of an occasional lapse from strict veracity on Jefferson's part. Boyd was finding that his general assessment of Jefferson's character didn't stand up to his investigations into Jefferson's activities in the period 1791–92. Boyd, like Dumas Malone and other biographers, had taken Jefferson at his own valuation, as a person shrinking from controversy and from the political melee. But the founder and patron of the *National Gazette* was a devoted and skillful organizer of controversy and a ruthless, elusive, and devious participant in the political melee, and Jefferson's editor could no longer avert his eyes from this.

Julian P. Boyd died shortly after completing volume 20, and this might not be entirely a coincidence. To discover at that stage of his monumental work that the idol has feet of clay is the kind of shock that might deprive a scholar of the will to live. But his twenty volumes remain the greatest mine of information that we have on Jefferson. That Boyd misinterpreted *some* of the information matters little in comparison with the immensity of his editorial achievement.

IV

Philip Freneau was of course an ardent admirer of the French Revolution. Jefferson and Madison would not have made him editor of the *National Gazette* if he had not been. As a not-unfriendly student of both Jefferson's and Freneau's has put it: "Freneau was a thorough Jeffersonian and in the Gazette Jefferson's opinions were reflected as in a mirror."[20] Jefferson fed Freneau appropriate material on the French Revolution. "Appropriate material" did not include William Short's reports from Paris. Boyd writes:

> It would be a mistake, however, to assume that the need for confidentiality alone caused Jefferson to withhold from Freneau every part of the long, perceptive, and highly important dispatches of William Short. In his intimate knowledge of affairs in France, in his appraisals of leading public figures, and in his ability to anticipate the course of events, Short provided Jefferson with the most important budgets of information of any of the American representatives abroad. Gouverneur Morris, who preferred to communicate with the President because he thought information channeled through the Secretary of State would be biased, also provided much useful intelligence about the drift of affairs in France. But both Short in his modest, studious accounts and Morris in his self-confident but generally accurate appraisal of men and measures, were in substantial agreement about the extreme revolutionists and the likelihood that they would destroy the bright hopes for the French republic. The nature of their skeptical reports, added to the need for confidentiality, helps to explain why Jefferson declined to allow Freneau in any instance to make use of any part of the dispatches of these two astute observers of the European scene.[21]

The following is an instructive example of how Jefferson and Freneau between them used to manage material received from France for the instruction of readers of the *National Gazette:*

> A few days before the first issue of the *National Gazette* appeared, Jefferson received from William Short a number of French journals to show to what extremes their editors went in appealing to popular prejudices. "At any other period," Short declared, "such publications would be disgusting and unworthy of being read." In the second issue of his paper Freneau quoted one of these journals, *L'Argus Patriote,* and referred to it as "a French paper of estimation." A few days later he printed an extract from it asserting that liberty of the press was dead in England, its carcass gnawed upon by worms, but it had been revived in France, the freest nation in all the universe, whose constitution had been brought to perfection.[22]

Under Freneau, and under the discreet patronage of the Secretary of State, the offices of the *National Gazette* became the hub of French Revolutionary activity in the capital of the United States in 1792–93. As Samuel Forman writes: "Besides being its greatest literary champion, Freneau was in other ways a conspicuous figure among the promoters of the French cause. His editorial office was a rendezvous for French sympathizers; he solicited and collected funds to be sent to France acting as agent, for the 'French Society of Patriots of America.'"[23]

For "French cause" read "French Revolutionary cause" and for "French sympathizers" read "French Revolutionary sympathizers." And in the title of that French Society, the term "patriots" should be understood in its technical French Revolutionary sense, (below, p. 189).

Jefferson was the patron of all this activity in and around the *National Gazette*. Republicans were aware of this, and grateful to Jefferson for it. From others, and from Washington in particular, the nature and extent of the patronage had to be dissimulated. In Frank L. Mott's book *Jefferson and the Press,* the chapter on the story of the *National Gazette* is followed by a chapter of commentary aptly entitled "Sub Rosa." In this, Mott writes:

Jefferson apparently attempted to keep his ventures in this chess game of counterinfluences—his efforts at vote-getting, his play of one man against another, his management of both public and personal pressures—under cover and secret. Few public men have ever been more industrious letter writers, and much of his correspondence was punctuated by pleas for secrecy. It is as though he felt a certain dichotomy in his political career—a cleavage between the Jefferson of history, and, on the other hand, Jefferson the political manager, whose smaller intrigues, necessary though they seemed at the time, were more or less distasteful and might better be private and easily forgotten.

This secretive characteristic has sometimes been condemned by writers upon Jefferson's career and personality, and with some appearance of justice. Yet one must consider the nature and necessities of practical politics. Is there a moral question involved? Jefferson wrote De Foronda that he had always acted in good faith, "having never believed that there was one code of morality for a public, and another for a private man." One cannot fully understand this technique of almost furtive secrecy without an appreciation of Jefferson's native sensitiveness, his dislike of brawling, his preference for calm interchange of opinion. "The way to make friends quarrel," he once wrote to Washington, "is to put them in disputation under the public eye." A fighter like Andrew Jackson puts all his cards on the table and openly

Portrait of William Short, by Rembrandt Peale (American, 1778–1860), 1806. Oil on canvas, 31 x 25 in. Courtesy of Muscarelle Museum of Art, College of William and Mary in Virginia, U.S.A.; gift of Mary Churchill Short, Fanny Short Butler, and William Short. Short was regarded by Jefferson as his "adopted son," but severely rebuked by him for his attitude to the French Revolution. "The tone of your letters had for some time given me pain, on account of the extreme warmth with which they censured the proceedings of the Jacobins of France. . . . You have been wounded by the sufferings of your friends, and have by this circumstance been hurried into a state of mind which would be extremely disrelished if known to your countrymen" (TJ to WS, 3 January 1793; chapter 4, pp. 145–47).

challenges all opponents; a Jefferson must employ a more subtle course of conduct.

Here is the chief difference between Alexander Hamilton's journalism and that of Jefferson. Hamilton wrote for the papers as openly as the customs of the time allowed, and was well known to have had a hand in the establishment of three or four of them. Jefferson wrote scarcely anything directly for the papers; and when he procured the insertion of anything, he did it by oblique methods.

For many years after his relations with the *National Gazette,* Jefferson was fond of declaring that he never wrote a line for the newspapers. Sometimes he added an exception: "without subscribing my name." By this he unquestionably referred to official papers of one kind or another, since

Gouverneur Morris, by Gilles-Louis Chrétien, after Edme Quenedey, 1789. Engraving. Courtesy of Print Collection, Miriam and Ira D. Wallach Division of Arts, Prints and Photographs, The New York Public Library; Astor, Lenox and Tilden Foundations. Morris was the Minister Plenipotentiary of the United States in Paris, 1792–95. Jefferson was Washington's Secretary of State at the time of this appointment, about which Jefferson was not consulted by Washington. Shortly after Morris's appointment, Jefferson blamed Morris for Washington's "want of confidence in the French Revolution." "The fact is that Gouverneur Morris, a high flying Monarchy-man, shutting his eyes and his faith to every fact against his wishes, and believing everything he desires to be true, has kept the President's mind constantly poisoned with his forebodings" (TJ's note of 12 March 1792; chapter 4, p. 130).

these were the only signed pieces which appeared in the newspapers of the period. He made such a declaration to Washington in the letter concerning his relations to Freneau, already quoted; and he repeated it in another letter after he had left the Cabinet. A little later he wrote to Samuel Harrison Smith, lately of the Philadelphia *New World,* who had evidently been urging him to reply to certain personal calumnies in the papers: "At a very early period in my life I determined never to put a sentence into any newspaper. I have religiously adhered to the resolution through my life, and have great reason to be contented with it." There are many similar statements in Jefferson's letters; one other may be quoted: "I only pray that my letter may not go out of your own hands, lest it should get into the newspapers, a bear-garden scene into which I have made it a point to enter on no provo-cation."[24]

V

In January 1792, the Secretary of State informed Gouverneur Morris that the President's decision to nominate him as Minister Plenipotentiary to France had been approved by the Senate. This decision was a setback to Jefferson, and another mark of Washington's lack of confidence in his Secretary of State in matters pertaining to the French Revolution. Charles T. Cullen—Boyd's successor as editor of the Jefferson papers—writes:

> Morris' nomination to succeed Jefferson as minister to France came as a distinct shock and surprise to the Secretary of State. Washington decided on this nomination without consulting Jefferson beforehand and remained adamant in the face of an effort by Jefferson to persuade him to dispatch Thomas Pinckney to Paris instead. Morris' nomination was a source of great unease to Jefferson because of the aristocratic New Yorker's well-known contempt for the French Revolution.[25]

In his letter notifying Morris of his appointment, Jefferson said:

> To you it would be more than unnecessary for me to undertake a general delineation of the functions of the Office to which you are appointed. I shall therefore only express our desire, that they be constantly exercised in that spirit of sincere friendship and attachment which we bear to the French Nation; and that in all transactions with the Minister, his good dispositions be conciliated by whatever in language or attentions may tend to that effect. With respect to their Government, we are under no call to express opinions which might please or offend any party; and therefore it will be best to avoid them on all occasions, public or private. Could any circumstances require unavoidably such expressions, they would naturally be in confor-mity with the sentiments of the great mass of our countrymen, who having first, in modern times, taken the ground of Government founded on the will of the people, cannot but be delighted on seeing so distinguished and so esteemed a Nation arrive on the same ground, and plant their standard by our side.[26]

On 2 March 1792, the French minister to the United States submitted to Washington a letter from Louis XVI announcing his acceptance (19 September 1791) of the constitution drafted by the National Assembly.

This document, signed by the recaptured "constitutional monarch," opened with the words: "Very dear, great friends and allies. We make it our duty to inform you that we have accepted the Constitution which has been presented to us in the name of the nation, and according to which France will be henceforth governed."[27]

The "henceforth" contemplated in the letter turned out to be a period of eleven months at the end of which the constitution in question was scrapped, and the monarch deposed, at the bidding of the Paris mob. These events and the subsequent executions of the King and Queen had all been predicted by Burke.

Washington's reply was drafted by Jefferson, in conformity with what he knew to be Washington's attitude. Charles T. Cullen wrote:

> After submitting both documents to the House and the Senate on 5 Mch. 1792, Washington, who expected Congress to take no action on them, instructed TJ to draft a reply for him to the king's letter. TJ drafted a letter for Washington which, while scrupulously refraining from any comment on the merits of the Constitution of 1791, congratulated the king for accepting this charter and expressed good wishes for the freedom and safety of the French monarch and the French nation. The Secretary of State deliberately avoided even the slightest hint of praise for the French Constitution because of his recognition that the President was much less sanguine than he about the course of the French Revolution. Washington signed this letter on 10 Mch. 1792 and, before dispatching it to France, revealed its contents to Ternant, who took pleasure in every part of it save for its failure to laud the 1791 Constitution.

The House of Representatives, led by Madison, now intervened to bring about a somewhat warmer response to the message from Paris. Cullen:

> Before it was actually sent to France, however, the letter TJ drafted for the President had to be significantly altered owing to the actions of Congress. At first neither house of Congress made any response to Washington's message and the accompanying translation of the French king's letter. The Senate merely tabled these documents, and the House twice refused motions to deliberate on them, preferring instead to leave to the President the task of framing a suitable response to the king. But on 10 Mch. 1792— perhaps not coincidentally the same day Washington informed Ternant of the substance of his generally noncommittal reply to Louis—the House cast aside its previous restraint and took up the subject of the king's letter. Led by partisans of the French Revolution, including James Madison, the House

Portrait of James Madison, by Gilbert Stuart, 1804. Courtesy of Colonial Williamsburg Foundation. Throughout the period covered by *The Long Affair,* Madison was Jefferson's closest collaborator, even from 1790 to 1793, when Jefferson was a member of Washington's first administration and Madison was leading the Republican opposition in the House of Representatives. "Madison had become Jefferson's unquestioning disciple, in all that pertained to the French Revolution, from the time of Jefferson's return to America at the end of 1789" (chapters 3 to 6).

passed a resolution expressing satisfaction with the king's notification of his acceptance of the Constitution and asking the President "in his answer to the said notification, to express the sincere participation of the House in the interests of the French Nation, on this great and important event; and their wish, that the wisdom and magnanimity displayed in the formation and acceptance of the constitution, may be rewarded by the most perfect attainment of its object, the permanent happiness of so great a people." It then appointed a committee to present this resolution to the President.

After mentioning a somewhat similar but "noticeably more restrained" resolution from the Senate, Cullen concludes his account of these transactions:

> Washington was infuriated by the House's action. He regarded it as a flagrant example of legislative encroachment on the executive authority to conduct foreign affairs and feared that incorporating the substance of the House's resolution in his reply to the king would unduly involve the United States in the internal affairs of France. Consequently, his first inclination was sternly to admonish the committee appointed by the House to meet with him that he had sent the king's letter of notification to the House strictly for its information. Washington softened his stand, however, after TJ advised him that support for the French Revolution was so widespread in America that few people would view the House's action as an encroachment on presidential authority. Thus Washington notified the members of the House committee on 12 Mch. 1792 that on his orders TJ had retrieved the initial response to the king from the vessel on which it had been dispatched, so that "another might be written communicating the sentiments of the House agreeably to their request" (Washington to House Committee, 12 Mch. 1792, DLC: Washington Papers, Legislative Proceedings). On the following day TJ submitted to the President a revised letter to Louis XVI, which differed from the original text insofar as it contained a reference to the resolutions of the House and Senate respecting royal acceptance of the French constitution and enclosed copies of them. Washington signed this letter on 14 Mch. 1792, thus avoiding a clear presidential statement on the course of the revolution in France.[28]

Clearly Washington, warned by Jefferson, had flinched from the possible consequences of a confrontation with the House of Representatives over the French Revolution. This is a significant index of the strength of pro–French Revolution sentiment in the United States, early in 1792. Yet in general Jefferson was aware that Washington did not share his views.

Jefferson (unrealistically) put all the blame for this on Gouverneur Morris, instead of on the actual course of the Revolution in 1791–92. Of a consultation with Washington on 12 March 1792, over the message from Louis XVI, Jefferson wrote:

> Why indeed says he I begin to doubt very much of the affairs of France. There are papers from London as late as the 10th. of Jan. which represent them as going into confusion.—He read over the letter he had signed, found there was not a word which could commit his judgment about the constitution, and gave it me back again.— This is one of many proofs I have had of his want of confidence in the event of the French revolution. The fact is that Gouverneur Morris, a high flying Monarchy-man, shutting his eyes and his faith to every fact against his wishes, and believing every thing he desires to be true, has kept the President's mind constantly poisoned with his forebodings. That the President wishes the revolution may be established I believe from several indications. I remember when I recd. the news of the king's flight and capture, I first told him of it at his assembly. I never saw him so much dejected by any event in my life.[29]

Of course, Washington did wish the revolution to "be established"— as a constitutional monarchy—and that is precisely why he was "so much dejected" by "the news of the king's flight and capture" which revealed that "constitutional monarchy" in France was an unsustainable fiction. But for Jefferson in the early 1790s, the French Revolution, irrespective of what forms it might take, could do no wrong.

Concerning the flight to Varennes, Jefferson commented in a private letter: "it would be unfortunate were it in the power of any one man to defeat the issue of so beautiful a revolution."[30] But it was not just "one man" who was compromised by the royal flight. The National Assembly itself, up to then the motor of "the beautiful revolution," was now incapacitated.

On 6 April 1792, Gouverneur Morris, then in London, acknowledged Jefferson's notification of his appointment, which he had received on that day. Formally, Morris accepted the Secretary of State's admonitory advice, but pointedly distanced himself from the Jeffersonian approach to the French Revolution.

> Nothing can be more just than your Observations respecting the Propriety of preserving Silence as to the Government of France; and they are peculiarly applicable to the present state of Things in that Country. Changes are now so frequent, and Events seem fast ripening to such awful Catastrophe,

that no Expressions on the Subject, however moderate, would be received with Indifference.[31]

William Short had been appointed Minister Plenipotentiary at The Hague and was awaiting Morris's arrival in Paris in April. On 22 April, Short reported another major development in the French Revolution, the National Assembly's declaration of war on "the King of Hungary and Bohemia," that is, the Austro-Hungarian Empire. This opened a phase, not only of military activity, but of intense international ideological warfare, intended to precipitate class war inside all other countries. In this "Girondin" phase of the French Revolution the governing slogan was "Peace to the peasants' huts! War on the castles!" Soon afterward the French Revolution was at war with Holland, making an eventual war with Britain probable. As an issue in other countries, including the United States, the French Revolution was getting much hotter.

On 15 May, William Short, on the eve of departure from Paris, reported adverse reactions there to the appointment of Gouverneur Morris. Short here shows himself aware that Jefferson had been overruled in that matter.

Those who were best acquainted with America considered it as a calculation of the President on the present revolution, and were alarmed because they considered it as arguing his supposing it would fall through and yield [sic] to those to whom Mr. Morris wd. probably be agreeable. Some of these and among them *the Marquis la Fayette* affirmed it was impossible *the President* could know on what footing *Morris* stood here, and particularly how disagreeable he was to all those who were friends to the revolution, from the manner in which he spoke of it and them on all occasions and in all companies. The person abovementioned [Lafayette] expressed his surprize and grief that you had not mentioned this as you could not but be persuaded of it from what you had seen here yourself. He seemed particularly hurt as he thought it indicated an opinion that the revolution here was falling through, and as no body respects more your opinion or that of [the] *President* than he does in such matters, and as nobody is more interested in the success of the revolution than he is, it seemed to make an impression on him which he expressed with much openess, but of which it was evident he concealed a part. He told me he intended writing to [the] *President* respecting it. Whether he has done it or in what style I cannot say. He said he considered it more to be attributed to you than anybody else, as having been here, and knowing the ground, it would have been easy for you to have prevented it. I told him I apprehended and was persuaded you had made a point of taking no part in the diplomatic appointments—but it wd. be as easy to convey an idea of Color to the blind, as to make a Frenchman concieve that a minister of foreign affairs could be without influence in the nomination of foreign ministers.[32]

On 23 May, Jefferson wrote an exceptionally long and earnest letter, containing a kind of remonstrance, to George Washington. The letter contains not a syllable of direct reference to the French Revolution but is of great importance with regard to the context—in particular the sectional context—in which the American debate over the French Revolution is being conducted in the early 1790s. For this reason, examination of this letter and quotations from it are needful for the purposes of our present study. Jefferson's letter opens with a respectful plea, and one that seems to imply that Washington had been keeping him at a distance in the early part of 1792:

> I have determined to make the subject of a letter, what, for some time past, has been a subject of inquietude to my mind without having found a good occasion of disburthening itself to you in conversation, during the busy scenes which occupied you here. Perhaps too you may be able, in your present situation, or on the road, to give it more time and reflection than you could do here at any moment.
>
> When you first mentioned to me your purpose of retiring from the government, tho' I felt all the magnitude of the event, I was in a considerable degree silent. I knew that, to such a mind as yours, persuasion was idle and impertinent: that before forming your decision, you had weighed all the reasons for and against the measure, had made up your mind on full view of them, and that there could be little hope of changing the result. Pursuing my reflections too I knew we were some day to try to walk alone, and if the essay should be made while you should be alive and looking on, we should derive confidence from that circumstance, and resource if it failed. The public mind too was then calm and confident, and therefore in a favorable state for making the experiment. Had no change of circumstances supervened, I should not, with any hope of success, have now ventured to propose to you a change of purpose. But the public mind is no longer so confident and serene; and that from causes in which you are no ways personally mixed.

The adverb "personally" in that last sentence, is crucial. For the "causes," which Jefferson goes on to denounce at length, consist of nothing less than the whole financial policy of Washington's first administration. The policy was being carried out by Alexander Hamilton, but without Washington's approval, Hamilton would not be Secretary of the Treasury. So the word "personally" is a polite fiction. While pleading with Washington to serve for a second term—lest worse befall, perhaps John Adams—Jefferson is obliquely telling Washington that he detests almost all the important things that have been done during Washington's first term.

Jefferson's charges against the Hamiltonian system need not be detailed here. They are standard Republican stuff and, as Jefferson himself acknowledges to Washington, "hackneyed in the public press." The part of this letter that is most relevant to our present study is the warning that the inflammation of sectional differences may lead to a civil war.

But the division of sentiment and interest happens unfortunately to be so geographical, that no mortal can say that what is most wise and temperate would prevail against what is more easy and obvious? I can scarcely contemplate a more incalculable evil than the breaking of the union into two or more parts. Yet when we review the mass which opposed the original coalescence, when we consider that it lay chiefly in the Southern quarter, that the legislature have availed themselves of no occasion of allaying it, but on the contrary whenever Northern and Southern prejudices have come into conflict, the latter have been sacrificed and the former soothed; that the owers of the debt are in the Southern and the holders of it in the Northern division; that the Antifederal champions are now strengthened in argument by the fulfilment of their predictions; that this has been brought about by the Monarchical federalists themselves, who, having been for the new government merely as a stepping stone to monarchy, have themselves adopted the very constructions of the constitution, of which, when advocating it's acceptance before the tribunal of the people, they declared it insusceptible; that the republican federalists [Jefferson is clearly referring to Madison], who espoused the same government for it's intrinsic merits, are disarmed of their weapons, that which they denied as prophecy being now become true history: who can be sure that these things may not proselyte the small number which was wanting to place the majority on the other side? And this is the event at which I tremble, and to prevent which I consider your continuance at the head of affairs as of the last importance. The confidence of the whole union is centered in you. Your being at the helm, will be more than an answer to every argument which can be used to alarm and lead the people in any quarter into violence or secession. North and South will hang together, if they have you to hang on: and, if the first corrective of a numerous representation should fail in it's effect, your presence

Portrait of Alexander Hamilton, by John Trumbull, 1806. Courtesy of National Portrait Gallery, Smithsonian Institution/Art Resource, New York. Even while they were colleagues in Washington's first administration (1790–93), Jefferson and Hamilton were at loggerheads, with the French Revolution at the center of their quarrel. According to Hamilton, Jefferson "drank freely of the French philosophy on religion on science, on politics" (Prelude, p. 9; chapter 3, pp. 97–98; chapter 4, p. 135).

will give time for trying others not inconsistent with the union and peace of the states.[33]

Jefferson was, at this time, busy fanning that same Southern resentment (against Northern hegemony) about the power of which he is warning Washington. Of the attacks on Hamilton's policies (which were also Washington's) Charles T. Cullen quaintly observed, "This critique had been taking shape in the pages of the *National Gazette* since the beginning of 1792 and there can be little doubt that TJ was influenced by that paper's criticism of the underlying implications of the Secretary of the Treasury's economic program."[34]

But of course Jefferson and Madison had set up the *National Gazette* precisely in order to *mount* the kind of "critique" of Hamiltonian policy which Cullen innocently supposes to have "influenced" Jefferson. It looks as if the editor of volume 23 of *The Papers of Thomas Jefferson* had never read the Editorial Note at the end of volume 20 in which his predecessor, Julian P. Boyd, clearly sets out the part which the *National Gazette* was founded to play within the political strategies of Jefferson and Madison.

The exploitation of American enthusiasm for the French Revolution was integral to that strategy. This was an issue which united the (white) South (with a few exceptions) and tended to split the population of the North along class lines. So the *National Gazette* played up the French Revolution, and James Madison made adroit use of it in the House of Representatives. Jefferson, as Washington's Secretary of State, had to be more discreet, but he was in reality the mastermind of the whole operation.

When Jefferson warned Washington about the danger of confronting the House over the French Revolution, he was speaking of the power of emotions which he himself was doing more than any other American to keep alive and inflamed. And Washington knew this.

Washington kept on Hamilton and continued to support him, but Jefferson's plea—and, perhaps even more, his warning—are believed to have been among the factors which influenced Washington's decision to accept a second term.

In the summer of 1792 Jefferson is preoccupied—indeed, almost obsessed—by the contrast between what he sees as the triumph of Freedom in France, and its decline in the United States. He writes to Lafayette:

> Behold you then, my dear friend, at the head of a great army, establishing the liberties of your country against a foreign enemy. May heaven favor your cause, and make you the channel thro' which it may pour it's favors. While you are exterminating the monster aristocracy, and pulling out the

teeth and fangs of it's associate monarchy, a contrary tendency is discovered in some here. A sect has shewn itself among us, who declare they espoused our new constitution, not as a good and sufficient thing itself, but only as a step to an English constitution, the only thing good and sufficient in itself, in their eye. It is happy for us that these are preachers without followers, and that our people are firm and constant in their republican purity. You will wonder to be told that it is from the Eastward chiefly that these champions for a king, lords and commons come. They get some important associates from New York, and are puffed off by a tribe of Agioteurs which have been hatched in a bed of corruption made up after the model of their beloved England. Too many of these stock jobbers and King-jobbers have come into our legislature, or rather too many of our legislature have become stock jobbers and king-jobbers. However the voice of the people is beginning to make itself heard, and will probably cleanse their seats at the ensuing election.[35]

Lafayette probably never received this letter. Within two months of its dispatch, the progress of the French Revolution had driven him from France, to which he was not able to return until the Revolution was over. But in reality, around the time he wrote that glowing letter, Jefferson had already lost faith in Lafayette and was looking to more up-to-date embodiments of the French Revolution. He wrote to James Madison, less than two weeks after his letter to Lafayette:

This ministry, which is of the Jacobin party, cannot but be favorable to us, as that whole party must be. Indeed notwithstanding the very general abuse of the Jacobins, I begin to consider them as representing the true revolution-spirit of the whole nation, and as carrying the nation with them. The only things [sic] wanting with them is more experience in business, and a little more conformity to the established style of communication with foreign powers. The latter want will I fear bring enemies into the feild, who would have remained at home; the former leads them to domineer over their executive so as render it unequal to it's proper objects. I sincerely wish our new minister Gouverneur Morris may not spoil our chance of extracting good from the present situation of things.[36]

(Jefferson, when he wrote the letter, had not yet received Short's letter of 29 June in which Short described "the present situation of things as the late disgraceful and alarming crisis in Paris.")[37]

Jefferson was mistaken about his "Jacobins," a description which, however loosely applied, did not fit the harried Ministers of the Crown within the tragic farce of the constitutional monarchy of September 1791 to August 1792. They *talked* more like Jacobins than any of their ministerial predecessors but that did not fool the real Jacobins, who hounded these people (among others) to their deaths after 10 August 1792. But Jefferson was habitually vague about the actual events, politics, and personalities of the French Revolution. It was the *idea* of the French Revolution that entranced him, both in itself and because of its power in the politics of the United States.

Still, to mistake the last of the King's Ministers for "Jacobins" seems unusually wide of the mark. I think I may have found the source of the error, in a letter written to Washington from Paris by Gouverneur Morris on 4 February 1792. If we assume that—as seems not improbable—Washington had shown this letter to Jefferson, Morris's language would account for the mistake in Jefferson's letter to Madison. Morris, in his letter to Washington, referred to three of the leading figures in the Ministry—Duport, Lameth, and Barnave—as "the Chiefs of the old Jacobins," adding "I say the old Jacobins because the present Jacobins are the Republican party [and as such could not possibly be part of a Royal Ministry]."[38] Jefferson, who detested Morris, and would not have read his long letter with close attention (still on the assumption that Washington showed it to him), could have ignored the distinction made by Morris, and retained only the chimerical notion of a Jacobin Royal Ministry. But that Jefferson could entertain such a notion at all (however he may have acquired it) shows that the Secretary of State had been paying remarkably little attention to the actual course of events within the French Revolution since June 1791, despite the full and accurate reports he had been receiving from William Short. But then Thomas Jefferson did not *need* information about the French Revolution. He *knew* the French Revolution in its essence, by faith.[39]

William Short, in a letter written on the same day as that from Jefferson to Madison, referred to "the insupportable tyranny of the present domineering faction." He did not mean the Ministers but the real Jacobins (and, for the moment, Girondins) who were at that time denouncing the Ministers and preparing their downfall.

The downfall came on 10 August 1792. Gouverneur Morris, now in Paris as Minister Plenipotentiary, reported to Jefferson on 16 August on what may reasonably be called the Second French Revolution, involving the deposition of the King and the scrapping of the constitution of 1791. Morris's dispatch opens with the words: "My last was of the first Instant No. 5. Since that Period, another Revolution has been affected [*sic*] in this City. It was bloody."[40] Morris gives no details of that last, as Short would have done (to Jefferson's irritation). After some rather vague politi-

cal reflections Morris provides a whiff of the new revolutionary conditions prevailing in Paris:

> I do not go into the History of Things nor trouble you with a Recapitula-
> tion of Events. I enclose and shall send by the present opportunity the Ga-
> zettes since my last which will communicate all Particulars which you may
> desire to know. Since the Operations of the tenth the Logographe, Gazette
> Universelle, and Indicateur, are suppressed as indeed are all those who were
> guilty of *Feuillantisme,* that is Adherence to the *Club des Feuillans soi dis-
> ant constitutionel.* You must therefore make Allowances for what you find
> in the other Gazettes, written not only in the Spirit of a Party but under the
> Eye of a Party. The first must influence the most honest Printer in the Color-
> ing of some Facts and the second will restrain the boldest Printer in the
> publishing of other Facts. If it were necessary or could be useful I should
> communicate all the Particulars which come to my Knowlege but this invid-
> ious Task would answer no good End and long before my Letters could
> reach you Changes must inevitably take Place.[41]

Morris's dispatch ends with the words:

> Before I conclude this Letter permit me my dear Sir to request the orders
> of the President respecting my Line of Conduct in the Circumstances about
> to arise. Perhaps these orders may not reach me untill the Circumstances
> are past but even then they may serve as a Ground to Reason on in the
> Circumstances which succeed. If they arrive in Season they will releive my
> mind from a great Weight. At present I feel myself in a State of contingent
> Responsibility of the most delicate Kind. I am far from wishing to avoid
> any fair and reasonable Risque, and I rely on the Justice of Government at
> the same Time to mark out as exactly as possible the Conduct to be pursued
> as well as on its Goodness to judge favorably of Cases unforeseen. I am
> with sincere Esteem & Regard Dear Sir your obedt Servant.

Morris's specific request for "the orders of the President" is significant: he is not content to await the instructions of his direct superior, the
Secretary of State. Normally this might be an imprudent stipulation on
the part of a diplomatic officer in the field. But Morris knew that he was
on strong ground. He was an intimate friend of Washington's and Washington personally had appointed Morris as Minister Plenipotentiary in
Paris, over the head of his Secretary of State and against the Secretary's
known wishes. So the Minister Plenipotentiary knew that the Secretary of
State would have to pass on his request to the President, however Thomas
Jefferson, personally, might feel about this transaction.

This dispatch reached Jefferson on 24 October 1792.[42] On 22 August

Morris reported the flight of Lafayette: "He, as you will learn, encamped at Sedan and official Accounts of last Night inform us that he has taken Refuge with the Enemy. Thus his circle is compleated. He has spent his Fortune on a Revolution, and is now crush'd by the wheel which he put in Motion. He lasted longer than I expected."[43]

Morris went on to describe his own position as a resident diplomatist in the capital of what had been a Monarchy when he had been accredited, and was now a Republic:

> The different Embassadors and Ministers are all taking their Flight and if I stay I shall be alone. I mean however to stay unless Circumstances should command me away because in the admitted Case that my Letters of Credence are to the Monarchy and not to the Republic of France it becomes a Matter of Indifference whether I remain in this Country or go to England during the Time which may be needful to obtain your Orders or to produce a Settlement of Affairs here. Going hence however would look like taking Part against the late Revolution and I am not only unauthoriz'd in this Respect but I am bound to suppose that if the great Majority of the Nation adhere to the new Form the United States will approve thereof because in the first Place we have no Right to prescribe to this Country the Government they shall adopt and next because the Basis of our own Constitution is the indefeasible Right of the People to establish it.

This "moderate" position must have surprised Jefferson, who regarded Morris as a fanatical enemy of the French Revolution. Morris did indeed dislike the French Revolution, in *all* its phases. But he was much less fanatical *against* the Revolution than Jefferson was fanatical *for* it. Unlike Jefferson (when on the subject of the French Revolution) Gouverneur Morris had a good deal of common sense, and it shows in this impressive paragraph of his dispatch of 22 August 1792. Jefferson received that dispatch on 4 December 1792.

William Short (who, after Morris's appointment to Paris, had been transferred to the Hague, and promoted to Minister Plenipotentiary), continued to take an interest in the progress of the French Revolution. In a letter to Jefferson, on 24 August 1792, Short, unlike Morris, registers anger at the Second French Revolution. Short, again unlike Morris, had been well-disposed to the early, "Lafayette" phase of the French Revolution, and therefore grieved for what was happening to the "moderates" of 1789 at a time when, after 10 August 1792, even to be suspected of *indulgence* had become a capital offense. Whereas Morris thought these people had brought their troubles on themselves. Short opens his letter with the words: "My late letters and those which you will no doubt have recieved from Paris have prepared you for hearing of the arrestation, massacre or flight of all those who should be considered as the friends and supporters of the late constitution in France with a monarch at its head. The mob and demagogues of Paris had carried their fury in this line, as far as it could go."[44]

In a postscript Short reports on the latest developments, in similar style:

P.S. Since writing the above the French post has come in which brings intelligence from Paris from the 17th. to 20th.—every thing seems to have continued in the same horrid line. Arrestations without number of all descriptions of persons suspected of attachment to the late constitution, and the people of Paris menacing the assembly to immolate these victims without delay, if a tribunal was not immediately formed for judging them—and the assembly in consequence passing a decree for erecting this new tribunal, and declaring that the carrousel should be the place of execution. Robertspierre [one version of the name] and others of that atrocious and cruel cast compose the tribunal, named by a popular election. We may expect therefore to hear of such proceedings, under the cloak of liberty, *egalité* and patriotism as would disgrace any *chambre ardente* that has ever existed—humanity shudders at the idea.

This letter reached Jefferson on 31 October 1792 and, as we shall see, it infuriated him.

On 10 September 1792, Gouverneur Morris reported on the September Massacres. This time most of the victims were not themselves revolutionaries and Morris is moved by their horrible fate:

We have had one Week of uncheck'd Murders in which some thousands have perishd in this City. It began with between two and three hundred of the Clergy who had been shut up because they would not take the Oaths prescrib'd by Law, and which they said was contrary to their Conscience. Thence *these Executors of speedy Justice* went to the Abbaye where the Persons were confind who were at Court on the tenth. These were dispatchd also and afterwards they visited the other Prisons. All those who were confin'd either on the Accusation or Suspicion of Crimes were destroy'd. Madame de Lamballe was (I believe) the only Woman kill'd, and she was beheaded and embowelled, the Head and Entrails were paraded on pikes thro the Street and the Body dragged after them. They continued I am told at the Temple [where the former Royal family were now imprisoned] till the Queen look'd out at this horrid Spectacle. Yesterday the Prisoners from

Orleans were put to Death at Versailles. The Destruction began here about five in the Afternoon on Sunday the second Instant.[45]

This dispatch was received by Jefferson on 10 January 1793, but the news had reached him earlier through the American newspapers. The *National Gazette* took a robust editorial line against those who were trying to defame the French Revolution concerning the perfectly legitimate transactions carried out by Parisians in the first week of September 1792. The *National Gazette* did not detail the transactions in question, as Gouverneur Morris had done, but it commented:

> The great scene that has passed in the capital of France is a lesson worthy of the serious attention of every monarch in Europe. It is sickening to hear our prostituted prints call the French barbarous and inhuman; because when justly incensed they have made examples of two or three thousand scoundrels, to rescue the liberties of millions of honest men, while the same ideots [*sic*] pretend to respect a *family* [i.e., the French royal family], the vain wars of whom have covered the earth with the blood of innocent individuals from one end of Europe to the other.[46]

We do not know whether Philip Freneau consulted his patron, Thomas Jefferson, as regards the editorial line to be taken by the *Gazette* in relation to the September Massacres. Probably not. But there is no evidence that the *Gazette*'s treatment of this episode (or indeed of anything else) was disapproved by either Jefferson or Madison in 1792. And, as we shall see, Jefferson's personal enthusiasm for the French Revolution was expressed most fervently shortly after the news of the September Massacres had reached him.

On 3 December 1792, Gouverneur Morris wrote to his friend Thomas Pinckney, of South Carolina, a letter which illuminates Morris's position with regard both to the French Revolution and the French people. Morris wrote: "Since I have been in this country I have seen the worship of many Idols and but little of the true God. I have seen many of those Idols broken and some of them broken to dust. I have seen the late Constitution in one short year admired as a stupendous monument to human wisdom and ridiculed as an egregious production of folly and Vice. I wish very much the Happiness of this inconstant people, I love them."[47]

Morris's use of the words "the true God" with reference to the French Revolution is curious. These are the words which were used by Jefferson, also with reference to the French Revolution (though without Morris's irony) in his letter to Tom Paine from Cowes in October 1789. Could Morris have known that Jefferson had used those words, and has he Jefferson in mind when he uses them himself, ironically? It is not impossible. Jefferson's correspondents tended to show others his letters, and to quote from them. Paine quoted Jefferson on the French Revolution in a letter to Edmund Burke. So that Jefferson's views might be relayed to Gouverneur Morris is not as improbable as it may sound.

On 21 December 1792, Gouverneur Morris sent Jefferson a percipient report on the progress and prospects of the French Revolution as these then appeared: "You will have seen that the Jacobine Club is as much at War with the present Government as it was with the preceding." The governing faction in France, from August 1792 to June 1793, is known in history as the Girondins, but more often referred to, in 1792, as Brissotins (after their then leader, Jefferson's acquaintance, Brissot de Warville). The Girondins, under pressure from the Jacobins, had now put Louis XVI on trial. Gouverneur Morris provides an excellent analysis of the political context of this show-trial:

> I come now to the Trial of the King, and the Circumstances connected therewith. To a Person less intimately acquainted than you are with the History of human Affairs, it would seem strange that the mildest monarch who ever fill'd the French Throne, One who is precipitated from it precisely because he would not adopt the harsh measures of his Predecessors, a Man whom none can charge with a Criminal or Cruel Act, should be prosecuted as one of the most nefarious Tyrants that ever disgraced the Annals of human nature. That he, Louis the sixteenth, should be prosecuted even to the Death. Yet such is the Fact. I think it highly probable that he may suffer, and that for the following Causes. The Majority of the Assembly found it necessary to raise, against this unhappy Prince, the National Odium, in order to justify the dethroning him (which after what he had suffered appeared to be necessary even to their Safety) and to induce the ready adoption of a Republican Form of Government. Being in Possession of his Papers, and those of his Servants, it was easy (if they would permit themselves to extract, to comment, to suppress, and to mutilate) it was *very* easy to create such Opinions as they might think proper. The Rage which has been excited was terrible, and altho it begins to subside, the Convention are still in great Streights, fearing to acquit, fearing to condemn, and yet urged to destroy their Captive Monarch.[48]

In the many cursory historical retrospects on the course of relations between Americans and the French Revolution, there is a tendency to assume that Americans were enthusiastic about the Revolution in its early, mostly bloodless, phases but were repelled when it turned violent. This is misleading. American enthusiasm for the French Revolution was at its height in the period that stretched from the reception of the news of the September Massacres to that of the reception of the news of the execution of the King (which occurred in January 1793); that is, the period from November 1792 to April 1793. The violent events were not the *cause* of the increase in enthusiasm, but neither had they offset it to any significant extent. What caused the increase in excitement was, first, the French Revolutionary victories of late 1792; beginning with Valmy in September 1792, and second, the news of the French declaration of war on "the king of England," immediately following the execution of Louis XVI.

In his study *Contemporary American Opinion of the French Revolution* (Baltimore, 1897), Charles Downer Hazen describes the mounting excitement of this period:

> Though Americans had been interested in the Revolution from the very outset for a variety of reasons, it was only toward the close of the year 1792 that this interest was publicly manifested. But when the monarchy was completely overthrown and the Republic proclaimed, all America was thrilled. From this time on the movements of the French armies were followed with great excitement, and when, toward the close of this year, the Republic had so far asserted itself as to have driven back the invaders, the Revolution seemed so far accomplished as to demand a public manifestation of joy on the part of the Americans.

There follow descriptions of "Civic Feasts" in honor of the French Revolution in New York, Boston, and Philadelphia in December 1792 and January 1793. Hazen adds "These celebrations were not local; they occurred in the South, in the North, in the Middle States; Philadelphia saw scores of them."

If American enthusiasm for the French Revolution had been a treasured political asset to Jefferson and Madison from 1789 to 1791, it appeared as a much greater asset from November 1792 to April 1793, inclusive. By late December, Jefferson even fancied that events had won over the President to his side, with regard to the French Revolution. This appears from a document in Jefferson's handwriting headed *Notes of a Conversation with George Washington,* Thursday, Dec. 27, 1792.

This document opens:

> Thursday Dec. 27. 92. I waited on the President on some current business. After this was over, he observed to me he thought it was time to endeavor to effect a stricter connection with France and that G. Morris should be

written to on this subject. He went into the circumstances of dissatisfaction between Spain, Gr. Brit. and us, and observed there was no nation on whom we could rely at all times but France, and that if we did not prepare in time some support in the event of rupture with Spain and England we might be charged with a criminal negligence. (I was much pleased with the tone of these observations. It was the very doctrine which had been my polar star, and I did not need the successes of the Republican arms in France lately announced to us, to bring me to these sentiments).[49]

The phrase "the very doctrine that had been my polar star" is illuminating. It is clear that Jefferson regarded as meritorious the *fixity* of his doctrinal attitude to the French Revolution, irrespective of what might be happening in and around France. And as a metaphorical instrument for conferring grandeur on an *idée fixe,* there is nothing to beat the polar star.

Unfortunately, Washington has left no record of this conversation, so that we have only Jefferson's account (or rather, *accounts,* see below, pp. 145–48), which is not likely to be understated. Washington's subsequent conduct (after that December conversation) does not suggest that his attitude toward the French Revolution was significantly warmer than it had been previously. But Washington did accept the National Convention as the legitimate government of France (as Gouverneur Morris had assumed Washington would do) and he authorized Jefferson to pay to the Convention the installments of the American debt to France (payments which had been suspended after the deposition of the Monarch).

Jefferson, however, was exhilarated, even to an alarming extent, by the change he thought was happening to Washington's thinking over the French Revolution. On 3 January, still under the impact of the December conversation, as he understood it, Jefferson sent to William Short the most extraordinary letter he ever wrote. Short was a young Virginian connected to Jefferson by marriage. Jefferson wrote, in 1789, that Short "put himself under my guidance at 19 or 20 years of age" (that is, in 1779 or 1780) and was virtually "my adoptive son."[50]

Short was Jefferson's private secretary in Paris from 1785 to 1789, and became Chargé d'Affaires at the Legation (no doubt on Jefferson's recommendation) after Jefferson's return to America. Short's reporting on the progress of the French Revolution had become negative after the "Lafayette" generation began to lose control in 1791. Jefferson had obviously been angry with Short for the "blasphemies" he had been sending in about the French Revolution since the spring of 1791, but had apparently not felt sufficiently confident of Washington's support, over this range of issues, to rebuke the Chargé d'Affaires in Paris for being insufficiently favorable to the French Revolution. Now Jefferson feels he has Washington behind him at last, and he lets Short have it. The letter in which he does so is sufficiently important, in the context of the present study, to be quoted in full, as follows:

Dear Sir   Philadelphia Jan. 3. 1793.

My last private letter to you was of Oct. 16. since which I have recieved your No. 103. 107. 108. 109. 110. 112. 113. and 114. and yesterday your private one of Sep. 15. came to hand. The tone of your letters had for some time given me pain, on account of the extreme warmth with which they censured the proceedings of the Jacobins of France. I considered that sect as the same with the Republican patriots (of America), and the Feuillants as the Monarchical patriots (of America), well known in the early part of the revolution, and but little distant in their views, both having in object the establishment of a free constitution, and differing only on the question whether their chief Executive should be hereditary or not. The Jacobins (as since called) yeilded to the Feuillants and tried the experiment of retaining their hereditary Executive. The experiment failed completely, and would have brought on the reestablishment of despotism had it been pursued. The Jacobins saw this, and that the expunging that officer [in English, executing the King] was of absolute necessity, and the Nation was with them in opinion, for however they might have been formerly for the constitution framed by the first assembly, they were come over from their hope in it, and were now generally Jacobins. In the struggle which was necessary, many guilty persons fell without the forms of trial, and with them some innocent. These I deplore as much as any body, and shall deplore some of them to the day of my death. But I deplore them as I should have done had they fallen in battle. It was necessary to use the arm of the people, a machine not quite so blind as balls and bombs, but blind to a certain degree. A few of their cordial friends met at their hands the fate of enemies. But time and truth will rescue and embalm their memories, while their posterity will be enjoying that very liberty for which they would never have hesitated to offer up their lives. The liberty of the whole earth was depending on the issue of the contest, and was ever such a prize won with so little innocent blood? My own affections have been deeply wounded by some of the martyrs to this cause, but rather than it should have failed, I would have seen half the earth desolated. Were there but an Adam and an Eve left in every country, and left free, it would be better than as it now is. I have expressed to you my sentiments, because they are really those of 99 in an hundred of our citizens. The universal feasts, and rejoicings which have lately been had on account of the successes of the French shewed the genuine effusions of their hearts. You have been wounded by the sufferings of your friends, and have by this circumstance been hurried into a temper of mind which would be extremely disrelished if known to your countrymen. The reserve of *the Prest. of the U.S.* had never permitted me to discover the light in which he viewed it, and as I was more anxious that you should satisfy him than me, I had still avoided explanations with you on the subject. But your 113. induced him to break silence and to notice the extreme acrimony of your expressions. He added that he had been informed the sentiments you expressed *in your conversations* were equally offensive to our allies, and that you should consider yourself as the representative of your country and that what you say might be imputed to your constituents. He desired me therefore to write to you on this subject. He added that he considered *France as the sheet anchor of this country and its friendship as a first object.* There are in the U.S. some characters of opposite principles; some of them are high in office, others possessing great wealth, and all of them hostile to France and fondly looking to England as the staff of their hope. These I named to you on a former occasion. Their prospects have certainly not brightened. Excepting them, this country is entirely republican, friends to the constitution, anxious to preserve it and to have it administered according to it's own republican principles. The little party above mentioned have espoused it only as a stepping stone to monarchy, and have endeavored to approximate it to that in it's administration, in order to render it's final transition more easy. The successes of republicanism in France have given the coup de grace to their prospects, and I hope to their projects.—I have developed to you faithfully the sentiments of your country, that you may govern yourself accordingly. I know your republicanism to be pure, and that it is no decay of that which has embittered you against it's votaries in France, but too great a sensibility at the partial evil by which it's object has been accomplished there. I have written to you in the stile to which I have been always accustomed with you, and which perhaps it is time I should lay aside. But while old men feel sensibly enough their own advance in years, they do not sufficiently recollect it in those whom they have seen young. In writing too the last private letter which will probably be written under present circumstances, in contemplating that your correspondence will shortly be turned over to I know not whom, but certainly to some one not in the habit of considering your interests with the same fostering anxieties I do, I have presented things without reserve, satisfied you will ascribe what I have said to it's true motive, use it for your own best interest, and in that fulfill completely what I had in view. With respect to the subject of your letter of Sep. 15. you will be sensible that many considerations would prevent my undertaking the reformation of a system of which I am so soon to take leave. It is but common decency to leave to my successor [Jefferson at this time believed his own retirement as Secretary of State to be imminent; it did not in fact take place until the end of the year] the moulding of his own business.—Not knowing how otherwise to convey this letter to you with certainty, I shall appeal to the friendship and honour of the Spanish commissioners here, to give it the protection of their cover, as a letter of private nature altogether. We have no remarkeable event here lately, but the death of Dr. Lee: nor have I any thing new to communicate to you of your friends or affairs. I am with unalterable affection & wishes for your prosperity, my dear Sir, your sincere friend and servant.

P.S. Jan. 15. Your Nos. 116. 117. and Private of Nov. 2 are received.— Congress have before them a statement of the *paiments to France*. It appears none were made from *Dec. till Aug. nine*. This long previous suspension and *paiment* the day before the *tenth August begot suspicions on Gov. Morrise. Hamilton cleared* him and leaves it *on you by denying that Morris* had any thing to do with it, and *he clear[s] himself by saying that you had no order[s] from hence either for the suspension or paiment. Contrive to convey to me the truth of this* and I will have it so used for your justification as to clear you with all and injure you with *none.*[51]

That postscript—the sting in the tail—was so alarming to Short that almost the whole of his reply to this letter is confined to the postscript.[52] The postscript is of course of much less interest to us here than the body of the letter, dealing as it does directly with the French Revolution. But the postscript is of some interest in the context of Hamilton-Jefferson relations, which do have a bearing on the French Revolution as an issue in American politics. In that context Short had unwittingly committed a monumental indiscretion. He had actually boasted *to Jefferson* about a flattering comment on his reports from Paris which had been made to him *by Hamilton.*[53] For Jefferson, this was adding gall to the wormwood of the dispatches themselves. Jefferson followed up his letter of 3 January with another letter in which he explicitly warns Short against the adverse political consequences, to him personally, which might result from dealings with Hamilton:

Be cautious in your letters to the Secretary of the treasury. He sacrifices you. On a late occasion, when called on to explain before the Senate his proceedings relative to the loans in Europe, instead of extracting such passages of your letters as might relate to them, he gave in the originals in which I am told were strong expressions against the French republicans. . . . I have done what I could to lessen the injury this did you, for such sentiments towards the French are extremely grating here. . . . The next Congress will be strongly republican. Adieu.[54]

As regards the body of Jefferson's letter of 3 January, it should first be noted that the version of the conversation with Washington that is given in the letter to Short is different in several respects from the version contained in the *Notes*. The *Notes* do not record any references by Washington concerning Short: the letter reports Washington as commenting severely on Short's dispatches and alleged conversations. Also Washington's position on the French Revolution is made to appear more strongly favorable in the letter than in the *Notes*. The expression "*France as the sheet anchor of this country and its friendship as a first object*," italicized in the letter, does not appear in the *Notes* at all. The *Notes* have of course the higher evidential value, having been recorded on the day of the conversation itself, and as an aide-memoire only, and not part of a persuasive effort.

This "Adam and Eve" letter is also of interest as the only one in which Jefferson takes note of *successive phases* of the French Revolution. This might seem to invalidate the polar star idea, but it doesn't. The idea is that the French Revolution remains essentially always the same—as the holy cause of Liberty—despite alterations in its outward manifestations. This is fundamentally a theological approach—as, for many devout Roman Catholics, the consecrated bread and wine are inalterably the body and blood of Jesus Christ, whatever changes may occur in "the accidents," meaning the material components of the bread and the wine.[55] For Jefferson, at this time, the actual events of the French Revolution were "accidents" in that theological sense. The Revolution itself is not susceptible of change.

John Catanzariti, the editor of volume 25 of *The Papers of Thomas Jefferson* (Princeton edition) makes the following comment:

JEFFERSON'S "ADAM AND EVE" LETTER ON THE FRENCH REVOLUTION

Jefferson's celebrated letter to William Short of 3 Jan. 1793, the second page of which is illustrated in this volume, represented a profound shift in his attitude toward the French Revolution. During his ministry to France and for approximately the first thirty months of his tenure as Secretary of State, Jefferson's hopes for the French Revolution were tempered by his belief that centuries of royal despotism and religious authoritarianism made a constitutional monarchy along British lines the most desirable outcome of the revolutionary turmoil in France. But with the overthrow of the Bourbon monarchy in August 1792 and the establishment of the French Republic in the following month, his enthusiasm for the Revolution became almost unbounded, and the conviction grew in his mind that the success of French republicanism in Europe was necessary to thwart what he regarded as the monarchical designs of the Federalists in America. Despite the ensuing changes of regime in France, it took Napoleon Bonaparte's rise to power to convince Jefferson that his enthusiasm for the French Republic had been mistaken and that his earlier support for a French constitutional monarchy had been well founded.[56]

I find Catanzariti's comment to be wide of the mark in its main thrust, and also defective in other respects. Catanzariti does not connect the letter to Short with Jefferson's "*Notes of a Conversation with George Washington on French Affairs*," although references to that conversation play a central part in Jefferson's letter to Short.[57] The *Notes*, as well as the letter to Short, were written after Jefferson had become aware of "the overthrow of the Bourbon monarchy . . . and the establishment of the French Republic" in August and September 1792. Morris's report of the former event (17 August) was received by Jefferson on 24 October 1792.[58] Morris's dispatch of 22 August 1792—making it clear that it is with a republic, and not a monarchy that the Minister Plenipotentiary has to deal—was received by Jefferson on 4 December 1792, more than three weeks before that conversation with George Washington. Yet Jefferson, in his *Notes* on that conversation, is telling us—boasting indeed—that his attitude to the French Revolution has *not* been changed either by those events or by subsequent victories of French Revolutionary armies. Events *cannot* change his "doctrine" with regard to the French Revolution for it was "my polar star." *Nothing,* therefore, can change it.

Furthermore, the record, from October 1789 on (at least until late in 1793), fully bears out Jefferson's claim to fixity of doctrine with regard to the French Revolution. The "profound shift" in Jefferson's position on the French Revolution occurred not in January 1793, but at some point between July and October 1789. Before July 1789, Jefferson's attitude to the French Revolution was indeed subject to the kinds of reservations suggested by Catanzariti, and also subject to others (above, chapter 2). But by October it has frozen into a rigid faith attested by that "true god" passage in Jefferson's letter to Paine from Cowes. Significantly, the change is first attested in a letter written after Jefferson had left France and was on his way home to America. He had left the reality of the French Revolution behind him. What he brought with him to America was the French Revolution as an article of faith, in the name of which he could excommunicate heretics and purify America. This faith, like traditional religious faiths, is not, in essence, susceptible to change and is impervious to news.

What Jefferson is telling Short, in the "Adam and Eve" letter, is that no atrocity the French Revolutionaries could possibly commit could shake his faith in the French Revolution. Anything the French revolutionaries might choose to do—up to massacring the entire French population, minus two—would *ipso facto* represent Freedom. It is difficult to resist the conclusion that the twentieth-century statesman whom the Thomas Jefferson of January 1793 would have admired most is Pol Pot.

VI

What Catanzariti took for "a profound shift" in basic attitude was in reality no more than a sudden exhilarating release from constraints in the *expression* of a constant attitude. As Washington's Secretary of State, Jefferson had generally been cautious in the expression of his faith in the French Revolution, for Jefferson knew Washington did not share that faith (Washington was indeed no better than a heretic, from a Jeffersonian point of view, though it was not yet expedient to say so). But the conversation with Washington gives Jefferson the impression that things are moving his way fast, and that he can be much more outspoken about the French Revolution than he could have afforded to be previously.

We are told, most recently by James Roger Sharp,[59] that Jefferson, when he wrote that letter to Short, "was not fully aware of the violent turn the revolution had taken." This is quite untenable. As Secretary of State, Jefferson had been kept fully informed from as early as the spring of 1791, first by Short himself and then by Gouverneur Morris, of the growth of French Revolutionary violence. In November 1792—two months before the date of Jefferson's letter to Short—the American papers had carried the news of the September Massacres in Paris, in which six thousand prisoners are believed to have been murdered. The Philadelphian organ under Jefferson's patronage, Freneau's *National Gazette,* had scolded the Federalist papers ("our prostituted prints") for having described the French Revolutionaries as "'barbarous and inhuman' because when justly incensed they have made examples of two or three thousand scoundrels" (*N.G.,* 7 November 1792).

Jefferson's rebuke to Short is written from exactly the same point of view as Freneau's rebuke to the Federalist newspapers, although Jefferson's language is more refined than that of his protégé. Jefferson does not dispute the facts of French Revolutionary violence—which Short has been reporting. But he rebukes Short for daring to write about French Revolutionary violence *in a disapproving manner.* When I looked for J. R. Sharp's authority for this untenable interpretation, a footnote referred me to Dumas Malone (*Jefferson and the Ordeal of Liberty,* pp. 45–47). It is rather depressing to find Malone's protectively emollient *obiter dicta* about Jefferson still being treated as authoritative sources, as late as 1993.

The almost manic enthusiasm for the French Revolution which appears in the Adam and Eve letter was not destined to last. Jefferson continued indeed to appear in the role of a friend of the French Revolution, until that revolution came to an end in the late 1790s. But he never again was to write about the French Revolution with anything resembling the fanatical fervor of that letter of 3 January 1793.

The reason for the change had nothing to do with levels of French Revolutionary violence. It was a purely geographical phenomenon. In the summer of 1793—as we shall see in the next chapter—the French Revolution became a reality *in the New World.* For Jefferson, that revolution was never the same again. Up to then, the French Revolution had been for him both an article of faith and a useful issue in American politics. In both respects the French Revolution, so conceived, had been comfortably insulated from reality. Atrocities attributed to it could be publicly denied—being attributed to British propaganda—and privately condoned. The French Revolution was thousands of miles away, and Jefferson was free to make whatever he liked of it. But in the summer of 1793, the French Revolution came to the New World. —Nothing in the relations between America and the French Revolution was ever quite the same again after the mission of Citizen Charles-Edmond Genet in the summer of 1793, and the news, that same summer, of the triumph of the slave revolt in the French possession of Saint-Domingue.

FIVE

FRENCH REVOLUTION
IN AMERICA

The Mission of Citizen Charles-Edmond Genet
April 1793–January 1794

In April 1793, Jean-Baptiste Ternant, Minister Plenipotentiary of the French Republic to the United States, was in Philadelphia, awaiting the arrival of his successor, Citizen Charles-Edmond Genet. On 18 April, Ternant reported to the Citizen Minister of Foreign Affairs of the Republic:

> The President is back here [from Mount Vernon, to Philadelphia] since yesterday—the English war [with France] is giving more and more concern to the American Government, and I have reason to believe that it is about to proclaim its neutrality; on the basis of the press reports that war has broken out [*sur la seule notoriété de la guerre*] and without waiting for official notification from the belligerent powers. The extreme probability of such a position of the United States, in such a case, was reported in several of my former dispatches [which had been unanswered]. I am greatly distressed [*jugez si je dois souffrir*] to be left without information with regard to future French policy towards America [*le parti que la France veut adopter relativement à l'Amérique*]. Also at seeing that my successor, although nominated last November, is still not at his post on April 18—I have pledged myself to remain at my post, and I shall keep that pledge faithfully, but as soon as I am released by the arrival of Citizen Genest [*sic*] I hope I shall have sufficient resolve, despite my extreme poverty, never again to be the agent of any Government whatever [*ne plus être l'agent d'aucun gouvernement quelconque*].[1]

Jean-Baptiste Ternant had reason to be sick at heart. His life had been a diplomatic misery since news of the events of August 1792 had reached America, towards the end of the same year.[2] Ternant had served in the American Revolution, under Steuben, and on his appointment as Minister Plenipotentiary (August 1791) had been recommended to Washington by Lafayette. Washington had regarded him as "an old friend." But a year later to be known as a friend of Lafayette was to be in deep disgrace with the authorities in Paris. Among the Girondins, "*Fayettiste*" was the worst possible term of opprobrium. (We shall see below, p. 181, how this term was to be applied by Ternant's successor to Washington himself.) The best that Ternant could look forward to, had he returned to France, was a life of provincial obscurity; the guillotine was a distinct possibility. So he stayed on in America (as his successor was also to do). Ternant lived until 1816.

On 20 April, Ternant wrote again to his Citizen Minister, this time to announce the arrival of his successor in the United States, but not in the capital, to which he was accredited. Ternant wrote, with exasperation:

> A ship from Charleston has finally brought me a letter dated 11th of this month in which Citizen Genet announces his arrival in that city, and his immediate departure for Philadelphia. It will take him at least 22 days to make that wearisome journey; and as he probably left on the 12th, I can't expect to see him here until the opening days of May. It is much to be regretted, since he is entrusted, as he says himself, with important negotiations, that he should have taken the longest possible route to reach the place in which these negotiations have to be conducted.[3]

Actually, Genet spent eleven days in Charleston, and twenty-nine days en route, reaching Philadelphia on 16 May. This was a deliberate progress for a set purpose: to excite, display, and exploit American enthusiasm for the French Revolution. This was no ordinary diplomatic mission, from one government to another. This was a mission from one nation to another; from one people to another; from one republic to another; from one revolution to another. Meeting the people was more important than meeting the President. So Genet took his time and met the people. The general idea was that the President—usually referred to by Genet simply as General Washington—would be more receptive of Citizen Genet's message from the French Republic, after Washington had witnessed the enthusiasm of his own people for Citizen Genet, and for the French Revolution incarnate in the person of the Citizen.

Jefferson and Madison were later to have cause to deplore Genet's manner of appealing to the people but they were delighted with his initial progress. On 28 April 1793, Jefferson wrote to Madison: "We expect Mr. Genest here within a few days. It seems as if his arrival would furnish occasion for the *people* to testify their affections without respect to the cold cautions of their government."[4] This is of course precisely what

Genet intended. The meeting of minds, across great distances, is remarkable, at this stage of the Genet-Jefferson interaction. On 29 May, Madison is eager for publication of Genet's addresses.

> The sentiments expressed by Genest would be of infinite service at this crisis. As a regular publication of them cannot be expected till the meeting of Congress, if then, it will be wished they could in some other mode make their way to the press. If he expressed the substance of them in his verbal answer to the address, or announces them in open conversation, the Printers might surely hand them to the public. The affection to France in her struggles for liberty would not only be increased by a knowledge that she does not wish us to go to war; but prudence would give its sanction to a bolder enunciation of the popular sentiment.[5]

At this stage, then, Jefferson and Madison regarded Genet's arrival as constituting a most valuable reinforcement for the American Republican cause. They were in a mood to egg him on. But they were soon to find that egging on was not exactly what Citizen Genet required.

Genet was, personally, a most attractive avatar of his cause: young, handsome, dashing, outgoing, sincerely eloquent; a romantic representative of the French Revolution in its most romantic phase. Women fell in love with him, at the mere sound of his approach. The lady whom he was to marry—Cornelia, daughter of Governor George Clinton of New York—let it be known that she was in love with him before ever she set eyes on him, just on the strength of what she heard about him, as he journeyed north from Charleston.

Arousing popular enthusiasm was the most essential part of Citizen Genet's mission, and he was extremely good at this. But his mission also involved more practical activities, and he set about these energetically from the moment of his arrival in Charleston. Harry Ammon writes:

> Within a few days after his arrival, Genet commissioned four privateers. Christened most appropriately, *Republican, Anti-George, Sans-Culotte,* and—the finest touch of all—*Citizen Genet,* they were soon sending into Charleston English ships captured as prizes. The Minister also made the initial arrangements for an expedition to be launched against Spanish Florida. The details of this operation were entrusted to the French Consul, Michel Ange Mangourit, whose patriotism met Genet's approval.[6]

Ammon says that Genet took these steps while "totally ignorant of the administration's position." But Genet was not "totally ignorant" of this. He knew the administration's position very well, *as the position was represented in the Republican press,* of which the bellwether was Jeffer-

son's *National Gazette*. For more than a year before Genet's mission began, those French Revolutionaries who were interested in America had
been receiving through that press the Jeffersonian picture of Washington's
first administration. Genet's chief, and Jefferson's old acquaintance Brissot de Warville, was thoroughly familiar with that picture. Washington's
administration—as the Republican press could tell you—contained one
good man, whose heart and soul was with the French Revolution. This
was Thomas Jefferson. It also contained one bad man, in the pay of the
King of England. This was Alexander Hamilton.[7] Then there was Washington, a good man but unaccountably open to the evil influence of Hamilton. Since 1791, French diplomatic representatives had been taken into
Jefferson's confidence in these matters. So it was not that Genet was totally ignorant of the administration's position. He knew that position, in
the Republican version of it, and that is what Genet, with the approval
of the Republican leaders, wanted to change. He was confident that it
could be changed, when he had demonstrated the extent of the power
that the French Revolution possessed over the hearts and minds of the
American people. And there was also direct action to be taken, on behalf
of the French Revolution, in the ports of the United States and in the
adjacent territories of Spanish Florida and Louisiana.

Citizen Genet was not an ignorant blunderer, as he has sometimes
been represented. He was a revolutionary, acting consistently on revolutionary premises. He didn't, as a revolutionary, need the permission of the
American administration for any project he might undertake on behalf of
the French Revolution. What he needed was the permission of a superior
power: the American people, which was held to be heart and soul with
the French people. For Citizen Genet, as for other revolutionaries, "the
people" always meant that part of the people which was on the side of
the Revolution; the others didn't count. So the plaudits of the people of
Charleston constituted a fully adequate mandate for military action in
Charleston Harbor. If Washington's administration were to contest the
legitimacy of that act, it would be revealing its own lack of legitimacy,
since it would be going against the source of all legitimacy: the people.
This was not only sound revolutionary logic, in a general way. It was specifically the logic and the *modus operandi* of the French Revolution in all
its phases: as Burke had known as early as September 1789. By mobilizing
"the people" against the Executive, the Ancien Régime had been destroyed. In August 1792, the constitutional monarchy had been destroyed
by the same revolutionary logic and the same methods. And in June
1793—the month after Citizen Genet's arrival in Philadelphia—the Girondin version of the Republic was to be swept away by Robespierre's

Jacobins and the people had marked out Genet's friends for the guillotine. But neither Genet nor Washington's administration learned of those developments until near the end of 1793, by which time Genet's mission was coming to an end anyway; for American reasons, not French ones.

It came later to be maintained by Republicans that Genet had exceeded his instructions. The French Revolution was absolutely all right, as always. It was one misguided individual, the regrettable Charles-Edmond Genet, who was alone responsible for everything that had gone wrong, in the relations between America and France in the summer of 1793. That was the retrospective thesis that came to be adopted by Jefferson and the Republicans. That Genet had exceeded his instructions became a Republican article of faith. So let us take a look at the instructions in question. These were not, of course, known to the Washington administration in 1793. They appear to have been released by Genet himself after his recall, but attracted little notice at the time. They were published in full by Frederick Jackson Turner for the American Historical Association in 1903 (*AHA* [1903], pages 202–11 in the original French). The passages that follow are my own translation.

The first thing to note about these instructions is the capacity (*qualité*) in which Genet is to act. He is described as "Minister Plenipotentiary of the French Republic to [*près*] the Congress of the United States." Harry Ammon describes this as "a minor error, which reflected the Girondin vagueness about American institutions."[8] I don't think this is either minor or an error. Brissot de Warville, at this time the leading figure among the Girondins, had made a study of American affairs, and must have known, at least in outline, of the system of government established by the American Constitution, and by now in operation for more than three years. There is vagueness here, but it is calculated vagueness, *revolutionary* vagueness. The institutions of other countries were perceived on behalf of the French Republic as legitimate only in the degree that they resembled the pan-Revolutionary archetype: the French Republic, One and Indivisible. In that respect the *Congress* has legitimacy, through its resemblance to the National Convention. On the other hand, the idea of a Chief Executive, elected by the people, has no analogue in French Revolutionary terms and therefore no revolutionary legitimacy. The form of accreditation of Citizen Genet is certainly mistaken, *in American terms*. But it is not at all mistaken *in French Revolutionary terms*. In appealing to Congress, over the head of the President (as he was soon to do) Citizen Genet was acting, not only in accordance with the letter of his istructions, but also with their spirit. And also with the spirit of the

French Revolution, which was a strongly nationalist spirit and never more profoundly nationalist than when, as under the Girondins, it abounded in the rhetoric of the most exalted *internationalism.*

In that spirit, Genet will appeal to Congress against the Executive, and he will continue to accredit Consuls to Congress, even after the Executive has instructed him to refrain from doing so. This is not a series of personal blunders: it is the unfolding of revolutionary policy.

The opening paragraph of Genet's instructions makes clear that he is expected to be, not just an envoy accredited to a governmental institution, but also and primarily, a revolutionary missionary to the American people. Having referred to the links which unite "the French Nation" to "the American People," the instructions require Citizen Genet "to devote his energies to fortifying the Americans in the Principles which have induced them [*les ont engagés*], to unite themselves to France."

Genet would not have needed to be told that "fortifying" the Americans in these "Principles" included instructing them on what those Principles actually were. This was standard, both in doctrine and practice, during the ideologically expansionist phases of the French Revolution, the most exuberant of these phases being that of the Girondins in 1793.

The instructions next prescribe for Citizen Genet "a route diametrically opposed to that along which his Predecessors have been constrained to crawl" [*ramper*]. The instructions continue: "The Executive Council, faithful to its duty, obedient to the will of the French People, authorizes Citizen Genet to declare candidly and honestly [*avec franchise et loyauté*] to the Ministers of Congress . . ."

The French Revolution schema of a legitimate American political system, united with the French one, is perfectly clear. The American administration is legitimate only if its members regard themselves as "Ministers of Congress"; and behave as such. Congress itself is legitimate only if it shows itself as "obedient to the will of the people." The envoy of the French Revolution, applauded and thereby accredited by the American people, is *ipso facto* constituted arbiter of the legitimacy or illegitimacy of both Ministers and Congress. It is implicit in the logic of the instructions, and of the Revolution from which they emanate, that if Congress and its supposed "Ministers" fail to comply with the directives conveyed to them by the envoy of the French Revolution, a new American Revolution would be in order, to be conducted on French Revolutionary lines.

Citizen Genet is to seek to develop previous negotiations for a commercial treaty into something far more ambitious and revolutionary: "a national pact in which the two peoples would completely combine into one [*confondroient*] their commercial interests with their political interests and establish an intimate concert [*concert intime*] in order to promote [*favoriser*] in all connections [*sous tous les rapports*] the Empire of Liberty."

The words "national pact" deserve comment. Within the "intimate concert" of "the Empire of Liberty" are America and France to become *one nation*? It might seem so but if that is the case, the momentous fusion is not to take place immediately, for the "national pact" is to require that the ships of certain powers are "not to be received in the ports of the two contracting Nations" [as the powers in question are clearly meant to include Britain, this part of Genet's instructions would have automatically involved the United States in war with Britain.]

Warming to their work; the members of the Executive Council go on to describe how the Empire of Liberty might be made up, territorially speaking, under the binational "national pact":

> This pact which the French People would support with all the characteristic energy of which it has already furnished so many proofs, would lead rapidly to the liberation of Spanish America, would open the navigation of the Mississippi, would deliver our brothers-of-old [*anciens frères*] from the tyrannical yoke of Spain, and perhaps reunite to the American Constellation the beautiful star of Canada. However vast this project may be, it will be easy to execute, if the Americans want it, and Citizen Genet must devote himself to encouraging them to do so.

This part of Genet's instructions may seem wildly chimerical, and is so for the 1790s, if seen in its full extension (including all of "Spanish America" and Canada). But in a more limited sense (initially at least) the construction of an Empire of Liberty through the territorial expansion of the United States was the most realistic part of Genet's instructions, because inherently attractive to many Americans, and most notably to Thomas Jefferson. If Americans could—with French aid in money, ships, and arms—open the Mississippi entirely to American navigation, acquire Spanish Florida and much of Louisiana, that would be a most satisfactory outcome in the eyes of most Americans and also one that, handled with discretion and without *official* American backing, need not provoke hostilities with Spain's ally, Great Britain.

From a Jeffersonian point of view, this would have other additional advantages. It would greatly enhance the prestige of the French Revolution among the American people, and this would not only advance the cause of Liberty, philosophically speaking, but would be greatly beneficial to the Republican Party in electoral terms. So Jefferson, as we shall see, not merely encouraged Citizen Genet to think along those particular lines, but actually assisted him, operationally (below, pp. 171–75).

If Genet had stuck to "Empire of Liberty"–type operations, had speedily desisted from overtly autonomous operations on and from the territory of the United States, and had allowed himself to be guided by Thomas Jefferson—the most powerful and prudent of the American well-wishers to the French Revolution—his mission might have been a great success. Fortunately or unfortunately for America, Citizen Genet found himself unable to order his priorities in that manner. (I shall consider the reasons for that inability a little later.)

To return to the instructions from the Executive Council, the passage about the Empire of Liberty is followed by one in which the reasons for France's declaration of war on "the King of England" are explained. The formula is a classic of French Revolutionary thinking and does much to explain both the conduct and the eventual failure of Citizen Genet's mission to the United States. The relevant passage in the instructions was:

> The English Ministers, instead of associating themselves with the glory of France, instead of realizing that our liberty, as well as that of the Peoples whose chains we have broken, guarantees Forever [à Jamais] that of their country [Patrie] allow themselves to be influenced by our enemies, who are also those of the Liberty of Peoples.

Note the implications that other nations yearn to be associated with the glory of France, implicitly superior to anything which the other nations may possess of their own in that line; also that other nations would be content to have their liberty "guaranteed" for them by France (and defined for them by their guarantor) rather than to have their liberty cherished and defended by themselves, in their own way and on their own terms.

Those numerous Americans who admired the French Revolution, or what they thought of as the French Revolution, would hardly have been happy with that formulation, if they had known about it, and been able to ponder its implications for themselves.

The instructions conclude by instructing their Minister Plenipotentiary about matters of protocol and precedence. In an earlier part, and in a general context, the instructions had spoken of "flinging away far from us everything that pertains to the old Diplomacy." In the concluding part, it is made clear that the rejection of the old Diplomacy does not apply to the precedence to which a diplomatic representative of France was traditionally entitled [i.e., under the defunct Ancien Régime]. Having told Citizen Genet to avoid "the ridiculous disputes which took up the time of the old Diplomacy," the Executive Council explains how he is to conduct himself, as Minister Plenipotentiary of France (as well as of the Republic) should any such dispute arise. There is a general policy to be followed by all Ministers of the French Republic in such cases:

> The intent of the Council is that the Ministers of the Nation declare openly and proudly [*hautement*] that the French People sees in all the Peoples brothers and equals, and that it wishes to set aside [*écarter*] all idea of supremacy and precedence, but that if any State misunderstanding the generosity of [French Revolutionary] principles, were to claim any special distinction, and were to put itself in a position to acquire such a thing by direct or indirect diplomatic representations [*démarches*], the Ministers of the French People would then demand all the prerogatives enjoyed in every time by the French power [*la puissance Française*], the Nation being determined that, in such a case, its Ministers defend these prerogatives, in the knowledge that She [*Elle, la Nation*] will know how to ensure that they are respected [*les faire respecter*].

In short, all Peoples are equal, but some Peoples are more equal than others.

The above are the principal promises contained in the main body of the Executive Council's far-reaching instructions to the Revolutionary plenipotentiary to the United States. But there is also a "supplement" to the instructions, which is even more illuminating than the main body of this document with regard to French Revolutionary attitudes to the United States, in the epoch of maximum French Revolutionary ideological expansion (1793).

The supplement begins by acknowledging that the Minister Plenipotentiary, in attempting to carry out his Instructions, may run into American resistance, at a high level (or what would have been regarded as "a high level" before the advent of the doctrine of the supremacy of the people). The first paragraph of the supplement runs:

> The Executive Council wishes a new treaty, on wider and more fraternal foundations than those of 1778, to be concluded as soon as possible. However, the Council has to recognize that during the present crisis of Europe a negotiation of this nature may be subject to many delays whether as a result of secret maneuvers of the [British] Minister and the English partisans at Philadelphia or because of the timidity of several leaders of the American Republic who, despite their well-known patriotism, have always shown the strongest aversion for any measures which could mean the displeasure of England.

Always? Even during the American Revolution? Yes, apparently, for the Executive Council goes on to tell its plenipotentiary the argument by which he is to overcome the timidity of George Washington and his colleagues:

> He will make the Americans realize that the engagements which may appear onerous to them are no more than the just price of *the independence which the French Nation won for them* [emphasis added] and the more severe he shows himself to be on these points, the more easy it will be to induce them to conclude a new Treaty.

Citizen Genet has often been accused of exceeding his instructions, but he fell well short of them in this particular. This was prudent on his part. Had he insisted on explaining to the crowds that came out to meet him on the road from Charleston to Philadelphia in that month of May that the Americans owed their liberation, not in any degree to their own exertions and sacrifices, but entirely to the French nation, the representative of the nation in question might never have reached Philadelphia alive.

The enthusiasm of Jefferson and Madison for the French Revolution would have been sensibly abated had they known that in the authoritative opinion of the Executive Council of the French Republic, Americans must be grateful, and pay, for "the independence which the French Nation won for them." It was, of course, a standard theme of American Republican oratory that Americans should be grateful for the support the French had given to the American Revolution, and that the Federalists were ingrates in that regard. But none of the Republican orators could have suspected just *how much* gratitude the French Revolutionaries expected from Americans, or on what grounds.

I

We have studied Citizen Genet's Revolutionary instructions. Now let us watch him as he sets about implementing them. Our best source here is Genet's own copious and spirited dispatches, redolent as these are both of his own ardent and sanguine temperament, and of the French Revolutionary ideology so congenial to that temperament. The dispatches quoted below are translated from the original French texts in *AHA* (1903). As the dispatches are dated, and are printed in chronological order, I have dispensed with page references.

Genet's first dispatch is dated from Charleston, 16 April 1793. He announces his intention of proceeding overland towards Philadelphia, intending to pass by Mount Vernon, where he hoped to meet "General Washington" and hand over to him "the letters of which I am the carrier." In fact, Washington had already left Mount Vernon, on 13 April, to go to Philadelphia where, with his Cabinet, he prepared the Proclamation of Neutrality which issued on 23 April (below, pp. 164–66).

The part of Genet's first dispatch which will have had most interest for the Executive Council is the discreetly worded postscript: "Citizen Mangourit, consul at Charleston, is an excellent patriot, Citizen Minister. He has prepared the ground very well, and I have left with him all the instructions necessary to direct his zeal toward the objective aimed at by the Council in the different negotiations for which it has made me responsible."

The Council will have understood from that postscript that the implementation of the plans for the first stage of the Empire of Liberty—the conquest of Louisiana—are in good revolutionary hands.

In his second dispatch, dated from Philadelphia on 18 May, Genet announces that he has delivered his letters of credence to "the President of the United States," an official whose existence is ignored in those same letters. Genet does not say, in this letter, how Washington received him, but he later described the reception as cold, and we know this was Washington's intention. After contemplating that progress from Charleston, Genet consoles himself with the thought of his popular success: "My journey was a succession of civic feasts without interruption and my entry into Philadelphia a triumph for liberty. The real Americans are brimming over with joy."

Les vrais Américains . . . This is not just an idiosyncratic phrase of Genet's own. It is a critically important element within the French Revolutionary ideology. In every country, the partisans of the French Revolution are the only "real" whatever it is. Thus the great French Revolutionary historian Jules Michelet in his account of the liberation of Belgium by the French Revolutionaries, distinguishes between *les vrais Belges* and *les faux Belges.* By any conventional statistical computation, the *faux Belges*—that is, the Belgian opponents of the French incursion—were in a majority but in terms of the French Revolutionary ideology, this is an illusion. The *faux Belges,* not being really Belgian at all, can not properly be entered into the computation. The only Belgians who are really Belgians, in the logic of ideology, were *les vrais Belges,* the friends of the French Revolution. Similarly, Citizen Genet is secure in the knowledge that he has the support of the American people, since those who do not welcome him are not *de vrais Américains*. (He was later to wonder whether George Washington was *un vrai Américain*.)

A postscript to this dispatch runs: "Tomorrow, Citizen, I shall have my first ministerial meeting with Mr. Jefferson, Minister for Foreign Affairs. His principles, his experience, his talents, his devotion to the cause which we uphold, all inspire me with the greatest confidence in him and make me hope that we shall reach the glorious goal which the general interest of humanity must make us desirous of attaining."

That was in Dispatch No. 2. Dispatch No. 3, dated 31 May, has nothing to say about that interview with Jefferson. We can safely infer that Jefferson did not fully meet Genet's expectations, even then. No doubt Jefferson mingled a few words of caution with his compliments, and that would not have gone down too well. Also, Jefferson's official demeanor towards the first Envoy of the French Republic may have been less warm than Jefferson personally would have wished. In March, before Genet's arrival at Charleston, there had been discussions as to how to receive him. Washington had told Jefferson that "Mr. Genet should unquestionably be received, but he thought not with too much warmth or cordiality, so only as [to] be satisfactory to him."[9]

Jefferson must have been taken aback by this. It did not tally with his understanding, after his December conversation with the President, that Washington had become a convert to the cause of the French Revolution. So Jefferson was already aware that relations with Genet were going to require delicate handling. This awareness may have been apparent in the Genet-Jefferson interview.

No official chill in Philadelphia can damp the ardor of the Revolutionary Proconsul, as he takes America by storm: "All America [*L'Amérique toute entière*] has risen up [*s'est levée*] to recognize in me the Minister of the French Republic: the voice of the People continues to neutralize President Washington's declaration of neutrality. I live here amid perpetual feasts [Dispatch No. 3, 31 May 1793]."

Dispatch No. 3 ends on a practical note: "The privateer [*corsaire*] Le Sans Culotte which I armed at Charleston has captured eight large English vessels."

Le Sans Culotte was operating out of American waters, as were other vessels armed by the Minister Plenipotentiary and by the French Consuls who cooperated enthusiastically with his revolutionary programme. Genet obviously assumed that the American administration, cowed by the demonstrations of the people's will, would not dare to interfere with the development of his program. Most writers on the subject attribute this mistaken assumption to the personal vanity of Charles-Edmond Genet. Genet's vanity was indeed a somewhat enlarged organ, but his mistaken assumption was one which he shared with the other French agents—mostly consular—in the United States at this time. It was an assumption drawn not from any merely personal source, but from a collective experience and a collective ideology: those of the French Revolution. To all French Revolutionaries it was axiomatic that an Executive must bow before the popular will, as manifest in popular assemblies and demonstrations. French Revolutionaries, contemplating the American scene in 1793, had a subliminal tendency to assimilate George Washington to Louis XVI. This was not conducive to a realistic assessment of American affairs.

In Dispatch No. 4—19 June 1793—Genet for the first time takes Washington personally to task, and announces his intention to appeal to Congress against him:

> Everything has succeeded even beyond my hopes: the real Republicans [*les vrais Républicains*] are triumphant, but old Washington [*le vieux Washington*], who differs greatly from the man whose name has gone down in history, does not forgive me my successes, and the enthusiasm with which the whole Town [of Philadelphia] thronged to my house, while a handful of English merchants were thanking him for his proclamation [of neutrality]. He is putting every kind of obstacle in my way, and obliges me to work secretly for the convening of Congress, in which the majority, under the leadership of the finest minds [*les premières têtes*] of the American union will be decidedly in our favor.

Les premières têtes . . . This is clearly a reference to Jefferson and Madison, whom Genet still believes to be on his side, at this point in his mission. This seems to be a good point at which to turn to the contemplation of that mission, as it developed in the spring and early summer of 1793, from American points of view.

II

As we have seen, the Proclamation of Neutrality occurred before Genet had presented his credentials. The early debate over Genet's mission centered on whether tolerance of certain activities of his in the long interval between his arrival in the United States and the presentation of his credentials was compatible with American neutrality.

As Harry Ammon puts it: "In the spring of 1793, basic policy towards France was shaped more by the Secretary of the Treasury, whose influence over the President seemed unshakable, than by the Secretary of State." [10] Hamilton, as well as Jefferson, had informed Washington of the French declaration of war against England and it was Hamilton who, a few days afterward, asked his confidant, Chief Justice John Jay, to draft a proclamation of neutrality. The proclamation, in its final form, was based on Jay's draft, and the questions put by Washington to the Cabinet concerning the question of neutrality, were drawn up by Hamilton, as Jefferson noted.

For Jefferson, the climate in the Cabinet room, while neutrality was being discussed in April 1793, must have been stiflingly Hamiltonian, laden with heresy.

Jefferson did not advocate entry into war, against monarchist England, on the side of the French Republic, although the mystical "Adam and Eve" side of him must surely have been attracted to the concept of a Franco-American alliance in the cause of Liberty. But Jefferson knew that that was out of the question: Washington would not have it, and if Washington would not have it, the country would not have it either. The Cabinet were agreed (for different reasons) that America should stay out of the war that had just begun in Europe. Jefferson accepted neutrality, in practice. But he sought to avoid a *proclamation* of neutrality. Granted the popularity of France, and the unpopularity of Britain, among the American public, a proclamation of neutrality would appear as a snub to France, and a victory for Britain. And American Republicans might begin to wonder what exactly Thomas Jefferson was doing, in an administration that behaved in that way. As Jefferson put it in a letter to Madison near the end of April "I fear that a fair neutrality will prove a disagreeable pill to our friends, tho' necessary to keep us out of the calamities of a war. [11]

In these rather trying circumstances, Jefferson, like the pragmatist he usually showed himself to be, when difficult political decisions had to be taken, fought a skillful rearguard action. Finding he could not avert a proclamation of neutrality, in substance, he managed to keep the *word* neutrality omitted from the proclamation. He also managed to eliminate from the final text some strictures on French Revolutionary proceedings which had figured in Jay's draft. More substantially, Jefferson sketched a fall-back position. He questioned the constitutionality of such a proclamation. Was it not an invasion of Congress's power to declare (or not to declare) war? Jefferson did not convince any of his Cabinet colleagues on that point, but he did convince James Madison. The Republicans therefore found a way of dissociating themselves from the Proclamation—by holding it to be *ultra vires*—but without challenging neutrality in practice. As Alexander DeConde puts it:

> If the administration was not favorably disposed toward republican France, popular sentiment was. This sentiment would, perhaps, spread to Congress and help to mold foreign policy. In the newly elected Congress, Republicans would, for the first time, have a dominant voice; they would control the House, and the Senate would be divided about evenly with Federalists. By supporting a call for a special session and emphasizing the role of Congress in the formulating of foreign policy, Jefferson would hasten the day when his party would have an important voice in the conduct of foreign policy and could perhaps counterbalance Federalist predominance in the Executive Branch.[12]

It can be seen that there was much in common between the direction of Jefferson's thinking and that of Genet in April–June of 1793. Both were contemplating an appeal to Congress against an Executive decision—the Proclamation of Neutrality. Genet's ideas on that subject were far more dramatic, and less well-informed, than those of Jefferson. Still there was a shared general direction of the thinking of these two partisans of the French Revolution, in this early phase of Citizen Genet's mission. And we have always to keep in mind that the *National Gazette,* known to be under Jefferson's patronage, staunchly supported Citizen Genet, throughout his mission. But what Citizen Genet failed to see was that the things the *National Gazette* were saying had a specific and limited function. That function was a domestic and propagandist one: to mobilize and develop support for the Republican Party, and in the process to encourage and draw upon the popularity of the French Revolution, this popularity being a major asset of the Republicans in their struggle against the Hamiltonian Federalists. So the *National Gazette* was not a reliable guide to the mind of the Secretary of State, when delicate policy decisions had to be taken. But Genet could never understand American politics. To that devout French Revolutionary, the very existence of forms of American politics, affected by domestic issues, was a betrayal of the Cause of Liberty, synonymous with the French Revolution.

In the early summer of 1793, however, the factors that would lead to a divergence and eventually a total break between Jefferson and Genet had yet to come into play. Indeed under the immediate impact of Genet's arrival, what is most apparent is a divergence between Jefferson's position as leader *in petto* of the Republican Party in the United States and his position as Washington's Secretary of State. In early May, Jefferson wrote to James Monroe in connection with some of the exploits of the newly arrived Minister Plenipotentiary of the French Republic:

> The war between France and England seems to be producing an effect not contemplated. All the old spirit of 1776 is rekindling. The newspapers from Boston to Charleston prove this; and even the Monocrat papers are obliged to publish the most furious Philippics against England. A French frigate took a British prize off the capes of Delaware the other day, and sent her up here. Upon her coming into sight thousands and thousands of the *yeomanry* of the city crowded and covered the wharves. Never before was such a crowd seen there, and when the British colours were seen *reversed,* and the French flying above them they burst into peals of exultation. I wish we may be able to repress the spirit of the people within the limits of a fair neutrality.
>
> In the meantime H. is panic-struck if we refuse our breach to every kick which Gr Brit. may chuse to give it. He is for proclaiming at once the most abject principles, such as would invite and merit habitual insults. And indeed every inch of ground must be fought in our councils to desperation in order to hold up the face of even a sneaking neutrality, for our votes are generally 2 1/2 against 1 1/2.[13]

Jefferson sent the letter addressed to Monroe, unsealed, to James Madison, with the injunction: "Seal and forward Monroe's letter [i.e. the letter *to* Monroe] after reading it." Monroe was the most Francophile of the Republican leaders, and therefore the one most likely to criticize Jefferson for remaining on in Washington's Cabinet after the Proclamation of Neutrality. Jefferson is letting Monroe know that his own heart still beats in the right place with regards to the French Revolution, and that he is defending that cause, under heavy pressure, in the Cabinet. Jefferson, whose correspondence with Madison was less enthusiastic in tone, wants Madison to know exactly what he is saying to Monroe. Jefferson's difficult task of leading the anti-Government Republican Party, from within Washington's Cabinet, was carried out mainly through correspondence with Madison and Monroe. Jefferson was a master of epistolary political management, but his powers were stretched by the inherent difficulty of simultaneously exploiting and trying to control popular enthusiasm for the French Revolution.

A week after sending off that letter, Jefferson, as Secretary of State, found himself required, by Washington's decision, to write to the British Minister Plenipotentiary, George Hammond, formally condemning the very action about which (in a private, or rather party-political, character) he had written in such a gleeful vein to James Monroe.

Secretary of State to George Hammond:

The capture of the British ship Grange, by the French frigate l'Embuscade, has, on inquiry been found to have taken place within the Bay of Delaware and Jurisdiction of the United States, as stated in your memorial of the 2d instant. The government is, therefore, taking measures for the liberation of the Crew and restitution of the ship and cargo.

It condemns in the highest degree the conduct of any of our citizens, who may personally engage in committing hostilities at sea against any of the nations, parties to the present war, and will exert all the means with which the laws and constitution have armed them to discover such as offend herein and bring them to condign punishment. . . .

The practice of commissioning, equipping and manning Vessels, in our ports to cruise on [behalf of] any of the belligerent parties, is equally and entirely disapproved, and the government will take effectual measures to prevent a repetition of it.[14]

Hamiltonian language there, not Jeffersonian, and George Hammond, always well briefed by Hamilton, understood this perfectly.

On the same day, the Secretary of State wrote to Jean-Baptiste Ternant, who was still Minister Plenipotentiary as Genet did not present his credentials until three days later. After laying down some general principles, the letter comes to the point: "I am, in consequence charged by the President of the United States to express to you his expectation, and at the same time his confidence that you will be pleased to take immediate and effectual measures for having the ship Grange and her cargo restored to the British owners, and the persons taken on board her, set at liberty."[15]

The case of a prize taken by another "Genet" privateer, *The Little Sarah,* was already under consideration (below, pp. 196–98). So the new Minister Plenipotentiary, even before presenting his credentials, was already in deep trouble with the administration which received those credentials.

With the administration collectively that is. The Secretary of State, while obliged to protest officially about Genet's actions, was privately still delighted with Genet. On the occasion of the presentation of the Minister's credentials, Jefferson wrote to Madison:

[Ternant] delivered yesterday his letters of recall, & Mr. Genet presented his of credence. It is impossible for anything to be more affectionate, more magnanimous than the purport of his mission. "We know that under present circumstances we have a right to call upon you for the guarantee of our islands. But we do not desire it. We wish you to do nothing but what is for your own good, and we will do all in our power to promote it. Cherish your own peace & prosperity. You have expressed a willingness to enter into a more liberal treaty of commerce with us; I bring full powers (& he produced them) to form such a treaty, and a preliminary decree of the National convention to lay open our country & it's colonies to you for every purpose of utility, without your participating the burthens of maintaining & defending them. We see in you the only person on earth who can love us sincerely & merit to be so loved." In short he offers everything & asks nothing. Yet I know the offers will be opposed, & suspect they will not be accepted. In short, my dear Sir, it is impossible for you to conceive what is passing in our conclave: and it is evident that one or two at least, under pretence of avoiding war on the one side have no great antipathy to run foul of it on the other, and to make a part in the confederacy of princes against human liberty.[16]

Jefferson, it seems, has not yet noticed that the reason Genet "asks for nothing" is that he takes whatever he wants, without asking, in the name of the French Revolution.

In the light of Jefferson's effusiveness about his first meeting with Genet, it seems curious that *Genet* had nothing to say about his first meeting with Jefferson. Perhaps the Minister Plenipotentiary, who offers everything and asks nothing, was disconcerted to find his professions taken literally, since this was by no means the spirit of his instructions.

On 23 May, eight days after having formally protested at the maritime transaction of Citizen Genet, Jefferson wrote in a very different vein in the guise of a personal letter to his friend (soon to be his son-in-law), John Wayles Eppes: "You have missed seeing what has highly gratified the great mass of Philadelphians, British prizes brought in by French armed vessels. Thousands & thousands collected on the beach when the first came up, & when they saw the British colours reversed & the french flying above them they rented the air with peals of exultation."[17]

Officially, the Secretary of State is obliged to keep up pressure on the Minister Plenipotentiary on the matter of those ships: "The expressions of friendly sentiment, which we have already had the satisfaction of receiving from you leave no room to doubt that the conclusion of the President, being thus made known to you these vessels will be permitted to give no further umbrage by their presence in the Ports of United States."[18]

The sheer *brio* of Genet's dealings with the British had at first some charms for Jefferson as we have seen. But by late June, with Genet still busy arming privateers in American waters, recruiting American citizens, and disregarding governmental warnings, Jefferson realized that Genet was becoming a dangerous liability to the Republican cause, and that leading Republicans would have to be alerted accordingly. In a letter to James Monroe, on 28 June 1793, Jefferson wrote:

> I do not augur well of the mode of conduct of the new French minister; I fear he will enlarge the circle of those disaffected to his country. I am doing everything in my power to moderate the impetuosity of his movements, and to destroy the dangerous opinion which has been excited in him, that the people of the U.S. will disavow the acts of their government, and that he has an appeal from the Executive to Congress, & from both to the people.[19]

Of course, the "dangerous opinion" in question was one which the Republican press and the associated Democratic and Republican Societies were busy propagating throughout that summer. Jefferson, Madison, and Monroe were at that very time preparing "an appeal from the Executive to Congress" over the Proclamation of Neutrality. But all that was *American* politics. It was a different matter for the representative of a foreign government to join in. Jefferson is prescient here. Genet at this time is at the height of his popularity with Republicans, but Jefferson sees that this popularity can boomerang against the Republicans, if Genet's activity comes to be seen as foreign interference. Of course, from Genet's point of view, it wasn't foreign interference at all. Genet was not a mere representative of any old foreign government. He represented *the French Revolution,* which was the cause of all humanity. Genet was confident that all *les vrais Américains* would view his conduct in that light. Unfortunately—as with the Belgian experience—*les vrais Américains* were outnumbered by *les faux Américains,* though that was not how it looked in the early summer of 1793.

In writing to Monroe, Jefferson was careful in his language: he knew it would not be easy to cure Monroe of his illusions about Genet. Writing (about a week later) to Madison, who is completely under Jefferson's spell at this time, Jefferson is more outspoken. He writes:

> Never in my opinion, was so calamitous an appointment made, as that of the present minister of F. here. Hotheaded, all imagination, no judgment, passionate, disrespectful and even indecent towards the P. in his written as well as verbal communications, talking of appeals from him to Congress, from them to the people, urging the most unreasonable and groundless propositions, and in the most dictatorial style etc. etc. etc. If ever it should be necessary to lay his communications before Congress or the public, they will excite universal indignation. He renders my position immensely difficult. He does me justice personally, and, giving him time to vent himself

and then cool, I am on a footing to advise him freely, and he respects it. But he breaks out again on the very first occasion, so as to shew that he is incapable of correcting himself.[20]

Jefferson's complaints are fully justified. But it wasn't *just* Genet. Genet is acting both on the letter and in the spirit of his instructions from the Executive Council. Genet and the French consular corps in the United States—*bons patriotes* all—are fervent devotees of a common ideology. Through them, what was working in the United States that feverish summer was the French Revolution itself, making itself at home on American soil and in American territorial waters.

Jefferson could have seen that if he had wanted to, but he didn't, or if he did, he never let on. It was politically expedient to put *all* the blame on Genet, personally, so that is what Jefferson did.

Yet, in relation to the "Empire of Liberty" project, Jefferson is still close to Genet. A dispatch of Genet's, dated 25 July 1793, refers to a meeting with Jefferson. Genet's dispatch opens with a reference to the general political context of his endeavors with respect to Louisiana:

> Since the Executive Council had foreseen that the Federal Government of the United States would not immediately embrace, with all the warmth we could wish, the lofty objectives [*les grandes vues*] whose execution the Council had entrusted to me, the Council had instructed me—while awaiting the moment in which the American People would force its Government to make common cause with us—to take every measure in my power to sow the seeds, in Louisiana and the other provinces of America bordering on the United States, of the principles of liberty and independence.

Genet went on to describe contacts made with Louisiana, and certain proposals made by General Clark, the designated leader of the rebellion against Spain. Genet took these proposals to Jefferson:

> Before committing myself completely to these proposals, I thought it my duty to ascertain the attitude of the American Government, and engage it to unite itself with us [*sic*]. Mr. Jefferson seemed to have a lively sense of the utility of such a project, but he told me that the United States had entered into negotiations with Spain in the hope of acquiring a trading post below New Orleans and that, unless these negotiations were broken off, a regard for propriety [*la délicatesse des Etats Unis*] would not permit the United States to take part in our operations. However, he gave me to understand [*il me fit entendre*] that a little spontaneous irruption of the inhabitants of Kentucky into New Orleans could get things moving [*pourrait avancer les choses*]. He put me in touch with several Congressmen [*députés*]

from Kentucky, and especially Mr. Brown [later referred to as "Senator Brown"] who, convinced that his country would never flourish until the navigation of the Mississippi was free, adopted our plans with as much enthusiasm as an American is capable of manifesting.

A botanist called Michaux was also made privy to the plot: "I obtained letters for him from Mr. Jefferson and from Senator Brown for the Governor and the most influential men of Kentucky."

Jefferson has left his own version of this conversation, though his account bears an earlier date (5 July 1793). The difference in the dates is probably not significant. Genet does not say when the conversation took place and was probably reporting it after a delay. Jefferson's account of the conversation follows:

Mr. Genet called on me and read to me very rapidly instrns he had prepared for Michaud who is going to Kentucky, an address to the inhab. of Louisiana, & another to those of Canada. In these papers it appears that besides encouraging those inhabitants to insurrection, he speaks of two generals at Kentucky who have proposed to him to go & take N. Orleans if he will furnish the exp. about £3,000 sterl. He declines advancing it, but promises that sum ultimately for their expenses, proposes that officers shall be commissd. by himself in Kentucky & Louisiana, that they shall rendezvous *out of the territories of the U.S.* suppose in Louisiana, & there making up a battalion to be called the —— —— of inhabitants of Louisiana & Kentucky and getting what Indns. they could, to undertake the expedn against N. Orleans, and then Louisiana to be established into an independant state connected in commerce with France and the U.S. That two frigates shall go into the river Mississipi and cooperate against N. Orleans. The address to Canada, was to encourage them to shake off English yoke, to call Indians to their assistance, and to assure them of the friendly disposns of their neighbors of the U.S.

He said he communicated these things to me, not as Secy. of State, but as Mr. Jeff. I told him that his enticing officers & souldiers from Kentucky to go against Spain, was really putting a halter about their necks, for that they would assuredly be hung, if they commd. hostilities agt. a nation at peace with the U.S. That leaving out that article I did not care what insurrections should be excited in Louisiana. He had, about a fortnight ago sent me a commn for Michaud as consul of France at Kentucky, & desired an Exequatur. I told him this could not be given, that it was only in the *ports* of the U.S. they were entitled to consuls, & that if France shd have a consul at Kentucky Engld and Spain would soon demand the same, & we shd have all our interior country filled with foreign agents. He acquiesced, & asked me to return the commission & his note, which I did. But he desired I would give Michaud a lre of introduction for Govr. Shelby. I sent him one a day or two after. He now observes to me that in that letter I speak of him only as a person of botanical & natural pursuits, but that he wished the Govr. to view him as something more, as a French citizen possessing his confidence. I took back the letter, & wrote another. See both.[21]

Scholars who have made special studies of the Genet mission, and have adverted to apparent discrepancies in the two versions of the Louisiana episode, interpret these with varying emphases. Harry Ammon (in *The Genet Mission*) is curiously ambivalent on this point. In the first paragraph, below, Ammon seems to give total credence to Jefferson, while in the second paragraph he allows substantial credence to Genet's version:

> As frequently happened Genet's account of this conference differed considerably from that of the Secretary of State. Writing to the Minister of Foreign Affairs three weeks later, Genet reported that Jefferson, who appreciated the value of the undertaking, had merely indicated that the United States could not participate in view of the negotiations about the navigation of the Mississippi in progress in Madrid. Nonetheless, Genet reported, Jefferson had made it clear that "a little spontaneous irruption" of the Kentuckians would not compromise the United States. Jefferson, he told his superiors, had also advised him about the best means of executing the project and promised to use his influence to ensure its success. Obviously the Secretary's warning about involving American citizens had not made the slightest impression on the Minister. This distortion of Jefferson's comments (for the account left by Jefferson is undoubtedly accurate) was due to Genet's desire to impress his superiors with his achievements and to his habit of exaggeration. Yet at the same time he cannot be entirely blamed for his reading of Jefferson's observations.
>
> Under the circumstances, a diplomat of a less impulsive temperament might well have concluded that the Secretary of State was only registering a formal disclaimer against the employment of American citizens while in fact condoning the undertaking. It was a low-key meeting, and it seems likely that Jefferson's warning was not delivered with the heavy stress given the ban on outfitting privateers. If Genet's project had succeeded in liberating Louisiana with the consequent benefits to the United States, would Washington have really hung the participating Kentuckians? The only advice Jefferson seems to have given Genet was to suggest that he confer with Senator John Brown of Kentucky, who gave the French Minister letters of introduction for Michaux.[22]

Samuel Flagg Bemis, in his account of Jefferson's tenure as Secretary of State, accepts that Jefferson did indeed knowingly assist Genet with his Louisiana project:

> Jefferson at first had looked upon Genet with kindest feelings as a man representing the new French republic, with whom it was the interest of the United States to maintain the friendliest relations. He gave him private tutelage as to just how the political winds blew in the American Government, even as Hamilton had sometimes apprised the British minister; and he wrote letters of introduction to Governor Shelby of Kentucky, at Genet's request, presenting the latter's agent, Michaux, as a French citizen possessing Jefferson's confidence. He did this when he well knew from Genet's own lips that Michaux was the bearer of instructions to "two generals in Kentucky" who were organizing with French commissions, and expenses paid by France, an expedition to set out against Louisiana; and after he had seen proclamations which were given to Michaux to be delivered in Canada and Louisiana, inviting the inhabitants to revolt against Great Britain and Spain. Understanding from Genet that the Kentucky expeditions were to rendezvous outside the territory of the United States, Jefferson told him he "did not care what insurrections should be excited in Louisiana."[23]

Alexander DeConde (in *Entangling Alliance*) takes the same view.

In hopes of enlisting Jefferson's support, Genet sounded him out, "not as Secy. of State, but as Mr. Jeff.," on his attitude toward French frontier schemes, particularly as set forth in Genet's instructions to Michaux and his manifesto to Canadians which urged them to shake off England's yoke and to rely on American friendship.

Under the impression that the Kentucky expeditions were to assemble outside the United States, Jefferson cautioned that Americans enlisting in the Louisiana project would "be hung, if they commd. hostilities agt. a nation at peace with the U.S.," then added significantly that he "did not care what insurrections should be excited in Louisiana." According to Genet, he indicated also that "a small spontaneous irruption of Kentuckians into New Orleans would advance" the treaty negotiations then going on in Spain and might help in persuading Spain to concede a treaty along lines suggested by the United States.

At Genet's request, Jefferson now revised a letter of introduction for Michaux to Governor Isaac Shelby of Kentucky. The original letter had recommended Michaux merely as a botanist, the revision implied that he had Jefferson's confidence. The Secretary of State did this even though he knew that Michaux was to carry manifestos calling for rebellion against

English rule in Canada and against Spanish rule in Louisiana as well as instructions for organizers of the invasion of Louisiana.[24]

I have no doubt that the Bemis and DeConde readings are correct. Even if we rely solely on Jefferson's own version, we know that Jefferson allowed Genet to converse with him, "not as Secy. of State, but as Mr. Jeff." A more fastidiously loyal Secretary of State would have shown the presumptuous envoy the door at that point. "Mr. Jeff." hung on in there, thus opening the door to conspiracy. It seems that, at this point, near the end of Jefferson's tenure as Secretary of State (he retired on 31 December 1793), "Mr. Jeff." is beginning to conduct a foreign policy of his own, separate from and at variance with the less-congenial policy he was constrained to carry out as Secretary of State in Washington's Cabinet. After Jefferson's retirement, Washington put a stop to these Western schemes.[25]

In encouraging Genet's Western projects, Jefferson may well have hoped to divert Genet from his unacceptable activities in the territory and in the territorial waters of the United States. If so, his hopes were going to be decisively dashed.

III

In July of 1793, most Americans were unaware that relations between their government and the Minister Plenipotentiary of the French Republic were under severe stress. The Democratic and Republican Societies, which had begun to swarm—with the active encouragement of Jefferson and Madison—even before Genet's arrival, took Genet rapturously to their bosom. The Fourth of July in 1793 was an occasion for many Republican manifestations, emphasizing the continuity and affinity of the American and French Revolutions, and celebrating French and American friendship. Federalists also had to have their Fourth of July celebrations, of course, but these were hundred-per-cent American things in that year as in others. For the modern reader considering reports of 4th July celebrations, the distinction may not always be clear, if only because one emblem had been common to both revolutions and could be used, in retrospect, to symbolize both or either; these two cases being as different as chalk from cheese. "Both" celebrations were Republican, in 1793. "Either" [meaning American only] celebrations were Federal. The emblem that could be common to the two types of celebration was the cap of liberty.

When I first read the report of how George Washington had joined in a celebration of 4th July 1793, I fancied for a moment that even Washington had succumbed to the Francophile frenzy of that summer. The report ran, "And in the town of Alexandria the President of the United States drank with his Virginia neighbours the toast 'Prosperity to the French Republic,' while the cap of liberty was placed above the American flag and a standard below bore a zestful effusion in praise of liberty."[26]

The toast is anodyne enough. What startles is that cap of liberty—until you remember that the cap in question had been an American emblem before it became a French one. But of course Washington's *Republican* Virginian neighbors—probably about half of the total—would see the cap of liberty as a symbol of the continuity of the two great revolutions, and could hope that Washington saw it in the same light. Actually, he didn't. That celebration in Alexandria was helpful to the Federalists, not the Republicans, for it adopted an address of confidence in Washington "as the virtuous leader of the Republic."[27]

Hardly any of Washington's Virginia neighbors could object to that, of course, but it carried with it an implied rebuke to the Republican press, then sniping at Washington's administration, and supportive of Genet.

If we accept Jefferson's date (5th July) for that "Louisiana" conversation, that was just on the eve of the episode that was eventually to lead to Genet's recall. This episode concerned a British ship known as *The Little Sarah,* which had been captured by Genet's *l'Embuscade* and renamed *La Petite Démocrate. La Petite Démocrate* had been brought to Philadelphia for its armaments to be augmented. How the story developed in early July 1793 is summarized by Harry Ammon:

> It was not until late on Saturday July sixth—the day after Jefferson's session with Genet—that Governor Mifflin reported that the *Petite Démocrate* was not only armed but that she was ready to sail with a crew of 120 including some American citizens. A special messenger was sent to Jefferson's summer home just outside the city, but it was too late in the day for him to return to the capital before the following morning. Concerned that the *Petite Démocrate* might depart before the Secretary of State could return and concerned about the repercussions of a direct defiance of presidential orders, Governor Mifflin, who was well disposed to the French cause, sent Alexander J. Dallas, the Pennsylvania Secretary of State, to ask Genet to detain the vessel, stressing the importance of holding the *Petite Démocrate* in port until Washington (then en route to the capital from Mount Vernon) should reach the city. Having been on friendly terms with the Minister, Dallas was appalled as Genet in a "great passion" refused to hold the ship in port and proclaimed his intention of defending the rights of France by an "appeal from the President to the people."

On Sunday, July 7, when Jefferson arrived in the city, he first conferred with Mifflin and Dallas before visiting the French Minister. The conference between the Secretary of State and Genet was a long and acrimonious session, doubly taxing for Jefferson who was far from well. When Jefferson asked that the ship be detained for a few days pending the President's return, Genet reacted angrily. "He took up the subject instantly in a very high tone," Jefferson reported to the President, "and went into an immense field of declamation and complaint. I found it necessary to let him go on, and in fact could do no otherwise; for the few efforts, which I made to take some part in the conversation were quite ineffectual." The Minister reviewed with interminable detail the arguments of his earlier protests. Jefferson finally broke in, as Genet, in a calmer tone, complained about the President's failure to summon Congress to determine the extent of American treaty obligations. When the Secretary explained that the interpretation of treaties was within the President's constitutional powers, the response was impertinent: "He [Genet] made me a bow, and said that indeed he would not make me his compliments on such a constitution, expressed the utmost astonishment at it, and seemed never before to have had such an idea." Since Genet appeared to "have come into perfect good humor and coolness," the Secretary "observed to him the impropriety of his conduct in persevering in measures contrary to the will of the government, and that too within its limits, wherein they unquestionably had the right to be obeyed." The French Minister had a right to protest, but once rulings were made he must obey the President's orders until he received additional instructions from France. Genet listened silently and Jefferson thought he had finally impressed him with the seriousness of the situation. Although Genet would not promise to detain the privateer, Jefferson accepted the Minister's statement that the *Petite Démocrate*, which would shortly move to a new anchorage, was not yet ready to put to sea, as an implicit commitment to keep her in port until the President arrived. He based this conclusion on Genet's "look and gesture, which showed that he meant I should understand she would not be gone before that time."[28]

On 9 July, while Knox, the Secretary for War, was arming a battery on Mud Island to prevent the departure of *La Petite Démocrate*—and vindicate American neutrality—Genet's prize slipped down the river and out of reach. On the same day, Genet wrote to Jefferson to tell him that *La Petite Démocrate* was about to sail, which it promptly did, its mission being to attack British shipping. After Jefferson had reported these proceedings to Washington (11 July), Washington was extremely angry, and with Jefferson as well as with Genet. It was, after all, Jefferson's reliance on "a look and gesture" of Genet's which had allowed *La Petite Démocrate* to slip away to sea.

The Cabinet was divided over what to do about Genet. Hamilton wanted the President to announce publicly his intention of requesting Genet's recall. Washington was reluctant to go so far, no doubt for fear of the consequences of provoking Jefferson's resignation, over transactions connected with the French Revolution. Jefferson's resignation, in such a context, would have had explosive repercussions throughout America in the summer of 1793. Neither Jefferson nor any other member of the Cabinet wanted that. In order to gain time, the Cabinet, on Jefferson's recommendation, decided to put a number of questions to the Supreme Court, leaving the matter of recall in suspense until they were answered.

Genet was shaken, but by no means chastened, by the repercussions of his defiance of the Government, and of Jefferson, in the matter of *La Petite Démocrate*. In a dispatch dated 31 July 1793, Genet writes:

> Mr. Jefferson is the only one I can regard as being on my side [*le seul dont j'aye à me louer*]. He is the object of the hatred of the President and of his Colleagues, although he has had the weakness to sign opinions which he condemns [*sic*], "privately." In any case, before long we shall be avenged: the representatives of the people are about to assemble, and it is from them that will come the thunderbolts which will lay our Enemies low [*qui terrasseront nos Ennemis*] and will positively electrify all America. . . . My real political campaign will open with the Congressional session, and it is then that you will judge your Agent.

One can imagine Jefferson shuddering if he had been able to read these lines. It would be impossible to think of a more disastrous Congressional lobbyist than Citizen Genet. The only safe way of maintaining American enthusiasm for the French Revolution was to keep the French Revolution at a distance, seen through a warm haze. Any whiff of the real thing was fatal. Genet's high-handed *modus operandi* kept providing such whiffs.

By early August, Washington was clearly very angry indeed, not only with Genet, but with the Republican press, and implicitly with Jefferson. In notes under the date 2 August, Jefferson gives an account of a Cabinet meeting. The relevant part of the account runs:

> Knox in a foolish incoherent sort of a speech introduced the Pasquinade lately printed, called the funeral of George W—n (Washington) and James W—n (Wilson); King & judge &c. where the President was placed on a guillotine. The Presidt was much inflamed, got into one of those passions

when he cannot command himself, ran on much on the personal abuse which had been bestowed on him, defied any man on earth to produce one single act of his since he had been in the govmt which was not done on the purest motives, that he had never repented but once the having slipped the moment of resigning his office, & that was every moment since, that *by god* he had rather be in his grave than in his present situation. That he had rather be on his farm than to be made *emperor of the world* and yet that they were charging him with wanting to be a king. That that *rascal Freneau* sent him 3 of his papers every day, as if he thought he would become the distributor of his papers, that he could see in this nothing but an impudent design to insult him. He ended in this high tone. There was a pause.[29]

That must have been an awkward pause. Everyone round that table knew the close working relationship between Jefferson and Philip Freneau, editor of the *National Gazette* (above, chapter 4). When Washington called Freneau a scoundrel, he was coming perilously close to calling *Jefferson* a scoundrel.

In the following week tempers were allowed to cool, when the Cabinet reached agreement in the matter of Genet's recall (after the Supreme Court had refused to give an opinion on the matter). Shortly before 12 August 1793, Washington approved Jefferson's recommendation that the request for Genet's recall be made in a moderately worded letter to the American Minister in Paris. This meant of course that Washington had decided to get Genet recalled, and that he had also decided to let Jefferson handle the matter in such a way as to do as little damage as possible to American relations with the French Republic.

On 18 August, Jefferson sent to Madison a copy of the draft of the message requesting Genet's recall. In his covering letter, Jefferson said, "The addresses in support of the proclmn. [of neutrality] are becoming universal, and as universal a rising in support of the President against Genet."[30] Jefferson added: "You are free to shew the enclosed to Colo. Monroe."

The implied message from the leader of the Republican Party to his chief lieutenants is clear: Genet is now more of an embarrassment to the Republican Party than he is to the administration. Leading Republicans are to prepare the minds of Party members for the news of the request for the recall, and to preempt any tendency to agitate in favor of Genet.

Meanwhile French ships in American ports were doing their best to introduce the French Revolution to America. At Boston in August the French ship *Concorde* exhibited a banner "proscribing" eleven prominent American citizens as "aristocrats" and enemies of France. Even for Amer-

Philip Morin Freneau, by Frederick Halpin. Freneau was editor, under Jefferson's patronage, of the *National Gazette* (founded 6 October 1791), whose pages reflected his "uncritical acceptance of all propaganda favourable to the progress of the revolution in France"—Julian P. Boyd. By August 1793, Washington had had more than enough of the French Revolution and of Philip Freneau. In a Cabinet conversation recorded by Thomas Jefferson, Washington called the editor of the *National Gazette* "that rascal Freneau" (TJ's notes, 2 August 1793; chapter 5, pp. 178–79).

ican Republican sympathizers, the French Revolution was coming much too close to America, in the late summer of 1793.[31]

On 25 August, Jefferson reinforced the message to Madison with a more explicit one to Monroe:

You will perceive by the enclosed papers that Genet has thrown down the gauntlet to the President by the publication of his letter & my answer, and is himself forcing that appeal to the public, & risking that disgust, which I had so much wished should have been avoided. The indications from different parts of the continent are already sufficient to shew that the mass of the republican interest has no hesitation to disapprove of this intermeddling by a foreigner, & the more readily as his object was evidently, contrary to his professions, to force us into the war. I am not certain whether some of the more furious republicans may not schismatize with him.[32]

Edmond Charles Genêt, by Gilles-Louis Chrétien, 1793. Engraving. Genet was first Minister Plenipotentiary of the French Republic to the United States (1793–94). "It is impossible for anything to be more affectionate, more magnanimous, than the purport of his mission"—Jefferson to Madison, 18 May 1793. "Never in my opinion, was so calamitous an appointment made, as that of the present minister of F. here"—Jefferson to Madison, 5 July 1793 (chapter 5, *passim*).

Monroe would not care to be associated with "the more furious republicans," though he was a little nearer to them than either Jefferson or Madison was.

"Schismatize": the religious type of invective hitherto applied solely to Federalists (and Burke) is here turned on Republican extremists. Jeffersonian Orthodoxy is shifting its center, under the pressure of the excessive proximity of the French Revolution.

The "gauntlet" that Genet had thrown down consisted of a letter Genet had addressed to the President and caused to be published, after a report that Genet had threatened an appeal to the President. According to Genet's dispatch of 15 August to his Citizen Minister:

> Up to now, the *Fayettiste* Washington has annulled all my efforts by his system of neutrality. . . . The friends and adherents [of England] in the Council, alarmed by the extreme popularity which I am enjoying, are spreading a rumor that I wish to stir up the Americans to revolt against their Government, and this weak Government, always afraid of the English,

would deserve such an appeal. . . . But as the thing [*le fait*] is false, I have just written to General Washington a very strong letter declaring that I ask him to render homage to the truth by declaring that I have never threatened him with anything of the kind [*d'une pareille demande*]. I am awaiting his response, which I shall make public, and soon afterwards I shall also publish my correspondence with M. Jefferson, a man endowed with good qualities, but weak enough to sign things which he does not think and to defend officially threats [*sic,* against Genet] which he condemns in his conversations and anonymous writings.[33]

On this letter Harry Ammon aptly comments:

All this must have baffled French officials, for the tone of previous dispatches and all his talk about the ultimate effect of public opinion gave the impression that he did plan some kind of appeal. After all was not the promised publication of his correspondence a plea for popular support? Genet seemed to be denying what in fact he was actually doing—seeking popular backing to override Washington's policies.[34]

What had angered and alarmed Genet was a letter which had appeared in the New York *Diary* (and was reprinted throughout the country) by Chief Justice John Jay and Senator Rufus King, who affirmed that Genet had threatened to disregard the President and appeal directly to the people.

The person to whom the threat was allegedly made was Alexander Dallas (Secretary of State of Pennsylvania) and the occasion was the imminent departure of *La Petite Démocrate* for Philadelphia. Dallas, who was a strong Republican, soon denied Genet had ever, in his presence, threatened such an appeal. But Jay and King knew themselves to be on strong ground. Dallas might deny the story, but *Jefferson* would not. Jefferson himself had reported to Washington on 10 July 1793 at the height of the *Petite Démocrate* affair: "On repeating to him [Governor Mifflin of Pennsylvania] and Mr. Dallas what M. Genet had said we found it agreed in many particulars with what he had said to Mr. Dallas; but Mr. Dallas mentioned some things which he [Genet] had not said to me, and particularly his [Genet's] declaration that he would appeal from the President to the people."[35] Anything Washington knew concerning Genet, Hamilton also knew at this time. And Hamilton must have briefed Jay and King. There was no such thing as Cabinet secrecy in Washington's divided Cabinet towards the close of his first term as President. Both Jefferson and Hamilton leaked away purposefully to their chosen confidants. Jay and King, devoted Federalists both, were in Hamilton's confidence. They knew the Republicans could not discredit their story, because it had been authenticated by Jefferson himself. Also, it was by now in Jefferson's interest that the story should be believed—and before the news of the Government's request for Genet's recall broke. Jefferson knew that he was in danger of being denounced by "the more furious republicans" for being a party to the request for Genet's recall—Genet being still hugely popular with the radical Republican rank and file. So it was expedient to spread the word that Genet had put himself out of court by threatening to appeal to the people against the President. In a letter to Madison on 1 September, Jefferson explicitly confirmed that Genet had made this threat: "You will see much said & again said, about G.'s threat to appeal to the people. I can assure you it is a fact."[36]

That did it, as far as Madison was concerned; Monroe followed, after some hesitation. Jefferson's leadership of the Republican Party was not shaken by the ditching of Genet, despite Genet's personal popularity among the rank and file: a popularity which he retained, in an inconsequential sort of way, right up to the end of his mission (January 1794). But all Republican *politicians* could see that Genet had become an embarrassment to the Party, after his threat to appeal to the people against the President had been made known, and once it was clear that the Party leaders were not in a position to challenge the truth of the report.

Some readers may wonder that so much should be made of that threat by Genet. After all, the main business of the Republican Party had been the mounting of an appeal to the people against policies of the Washington administration which Republicans found obnoxious. And Genet had been an enthusiastic—and in the beginning a most welcome—participant in this appeal to the people. As Meade Minnigerode put it:

> His drive from Charleston to Philadelphia had been an appeal to the people, every gesture from every balcony from which he had ever spoken had been an appeal to the people. Congress, the people—he assumed them to be synonymous, far more so than the President and the people. Every time that Jefferson advised him to wait for the new Congress, that was an implied appeal to the people; in every public address when he remarked on the sanctity of treaties, that was an actual appeal to the people; in his personal talk he must have expressed the thought on countless occasions. It was almost silly to make a fuss over any one individual instance, when his whole procedure was a continuous appeal to the people.[37]

The answer is that Genet's threat, through Dallas, was unacceptable for two reasons. First, it was *explicit* in that it was against Washington personally and named him. Second, it was *by a foreigner,* not an American.

The Republican campaign against certain policies that were central to Washington's administration had been carefully conducted, under Jefferson's guidance, in such a manner as to spare Washington personally, and even to treat him with great outward respect. The *identified* targets were Hamilton and Adams and their friends. It was the age-old tactic of the politic and dissatisfied: "The King is great and good, but he is surrounded by evil counsellors." The equally age-old question—"If the King is so great and good, why then does he keep on these evil counsellors?"—was left unanswered, in the age-old way. That was the politic way to conduct an appeal to the people and the politic way was also the Jeffersonian way. Genet's frontal attack was therefore a blunder, in terms of Republican strategy.

Also—the second reason—it was doubly a blunder because it was perpetrated by a foreigner, the most conspicuous foreigner in America at the time. Jefferson knew that the Republican Party would be ruined if it appeared to follow a foreigner in a personal frontal attack, on the best loved of all Americans, then President of the United States. That is just what the Hamiltonians hoped to see—as witness that little letter of John Jay and Rufus King—and that is what had to be averted at all costs. So Jefferson prepared, with as much expedition as prudence would permit, to jettison the man who was still the darling of the Republican press and of the Democratic and Republican Societies: Citizen Charles-Edmond Genet.

Genet's "gauntlet"—in the shape of his letter to the President—reached the Secretary of State at a time when that official was still working on the draft of the letter requesting Genet's recall, a matter of which Genet still knew nothing. Jefferson may have permitted himself a smile when he received Genet's letter. That letter—and above all Genet's publication of it—made things easier for Jefferson, by demonstrating to Republicans that Genet was impossible to deal with. Genet's threat to appeal to the people against the President had been unacceptable, but his appeal to the President to confirm that Genet had never threatened to appeal to the people against the President was ridiculous. Jefferson's reply of 16 August—which was published in the New York *Daily Advertiser* on 22 August and in the *Gazette of the United States* on 24 August—breathed disdain for Genet and deference for the President: just what the political conjuncture required:

The President . . . has received the letter . . . addressed to him, . . . and I am desired to observe to you that it is not the established course for the diplomatic characters residing here to have any direct correspondence with him. The Secretary of State is the organ through which their communications should pass. The President does not conceive it to be within the line of propriety or duty for him to bear evidence against a declaration which, whether made to him or others, is perhaps immaterial: he therefore declines interfering in the case.[38]

This was written on the same day that the Secretary of State sent off to Gouverneur Morris the letter requesting Genet's recall. Thomas Jefferson was finished with Citizen Genet.

Jefferson has been charged with perfidy over his dealings with Genet. Meade Minnigerode, having correctly identified Jefferson's report to Washington of Genet's "threat" (made in the presence of Dallas) as the breaking point for Genet, goes on to describe this action as "neither sincere nor candid, because it was only intended to serve a timely purpose, to ruin Genet, behind his back, now that Jefferson was afraid of him."[39] It is quite true that, in passing on that information, Jefferson knew that he was doing Genet a bit of no good. But by the time he passed on that information, Jefferson owed Genet absolutely nothing. In the matter of the sailing of La Petite Démocrate, Genet had deliberately flouted the authority of the Government of the United States, and ignored the urgent pleas made to him by Jefferson to refrain from acting in such a wantonly provocative manner. After that, why should Jefferson not wash his hands of this wildly undiplomatic envoy? It is true that Jefferson was, by now, "afraid" of Genet but only in the sense that Genet was fast becoming an incubus to the Republican Party and the Republican cause. And it was surely the duty of the Republican leader to get rid of such an incubus— if it could be done diplomatically, which it was.

Attentive readers of this book, who have got this far, will have noticed that I am not in agreement with the pious Jeffersonians who assume that Thomas Jefferson was incapable of duplicity. There can be very few successful politicians who have suffered from such an incapacity, and I do not find that Thomas Jefferson was disadvantaged in this particular way.

In 1792–93 Washington and Hamilton had plenty of reason to complain about Jefferson's duplicity, in covertly masterminding a press and propaganda campaign against policies pursued by an administration of which Jefferson himself was a member. But I can't see that Genet has much cause for complaint. Jefferson had helped Genet as far as he could, until Genet himself, through his French Revolutionary assumptions and arrogance, had put it out of Jefferson's power to help him any more.

There are no good grounds for finding fault with Jefferson's handling of the recall of Genet, as a political and diplomatic transaction. But the connection of this transaction with Jefferson's mystical vision of the French Revolution is another matter. Since 1789, Jefferson had seen the French Revolution as a providential instrument for the regeneration of America, in terms of the ideals of the Declaration of Independence: ideals of which Jefferson felt himself to be the custodian. In the light of that mystical concept of the relationship between the American and French Revolutions, the mission of Citizen Genet—which Jefferson had warmly welcomed in May of 1793—had to be tinged with sacral associations. That May, Citizen Genet, on his progress from Charleston to Philadelphia, through the cheering throngs of American Republicans, must have appeared, for some weeks, as a kind of political Messiah. And it must be a tricky business, psychologically speaking, to find yourself claiming that the Messiah has exceeded his instructions, and demanding the recall of the Messiah: a tricky business, psychologically as well as theologically.

In his retirement at Monticello, in 1794, Jefferson must occasionally have wakened at dawn to hear the cock crow. If the mystic in Jefferson still lingered, he may have found it hard to repress a mental picture of Peter denying Christ.

There was also another side to all this, affecting Jefferson's conception of the French Revolution itself. The French Revolution had given Genet his instructions and sent him to America. But then the French Revolution had recalled Genet (at Jefferson's request) and would have guillotined him (had not Washington intervened). Could this really be the *same* French Revolution? From 1789 to 1793, Jefferson had been insisting on the continuity and consistency of the French Revolution. But by the end of 1793 the "polar star" seems to be shifting a bit. All in all, the passage of the Genet meteor through the American skies must have been a devastating experience within the psyche of Thomas Jefferson.

Jefferson's handling of the Genet case was politically skillful and in every way appropriate; in the daylight world of politics, that is, and leaving aside the mystical and psychological dimensions. What was wildly inappropriate, *in American terms,* was Genet's arrogant treatment of Washington and Jefferson. But Genet's treatment of these Americans was entirely legitimate (if unfortunate) in terms both of his instructions and of the value system of the French Revolution. Within that value system, Washington and Jefferson were no more than petty local officials, to whom duties could be assigned, on behalf of the French Revolution, which they were then bound to carry out without question. In the majestic hierarchy of Liberty, people like Washington and Jefferson ranked—though they did not realize this—far, far below that awesome figure, the representative of the French Revolution itself.

According to the peculiar terminology and ideology of the French Revolution, Washington and Jefferson were—as long as they behaved themselves—*patriotes* belonging to *républiques soeurs.* Both were terms of art. *Patriotes,* in French Revolutionary usage, is a much more precise term than "patriots" in English. A *patriote* in any country is a person who puts the interests of the French Revolution first, absolutely and in all circumstances. It's *not* a question of putting the interests of France ahead of one's own country (as a Federalist might see it). The reality is that no country has any legitimate interests of its own, as distinct from those of the French Revolution. It is the French Revolution which defines what the legitimate interests of all countries are, and lays down the lines on which those interests are to be pursued. A *patriote,* in any country, was a person who understood and accepted this relationship.

Similarly, a *république soeur* was a country which unreservedly submitted to the French Revolution, *la soeur ainée, la grande nation.* In Europe all the *républiques soeurs* were deemed to have been liberated by the French Revolutionary armies, and were governed by local *patriotes,* who had established their credentials as such to the satisfaction of French Revolutionary officers. The most prized characteristic of a local *patriote* was gratitude to the French, for having liberated him. This gratitude was expected to be expressed with deferential fervor. Thus when a French Revolutionary army liberated a small town in Belgium, the Belgian *patriotes,* of course, came out to welcome them. All then sang the Marseillaise, but the French soldiers sang it standing up while the local *patriotes* sang it on their knees, in homage to their liberators. That was the kind of thing that was expected of a *patriote* in a *république soeur.*

In the perspective of French Revolutionary ideology and terminology, the United States presented a distressing anomaly. From the noises you heard in the streets, you might think this was a *république soeur,* brimming over with enthusiastic *patriotes.* But when you stayed around for a while, you found this was not so at all. The people who had the greatest reputation as *patriotes*—Washington and Jefferson—were deficient in the most basic characteristic of a *patriote*—unquestioning submission to the will of the French Revolution. They did not even seem to understand that submission was what the French Revolution required of them. Thus, in the affair of *La Petite Démocrate,* Washington and Jefferson saw Genet as defying the authority of the United States. But Genet, with equal sincerity, saw Washington and Jefferson as defying the only legitimate authority that existed, and applied universally, that of the French Revolution. No *république soeur* could have any authority that could avail against that of the French Revolution. The thing was preposterous.

Again, this was not just Charles-Edmond Genet speaking. It was the French Revolution speaking through Genet, and also through his colleagues, the consular agents. Minnigerode gives examples of revolutionary consular utterances:

> Gentlemen who, like the Consul at New York in the midst of the controversies over shipping, spoke of Jefferson as "this Minister of a day and of a Republic that owes us the light of day," who "dares to speak to men representing the most powerful nation on earth in the language of the old tyrants," and instructed the Secretary of State in person to address his complaints and "threats" henceforth to the French Minister. Or, like the Consul at Philadelphia, announced to the world that "no authority on earth has either the right or the power to interpose between the French nation and her enemies;" that "she alone is arbitress and judge of the offensive acts which . . . she is forced to commit against the despotic governments [confederated] to plunge her again into [that] slavery from which she alone has been able to free herself, although abandoned by her friends;" and that police seizure of French prizes by the courts of Pennsylvania in accordance with the President's orders was a procedure "hitherto unheard of," inaugurating what could only be a diplomatic discussion "by an arbitrary act of violence and by military execution."[40]

Thomas Jefferson had admired the French Revolution from afar before 1793, and he would continue to admire it from afar after 1793, though more circumspectly and more tepidly than before. But when the French Revolution actually visited the United States in 1793, in the person of those Girondin envoys led by Citizen Genet, Jefferson neither understood nor admired it, and the French Revolution neither understood nor admired *him*.

By the late summer of 1793, Genet personally was no longer a factor to be reckoned with, for Jefferson, but there remained the question of how to cope with the legacy of Genet. Basically, this was a matter of the management of the French Revolution as an issue in American politics. The Republicans needed to keep American enthusiasm for the French Revolution alive—as one of their major assets in their political war with the Federalists—but they also needed to keep it within bounds and leave the unfortunate Genet interlude behind them.

From late July on, the Hamiltonians—profiting from the repercussions of the *Petite Démocrate* episode—had been on the offensive and carrying out their own version of "an appeal to the people" with considerable élan, through public meetings and anti-Genet resolutions accompanied by a press campaign.[41] On 17 August the Hamiltonians carried the war to the capital of Virginia. A meeting in Richmond on that date strongly endorsed Washington's proclamation of neutrality and condemned "all attempts of foreign diplomats to communicate with the people except through the Executive." Madison and Monroe set out to counter the Hamiltonian offensive with belligerently anti-Federalist resolutions. Jefferson quickly called them to order. To get Genet forgotten, the Republican resolutions needed to be *basically similar* to those of the Hamiltonians, and different only in emphasis. Madison and Monroe complied. The Republican resolutions, like the Hamiltonian ones, would be warmly supportive of the President and include a statement affirming "the principle that foreign diplomats must conduct their negotiations with the executive" and refrain from "appeals to the people." With those points safely embodied, the resolutions could afford to be expressive of gratitude to France for past help, and of appreciation of the French alliance (of 1778–83).

Jefferson's deft handling of "the war of the resolutions" is evidence of the control he could exercise over his own party, in a time of difficulty and danger, and of his skill in damage limitation. As a political general, he had withdrawn his army in good order from an untenable patch of territory. Hamilton had won that battle, but Jefferson would win the war, seven years later. The pragmatist Jefferson, that is. The mystic Jefferson is not dead but in occultation after the summer of 1793.

When Congress met in December 1793, Genet appealed to it, as he had been threatening for so many months to do. His appeal fell completely flat. The Republicans had dropped him, at a signal from Jefferson, and the Federalists had never had any use for him. Several Congressmen—including Madison—did receive him, with noncommittal civility. Vice President Adams, the earliest declared and unrepentant American foe of the French Revolution, agreed to see him. Adams was singularly lacking in rancor—he forgave Jefferson for the *Rights of Man* episode. He also had a tendency to find French people rather diverting (especially those of advanced opinions). So Adams saw Genet and wrote about him in a letter to his daughter, Abigail Adams Smith. Adams described Genet as a "young gentleman of much ingenuity, lively wit and brilliant imagination, enamoured to distraction with republican liberty; very crude and inaccurate in his ideas of a republic and as yet totally uninformed about the operations of the human heart and the progress of the passions in public assemblies."[42]

On 11 October 1793—a week before the execution of the Queen of France—the Committee of Public Safety agreed to the American request for the recall of Genet. The news of Genet's recall, by the French authority, reached Philadelphia in mid-January 1794. For Jefferson and the Republicans this was a most happy outcome to the affair (at the level of daylight politics, for Jefferson). For Jefferson it meant that *the French Revolution itself* had approved his request for the recall of Genet, so that not even the most "furious" Republican could now claim that that request represented any kind of desertion of the French Revolution. For Republicans in general, the recall proved that Genet had indeed exceeded his instructions. Those who argued in that sense ignored the fact that the government which had recalled Genet was different from the one which had given him his instructions. So different indeed, that the one which recalled him had already guillotined all those who had given him his instructions. But American admirers of the French Revolution were not (generally speaking) curious about such transient and sordid details.

Genet, although recalled at Washington's request, remained in America, under Washington's protection. The new Jacobin Government demanded his arrest and deportation, but *le vieux Washington,* that miserable *Fayettiste,* refused because he knew that if Genet returned to France he would meet with the same fate as those who had given him the instructions which he had followed all too faithfully.

So Citizen Genet, alone of the Girondin elite, survived the triumph of the Jacobins. He married his Cornelia and lived peacefully in America for the rest of his days, without ever returning to France. There is no record that he ever expressed any gratitude to the man whom he had defied and maligned, and who in return had saved his life. But then, according to Genet's ideas, it was *Washington* who had been ungrateful—to France, which had liberated him, along with all the other ungrateful Americans. France was wonderful, when contemplated from America. Genet and Jefferson could still agree on that much.

SIX

THE LINGERING END OF THE LONG AFFAIR

Jefferson and the French Revolution

after Genet's Mission

1794–1800

Jefferson retired as Secretary of State on 31 December 1793. In January 1794 the news reached Philadelphia of the executions in Paris, in the previous October, of Queen Marie Antoinette, Madame Roland, and twenty Girondists.[1]

On 22 February 1794—Washington's sixty-third birthday—Genet's mission formally terminated. On the following day, the new Minister for the French Republic, Joseph Fauchet, presented his credentials. Fauchet was well received, his instructions from Robespierre's Committee of Public Safety being most satisfactory to Washington's administration. On behalf of the Committee, Fauchet disavowed "the criminal conduct of Genet and his accomplices," forbade all Frenchmen from violating American neutrality, and dismissed all the Consuls who had earlier taken part in arming privateers. Support for the western operations started by Genet (and abetted by Jefferson) was also withdrawn. The only part of Fauchet's instructions that was unacceptable was the request for the arrest and deportation of Genet himself—refused by Washington for humanitarian reasons—and Fauchet did not press this point.

The conciliatory attitude of the Committee of Public Safety towards the United States might seem at variance with the Terror then raging in France, on the orders of the same Committee, but in fact the conciliation of America and the Terror are cognate phenomena. Both reflect the same reality: the fact that Revolutionary France is under siege. A year later, Fauchet's successor, the Thermidorian envoy, Pierre-Auguste Adet, succinctly recalled the situation of Revolutionary France as it had been at the time of Fauchet's arrival:

It was in February 1794 that [Fauchet] arrived in America; France torn by terrorism, La Vendée in the paroxysm of its devastation, Toulon in the power of the English, the Austrians pushing their light troops into the Department of the Aisne, and already masters of Le Quesnoi, Valenciennes and Condé—such was the situation of the French Republic, as it then appeared in the American public press.[2]

In that forbidding situation, the great Committee of Public Safety, under the guidance of Robespierre and St. Just, pursued external and internal policies designed to reduce the number and the power of its enemies. The external policy was to conciliate those countries with which Revolutionary France was not actually at war. The most important of these countries was the United States, now valued mainly as a source of grain for the besieged French Republic. The internal policy was the Terror. The Terror was not directed mainly at aristocrats (in the sense of nobles), since almost all of these either had been killed already or had fled the country. It was directed at a number of stigmatized categories, including deviant revolutionaries of various tendencies: peasants suspected of hoarding grain; speculators and war profiteers, and—mingling with all the other categories—spies, *les agents de Pitt.*

Foreign sympathizers with the French Revolution, whom the Girondins had taken to their bosom, were automatically suspect to the Jacobins: potential *agents de Pitt,* every one of them. Many of them went to the guillotine, after June 1793. These included the most celebrated of the cosmopolitan French Revolutionaries, the Prussian-born Anacharsis Clootz, who had brought a many-hued "delegation of the human race" to the bar of the Convention, amid scenes of Girondin enthusiasm. All that was out, under the Jacobins. Tom Paine himself was suspect. As well as being a foreign sympathizer with the Revolution—in itself a suspect condition by now—Paine belonged in a specific category now found to be counter-revolutionary: *la faction des indulgents.* This meant that Paine had, with great courage, argued and voted in the National Convention against the execution of Louis XVI. Paine was imprisoned under the Jacobin Terror and would probably have been executed had he not been saved by the fall and death of Robespierre in July 1794.

The Jacobins, who hounded down those foreign sympathizers with the Revolution who had taken up residence in France, had nothing much against those foreign sympathizers with the French Revolution who had had the sense to remain where they belonged, in their own countries. Not much *against* these people, but not much *for* them, either. Fauchet's instructions from the Committee of Public Safety, unlike those of his predecessor from the Girondin Executive Council, resemble those of a conventional non-Revolutionary diplomatist.[3] Fauchet (and colleagues associated with him) are instructed "to observe scrupulously the forms laid down for official communications between the President of the United States and foreign representatives, and to refrain from any move [*aucune démarche*] which could offend free Americans with regard to the form of Government which they have established for themselves."

In practice: no popular demonstrations, no direct encouragement of the Democratic and Republican Societies; no anonymous contributions to the Republican press; nothing whatever that could carry the slightest whiff of Genet about it. In its Jacobin phase, the French Revolution is not for export.

In one of his early dispatches (signed also by three associates), Fauchet analyzes what had gone wrong under his predecessor:

> Here are reflections on reading of the plans, projects and operations of Citizen Genet. It seems that he came out vigorously in favor of a party opposed to the Government of the United States, and that he even encouraged that party to become more vehement in its opposition [*qu'il a même exaspéré ce parti*]. That he offended all the leaders of the Executive Power, without considering the consequences of his acts [*sans examen*]. We thought we could observe, in several of those whom he used to see, or with whom he was in correspondence, more hatred of Washington than love of France. In others, we saw a real enthusiasm for the cause of liberty. These last are faithful to principle, not men, as they made clear to us [Jefferson is probably included in this last category]. And what have been the results of Genet's Excesses [*son Exagération*] and those of his agents? Divisions which could have become fatal to America and France, the desertion of all the dispassionate persons [*les gens sans passion*] who up to then had been friends of France, and who are rallying to her cause, since our arrival here. [Under Genet] decent people, our soldiers, our officers, our frank and faithful Republicans, when they heard French officials proclaim that the American Government was Aristocratic, that it had sold out to the English etc., went around everywhere repeating and even improving on the language of the Ministers and the Consuls. . . . [It's not easy to] persuade these people that, in a neutral country, we must refrain from making judgments—favorable or unfavorable—on the laws which govern it, that each People is entitled to the Government it chooses for itself; that it is the insistence on converting other Peoples before finishing our own revolution that has brought down so many evils upon us. If you try to tell them all that, these people think you don't love your country. The conduct of the Consuls was every-

where the same. Suppose they make a demand contrary to the laws of the Country, and suppose it is refused? Immediately off they go protesting, yelling about Anglomania and accusing the Government of taking the side of the English. [However] the Proclamation indicated in our instructions, which forbids all Frenchmen to violate the neutrality of the territory of the United States, has had the best possible effect.[4]

With such instructions and such dispositions, Fauchet, in shining contrast with his predecessor, made an excellent impression on Washington's administration. Madison reported on this development, from Philadelphia, to Jefferson, now in Monticello, and ostensibly in retirement (and mostly really also, for 1794). Madison is obviously not altogether pleased by the sudden, dramatic improvement in the climate of Franco-American relations. He writes:

> Genèt [*sic*] has been superseded by Fauchèt [*sic*], the Secretary to the Executive Council. The latter has not been here long eno' to develope his temper and character. He has the aspect of moderation. His account of things in France is very favorable on the whole. He takes particular pains to assure all who talk with him of the perseverance of France in her attachment to us, and her anxiety that nothing which may have taken place, may lessen it on our side. In his interview with the President, he held the same language; and I am told by E. R. [Edmund Randolph, TJ's successor as Secretary of State] that the P. not only declared explicitly his affectionate solicitude for the success of the Republic, but after he had done so with great emphasis, desired, in order to be as pointed as possible, that his expressions might be repeated, by E. R. who acted as Interpreter. Fauchet does not speak our language. La Forest comes over with the Minister as Consul General: And Petry, formerly Consul of S.C. as Consul for this place. The political characters of these gentlemen as heretofore understood, give some uneasiness to the Republican party; and the uneasiness has been increased by the homage paid by the leaders of the other party to the new Minister. They may probably aim at practising on him, by abusing the madness of Genèt and representing the Republicans as rather his partisans, than the friends of the French cause. But if he is not an uncommon fool, or a traytor, it is impossible he can play into their hands, because the Anglicism stamped on the aristocratic faction must warn him of its hostility to his objects.[5]

It is symptomatic of the condition of Republican values and feelings at this time that Madison should be preparing to regard the diplomatic representative of a foreign power as a potential "traytor" (to the French

Republic) if he should remain on friendly terms with the Government of the United States. But Madison's concern is understandable. As a factor in American politics, American enthusiasm for the French Revolution was of service to the Republicans only if relations between the French Republic and Washington's administration were known to be strained. That enthusiasm continued through 1794, as Fauchet himself observed. But what good was that enthusiasm to the Republican cause if it was enthusiasm for a version of the French Revolution which was known to be on excellent terms with the Federalists in power in Washington? From a Republican point of view, the arrival of Citizen Fauchet, replacing Citizen Genet, after the retirement of Jefferson as Secretary of State, presented a most unwelcome paradox. The Federal administration was now entirely under Federalist control. And it was on much better terms with the representatives of the French Revolution than the administration had been in which the best-known American admirer of the French Revolution, Thomas Jefferson, had been Secretary of State. This was in no way Jefferson's fault, of course. If it was anyone's fault, it was the fault of the French Revolution itself, with its abrupt and savage contortions and changes of course. But that thought was still unutterable, though not perhaps unthinkable, to American Republicans with their heavy baggage of rhetorical commitment to that holy but unpredictable cause.

Jefferson was more philosophical about the transformation in Franco-American official relations than Madison could be. Jefferson acknowledged receipt of Madison's letter of 2 March—along with three other Madison letters—in a letter dated "Monticello, April 3, 1794." In this letter, Jefferson does not refer to Fauchet, Genet, the execution of Brissotins—all topics referred to by Madison—or advert to any other aspect of the French Revolution. An implicit reply, of a general character, is contained in the last paragraph of this letter of Jefferson's:

> I have never seen a Philadelphia paper since I left it, till those you inclosed me; and I feel myself so thoroughly weened from the interest I took in the proceedings there, while there, that I have never had a wish to see one, and believe that I never shall take another newspaper of any sort. I find my mind totally absorbed in my rural occupations. We are suffering much for want of rain. Tho' now at the 3d. of April, you cannot distinguish the wheat feilds of the neighborhood yet from hence. Fruit is hitherto safe. We have at this time some prospect of rain. Asparagus is just come to table. The Lilac in blossom, and the first Whip-poor-will heard last night.[6]

It would be a mistake to attribute Jefferson's apparently apolitical stance at this time to affectation. One of the sources of Jefferson's greatness as a political leader is his capacity to be *genuinely* apolitical—and happily so—at times when, as in the first half of 1794, political activity on his part would be unlikely to serve any useful purpose. (The next Presidential election was still more than two years away.) This capacity of his derived from the great strength and versatility of his interests outside of politics. Unlike most other politicians, Jefferson was never bored or fretful when away from the political arena. He had too many other interests for that: farming, building, scientific and technological inquiry, his collections of books and works of art, his nail factory at Monticello. He could think about politics all the more effectively because he did not have to think about it all the time. These capacities and propensities gave to his political leadership its distinctive style, based on a capacity to wait unobtrusively, for as long as necessary, and then pounce decisively.

Jefferson's enjoyment of nonpolitical life at Monticello was genuine, but Monticello was also strategically placed for the consolidation of Jefferson's Virginian power base. National politics were unpropitious, and likely to remain so, for most of Washington's second administration, but Virginian politics, unobtrusively pursued, were congenial, and could be rewarding. As James Monroe's biographer writes, concerning the period immediately following Jefferson's return to Monticello:

> Jefferson had realized that the leadership of the great opposition party could best be exercised by a man not hampered by the restraints of official position. And he knew, too, that if ever the young liberal party needed strong leadership it was now, in the moment of crisis precipitated by Genêt's ill-advised patriotism. By the middle of October, Jefferson was back in Virginia and in full control of the local situation. At Monticello, the spermaceti candles burned late into the night as Jefferson sat with Monroe and Madison discussing the strategy to be followed in Philadelphia and Richmond.[7]

I believe that, by refraining from all comment on the "French Revolution" aspects of Madison's letter, Jefferson is silently conveying a political message: that the French Revolution is unlikely to be a particularly rewarding topic for the Republican leadership for some time to come. Also, I don't think Jefferson himself now finds the French Revolution as attractive a topic as it has formerly been. This was partly, but not entirely, due to the *arrière-goût* of the Genet affair. But there was also the question—probably more deeply worrying—of the relation of the French Revolution to the successful slave revolution in Saint-Domingue in July 1793. This question is examined in chapter 7. So, probably for both political and personal reasons, Jefferson shows no interest in what Madison has to say about Fauchet.

Madison was basing his hopes for Fauchet on the assumption that Fauchet (if not a fool or a "traytor") must soon be repelled by the "Anglican" tone of the "aristocratic faction." These hopes were not fulfilled. Fauchet continued to get on well with the Federalists, and came to admire Washington and Hamilton. As for the "Anglicism" constantly attributed by Republicans to Federalists, Fauchet could see that this consisted of no more than a strong and rational desire not to be embroiled in war with Britain. But Fauchet's instructions did not require him to try to embroil the United States in war with Britain. On the contrary, they required of him, most strictly and precisely, to see to it that American neutrality was fully respected by all the French who might be in, or come to, the United States.

As long as Fauchet obeyed these instructions—which he punctiliously did for as long as he believed those who had given him his instructions to be still in power—he would have no trouble with the "Anglicanism" attributed to the Federalists.

Madison was also wrong in supposing—as he appeared to do—that the assumptions and tone of the "aristocratic faction" would necessarily grate on the revolutionary sensibilities of the envoy of the Jacobins. True, the words "aristocracy" and "aristocrats" were anathema to the Jacobins, just as they had been to the Girondins. But conceptually—as distinct from lexically—the Jacobins were themselves aristocrats. They were aristocrats in the original etymological sense of the word aristocracy: "the rule of the best." Like all other healthy aristocrats, the Jacobins believed that they themselves were the best, and that that gave them the right to rule.

The Jacobins were an aristocracy of a special kind: an elite of *virtue*. The Jacobins continued to speak of *"la liberté,"* as all previous generations of French Revolutionaries had done. But under the Jacobins, it is understood that *la liberté* must always be associated with *la vertu*. And the virtuous, who alone had the right to define what *la liberté* must entail, were a minority. Robespierre himself, accepted by all Jacobins as the embodiment of *la vertu,* is explicit on that point. In one of those fulminating aphorisms of his, in the manner of his mentor Jean-Jacques Rousseau, Robespierre proclaimed: *"La vertu est toujours en minorité sur la terre."*

The Jacobins, then, regarded themselves as an elite minority, entitled by their superior moral character, courage, and abilities (*la vertu* subsumed all three) to rule over the rest of the people, for their own good. These views were not altogether dissimilar to those held by John Adams and Alexander Hamilton, in relation to their own role in American society. We do not know whether leading Federalists were aware of this ideological resemblance, but they clearly found the Jacobin *style*—which was that of a self-conscious elite—a refreshing change from Girondin rabble-rousing. The Jacobin style was cool and reserved, distrustful of enthusiasm; more like an English-speaking gentleman than a gushing, gesticulating Frenchman. So Federalists and Jacobins got on quite well in America.

Fauchet was a good diplomatist; one of the best, whether French or American, whom we encounter in the course of this story. As a good diplomatist should, he cultivated the opposition as well as the ruling party, but with discretion, and without abetting their political efforts. He took to James Madison, in particular, seeing in him a shining representative of the American branch of an international elite of virtue, represented in France by the Jacobins. Moved by this conception he paid to James Madison the highest compliment that could be offered by a Jacobin representative. In a dispatch to his Minister in June 1794, Fauchet referred to *"Madison le Robespierre des Etats Unis."*[8] Fortunately, the Federalists never learned of this.

I referred earlier to the rather widespread assumption that Americans were at first attracted to the French Revolution by its early idealism, but later repelled by its excesses. In general, this assumption doesn't fit very well, but it is particularly hard to accommodate it to the realities of Franco-American relations in the first half of 1794. This was a particularly halcyon period for Franco-American relations both at official and popular levels. Officially, the Jacobin envoy of the Committee of Public Safety had been made welcome, and relations between Paris and Philadelphia were smoother than during any other phase of the existence of the French Republic. At the popular level, manifestations of enthusiasm for the French Revolution continued on a grand scale, as Citizen Fauchet noted with satisfaction, though without joining in.

As far as Franco-American relations were concerned, everything in the garden was fine. Yet throughout this very period, in France itself the Terror was at its height, and Americans were aware of this, from the first month of 1794 on. If ever there was a time to be revolted by the excesses of the French Revolution, that period was the first half of 1794, when those excesses had become the norm. Federalists may have been revolted, but if any Republicans were, none of them showed it at the time.

News of the Terror does not seem to have caused any appreciable diminution in popular enthusiasm for the French Revolution from the extremely high levels that enthusiasm had attained in 1793. Fauchet was only one of many observers who had noted this. And the enthusiasm continued into the second half of 1794. Moreau de St. Méry, a French emigré, has left a record of the 1794 Fourth of July celebration in New York:

July 4, 1794. From the house of Talleyrand and Beaumetz at the side of the square facing the house of Governor Clinton in Broadway, we saw the annual fête of American independence. The Governor and the people who accompanied him in this fête were preceded by a long procession of French Jacobins, marching two by two, singing the *Marseillaise* and other republican songs. Both times, going to the fête and bringing the Governor back from it, they interrupted themselves to address invectives to us in the windows where they saw us, Talleyrand, Beaumetz, Cazenove, La Colombe, Baron de la Roche and me. The Minister of France to the United States, Genêt, brother of Mme. Campan, was in the procession; and sang and insulted us like all the others.

We wept for our country and for him![9]

That was five days before the fall of Robespierre. It seems clear that no atrocities the French Revolutionaries could commit, in France itself, had the power to tarnish the *idea* of the French Revolution, enshrined immaculately in the minds and hearts of good American Republicans. Much of this was a simple nationalist reflex: the French were fighting the British, so it was patriotic to cheer for the French. To be affected by news of French atrocities was *un*patriotic. Most of the alleged atrocities were deemed to have been made up by the British (a line Jefferson had adopted as early as October 1789). In other cases, the alleged victims deserved no pity. They were traitors and spies, in the pay of the British. American Republicans were not repelled by reports of the excesses of the French Revolutionaries during 1794. Most Republicans chose not to believe those reports. A few condoned the severities of the French Revolutionaries, and suggested that something of the kind might not be amiss in America, in dealing with those "Monocrats" and "Anglomen" around George Washington.

Federalists had their own reasons for not "overreacting" (as we would now say) to the reported excesses. Federalists had disliked and feared American enthusiasm for the French Revolution since early 1791, when Alexander Hamilton first realized how Jefferson and his friends were exploiting that enthusiasm as a weapon against the Federalists. That enthusiasm had reached a climax early in 1793, with the news of war between Britain and France, and the arrival of Citizen Genet. After that, the fall of the Girondins, and their destruction at the hands of the Jacobins, provided a respite for America, and for Washington's government in particular. It is true that the Jacobins were doing unspeakable things in France—and Federalists had no doubt of the truth of the reports—but they were scrupulously correct in all their diplomatic dealings with

America. Washington's government was content to settle for that. Protests against Revolutionary excesses would have brought a satisfactory phase in Franco-American relations to an abrupt end, would have been unpopular with most Americans, and would have benefited the American Republicans. (Nor would they have been likely to check or mitigate the Terror.) No prudent government would have embarked on a cause fraught with such adverse consequences, both domestic and international. Washington's government was an eminently prudent one. Franco-American relations remained entirely satisfactory during the entire period of the Terror, from the time when its existence became known in America to its end (January 1794 to July 1794). It was only *after* the fall of Robespierre that Franco-American relations again deteriorated.

Moreau de St. Méry, an astute observer, resident in America throughout this period, believed that Robespierre had actually been *popular* with Americans generally, because the American economy benefited from the wave of emigration caused by the Jacobin Terror:

> As for Americans of all classes and all conditions, they expressed sincere sorrow for Robespierre and were filled with consternation at his loss. This was their reason why:
>
> *Robespierre made France uninhabitable for all the French. Every man, every gold piece, escaped at the earliest moment, and both took refuge with us, who are in need of men, of money, of industry. Consider, therefore, how the death of such a one will harm us!*
>
> I heard this view uttered a hundred times with a frankness which never made it any easier to tolerate.[10]

However that may be, it is clear that the revulsion of Americans from the excesses of the French Revolution, so often assumed as a fact, did not actually manifest itself, to any significant extent, during the period in which these excesses were at their height.

I

Let us now consider Jefferson's recorded utterances with a bearing on the French Revolution in the period between his retirement as Secretary of State (31 December 1793) and his election as Vice President of the United States (November 1796).

In this period, Jefferson's direct references to the French Revolution are few. In the whole of 1794, there is only one such reference. It is in a letter of May 1794 to a Pennsylvanian, Tench Coxe, then an ally of Jefferson's:

Your letters give a comfortable view of French affairs, and later events seem to confirm it. Over the foreign powers I am convinced they will triumph completely, & I cannot but hope that that triumph, & the consequent disgrace of the invading tyrants, is destined, in the order of events, to kindle the wrath of the people of Europe against those who have dared to embroil them in such wickedness, and to bring at length, kings, nobles, & priests to the scaffolds which they have been so long deluging with human blood. I am still warm whenever I think of these scoundrels, tho I do it as seldom as I can, preferring infinitely to contemplate the tranquil growth of my lucerne & potatoes.[11]

Jefferson here focuses on what he hopes will be the results of the French military victories, which he correctly predicts. He does not comment on the condition of the French Revolution in France itself, where the Terror was still raging at the time when he wrote his letter to Coxe. It was not "kings, nobles, & priests," but French Revolutionaries who were deluging scaffolds with blood in France, throughout the summer of 1794. And Jefferson implies that it would be not only legitimate but desirable to extend the Jacobin Terror to other countries.

But it is hard to believe that Jefferson fully means what he says in this letter. It rings hollow; there is something forced in the language; flat, mechanical, cliché-ridden. In the pre-Genet days Jefferson's rare but altogether spontaneous outbursts of revolutionary enthusiasm had zest and sparkle about them, and lively imagery. The "lions, tygers and mammouts" of 1788 have deserted the Jefferson of 1794, more or less as the circus animals were to desert W. B. Yeats. Jefferson, in the letter to Coxe, is no longer expressing a spontaneous exaltation of spirit. This is the leader of the Republican Party, repeating a standard Republican mantra to a Republican henchman. It is not "warmth," but boredom, that takes him back to the lucerne and potatoes. Lucky for his sanity that he had them.

In the summer of 1794, two controversies began which aroused strong feelings throughout the United States and which were associated in the public mind—on both sides—with the French Revolution. The first concerned the nomination of John Jay as Minister Plenipotentiary to the Court of St. James. The second was the Whiskey Rebellion in Western Pennsylvania.

John Jay was a noted Federalist and enemy of the French Revolution. (Readers may recall his role in the downfall of Citizen Genet.) In the spring of 1794, Washington had decided to send a special envoy to London with authority to conclude a treaty removing all controversies between Great Britain and the United States and averting, as far as possible, any danger of war between the two countries. On Hamilton's recommendation, the President nominated John Jay for this extremely important diplomatic mission. The Republican press and the Democratic and Republican Societies immediately opened an all-out attack on Washington's administration. As Jefferson was no longer a member of that administration, they needed to pull no punches. Washington's biographers write:

> Armed with the broad authority of his instructions, with Washington's best wishes, and with a private letter from Hamilton meant to amplify the conciliatory spirit behind the mission, Jay left for New York. A thousand cheering citizens escorted him to his ship on May 12, but by this time Republican criticism of the appointment was savage. Anti-administration newspapers challenged its constitutionality and prophesied a disgraceful outcome of the venture, and in the West effigies of Jay were pilloried and burned. The defensive tactics of Federalist editors served only to draw new venom from Republican pens. Nor was the President to be spared personally. Assaults upon his character from the press and from the rostrums of Democratic societies were the most severe Washington yet had known.[12]

The Jay mission provided the Republican press with splendid copy. The issues were clear-cut; reader responses were surefire. The Washington administration, now totally under the influence of the diabolical Hamilton, was truckling to the British and insulting Britain's valiant enemy, Revolutionary France. Thus the agitation could tap simultaneously the two deep American reserves of political emotion: hostility to Britain and admiration for Revolutionary France.

In a well-judged maneuver, Washington, almost simultaneously with the appointment of Jay, appointed James Monroe as Minister Plenipotentiary to the French Republic. Thus, Washington could claim to be evenhanded. It was true that he was sending to London a person who was known to be well-disposed to Great Britain. But what was wrong with that? Was Washington not sending *to Paris* a man who was known to be at least equally well-disposed to Revolutionary France? And this was indeed the case. Monroe was the most fervent of the prominent Republicans in his commitment to the French Revolution. He was a *vrai Américain*, as opposed to Jay, who belonged to the *faux* variety, from a French Revolutionary point of view.

Of course, the argument about evenhandedness was no more than a debating point, though quite a useful one. Jay was being sent to London to conclude a new treaty of major importance. Monroe's nomination to Paris was (at least on the surface) a routine diplomatic appointment. But besides its utility in debate, the Monroe appointment had at least four other political merits. Its primary function within the Federalist grand design was to keep the French as happy as possible while the government of the United States was getting on with what was to be known as the Jay Treaty. Also, the Monroe appointment was making an awkward point for the Republicans. If the Washington administration is really as awful as the Republican press says it is, why is one of the most senior and respected leaders of the Republican Party taking office under it? Again, as relations with France are bound to turn sour, if the Jay mission succeeds, it will be a Republican, and not a Federalist, who will have to take diplomatic responsibility for the failure of a negotiation with the French Republic. Finally, as Washington's biographers note, Washington "could take comfort in the knowledge that one of his most consistent critics would be in Paris, and not in Philadelphia, when Congress convened again." [13]

I think the political skills of George Washington have been greatly underestimated. The same is true of Thomas Jefferson. And I think the reason is the same in both cases. An aura of the sacred clings to the Victor of Yorktown as well as to the Author of the Declaration of Independence. And political skills—whose maneuvers are usually at least a little unedifying—are felt to be incompatible with the sacred dimension. Hagiography tends to creep in—though much more in the case of Jefferson than of Washington—and wherever it does, it blurs the politics. Which is a pity in the case of two great men who were—among other things—consummate politicians. [14]

Conversely, the Republican leadership does not seem to have noticed what the Washington administration was up to with the nomination of James Monroe. Monroe himself suspected nothing, and (more surprisingly) neither did Madison. The editor of the Jefferson-Madison correspondence writes:

> The only comfort for the Republicans was President Washington's appointment of James Monroe as minister to France. After the recall of Genet, France demanded the removal of Gouverneur Morris, who had lost favor with the French government because of his unfriendly views of the revolution. Monroe won confirmation easily, and Madison accompanied the minister and Mrs. Monroe to Baltimore, saw them off to France, then traveled to Virginia in June for the congressional recess. [15]

In taking Washington's appointment of James Monroe as a friendly gesture to the Republicans, both Madison and Monroe were being a bit unworldly. George Washington in the summer of 1794 could feel no inclination to make a friendly gesture to the Republicans, whose press was

George Washington, by Joseph Wright and John Trumbull, 1786. Courtesy of
the Massachusetts Historical Society. Washington at first welcomed the French
Revolution, but from the end of 1790 on, he viewed it with alarm and suspicion
(chapter 3). This led to a widening rift between Washington and Jefferson (chapters 3, 4, and 5). By 1796, Jefferson had come to see Washington as an apostate
to the cause of Liberty. "It would give you a fever were I to name to you the
apostates who have gone over to these heresies, men who were Samsons in the
field & Solomons in the council, but who have had their heads shorn by the harlot
England" (TJ to Philip Mazzei, 24 April 1796; chapter 6, p. 231).

giving him hell that summer. Washington was making use of the Republicans for Federalist purposes and Madison and Monroe allowed themselves to be used. Jefferson, if he had been attending to politics at this time (June 1794), would hardly have made this mistake. He would have been likely to discern the fine Italian hand of Alexander Hamilton. There is no more convincing proof that Jefferson's retirement from politics in the summer of 1794 was real, and not feigned, than the acquiescence of the Republican leadership in an appointment and a mission which were an integral, well-camouflaged part of the Federalist grand design for a treaty with Britain.

We now come to one of those diverting and almost farcical set pieces in Franco-American relations which enliven this story from time to time, and also illuminate its background. The episode, as we shall see, is in line with the public encounter between Voltaire and Benjamin Franklin in 1778 (as described by John Adams; see Prelude) and the communications between the French National Assembly and the U.S. Congress concerning commemoration of Franklin in 1791 (see chapter 3). The new episode consists of the presentation of the credentials of James Monroe to the National Convention on 14 August 1794. The three episodes belong together in one genre which may be called *la mésentente cordiale,* cordial misunderstanding.

(This episode will take us away for a time from Thomas Jefferson, who is in any case in temporary retirement from the political scene. But the episode is quite instructive about the general context of our study: the interaction between American politics and the French Revolution.)

Diplomatic representatives do not, of course, normally get to present their credentials to legislative bodies, as James Monroe did. Their business is normally solely with the Executive power. The spectacular departure from this principle that occurred in the case of James Monroe came about in this way: Monroe arrived in Paris in early August, barely a week after the fall and execution of Robespierre, on 28 July. This was a time of maximum turmoil, fear, and confusion. Monroe—a friend to what he believed to be the French Revolution, but an innocent American gentleman at heart—behaved with complete diplomatic propriety in a trying situation. He first awaited the return of his predecessor, Gouverneur Morris, who was away from Paris at the time of Monroe's arrival. (Morris had been recalled by Washington at the end of 1793 in return for the agreement of the Jacobin Government to recall Citizen Genet. Morris, personally, still retained Washington's full confidence.) On Morris's return, Monroe and he went together to the Foreign Affairs Office, "where Morris formally notified the [French] Commissary of his recall and of

Monroe's succession. The new envoy left a copy of his credentials, with a request for the earliest possible reception."[16]

All perfectly *protocolaire* and perfectly futile, in the Paris of August 1794. No reply was ever forthcoming from the Commissary of Foreign Affairs or from the new post-Robespierre Committee of Public Safety, still supposed to be the Executive. Poor Monroe was soon in a fever of speculation as to the reasons for the non-reply. Some of his speculations were of Byzantine complexity. As he later wrote to Edmund Randolph (who had succeeded Jefferson as Secretary of State), he thought that the Committee might have reasoned that as "my principles were with them, I ought on that account to be more dreaded; for if they confided in me, I should only lull them asleep as to their true interests, in regard to the movements on foot; and under this impression I was viewed with a jealous eye, and kept at the most awful distance."[17]

This is a classic example of the incapacity of an American lover of "the French Revolution" (in the abstract) to achieve any understanding of the French Revolution in its actual workings. The reason why Monroe could get no reply from the Executive in August 1794 is in reality quite simple. There *was* no Executive, in the Paris of August 1794.

The government that had just fallen—the great Committee of Public Safety, under Robespierre—had been the strongest (and also the grimmest) Executive the French Revolution was ever to know, and it had not yet been succeeded by anything sufficiently coherent to deserve the name of Executive. There was indeed a body that bore the fearsome title, Committee of Public Safety, but this was now a mere agglomeration of individuals who had had nothing in common except fear and hatred of Robespierre. With Robespierre gone, the only bond is also gone, and each of these individuals is living in fear of his life. At any moment, this Revolution of theirs may take some new and sickening lurch, to the Right or the Left. These terror-stricken people are waiting to see which way the cat will jump. And it is the most fearsome cat on earth. These people are not thinking about the "principles" of the new envoy from America or about the dangers of "confiding" in him (*confiding*!). They are thinking about one topic only, and very earnestly indeed about that one. The topic is: how to keep my head on my shoulders until the end of the month. The best way of achieving that is to do nothing at all, since *any* move may turn out to be the pretext for my destruction.

So the envoy from America gets no reply, from the Executive that isn't there. Then Monroe gets this bright idea of an appeal to the Convention. It was not his own idea. According to Monroe's biographer: "It had been suggested to him by certain persons familiar with the workings of the governmental machinery [*sic*] that an appeal be made directly to the legis-lative body, the National Convention. So, on 13 August, Monroe sent a letter to the President of the National Convention, expressing his desire to be received."[18]

Who were the "certain persons"? The new and still unaccepted envoy cannot have been on confidential terms with many people in the scary Paris of August 1794. But there was one person, with whom we know Monroe to have been in touch at this time, who was fully "familiar with the workings of the governmental machinery." This was Gouverneur Morris, who understood the workings of the French Revolution so well that he had become *persona non grata,* comprehensively disliked by revo-lutionaries of all the phases, from Lafayette in 1791 to the successors of Robespierre in 1794. It is probable that Monroe got the idea of appealing to the Convention from Morris. Morris was a kindly person and he would have wished to help the hapless envoy out of the black diplomatic hole in which he found himself in the early part of August 1794. Also, he had no political reason for *not* helping Monroe, different though Monroe's poli-tics were from his own. Morris knew Washington's mind and intentions well enough to realize that Monroe was a Republican envoy serving a Federalist purpose. Monroe was intended to keep the French as happy as might be possible, while the real diplomatic business was being conducted by Jay in London: the framing of a treaty between the United States and Great Britain.

As for Monroe, he had adequate reasons for concealing the identity of his adviser. Gouverneur Morris was everything that all good Republi-cans detested: he was an aristocrat, a monocrat, an Angloman, a heretic, and an apostate. If Jefferson had known that James Monroe had been taking advice from Gouverneur Morris in Paris, he would have suspected the worst. And he would have been right. James Monroe in Paris was unwittingly doing the work of the Federalists: Washington, Hamilton, and Gouverneur Morris.

Monroe's communication was immediately acted on by the Conven-tion. As the journal of the National Convention for 15 August 1794 re-cords:

Citizen Monroe, Minister Plenipotentiary of the United States of America to [*près*] the French Republic, is admitted to the hall at the sitting of the National Convention. He takes his place in the midst of the representatives of the people, and remits to the President of the Convention a translation of his discourse addressed to the National Convention. It is read by one of the secretaries. The expressions of fraternity and union between the two

peoples, and the interest which the United States takes in the French Republic are heard with a lively sensibility and with applause. The letter of credence of Citizen Monroe is also read, as well as those written by the American Congress and addressed to the President of the National Convention
and to the Committee of Public Safety. In witness of the fraternity which
unites these two peoples, French and American, the President gives the *accolade* [fraternal embrace] to Citizen Monroe.[19]

The Congressional messages are interesting. Quite contrary to a pattern established since 1791 (with the Franklin commemoration business),
the Senate, in the message read to the Convention, is even more effusive
about the French Revolution than the House of Representatives is:

Senate . . . tender to the Committee of Public Safety, their zealous wishes
for the French Republic; they learn with sensibility every success which pro-
motes the happiness of the French nation; and the full establishment of their
peace and liberty will be ever esteemed by the Senate as a happiness of the
United States and to humanity.

One might think that the Republicans had somehow gained control
of the Senate, but this was far from being the case. The Senate, at this
time, was thoroughly responsive to the wishes of the administration. It
was heartily supportive of the idea of a treaty with Britain, and bitterly
hostile to the French Revolution. Only one thing could have produced
those "zealous wishes for the French Republic" from the U.S. Senate in
this period, and that was a recommendation from Washington's administration. The message, probably conveyed through Hamilton, would have
been to the general effect: "Would you mind buttering up the French for
us, for the next few months, to keep them quiet while we get on with the
Jay Treaty?"

Monroe seems to have suspected nothing, although he was himself a
member of the Senate, and ought to have known his colleagues' real
views. But he seems to have been a rather simple soul, at least at this point
in his career.

Monroe's biographer narrates the sequel to the President's accolade
(a sequel which seems to have included another accolade):

Monroe emulated the tone of the Secretary's rather florid effusions.
"Citizens, President and Representatives of the French People," he began,
"My admission into this Assembly . . . to be recognized as the Representative of the American Republic, impresses me with a degree of sensibility
which I cannot express. I consider it as a new proof of that friendship and

regard which the French nation has always shewn to their ally, the United States of America. . . . America had her day of oppression, difficulty, and war, but her sons were virtuous and brave and the storm which long clouded her political horizon has passed and left them in the enjoyment of peace, liberty, and independence. France, our ally and our friend and who aided us in the contest, has now embarked in the same noble career; and I am happy to add that whilst the fortitude, magnanimity and heroic valor of her troops command the admiration and applause of the astonished world, the wisdom and firmness of her councils unite equally in securing the happiest results." . . .

The reply to this oratorical bouquet was delivered by the President of the convention, who used equally glowing terms, and after the ceremony of the embrace had taken place "in the midst of universal acclamations of joy, delight, and admiration," the following decree was passed:

"The reading and verification being had of the powers of Citizen James Monroe, he is recognized and proclaimed minister plenipotentiary of the United States of America to the French Republic. . . . The letters of credence of Citizen James Monroe . . . those which he has remitted on the part of the American Congress . . . the discourse of citizen Monroe, the response of the President of the Convention shall be printed in the two languages, French and American, and inserted in the bulletin of correspondence. . . . The flags of the United States of America shall be joined with those of France, and displayed in the hall of the sittings of the Convention in sign of the union and eternal fraternity of the two people." [20]

On the French side, these curious proceedings constituted a kind of ritual of regeneration.[21] The surviving *conventionnels* had been Robespierre's accomplices in the Reign of Terror; and then his murderers. What they wanted most was to have that whole bloody chapter forgotten as soon as possible. A ceremony signifying the recovery of the lost innocence of the French Revolution was urgently required. And what more suitable ceremony could there be than this Arcadian one, of an exchange of sentimental effusions with a Noble Savage from the American woods, symbolizing that unspoiled innocence of nature, about which Jean-Jacques Rousseau had so movingly written?

Gouverneur Morris's deep understanding of the French Revolution had allowed him to see a great window of opportunity for James Monroe.

But what a pity John and Abigail Adams could not have been present for that ceremony in the National Convention! The pens that gave us those pictures of Franklin, Voltaire, and Madame Helvétius (see Prelude) could have chronicled that scene in a manner for which the account in the journal of the National Convention offers only a poor and wooden substitute.

Those proceedings were public, and reports of them soon reached Britain. The laconic John Jay reported from London that the English reaction was "disagreeable." Monroe had to be rebuked, so that the rebuke could be shown to the British. In reality, Washington was not displeased. The flattery of the French was part of his plan, and even the British reaction to it seems to have fitted in quite well to Washington's program. Washington wrote to John Jay:

> "Considering the place in which they were delivered and the neutral policy the country had to pursue, it was a measure that does not appear to have been well devised by our minister." But he saw a possible beneficial result: "Yet, under the existing circumstances, the expression of such reciprocal good will was susceptible of two views, one of which even in the pending state of negotiations (by alarming as well as offending the British Minister) might have no unfavorable operation in bringing matters to a happy and speedy result." [22]

II

In the autumn of 1794 the main political topic in America was the Whiskey Rebellion in western Pennsylvania. This was a local revolt against the excise tax on whiskey. In August, the local militia joined with the insurgents, swelling their numbers to seven thousand, for an advance on Pittsburgh.

> Viewing forcible resistance to federal laws as a threat to the Union, President Washington issued a proclamation ordering the insurgents to disperse and sent federal commissioners to offer amnesty in exchange for pledges to comply with the law. To assure compliance, he also called up 12,950 militia-men from four states and took up personal command of the federalized militia in order to dramatize the critical situation in the West. [23]

The links between the French Revolution and the Whiskey Rebellion consisted of the Democratic and Republican Societies and the Republican press. These continued to be enthusiastic for the French Revolution, and were felt by Federalists and by Washington to have encouraged violent opposition to the Federal Government. Lance Banning writes:

> The rioting in Western Pennsylvania was acutely embarrassing to the Republicans, and they were quick to join in the general condemnation of

resistance to the laws. Still, the fact of resistance, along with the administration's powerful response to the insurrection, were opportunities too good to pass for renewed attacks on Federalist policies and motives. While they condemned the rioters, Republicans everywhere took pleasure in attributing the riots to "the arts, intrigues, and villanies of men in power." In one form or another, writer after writer maintained that "the insurrection may fairly be counted the first fruit of the blessed harvest sown by the advocates of the funding and banking systems." [24]

Although the Republican press generally did not support the Whiskey Rebellion, they thought Washington's mobilization of force against it excessive (as Jefferson did). In western Pennsylvania itself local Democratic Societies were the foci of the Rebellion (below, pp. 212–14). In Federalist eyes, all this Republican agitation was evidence of a Jacobin plot against the United States. Federalists believed that Citizen Genet had actually started the Republican and Democratic Societies. While this was not the case, the Societies had certainly given Genet enthusiastic encouragement while he was defying the Federal Government. Seeing that some of the same societies were now encouraging the Pennsylvanian rebels, Federalist belief in a Jacobin plot is understandable. Of course, the Jacobins had not been in power in France when Citizen Genet was sent to the United States. It was actually the Jacobins who *recalled* Citizen Genet and who forbade his successor to engage in any activities contrary to the wishes of the Federal Government. By the time the Whiskey Rebellion got going, the Jacobins were no longer a power in France, and had become a persecuted minority there. But for the American enemies of the French Revolution, *all* French Revolutionaries were Jacobins, permanently.

Washington put much of the blame for the Pennsylvania insurrection on the rebellious spirit evoked by the Democratic Societies. He wrote to John Jay on 1 November:

> The self-created societies, which have spread themselves over this country, have been laboring incessantly to sow the seeds of distrust, jealousy and, of course, discontent, thereby hoping to effect some revolution in the Government. . . . That they have been the fomenters of the Western disturbances admits of no doubt in the mind of anyone who will examine their conduct. . . . I shall be more prolix in my speech to Congress, on the commencement and progress of this insurrection, than is usual in such an instrument. [25]

It was claimed by Republicans that the link between the French Revolution and the Whiskey Rebellion was a Federalist invention. But we know that the link existed in the minds of the ringleaders of the Whiskey Rebellion, David Bradford and James Marshall. The authors of *The Age of Federalism*, drawing on the account of Hugh Henry Brackenridge (who represents himself as having tried to counter the influence of the extremists) write:

> Brackenridge goes on to describe the meeting of 226 elected delegates from the entire region at Parkinson's Ferry on August 14. Bradford and Marshall were all for setting up a "committee of public safety" with powers to govern the region on the basis of unyielding opposition to the excise law, and to prepare if necessary for war. (They had all been reading about the French Revolution in the *Pittsburgh Gazette*.) News of the approach of Washington's commissioners which arrived in the course of the meeting, together with the proclamation which announced the President's intention to call out the militia, was angrily received. Only through the painstaking finesse of Brackenridge, Gallatin, and other moderate spirits was the proposed committee of public safety renamed the "standing committee" a special conference committee appointed to meet the commissioners and hear their proposals. These conferences took place between August 20 and 23, and largely through the efforts of Brackenridge and Gallatin, who were members of it, the conference committee agreed to recommend to the standing committee of sixty that the people of the region should make their submission.
>
> But Brackenridge was darkly pessimistic, and when the committee of sixty met at Brownsville on August 28 to hear the conference committee's report, everything trembled in the balance. There was fiery talk; the would-be Robespierre, Bradford, warned of setting up guillotines (none of them yet knew that Robespierre himself had just been guillotined), and declared, "We will defeat the first army that comes over the mountains and take their arms and baggage." [26]

On 18 November, Washington was able to report to Congress on the bloodless suppression of the rebellion. His reference to the Societies was economical, and deadly. The excise law, he said, had been accepted with "reason and patriotism" by most Americans, but in four counties of Pennsylvania there appeared "symptoms of riot and violence" as "certain self-created societies assumed the tone of condemnation [of the excise]." [27]

On 23 December, John Adams brought the Senate in a group to Washington's house, and read aloud the statement adopted by the Senate on the day before. The Senate, said Adams, approved unequivocally the use of militia by the President and, moreover, shared his condemnation of the proceedings of "certain self-created societies." [28]

The House of Representatives approved the repression of the rebellion, but decided—by a narrow margin—not to follow the example of the Senate in joining in the condemnation of "certain self-created societies." Madison reported to Jefferson with some overstatement: "The attack on the most sacred principle of our Constitution and of Republicanism, thro' the Democratic Societies, has given rise to much discussion in the H. of Reps. and has left us in a critical situation." Madison explains to Jefferson the principle on which he had handled the drafting of the Address. "The draught was made as strong as possible on all proper points, in order the better to get it thro', without the improper one [i.e. the reference to "self-created societies"]."[29] Madison enclosed with his letter to Jefferson a copy of the Address, voted by the House in November. The first two paragraphs of this document ran:

> The House of Representatives calling to mind the blessings enjoyed by the people of the United States, and especially the happiness of living under Constitutions and laws which rest on their Authority alone, could not learn with other emotions than those you have expressed, that any part of our fellow Citizens should have shewn themselves capable of an insurrection.
>
> We feel with you the deepest regret at so painful an occurrence in the annals of our country. As men regardful of the tender interests of humanity, we look with grief, at scenes which might have stained our land with civil blood. As lovers of public order, we lament that it has suffered so flagrant a violation: as zealous friends of republican government, we deplore every occasion, which in the hands of its enemies, may be turned into a calumny against it.[30]

In his reply to the House, Washington managed to insert a confirmation and expansion of his original warning about the Societies into an acknowledgment of the professed sentiments of the House on the suppression of the rebellion. "It is far better," said Washington, "that the artful approaches to such a situation of things [i.e. actual rebellion] should be checked by the vigilant and duly admonished patriotism of our fellow-citizens, than that the evil should increase until it becomes necessary to crush it by the strength of their arms."[31]

It would be hard to conceive of a more firm and graceful implicit rebuke to the House for its failure to endorse the condemnation of the "self-created societies." The delightful phrase "duly admonished patriotism" accurately describes the condition of the Republican majority in the House at this time. We know that the Address would not have been as "strong" [in support of the President] as it was, had it not been for the President's "admonition," and the urgent need to keep the House from endorsing the same. The first two paragraphs of that Address are indeed so "strong" in a Federalist sense that they would have met with a hostile reception, had they been read out at a meeting of any of the Republican and Democratic Societies at the time.

And Jefferson himself was fuming, for a while. In a letter to Madison in late December Jefferson describes Washington's reference to "self-created societies" as "an attack on the freedom of discussion, the freedom of writing, printing and publishing." He attributes the attack to the "monarchical" tendencies of Washington's administration: "Their sight must be perfectly dazzled by the glittering of crowns and coronets." Jefferson does not spare Madison himself.

> And with respect to the transactions against the excise-law, it appears to me that you are all swept away in the torrent of governmental opinions, or that we do not know what these transactions have been. We know of none which according to the definitions of the law have been any thing more than riotous. . . . The excise-law is an infernal one [which may become] the instrument of dismembering the Union, and setting us all afloat to chuse which part of it we will adhere to.

Jefferson has convinced himself that the repression of the rebellion—which was an accomplished fact by November—had in reality been a total failure and that the secession of western Pennsylvania is imminent: "that their detestation of the excise law is universal, and has now associated to it a detestation of the government, and that separation which perhaps was a very distant and problematical event, is now near, and certain and determined in the mind of every man."[32]

In reality, Madison's handling of the "critical situation" created by Washington's reference to "self-created societies" seems eminently sound, in relation to the long-term interests of the Republican Party. Unlike Jay's negotiation, and later Jay's treaty, the issue of the Whiskey Rebellion was not an auspicious one on which to mount a challenge to Washington's administration. This was not an issue on which Anglophobia could be plausibly tapped. Most Americans could see that if the western Pennsylvanians could get away with resisting taxation lawfully imposed by the Federal Government, anarchy could become a serious threat to the young United States. Washington had had no difficulty in raising from the militias of four states all the recruits he required for his and Hamilton's policy of subduing the rebels, by a massive show of force. The operation had been entirely successful and totally bloodless.

In the circumstances, if the Republicans in the House had made a frontal attack on the suppression of the Whiskey Rebellion, they would have isolated the Republican Party nationally, and neither Jefferson nor Madison might ever have become President. The best the Republican leadership could do, and the most they could achieve, was to maintain contact with their own following by averting a House vote in favor of condemning "the self-created societies." Madison, in November 1794, is behaving very much as Jefferson had done in August 1793, over Genet. He is conducting a tactical retreat from an untenable political patch. He is limiting damage, regrouping and awaiting a more favorable political conjuncture.

That being so, Jefferson's implied criticism of Madison, in his letter of 28 December, appears perverse, and parts of that letter even seem irrational—for example, the conviction that western Pennsylvania, in the aftermath of the Whiskey Rebellion, is about to secede from the United States.

In Jefferson's Paris days, towards the end of his brief affair with Maria Cosway, he wrote a strange quasi-valedictory letter to the lady, in the form of a lengthy dialogue between "Heart" and "Head." There was no discernible political dimension to the affair with Maria, (which is why I did not refer to it in chapter 1) but there was sometimes a "Heart and Head" aspect to Jefferson's politics. His relations with Genet had started under the sign of "Heart" and ended under "Head." And there was a "Heart" and "Head" side to the Whiskey Rebellion also. Heart was on the side of the Pennsylvanian rebels, because they *were* rebels, like Shays's followers in 1788, about whom Jefferson had written the Tree of Liberty passage in 1787. Head on the other hand knew that Madison's course had been the prudent one, politically speaking, and should not be publicly challenged. As in the case of Maria Cosway, Heart made its protest, and Head then took over. Madison knew his Jefferson, and declined argument on this subject, in a tactful manner. He wrote to Jefferson, on 26 January 1795: "I have read your favor of Decr. 28 but [not] till three weeks after the date of it. It was my purpose to have answered it particularly, but I have been robbed of the time reserved for the purpose." Madison then goes on to consider other issues, notably Hamilton's long Valedictory Report, which "is said to contain a number of improper things."[33] After that, the two Republican leaders quietly dropped the unfortunate topic of the Whiskey Rebellion.

As regards relations between Americans and the French Revolution, by far the most important aspect of the Whiskey Rebellion controversy was Washington's condemnation of the "self-created societies." The Democratic and Republican Societies, throughout 1793 and 1794, had been the most vociferous apologists for the French Revolution. Now Washington clearly implies that these Societies have been behaving in a manner that was unpatriotic and dangerous for the United States. As their most obvious common characteristic had been enthusiasm for the French Revolution, Washington, without mentioning the French Revolution at all, is creating a general impression that enthusiasm for the French Revolution is in itself suspect. And this is something new. Up to November 1794, Republicans had been able to claim Washington as being on their side in relation to the French Revolution. The demand for the recall of Genet did little to impair that view of the matter. Jefferson was there to attest that Genet had exceeded his instructions and the government of the French Republic had agreed to his recall (Americans in general did not know that the government which recalled him was different from the one that had given him his instructions). The view that Washington approved of the French Revolution seemed to be confirmed—and was intended to seem so—by Washington's nomination of James Monroe as Minister Plenipotentiary to France.

But that had been in May of 1794, and by November, Washington no longer feels a need to conciliate the Republican opposition in Congress, which he had resolved to keep as quiet as possible during the negotiations that were about to lead to the Jay Treaty. There is a remarkable coincidence here. Washington's "self-created societies" speech was delivered on the same day–19 November—as the Jay Treaty was signed in London. Washington could not know of the precise coincidence, but he did know that the treaty would be signed soon, that the struggle over its ratification would be a bitter one, and that the Societies would be the main foci of opposition to it in the country.

In the circumstances, the "self-created societies" speech can be seen as a preemptive strike, discrediting the Societies as unpatriotic, *in advance of* their anticipated offensive against the ratification of the Jay Treaty. They had laid themselves open to such a pre-emptive strike, through the flagrant involvement of local Democratic Societies in the Whiskey Rebellion. Washington's thrust against the societies is part of a message that contains no reference to France or England—the most popular topic of agitation by the Societies. The message is entirely concerned with a rebellion against the Government of the United States, and the unpatriotic posture of the Societies in relation to that rebellion.

There is no doubt that Washington did regard the conduct of the Societies as unpatriotic, and not merely in connection with the Whiskey Rebellion. But he would not have been likely to go public against them had he not judged it necessary to do so in the national interest of the

To Avoid a War with England, 1794–96. *The Times: A Political Portrait,* anonymous caricature, c. 1795. Collection of the New-York Historical Society. This is a Federalist cartoon, showing Jefferson, aided by James Madison and Albert Gallatin, trying to obstruct Washington's second administration. "They coupled Jefferson's name with those of Madison and Gallatin when he was quietly tilling his red soil in Albemarle, attributing to him leadership which he neither exercised nor claimed. Any disclaimers of his they may have heard of they attributed to insincerity"—Dumas Malone (chapter 6, p. 228).

United States. He believed the Jay Treaty, and stable peace with Britain, were supremely in the national interests of the United States in 1794–95. That was the main reason for the "self-created societies" comment. To stigmatize American manifestations of enthusiasm for the French Revolution was a side-effect of that comment, but an entirely acceptable one. After all, the French, and their friends in America, in attacking the Jay Treaty, would be drawing on the well-established popular enthusiasm for the French Revolution for all they were worth.

The Societies were never quite the same after the "self-created societies" reference. The years of 1795 and 1796 saw a mortal decline in their membership and activity—and in manifestations of enthusiasm for the French Revolution—as compared with 1793 and 1794. Washington's prestige was still enormous and his disapproval proportionately chilling. If Washington indicated there was something wrong with the Societies, most Americans—not strongly committed to either the Republican or the Federalist cause—would take his word for it.

The Republican leadership had been troubled by the Genet affair, in relation to the French Revolution, though they never expressly admitted this. But the decline in *popular* enthusiasm for the French Revolution does not date from Genet's recall, as some have claimed. That enthusiasm continued up to near the end of 1794. It is only under the chill breath of Washington's "self-created societies" reference, in November 1794, that American popular enthusiasm for the French Revolution at last begins to falter and to fade.

III

Meanwhile in Europe, the French Revolution has again entered a phase of military expansion which will be sustained—although with major setbacks at sea—until the Revolution ends in 1799 with the military dictatorship of the future Emperor, Napoleon Bonaparte. This is the period of maximum proliferation of the French protectorates known as the *républiques soeurs*: Batavian Republic, Cisalpine Republic, Parthenopean Republic, and so on. The real, as distinct from the nominal, relation of these sister republics to France was to become sharply defined under the Napoleonic Empire when each sister republic in turn was briskly converted into a monarchy, ruled over by a member of the Bonaparte family. In each of the new Bonaparte monarchies, the *patriotes* of the Revolutionary phase (above, p. 187) now became courtiers in the service of their friendly neighborhood Bonaparte king. But all that was still some years ahead in the spring and summer of 1795, when the friends of the French Revolution in America were still welcoming what they regarded as the liberation of the rest of Europe by the armies of the French Republic.

Thomas Jefferson is still of this number in 1795–96, apparently at least. On 27 April 1795, he writes to William Branch Giles, one of the senior Republican members of the House of Representatives:

> I sincerely congratulate you on the great prosperities of our two first allies, the French & Dutch [the latter of these having just been occupied by the former]. . . . I should have little doubt of dining [in occupied London] with Pichegru [general of the French Republic, recently victorious in Holland], . . . for I believe I should be tempted to leave my clover for awhile, to go and hail the dawn of liberty & republicanism in that island.

Jefferson goes on to welcome a promised visit to Monticello by Giles, but warns Giles that when he comes to Monticello, the talk will be mainly about farming: "I shall talk with you about it from morning till night, and put you on very short allowance as to political aliment. Now and then a pious ejaculation for the French & Dutch republicans, returning with due despatch to clover, potatoes, wheat, &c."[34]

If this can still be classed as enthusiasm for the French Revolution, it is enthusiasm of a very different order to that of the peaks of Jefferson's French Revolutionary ardor in the period from October 1789 to January 1793. What was once "the true god," the "polar star," "the holy cause" of the Adam and Eve letter,[35] to which most of the human race could be legitimately immolated has now dwindled to being the subject of a "pious ejaculation" or two to be inserted occasionally into the discussion of really serious business concerning "clover, potatoes, wheat, &c." What a comedown! Genet had done some damage. But so, as we shall see, had Robespierre.

Two days after his letter to Giles, Jefferson wrote another letter, to Démeunier, a refugee from an earlier phase of the French Revolution. Jefferson tells Démeunier, "Being myself a warm zealot for the attainment & enjoiment . . . of as much liberty, as each may exercise without injury to the equal liberty of his fellow citizens, I have lamented that in France the endeavours to obtain this should have been attended with the effusion of so much blood."

Jefferson had never publicly lamented this, and in the Adam and Eve letter of 3 January 1793, he had legitimized further effusion of blood on a colossal scale: "I was intimate with the leading characters of the year 1789. So I was with those of the Brissotine party who succeeded them: & have always been persuaded that their views were upright."

While the Jacobin Terror was actually in progress, Madison had conveyed—without comment—to Jefferson the news of the executions of these upright men. Jefferson, in his reply to Madison's letter, ignored the news about the fate of the Brissotines.

Jefferson continues in his letter to Démeunier:

Those who have followed have been less known to me: but I have been willing to hope that they also meant the establishment of a free government in their country, excepting perhaps the party which has lately been suppressed [the Jacobins]. The government of those now at the head of affairs appears to hold out many indications of good sense, moderation & virtue; & I cannot but presume from their character as well as your own that you would find a perfect safety in the bosom of your own country.[36]

(This is possibly the only certificate of "virtue" ever offered to the Thermidorian collection of accomplices and assassins of Robespierre who ruled France from late 1794 to 1799.)

In a letter to Tench Coxe, about a month later, Jefferson is more explicit about "the party which has lately been suppressed." Jefferson is still rejoicing about French military victories, but also uneasily aware, by now, of a rather large stain on the French Revolution itself:

> This ball of liberty, I believe most piously, is now so well in motion that it will roll round the globe. At least the enlightened part of it, for light & liberty go together. It is our glory that we first put it into motion, & our happiness that being foremost we had no bad examples to follow. What a tremendous obstacle to the future attempts at liberty will be the atrocities of Robespierre![37]

This is the first time that Jefferson acknowledges that any "atrocities" have *ever* been perpetrated by the French Republic. It is a significant stage in the slow and uneven crumbling of Thomas Jefferson's faith in the French Revolution.

IV

As the "ball of liberty" advanced in Europe, the new masters of liberty, the Thermidorian Directory, were becoming more exigent in their relations with the United States. By the beginning of 1795, poor Monroe is having a miserable time in Paris. In the fast-moving calendar of the French Revolution, August 1794 and its accolades are ancient history by now. By January 1795, the French are aware of the existence—though not yet of the content—of the Jay Treaty between Britain and the United States. The Thermidorians, intoxicated by victory, regard the Jay Treaty as a piece of impudence, on the part of a third-rate power, towards the new masters of Europe. From Paris, Gouverneur Morris warns Hamilton that the new rulers in Paris mean to annul the Franco-American treaties of 1778. In Philadelphia, Secretary of State Randolph notes a new and ominous tone on the part of Minister Plenipotentiary Fauchet, who had been so accommodating while France had been besieged and the Jacobins in power. At the end of May, Randolph writes to Monroe to tell him of the change in Fauchet:

> At the beginning of this month Mr. Fauchet took up the strain of complaining and has written an indecent letter in which he collects all the charges which he thinks himself qualified to maintain against the United States. . . .

I am sure that he meditates something against the treaty with Great Britain, but what, I do not yet see. . . . I confess that I little expected from Mr. Fauchet the conduct which he has pursued and probably will pursue before his successor arrives.[38]

On 15 June 1795, Fauchet's successor, Pierre-Auguste Adet, presented his credentials. Adet's instructions required him, in effect, to ally himself with the Republicans, at Congressional level, for the undoing of the Jay Treaty. There was to be no repeat of Genet; not at this stage. Adet is instructed to take care to observe scrupulously the forms established for communication between the President of the United States and foreign representatives, and he will take no step which could give offense to the inhabitants of the United States with regard to the form of government which they have chosen.[39]

Adet was not instructed to cultivate the Republican and Democratic Societies. Under the Thermidorians, who had overthrown Robespierre, revolutionary clubs were proscribed, because of the terrifying memory of the Jacobin Club. So the Societies, already stigmatized by the President of the United States, would be shunned by the envoy of the French Republic. It was with the Republicans at Congressional level that Adet was to ally himself, while maintaining "cool but decent" relations with the Federalists.

On 25 June 1795, Adet reports on the presentation of his credentials.

I handed my letters of credence to the President on 27 Prairial (15 June), in a special audience. Protestations of friendship for France, wishes for her success; assurances of most cordial attachment to the United States, some praise of the President: such was the text of the President's address and of my replies. I would have been touched by the apparent sincerity of his protestations if I had not already been instructed by public opinion, by men who are sincerely attached to our country, that France is the plaything of the cunning of the Cabinet of Philadelphia.

We can see the new envoy already straining at the leash of his instructions, for Adet goes on:

It is time, Citizen Representatives, to remove completely (d'arracher) the veil which my predecessors have torn, and to show the truth in the full light of day. My duty prescribes it; the interest of my country requires it, and I should be betraying its glory if I were to sit idly by while these people repay the benefits which my country had lavished on them, with the blackest ingratitude!

Adet's instructions are very different from those of Genet, but the temperament and style of the two envoys are similar. Adet now seems to upbraid the Citizen Representatives who have given him instructions:

> By what fatality, Citizens, did you not receive the dispatches sent to you by my predecessor on the conduct of the American Government towards us and on the only-too-well-founded fears inspired in him by the negotiation of John Jay? You could have given me instructions proper for directing me in a definite manner. My position is extremely difficult, Citizen Representatives. I must forcibly demand that the text of the Treaty be communicated to me, and that I allow my indignation to burst out, or else I must suffer in Silence, while awaiting a happier moment, the insult offered to our Country. After mature reflection I have concluded that the latter option, although hard to reconcile with republican pride, was required of me by duty and prudence: I have taken this option, and I think that the development I am about to describe will cause you to approve my conduct.

Adet goes on to present his principals with an orthodox Jeffersonian analysis of the motivation of Washington's second administration:

> What motive can have led the federal Government to such means of breaking off the friendship which linked the American people to the French people, and to ally themselves with our enemy? It is easy to resolve this problem. The principal Agents of this Government have been tending for a long time towards absolute power. The ideas of nobility, of Power, ferment in many heads. The brilliant light [*éclat*] which surrounds the Throne is perhaps dazzling the imagination of the President; the desire to create a hereditary Senate, to distinguish between patrician and plebeian families, torment men who are already on the grip of the ridiculous affectations of our former nobility, and the liberty of America would perhaps today be no more than a word void of sense, if the French Revolution had not slowed down the progress of the ambition of the Executive power. . . .[40]

And so on for three more pages.

By early July—less than a month after the presentation of his credentials—the new envoy of the French Republic is already intervening actively, but at first deniably, in the politics of the United States. The U.S. Senate was then debating (behind closed doors, as was the Senate's practice) the Jay Treaty. Having failed to obtain a copy of the treaty from the Department of State, Adet took direct action: "I decided not to complain to the Executive, and to get an intermediary to buy from a Senator [*de faire acheter d'un Sénateur*] a copy of the Jay Treaty."[41] Adet then leaked part of the treaty to the American press. "I managed to transmit an Extract from the Treaty to Franklin's grandson [Benjamin Franklin Bache, editor of *L'Aurore Journal Patriote*] without his being able to suspect it came from me. He printed it in his sheet and on the following day it appeared in the other papers. Its publication has produced the effect that I expected."[42]

The Senate, none the less, ratified the treaty (leaving just one article in suspense) on 24 June. Popular demonstrations against the treaty followed, and Adet records them with relish:

> The People is far from having, concerning the Treaty between the United States and England, the same opinion as the majority of the Senate. The 4th July, anniversary of American independence, furnished unequivocal proofs of this. Jay was burned [in effigy] by the carpenters of the Vessels: he was shown holding a scales in his right hand; on the lighter scale was written *Liberty and Independence of America*: the heavier scale read *England's Gold;* in his left hand he carried the Treaty, and from his mouth came the words, *pay me what I ask and I shall sell you my country.*[43]

Anti-Jay riots, on a large scale, followed throughout the remainder of July in Boston, New York, and Philadelphia. Washington wrote to Hamilton on 29 July:

> The cry against the treaty is like that against a mad dog; and everyone, in a manner, seems engaged in running it down. . . . It has received the most tortured interpretations and . . . the most abominable misrepresentations. . . . The string which is most played on, because it strikes with most force the popular ear, is the violation, as they term it, of our engagements with France, or, in other words, the predilection shown by [the treaty] to Great Britain at the expense of the French nation. . . . Obviously it is the interest of the French . . . to avail themselves of such a spirit to keep *us* and *Great Britain* in variance. . . . To what *length* their policy may induce them to carry matters is too much in embryo at this moment to decide."[44]

The agitation against the treaty continued throughout most of the rest of 1795, combined with virulent personal abuse of Washington in the Republican press.

The campaign of abuse against Washington was conducted principally by Benjamin Franklin Bache, whose Philadelphia *General Advertiser and Aurora*, had replaced Freneau's *National Gazette* (defunct since 1793) as the principal organ of the Republican Party. The general direction of the attacks is summarized by James D. Tagg, who has made a study of this campaign:

The attacks were as varied as they were virulent. Included in the catalog of Washington's alleged shortcomings, failures, and crimes were: his cold, aloof, arrogant manner; his lack of intelligence and wisdom; and his love of luxury and display. According to his critics, he was both incompetent and unrepublican. He had been a poor general and a lukewarm patriot; he was ungrateful to France; he had conspired to destroy American liberty through a new alliance with Great Britain; and he had attempted to promote his own infallibility while disregarding the soveriegn will of the people.[45]

Tagg goes on to describe the role, in all this, of Bache, his paper, and other publications:

> After the collapse of [Freneau's *National Gazette*], Bache's newspaper, the Philadelphia *General Advertiser and Aurora* (the name *Aurora* was added in late 1794 and the paper was generally known by that name after that time), became the chief vehicle for the early, mild campaign against the President and the later hysterical campaign in which Bache hoped to destroy Washington completely. *Aurora* editorials attacking Washington ranged from small, two-line attacks to the massive serialized assault by the "Calm Observer" (John Beckley), who successfully showed, in 1795, that Washington had overdrawn his presidential salary. Nor did Bache restrict himself to the *Aurora*'s columns. As Washington's presidency drew to a close, Bache eagerly printed and distributed Paine's pathetic and vicious *Letters to Washington* (1796), and the long-discredited spurious letters of Washington which, according to Washington's worst enemies, proved the President's lack of enthusiasm for the American Revolution. To conclude the attack, Bache then wrote and published a rambling eighty-four-page pamphlet entitled *Remarks Occasioned by the Late Conduct of Mr. Washington . . .*, which summarized Washington's weaknesses, failures, and crimes.[46]

The involvement of John Beckley in this campaign is particularly interesting. Beckley was a close confidant and confidential agent of Jefferson's (see above, p. 111). His commitment to "a massive serialized assault" on Washington, in 1795, strongly suggests that Jefferson at this time not merely condoned the campaign against Washington, but was orchestrating it, from behind the scenes, in the 1795 phase of Jefferson's "retirement." But the agitation did not prevent the treaty from becoming law. On 2 September 1795 Adet responded:

> Citizen Representatives: My conjectures have proved to be correct; the President has just signed the dishonor of his old age and the slave [enslave-

ment?] of the United States. He has ratified the Treaty of Commerce and
Friendship with Great Britain, and Hammond, the English Minister, has left
New York for Europe, taking with him the certain pledge of Washington's
submission to the supreme will of George III.[47]

Up to the autumn of 1795, there is no record of any contact between
the Republican leaders and Adet, although it seems virtually certain that
Adet—in accordance with his instructions—would have been in touch
with Madison, and with other leading Republicans in Congress. The first
recorded contact, however, dates from September—October 1795, and it
is a contact with Jefferson. Dumas Malone writes:

> While following the path of privacy, he [Jefferson] may be charged with
> a departure from that of strict propriety in one case. Replying to a letter
> from the French minister, Adet, which had covered a communication from
> a Genevan savant, he went beyond the requirements of politeness. In view
> of his experiences with Genet, he may have been warranted in expressing
> the wish that his period of service in Philadelphia had overlapped that of
> the present French minister, but he said more than that:
>
>> . . . The interests of our two republics also could not but have
>> been promoted by the harmony of their servants. Two people[s]
>> whose interests, whose principles, whose habits of attachment,
>> founded on fellowship in war and mutual kindnesses, have so
>> many points of union, cannot but be easily kept together. I hope
>> you have accordingly been sensible, Sir, of the general interest
>> which my countrymen take in all the successes of your republic.
>> In this no one joins with more enthusiasm than myself, an enthusi-
>> asm kindled by my love of liberty, by my gratitude to your nation
>> who helped us to acquire it, by my wishes to see it extended to all
>> men, and first to those whom we love most. I am now a private
>> man, free to express my feelings, & their expression will be esti-
>> mated at neither more or less than they weigh, to wit, the expres-
>> sions of a private man. Your struggles for liberty keep alive the
>> only sparks of sensation which public affairs now excite in me. As
>> to the concerns of my own country, I leave them willingly and
>> safely to those who will have a longer interest in cherishing them.
>
> Since [Jefferson] ceased to be a private man by the end of another year
> and this French envoy was charged with participation in the effort to elect
> him President, [see below, pp. 238–40] this letter could have been very dam-
> aging if brought to light. There is no sufficient reason, however to attribute
> it to any personal political ambition.[48]

V

In the year of 1796 occurred the first contested Presidential election in the history of the United States. It was not until September of that year—with the news of Washington's retirement—that it became clear that there would be a contest. But the possibility of a contest was in the air throughout a year of intense political activity, in which Jefferson shows revived interest. It seems always to have been assumed that, if there was a contest, the contenders would be John Adams and Thomas Jefferson.

There was no campaign in the modern sense of the term, but there was increasing hostility between Republicans and Federalists. This was also a period of increasingly strained relations between the French Republic and the United States. The strain was partly due to the Jay Treaty, but it was probably mainly a result of the growing arrogance of the new French government, the Directory (set up in October), in its dealings with other countries during a period of dazzling military victories, including Bonaparte's conquest of Italy. The arrogance showed in a scheme for America put forward by the new Directory's Foreign Minister, Charles Delacroix. The authors of *The Age of Federalism* write:

> Delacroix in January 1796 produced a remarkable plan for America, largely pieced together from the dispatches of Adet, whereby France would "take advantage of the ferment that agitates the United States, to make them declare that power against England." This would be done by arousing the people ("while adroitly concealing the arouser," namely the French minister) to regain their liberty by unseating Washington and electing Jefferson, who would then "give the French Republic the influence she ought to have in America." America would thereupon break the Jay Treaty and enter the war; she would regain Canada for France; French naval forces would convoy American supplies to France and her colonies (he did not say where the ships would come from); the Americans, deprived of British manufactures, "will favor our industry and new channels will open for our commerce which from then on will be without competition." Every part of the scheme was the idlest fantasy. The Directory seems not to have taken it very seriously, though they saw no harm in letting Adet stir up whatever mischief he could in the coming American elections.[49]

Whether the Directory took the scheme seriously or not was not very material as far as the United States was concerned. The reality, in the conduct of Franco-American affairs in this election year is that Adet, with the approval of his immediate superior, Delacroix, acted as if this scheme was in force, and campaigned for Jefferson (see below, pp. 238–40).

The Foreign Minister also (whether with the authority of his colleagues or not) acted in accordance with his own scheme. In February 1796 he told Monroe that the alliance (dating from 1778) between France and the United States was broken (as a result of the Jay Treaty). Monroe's biographer, W. P. Cresson, writes:

> A February afternoon in 1796 found Monroe in the office of the Minister of Foreign Affairs. He had come to press some American claims of minor importance. Again, as on a previous visit, he had, instead, to listen to a monologue on the Jay Treaty. The French government had not become reconciled to it. In the interim since its ratification, the Foreign Office had been busy planning a retort, and it was ready. The Directory, Monroe was informed, had at length decided how to deal with the matter. The alliance between France and the United States was broken, and an envoy extraordinary would be forthwith sent to America to apprize the former ally of France of this development.
>
> Monroe tried his best to forestall such a move. He argued and pleaded with the Minister that such a step would produce the "most serious ill-consequences," that the enemies of both countries would welcome it with delight, and their friends "behold the spectacle with horror."
>
> The Minister countered with the argument that even aside from any treaty with Great Britain the French had "much cause of complaint," that the treaty was a gesture of absolute unfriendliness, and justified rupture of the alliance between the two countries. Nevertheless, concluded the Minister, Monroe's arguments were "strong and weighty with him," and he would present them to the Directory, "by whom, he doubted not, all suitable attention would be paid to them."
>
> Monroe deduced from the whole situation that the "minister, the government, preferred to have us as open (enemies) rather than perfidious friends." This comment leaves no question as to where his sympathies lay.[50]

The Republican leaders, early in the year, seem to have assumed that Washington would not run for a third term, though they could not yet act publicly on that assumption. In February, Madison wrote to Monroe in France that they intended to "post" Jefferson, the only candidate with whom they could hope to succeed. Dumas Malone comments:

> No Republican could have been expected to stand up to Adams except Jefferson. He also had been a notable Revolutionary Patriot and had served at a foreign court in Washington's official family with a distinction which could not be denied. His direct service to the Republican party until this time had been considerably less than that of Madison and far less than his

political enemies alleged. At the time of Genet he had helped save the party by wise counsel which was transmitted through Madison and Monroe. An avowed partisan in the treaty fight, he may have communicated some of his ardor to his close political friends, but he had exercised no particular influence on the course of events and had kept out of sight. His preferred status among the Republicans was owing far less to what he had done for them than to their belief in the firmness of his convictions and their confidence in his political sagacity. That his name was the greatest among them was also owing in no small degree to the advertisement his enemies had given him. No other man did more to build him up and turn him into a symbol than Hamilton did by extreme and unwarranted attacks. The party line which Hamilton laid down was followed thenceforth by his followers. *They coupled Jefferson's name with those of Madison and Gallatin when he was quietly tilling his red soil in Albemarle, attributing to him leadership which he neither exercised nor claimed.* Any disclaimers of his they may have heard of they attributed to insincerity.[51]

Dumas Malone's verdict (in the passage which I have italicized) is hard to reconcile with the correspondence between Jefferson and Madison (see *The Republic of Letters, passim*). From the moment of Jefferson's return to the United States at the end of 1789, Madison had consistently deferred to him (particularly with regard to the French Revolution), as he continued to do while Jefferson was Secretary of State. During that period—the time when the Republican press and the Republican and Democratic Societies were founded—Jefferson exercised his leadership mainly through Madison, but partly also through Freneau and the *National Gazette*. After Jefferson's retirement as Secretary of State, he took a holiday from politics, and during 1794 Madison was the only leader the Republicans had. But by 1795 and the Jay Treaty, Jefferson's political interest revives. By 1796, as the party's Presidential nominee, Jefferson is unquestionably leader of the party. And after his election as Vice President, and Madison's retirement, Jefferson is the active leader of the party, and busy preparing for the Presidential contest of 1800.

As early as the summer of 1792, when Philip Freneau commenced hostilities, Alexander Hamilton had correctly divined that his main enemy was his colleague in Washington's first administration Thomas Jefferson. And Hamilton was also being realistic in refusing to take a Jeffersonian disclaimer at face value.

On 28 February, Jefferson writes to John Adams, to thank him for a book: "I am to thank you my dear Sir for forwarding M. D'Ivernois' book on the French Revolution. I receive everything with respect which comes from him. But it is on politics, a subject I never loved, & now hate. I will not promise therefore to read it thoroughly."[52]

This is in sharp contrast with Jefferson's letter to Adet in the previous October. But it is possible that both letters accurately reflect the writer's feelings at the moment of writing. Jefferson's feelings about the French Revolution are clearly in a state of flux in 1795–96.

On 29 February 1796, the Jay Treaty (already approved by the Senate and ratified by the President) came before both Houses of Congress. The Republicans still hoped to make the Treaty inoperative through a refusal of the House of Representatives to appropriate funds required for its operation. The first move was a call by the House on the Executive to release to Congress all the documents bearing on the Jay negotiations. This was carried by sixty-one votes to thirty-seven, which looked like a substantial victory for the Republicans. (It was actually a hollow victory, for Washington politely declined to produce the documents, and there was nothing the House could do about it unless to start impeachment proceedings.) On 24 March 1796 Adet reported to Delacroix on this victory of the friends of the French Revolution (about whom, however, the Minister Plenipotentiary is beginning to entertain some doubts):

> This first gain, won in such an impressive manner by our friends, is of good augury for the future, and if I could permit myself to hazard some conjectures, I would say to you, Citizen Minister, that the Jay Treaty will shortly be condemned by the House [*la Chambre*] as unconstitutional and contrary to the interests and honour of the United States. The friendship and confidence which the Leaders of the Republican Party have shown to me up to this moment, the share I have had in their discussions in their projects and in their plans, my perfect knowledge of the means they intend to employ, would even put me in a position to give you positive assurances in this regard, were it not that I have always distrusted men and if I did not know to what extent the human mind is light changeable and subject to contradictions.[53]

That dying fall is curious; it looks as if the envoy has a hunch that his friends *les Chefs Républicains* were being overconfident, which was the case. But the main interest of the dispatch—and it is a considerable interest—is of course in what it tells us of the relations, in the spring of 1796, between the Minister Plenipotentiary of the French Republic and the American Republican Party. But can we believe Adet, or is he just boasting? Jefferson's letter to Adet in the previous October suggests that Adet is not exaggerating (or not much). Jefferson's letter seems to be *inviting* such a relationship as Adet is describing. We may take it, then, that this relationship was substantially as described by Adet, in the spring of 1796. And this is rather strange.

From 1789 to 1794, a cult of the French Revolution was in the interest of the Republicans, in terms of American internal politics. In view of the great contemporary popularity of the French Revolution among the American public, such a cult made political sense. But by 1796, the situation had changed radically. The main centers for the propagation of that cult had been the Democratic and Republican Societies. But the Societies had begun to wither early in 1795, partly from the touch of Washington's rebuke: "self-created societies" (December 1794) and partly because of the increasingly truculent attitude of the French government towards the United States. By the spring of 1796, the Societies were in terminal decline and so was the cult of the French Revolution, from its close and prolonged association with the Societies.

In the circumstances, it was extremely imprudent for *les Chefs Républicains* to be in anything like as close relations with the Minister Plenipotentiary of the French Republic as this dispatch of Adet's suggests. The most serious charge of the Federalists against Jefferson at this time was that he was "the head of a French party determined to change the entire system of Government."[54] If Adet's dispatch of 24 March 1796 had fallen into Federalist hands, it would have been generally accepted as clinching the Federalist case against Jefferson.

And the dispatch *could* have fallen into Federalist hands. It could have been intercepted at sea by the British, and subsequently handed over to Washington's administration, in order to confound a friend of France. Precisely that had happened in the previous year, to a dispatch of Adet's predecessor, Fauchet. The interception of that dispatch had blasted the career of Jefferson's successor as Secretary of State, Edmund Randolph.

In the circumstances, it seems the height of imprudence for Jefferson to maintain the kind of relations with Adet which are suggested by his letter of October 1795 and Adet's dispatch of March 1796. If Adet's dispatch had been intercepted and given to Washington, as Fauchet's had been, Jefferson would probably not have been elected Vice President in 1796, or President in 1800.

One has to wonder why Jefferson is behaving in such an imprudent, and even irrational, manner at this time, in his relations with Adet. My own hypothesis is that, amid the flux of differing ideas and feelings about the French Revolution which pass through Jefferson's mind (between his retirement as Secretary of State and his election as Vice President), the old mystical attraction to the French Revolution, though waning, can still exert more power over Jefferson than the general pattern of references in his correspondence in this period would suggest. There is still something in him which needs to be approved by that which had once been his "polar star." Some confirmation of this hypothesis will be found later.

On 23 April, Adet reported rumors of his own recall (which was not in fact decided until the following July and did not become effective until after the Presidential election). Adet claims that his recall accords with his personal wishes, and that he has remained in America only because of his duty. There follows a definition of the duties of a French Minister Plenipotentiary in the United States in the circumstances of 1796:

> I only consulted my duty when I came here, and only duty kept me here. Although I had made up my mind to seek my recall for this year, the way things turned out (*la tournure des affaires*), the trust which the leaders of the Republican Party reposed in me, the approach of the nominations for President, the necessity to get out the vote for a man devoted to France, the services which I could render to the Republic after his election—all imposed silence on the desire which I had had to return to my native land.[55]

In the event, Adet stayed long enough to have a good try at getting out the vote for Jefferson, as we shall see (below, pp. 238–40).

On 24 April 1796, Jefferson wrote a letter to an old friend and former neighbor, Philip Mazzei. Most of the political part of the letter consists of a standard Republican tirade against the Federalists ("an Anglican, monarchical and aristocratical party," etc., etc.). There is nothing in the letter to Mazzei which directly refers to the French Revolution. But there is one extraordinary sentence in this letter which does relate to the mystical French Revolution layer in the Jeffersonian psyche. The sentence runs, "It would give you a fever were I to name to you the apostates who have gone over to these heresies, men who were Samsons in the field & Solomons in the council, but who have had their heads shorn by the harlot England."[56]

The expression "apostates" has a precise meaning in the politico-religious lexicon of Thomas Jefferson in the period of the French Revolution. It applies to a former American Revolutionary (or supporter of the American Revolution) who rejects the French Revolution. "Heresies" applies to the ideas and utterances of such apostates. The "true god," forsaken by the apostates and heretics, is a single entity with two components: the American Revolution and the French Revolution, conceived as together making up one sacred phenomenon: the holy cause of liberty. That was the cause from which George Washington was an apostate.

This terminology shows that part of Jefferson's mind, even as late as the spring of 1796, is still worshipping the French Revolution. And this tends to confirm the hypothesis suggested above concerning the source of the influence of Pierre-Auguste Adet over Thomas Jefferson during the pre-election period of 1796.

Luckily for Jefferson, the "Mazzei" letter did not become public in advance of the Presidential election in November. But Mazzei apparently gave it to a Florentine paper, and the French Revolutionary journal *Le Moniteur* published a French translation of it on 24 January 1797. An English translation was published by the Federalist publication *Minerva* (founded by Noah Webster) on 14 May 1797. *Minerva* added a footnote: "The foregoing letter wears all the external marks of authenticity. Yet it seems hardly possible an American could be capable of writing such a letter. As the letter is circulating in Europe, we deem it just, if a forgery, to give Mr. Jefferson an opportunity to disavow it."

It was not a forgery and Jefferson never did disavow it publicly. Its publication in America was damaging to Jefferson because the Samson/ Solomon passage was taken to be an attack on George Washington. Dumas Malone resists this imputation: "Nowhere else did he describe the President as an apostate or charge him personally with subservience to the British, and it is most unlikely that he meant to do that now, even though his opinion of George Washington had reached its historical nadir." [57]

Malone does not explain what Americans, other than Washington, could be classified by Jefferson as having been "Samsons in the field and Solomons on the council." Jefferson's nineteenth-century editor Paul Leicester Ford entertained no doubt about whom Jefferson is targeting. In a footnote to the "Mazzei" letter, and after quoting *Minerva*'s editorial comment, Ford comments:

> Upon this publication in America, and Jefferson's failure to repudiate it, he was savagely attacked by the Federal press. He attempted no public explanation or palliation, but to his friends (see *post.*, letter to Madison, June 3, 1797) he sought to blame the translation for the stronger expressions, and many years later, in his letter to Van Buren (June 24, 1824) he tried to explain away the apparent allusions to Washington, even becoming insincere in his endeavors to prove that his references did not allude to his former chief. So far as this point is concerned, it is only necessary to note that the criticism on Washington in this letter is far less severe than Jefferson was writing to others in these years, and that Washington himself took the references so wholly to himself, that from the publication of this letter he ceased all correspondence and intercourse with his former secretary. Nor is it probable that Jefferson's attempt to discredit the public version at the

time was so much a repudiation of what he had written, as it was a political desire to avoid the unpopularity of being known as the critic of one whom he had himself to acknowledge had such personal popularity "that the people will support him in whatever he will do or will not do, without appealing to their own reason or to anything but their feelings toward him."[58]

I don't know of anything Jefferson is known to have written about Washington which could reasonably be rated as more severe than the Samson/Solomon passage with its conclusion about being "shorn" by a "harlot." On that point, I agree with Dumas Malone, but not with his inference that, since Jefferson is more severe here than elsewhere, he cannot have intended his reference to apply to Washington. There is nobody else it could possibly apply to, as Washington himself saw, drawing the appropriate conclusion.

Among the many characteristics which made Jefferson such an outstanding political success was a very healthy streak of luck. Had the Mazzei letter, or the Adet dispatch, been published in 1796, on the prelude to Jefferson's first Presidential contest, either one of them could have ended Jefferson's political career, right there. But Adet's dispatch was not published until the twentieth century, and the "Mazzei" letter was published in America in the aftermath of the 1796 election, and was largely forgotten by 1800, by which time, in any case, Washington was dead.

VI

On 30 April 1796 the House of Representatives, by failing to deny appropriations, completed the legislative part of the edifice of the Jay Treaty. From the (American) Republican point of view (which was also the point of view of the Minister Plenipotentiary of the French Republic) this was a most miserable outcome to the prolonged and once impressive Republican agitation against the treaty. In a letter to Jefferson shortly after the calamity, Madison bleakly surveys the state of Republicanism in the early summer of 1796:

We have had a calm ever since the decision on the Treaty. Petitions however continue to arrive, chiefly in favr. of the Treaty. The N. England States have been ready to rise in mass agst. the H. of Reps. Such have been the exertions and influence of Aristocracy, Anglicism, and mercantilism in that quarter, that Republicanism is perfectly overwhelmed, even in the Town of Boston. I hope it will prove but a transitory calamity; and that the discovery of the delusion, will ultimately work a salutary effect. The people have been every where made to believe that the object of the H. of Reps. in resisting the Treaty was—*War;* and have thence listened to the summons "to follow where Washington leads."[59]

In Madison's next letter to Jefferson, the diagnosis sounds even more despondent.

Congress are hurrying through the remnant of business before them, and will probably adjourn about saturday next. Petitions in favor of the Treaty still come in from distant places. The name of the President and the alarm of war, have had a greater effect, than were apprehended on one side, or expected on the other. A crisis which ought to have been so managed as to fortify the Republican cause, has left it in a very crippled condition.[60]

The same letter contains a passage which might have warned Jefferson against the perils of too close an association with Adet, but does not seem to have had that effect (see below, pp. 238–40). The passage runs:

The "Minerva" of N.Y. lately announced, with an affected emphasis, a letter from Paris to N.Y. intimating that influencial persons in the U.S. were urging measures on France, which might force this Country to chuse war agst. England, as the only alternative for war agst. France. It is probable that categorical steps on the part of F. towards us are anticipated as the consequence of what has been effected by the British party here, and that much artifice will be practised by it to charge them in some unpopular form, on its Republican opponents.

Madison felt that the Republicans had been defeated by Washington's personal prestige and popularity (thrown decisively against the Republicans at the end of 1794, with the "self-created societies" reference). Jefferson fully agrees with this interpretation. He wrote to Monroe in June, "Congress has risen. You will have seen by their proceedings the truth of what I always observed to you, that one man outweighs them all in influence over the people who have supported his judgment against their own & that of their representatives. Republicanism must lie on it's oars, resign the vessel to it's pilot, and themselves to the course he thinks best for them."[61]

Shortly after that letter to Monroe and conforming to the spirit of it, Jefferson made an effort to mend fences with Washington. The effort was not a success. Dumas Malone's account of it is unintentionally entertaining. It runs:

Meanwhile, he had written a long letter to the President and received a lengthy reply. In what turned out to be their last written exchange, each man characteristically lapsed into agricultural talk before he finished. Jefferson's initial purpose was to assure Washington that certain confidential information recently publicized in the *Aurora* did not come from him. His action, while certainly not improper, turned out to be unnecessary, since Washington denied harboring any suspicion that he had revealed official secrets. The President's conjectures pointed toward Edmund Randolph, though he did not say that in so many words. Jefferson's protestations were probably welcome, nonetheless, as his reiterated statement that he did not write for the papers doubtless was. But, having said that much, he should have hastened to talk of his peas and clover.

He would have been more consistent with his own policy of silence under attack if he had not referred to malicious charges against him by an unnamed person, readily identifiable as Henry (Light-Horse Harry) Lee. This person, he said, had tried to sow tares between him and Washington by representing him as "still engaged in the battle of politics, and in turbulence and intrigue against the government." Since these charges were quite untrue according to his lights, he described the supposed informer as a "miserable tergiversator." At the same time, while claiming that he avoided political conversation as much as he could without affectation, he admitted that he had never conceived that the fact that he had once been in public required him to belie or conceal his opinions when urged by others to express them. This attempt to prevent the deterioration of personal relations with Washington while maintaining his own political independence was hardly a happy one.

His suspicions of Lee were warranted. About two years earlier, when that erratic Virginian was governor of his state, he had passed on a second-hand report of Jefferson's dinner-table conversation. This related to the President's advisers and pro-British tendencies. Washington regarded it as derogatory but rejected it, and soon thereafter he showed his continued confidence in his former Secretary of State by offering him the mission to Spain. Now that Jefferson himself had opened up the subject, Washington, without intimating the source, admitted that he had heard something. This was that Jefferson had described him to "particular friends and connections," and they in turn had "denounced" him, as "a person under a dangerous influence," the claim being that all would be well if he listened to "some other opinions." Particular friends very probably had said something like that, but they did not need to get from Jefferson the idea that the President had suffered from bad counsel. There were differences of opinion among Republicans as to how "dangerous" it was, but Jefferson was certainly not the only one who deeply distrusted Hamilton. Moreover, the assertion that the President had been badly advised could not be fairly construed as a manifestation of disloyalty to him, even though he thought so.

Washington's own reply implied that he expected more than he had a right to, but it was an impressive statement, even a noble one:

> ... My answer invariably has been, that I have never discovered any thing in the conduct of Mr. Jefferson to raise suspicions, in my mind, of his insincerity; that if he would retrace my public conduct while he was in the Administration, abundant proofs would occur to him, that truth and right decisions, were the sole objects of my pursuit; that there were as many instances within his own knowledge of my having decided against, as in favor of the opinions of the person evidently alluded to; and moreover, that I was no believer in the infallibility of the politics, or measures of any man living. In short, that I was no party man myself, and the first wish of my heart was, if parties did exist, to reconcile them.

This is an admirable description of his position while Jefferson was in office with him, and it is a sufficient answer to the unwarranted claim, sometimes advanced by admirers of Hamilton, that the Secretary of the Treasury was then the master of the administration. But it did not allow for the changed situation, as the moving passage that followed it clearly showed. Not until the last year or two, he said—that is, not until the departure of Jefferson had upset the balance of the government—had he conceived to what lengths parties would go. And not until very lately—that is, until the fight over Jay's Treaty—could he have believed that he would be charged with being an enemy to one country (France) and under the influence of another (Great Britain), or that he would witness such gross misrepresentations of his administration. These were described, he said, "in such exaggerated and indecent terms as could scarcely be applied to a Nero, a notorious defaulter, or even to a common pickpocket."

Jefferson must have been touched by these words, for no one was more aware than he of Washington's extreme sensitiveness. He could appreciate it the more because he himself found personal differences almost intolerable and could hardly bear to be misunderstood. He was not above employing devious devices to avoid wounding one he had admired so much. Yet, his rather inept attempt to smooth things over, while asserting at the same time his right to voice private opinions which could be assumed to be critical of the administration, was an inevitable failure under the existing facts of political life, which Washington was still unable to understand.[62]

Washington knew that Jefferson had created and still inspired the Republican press which had been attacking Washington obliquely while Jefferson was still Secretary of State, and had been hounding him openly and unmercifully (mainly over the Jay Treaty) since Jefferson's retirement from that office. In the circumstances, Washington's reference to the "extravagant and indecent language" of the Republican press, like his reference to "that rascal Freneau" in 1793 is an oblique rebuke to Jefferson himself. To say that Jefferson "must have been touched" by this evidence of "Washington's extreme sensitiveness," is a good example of Malone's propensity to sentimentalize politics in general, and his hero in particular.

VII

On 7 July 1796, the French Minister of Foreign Affairs notified Monroe of the Directory's "final decision," in response to the Jay Treaty:

> Since the United States by the Jay Treaty had abandoned the neutrality principles laid down in the Treaty of 1778 with France, especially the "free ships make free goods" rule, "the Directoire considers the stipulations of (the) treaty of 1778, which respects the neutrality of (the) flag, as altered and suspended by this act; and that it would think itself wanting in its duty if it did not modify a state of things which would never have been consented to but upon the principles of strict reciprocity."
>
> On July 2, also, had been passed a decree providing that the French would treat neutral vessels "in the same manner as they suffer the English to treat them." The crowning blow was the recall of the French minister to the United States, Adet. No successor was appointed. Monroe appealed in vain to the Directory. Paris regarded the matter closed.[63]

By August, the Directory was seriously contemplating a kind of repeat of the Genet Mission. The instructions dated 5 August 1796 drawn up for Citizen Michel Ange Mangourit as Chargé d'Affaires to the United States occupy thirteen pages of Turner's edition of the correspondence of the French Ministers to the United States.[64] Some readers may recall Citizen Mangourit from chapter 3. As Consul in Charleston, South Carolina, Mangourit had been one of the most fervent of Genet's consular collaborators, on such matters as seizure of British shipping in American waters and the planning of an "irruption" from Kentucky into Louisiana. Mangourit had had the Genet seal of approval: "*Citoyen Mangourit, Citoyens, est un excellent patriote.*" The arrival in America of a notorious former collaborator of Genet's as Chargé d'Affaires of the French Republic would have been a disaster for the Republican Party in an election year.

Monroe appears to have succeeded in convincing the Directory of this, and the Mangourit idea was dropped.

On 17 September 1796, Washington published his Farewell Address. As regards party politics and international affairs the key words of the Address are: "Against the insidious wiles of foreign influence (I conjure you to believe me, fellow citizens), the jealousy of a free people ought to be *constantly* awake. . . . Excessive partiality for one foreign nation and excessive dislike of another cause those whom they actuate to see danger only on one side, and serve to veil and even second the arts of influence on the other." [65]

Even before the Farewell Address was published, Jefferson's name was already before the public as a candidate for the Presidency. Jefferson's hat (as might be expected) had been thrown into the ring by a hand other than Jefferson's own. A week before the Farewell Address, the following editorial paragraph appeared in *Aurora:* "It requires no talent at divination to decide who will be candidates for the chair. THOMAS JEFFERSON & JOHN ADAMS will be the men, & whether we shall have at the head of our executive a steadfast friend to the Rights of the People, or an advocate for hereditary power and distinctions, the people of the United States are soon to decide." [66]

Readers of the *Aurora* were already conditioned to know which sets of characteristics went with which candidates.

Shortly after the contest opened, the Minister Plenipotentiary of the French Republic was already electioneering for Jefferson, in Boston. On 24 September 1796, Adet reported to his Foreign Minister:

> Our friends in Massachusetts Bay had become singularly cold: they had interpreted the silence of the French Government in a manner unfavorable to us and had almost made up their mind to leave the coming election to their adversaries. I revived their stricken courage, I reanimated their lapses. I told them that the [French] Republic was far from abandoning them, as they had feared; that she had felt a lively indignation at the treaty concluded with Great Britain; that she had been aware of the price paid by the friends of liberty, and that she would certainly not abandon them to the mercy of England. It took no more than this to revive their zeal, and they promised me to do their best to vote Jefferson President and to reject John Adams. [67]

By October, Adet was using his diplomatic function for electoral purposes, in support of Jefferson. Dumas Malone writes:

> The week before the election in Pennsylvania, while Washington was away, the minister transmitted to Secretary of State Pickering a resolution

of the Directory stating that henceforth the French would treat neutral vessels in the same manner as these permitted the British to treat them. Upon its face the resolution may not seem unreasonable, but Adet's accompanying note undoubtedly does. Expecting his action to be regarded as a threat, he stated that he would cause this note to be published, and this he did in the *Aurora,* with the result that it was available to the public before it was submitted to Washington. Pickering properly objected to this presumption and asked for an explanation of the minister's allegations.[68]

Adet followed this up by an announcement of "the suspension of his own functions as a mark of the just discontent of the Directory." Adet's report to his Foreign Minister on these activities (14 November 1796) betrays an uneasy awareness that they may have not been having the effect intended.

> It is impossible for me to judge at present, Citizen Minister, of the effect that the measure adopted by the Directory [Adet's recall] will produce. At Philadelphia it markedly disturbed the English faction and for a moment it annoyed (*chagrina*) some of our friends. You will no doubt be astonished at this, Citizen Minister, but it is true that most of those here who call themselves Friends of the French approve the determination of the Directory solely because of the hatred they bear to Washington. All feel that the Directory's arguments are reasonable. But they are not equally satisfied to hear the Directory address the American Government in a tone which they would like to be the only ones entitled to use towards other peoples. They have been convinced for so long that the Americans are the first people on earth that they are amazed at the disappearance of the brilliant dreams which their imagination had presented to them as reality. They would perhaps have had some difficulty in forgiving the Directory for destroying these pleasant illusions, were it not for the fact that the Directory is furnishing them with the means for vengeance against Washington and the British faction.[69]

Adet, like Genet and Fauchet before him, is finding that the Americans are not worthy of the French Revolution.

On 5 December, while the outcome of the election was still uncertain, Madison wrote to Jefferson: "Adêts Note which you will have seen, is working all the evil with which it is pregnant. Those who rejoice at its indiscretions and are taking advantage of them, have the impudence to pretend that it is an electioneering manoeuvre, and that the French Govt. have been led to it by the opponents of the British Treaty."[70]

Yet the French Government *had* been "led to" it by "the opponents of the British Treaty." The discourse of *les Chefs Républicains* in their contacts with Adet had played a major part in the formation of the policy of Charles Delacroix on behalf of the Directory. The Republican leaders did not, of course, foresee the precise effects of their words on their French interlocutor or on the French Minister to whom that interlocutor reported. It was all part of the continuing comedy of errors, *la mésen-tente cordiale*.

Jefferson replied, on 17 December, to Madison's letter of the fifth, but did not advert to Madison's comment on Adet. In the context, the silence seems to suggest that he did not agree with Madison. We don't know what Jefferson thought about Adet's flamboyant exertions on his behalf in the months preceding the Presidential election of 1796, because there is no recorded utterance of Jefferson's on that subject. If my surmise is correct that he still felt a need, at some level of his psyche, for the approval of the French Revolution, then Adet's exertions must have been agreeable to Jefferson at that level. That could account for Jefferson's fail-ure to agree with Madison's anti-Adet outburst.

In any case, Jefferson would not have been worried by thoughts that Adet's indiscretions might cost him the Presidency. Thomas Jefferson, very sensibly, did not *want* the Presidency in 1796. The *Vice Presidency,* which he attained, suited him much better, in that year. He tells Madison, in that letter of 17 December 1796, why he does not want the Presidency at this time. Foreign affairs are the reason: "I think [foreign affairs] never were so gloomy an aspect since the year 83 [end of America's war with Britain]. Let those come to the helm who think they can steer clear of the difficulties. I have no confidence in myself for the undertaking."[71]

Jefferson was referring primarily to Franco-American relations, then bad and beginning to get worse. Jefferson knew that, as President, he would not be able to live up to French Revolutionary expectations of how a friend of France should behave. Adet himself was aware of Jefferson's limitations from a French point of view. As he reported to his Foreign Minister on 31 December 1796:

> I don't know whether, as people told me, we shall find in him a man entirely devoted to our interest. Mr. Jefferson likes us, because he detests England: he tries to be on good terms with us [*se rapprocher de nous*] be-cause he is less afraid of us than of Great Britain: but he would perhaps change his feelings [*Sentiment*] towards us, if tomorrow Great Britain ceased to frighten him. Jefferson, although a friend of liberty and fairness, although an admirer of the efforts which we have made to break our chains and dissipate the cloud of ignorance which weighs down on the human

race—Jefferson, I say is American and, as such [*à ce titre*] he cannot sincerely be our friend. An American is the enemy of all the European Peoples.[72]

On Adet's appreciation of Jefferson, Frederick Jackson Turner comments: "This shows unusual insight into Jefferson's real tendencies."[73] It does, and yet it leaves out a lot. Adet's assessment leaves out *the French Revolution,* rather a large matter. (The omission is significant. By the end of 1796, many Frenchmen, still nominally revolutionaries, were heartily sick of the Revolution. During the next decade, both Adet and Fauchet were happily serving the Napoleonic Empire.) Jefferson's faith in the French Revolution, strong in 1789–93, and indeterminately extant in 1796, had never been *exclusively* a matter of hatred of England (and hatred, not fear, was the emotion England inspired in Jefferson). It was *as an American* that Jefferson had cherished the French Revolution, for he believed it to be a providential agent in relation to America: the destined rekindler of the flame of 1776. Adet, astute as he was, was not the kind of man who could understand, or even believe in, the mystic side of Thomas Jefferson.

On one thing, however, Adet was certainly right. Jefferson could not be relied on to be "entirely devoted to our interests." That being so, Jefferson would, as he himself foresaw, have had a most miserable time as President of the United States from 1796 to 1800. The Vice Presidency, on the other hand, made an ideal vantage point. Biding his time was one of the many things at which Thomas Jefferson was very good indeed. And there is no better post for the exercise of that particular capacity than the Vice Presidency of the United States.

VIII

As relations between the United States and France worsen throughout 1797, while the war between England and France continues, Vice President Jefferson repeatedly asserts his commitment to neutrality, which he sees as threatened. In a letter to Thomas Pinckney on 29 May 1797, Jefferson writes:"When I contemplate the spirit which is driving us on here, & that beyond the water which will view us as but a mouthful the more, I have little hope of peace. I anticipate the burning of our sea ports, havoc of our frontiers, household insurgency, with a long train of et ceteras, which is enough for a man to have met once in his life."[74]

In this passage the spirit which is "driving us on here" is no doubt Federalism. The spirit which "will view us as but a mouthful the more" is certainly the France of the Directory, annexing country after country in this period.

One might perhaps infer from the "mouthful the more" passage that Jefferson has quite turned against the French Republic. But this would be simplistic. Jefferson has not yet overcome his *penchant* for indiscreet conversations with French Revolutionary envoys, and a record of one of these exists for June 1797. The envoy in question is Philippe-Henri-Joseph de Létombe, formerly a French Consul and now Chargé d'Affaires in Philadelphia since the departure of Adet. In his instructions to his (downgraded) successor, Adet reports a deterioration in the relations between his mission and the Republicans in Congress, in late 1796: "One saw the majority of the Republican Members in the last Congress fleeing (so to speak) from the Representatives of the Republic. During the Session I had with them, only distant relations and secret interviews. In the last session they avoided my house: today they informed of me that during the next session, they would not be able to communicate with me, even secretly."[75]

The nervousness of the Republican Congressmen about compromising contact with French diplomats in the months before the election of November 1796 makes Jefferson's silent tolerance of Adet's noisy and well-publicized efforts on his behalf, in the same period, all the more surprising.

In his instructions, Adet had advised Létombe to get around the nervousness of Republicans by the use of an *agent intermédiaire,* a private citizen. But Létombe soon found that in the case of Vice President Jefferson there was no need for any *agent intermédiaire.* In a report of 7 June 1797 to his Foreign Minister [still that same Citizen Charles Delacroix whose plans for the United States have already been referred to] Létombe wrote: "My conversation with the wise Jefferson [*le sage Jefferson*] was long and tranquil." Létombe records Jefferson's conversation: "The Country has broken in good faith and forever the chains which attached it to England: it is penetrated with gratitude to France and will never forget that it owes its liberation to France."

After references to Washington (positive), Genet (negative), and Hamilton (negative), the Vice President offers the French envoy a crisp assessment of the new President of the United States: "Mr. Adams is vain, irritable, stubborn, endowed with excessive *amour-propre,* and still suffering pique at the preference accorded to Franklin over him in Paris. . . . But his Presidency lasts only five [*sic*] years: he only became President by three votes, and the System of the United States will change along with him."[76]

It sounds as if Jefferson is already confident of his own election in 1800, but in the context this is not necessarily the case. Jefferson is trying to soothe the Directory, through Létombe, and the thought of his own victory-to-come (whether true or false) is part of the soothing strategy. Jefferson skillfully applies the kind of flattery that this strategy requires, when applied to French officials in a time of French victories. Létombe records Jefferson as saying:

> It is for France—great, generous, at the Summit of her glory—to be patient, to precipitate nothing, and everything will return to order. The links which unite and must unite forever the two Republics are relaxed, not broken. . . . The new Ministers Extraordinary [of the United States] are about to leave. The Vice President is persuaded and convinced that the Directory should receive them, listen to them; allow the negotiations to drag on and soften them by the Urbanity of [the Directory] proceedings.[77]

Jefferson's personal remarks about his President were indiscreet and *apparently* disloyal. But the substance of his advice was helpful to the Adams administration, to its envoys and to the national interest of the United States. And the occasion is an important one. Jefferson is trying to avert a war between France and the United States.

Létombe ends by reporting two proposals of Jefferson's. Both are old ideas, or dreams, of his. One is a project for reciprocity of citizenship rights between France and the United States. The other is a piece of advice for the Directory: "Let the Directory organize a descent on England and dictate in London the conditions of a peace which, by assuring the repose and happiness of the world, would be based on the Freedom of the Seas, the reciprocity of Commerce and the liberation of all colonies under the guaranties of their Metropolises."[78]

Jefferson, personally, is not emotionally neutral in the great conflict; he still desires the complete victory of one belligerent over the other. But *for the United States,* Jefferson now sees neutrality as the only possible option. To Elbridge Gerry, one of the new "Ministers Extraordinary" to France (whose path Jefferson was trying to smooth in his talk with Létombe) Jefferson writes (21 June 1797): "Our countrymen have divided themselves by such strong affections, to the French & the English, that nothing will secure us internally but a divorce from both nations; and this must be the object of every real American, and it's attainment is practicable without much self-denial."[79]

In a letter to Edward Rutledge a few days later, Jefferson uses similar language: "As to everything except commerce, we ought to divorce ourselves from them all."[80]

Jefferson's posture towards the French Republic, in this period, is fraught with tension. He is clear that the United States must divorce "from both belligerents." Yet he personally, though Vice President of the "divorced" United States, is dreaming of the total victory of one belligerent over the other.

That dream visits Jefferson in late June 1797, accompanied by the last clear manifestation of his old conception of the French Revolution as having a sacred mission. There are a few phrases, in his writing of this period, which might, or might not, derive from that conception: for example, his repeated use of "miraculous events" to describe the French military victories of the period. But in a phrase contained in a letter of 27 June 1797, the conception of a sacred mission appears without ambiguity. Jefferson wrote: "But nothing can establish firmly the republican principles of our government but an establishment of them in England. France will be the apostle for this." [81]

In the summer of 1797, the French Revolution has still a sacral mission, in the eyes of Thomas Jefferson. But the mission has been seriously downgraded. Back in the exalted days of 1789–93, the mission of the French Revolution, for Jefferson, had been the highest conceivable, that of restoring to America the purity of the American Revolution. By 1797, that lofty role can no longer be assigned to the French Revolution. Now the French Revolution has sunk into the role of the apostle for the establishment of Republican principles *in England*.

Evelyn Waugh once, with reference to Graham Greene, spoke of "the dark places where Mr. Greene's apostolate lies." The imagination of Thomas Jefferson could hardly conceive of any darker place than that in which he now supposed the apostolate of the French Revolution to lie.

Jefferson's urge to see the French Revolutionary armies "descend" on England lasted into the following year. It finds expression in three letters of February—March 1798. [82]

The first of these letters, dated 23 February 1798, is the most complex and the most interesting of all Jefferson's references to a topic which had preoccupied him since he first learned of the French Republic's Declaration of War on England (February 1793). Jefferson is replying to a letter from a gentleman, Peregrine Fitzhugh, who had apparently expressed some qualms about the subjugation of England by the French Revolutionary armies. In his reply, Jefferson explains that subjugation is not precisely what he has in mind:

The ensuing month will probably be the most eventful ever yet seen in Modern Europe. It may probably be the season preferred for the projected invasion of England. It is indeed a game of chances. The sea which divides the combatants gives to fortune as well as to valor it's share of influence on the enterprise. But all the chances are not on one side. The subjugation of England would indeed be a general calamity. But happily it is impossible. Should it end in her being only republicanized, I know not on what principle a true republican of our country could lament it, whether he considers it as extending the blessings of a purer government to other portions of mankind, or strengthening the cause of liberty in our own country by the influence of that example. I do not indeed wish to see any nation have a form of government forced on them; but if it is to be done, I should rejoice at it's being a freer one.[83]

They may not be "subjugated," but if the government forced upon them is "a freer one," Jefferson would rejoice. The concept that people might be "forced to be free" originated with Rousseau, in *Du Contrat Social* (first book, chapter 7, last paragraph). Jefferson never acknowledged any intellectual or moral debt to Rousseau but the debt is evident in this peremptory paradox. "Forced to be free" is a truly revolutionary concept, common to the French Revolution, and to its twentieth-century heir, the Russian Revolution.

IX

In October 1797, what came to be known as "the XYZ affair" produced consequences which led to a step further in the deterioration of the relations between the United States and the France of the Directory. Talleyrand, the new French Foreign Minister, attempted, through three *agents intermédiaires* (publicly identified only as "X., Y., and Z.") to extract large sums of money, both for public and private purposes, from the newly arrived envoys of the United States.

This sordid episode was characteristic of the deliquescent condition into which the French Revolution had sunk, as the decade and the century draw to their close. Outsiders might see the Directory as being "at the summit of glory"—because of the great military victories—but the Directory itself was aware that it was the Generals, not the Directory, who were reaping the glory. Bonaparte's dazzling victories of 1796 had made Italy his personal fief: his allegiance to the Directory was nominal, and perfunctory at that. The Directors and Talleyrand knew that their time was running out, and they used their time—as well as the appearance of overweening authority which they derived, briefly, from the victories of Bonaparte and others—to line their pockets.

One of the *agents intermédiaires,* Pierre Bellamy—the "Y" in "XYZ"—made use of "the French Party in America"—the Jeffersonian Republicans—in his efforts to blackmail the representatives of the United States. The authors of *The Age of Federalism* quote Bellamy:

> "Perhaps," he hastened to add, "you believe that in returning & exposing to your country men the unreasonableness of the demands of this government you will unite them in their resistance to those demands. You are mistaken. You ought to know that the diplomatic skill of France & the means she possesses in your country are sufficient to enable her with the French party in America to throw the blame which will attend the rupture of the negotiations on the federalists as you term yourselves & on the British Party as France terms you: And you may assure yourselves this will be done." [84]

When reports of the "XYZ" affair reached the United States in the spring of 1798, the humiliation of the American envoys by the French caused an *anti*-French upsurge of public opinion, at least as great as that pro-French upsurge of 1793 had been. Jefferson, in a letter to Madison (6 April 1798) acknowledges "such a shock on the republican mind, as has never been seen since our independence." [85]

Jefferson now doubles the functions of Vice President and leader of the Republican Party. In another letter to Madison (12 April 1798) he lays down the basis of Republican strategy at this most critical time: "All, therefore, which the advocates of peace can now attempt, is to prevent war measures *externally,* consenting to every rational measure of *internal* defence & preparation." [86]

Jefferson also foresees, very early on, how the *results* of the great Federalist wave may be turned to the benefit of the Republicans. He follows the line about "consent to every measure of *internal* defence" with: "Great expences will be incurred; & it will be left to those whose measures render them necessary, to provide to meet them."

Jefferson is at his best when things appear to be going best for his adversaries. His handling of the "XYZ" affair in 1798 recalls his handling of the Genet affair in 1793. And as in the Genet affair, he uses the tactic of *personalization,* in order to exonerate the French Republic. *Genet* had been solely responsible in 1793 and *Talleyrand* is solely responsible in 1797–98. The Directory is "above suspicion."

According to the authors of *The Age of Federalism:*

> The most extraordinary thing done in the extraordinary climate of the spring and summer of 1798 was the authorizing of a military establishment

more formidable than anyone would have thought possible a few months before. The regular army was augmented by an "Additional Army" of twelve thousand men, and a "Provisional Army" of ten thousand men was to be activated by the President in the event of actual war or invasion, or "imminent danger" of invasion.[87]

This was in accord with Jefferson's expectations; and also with his hopes for an eventual Republican revival. In a letter to John Taylor of Caroline (Virginia) in June, Jefferson is more emphatically neutralist than he had been before "XYZ":"Better keep together as we are, haul off from Europe as soon as we can, and from all attachments to any portions of it; and if they show their power just sufficiently to hoop us together, it will be the happiest situation in which we can exist."[88]

By October 1798, Jefferson notes that: "The X.Y.Z. fever has considerably abated through the country, as I am informed, and the alien & sedition laws are working hard."[89] That is that the security measures voted by the Federalists in response to the "quasi-war with France" are becoming unpopular with the public, and with the (Southern) states.

Though Jefferson does not advert to this, the Republicans in this period 1798–99 were actually organizing armed resistance to Federal activities regarded by them as unconstitutional. In his article "Republican Thought and the Political Violence of the 1790's," John R. Howe, Jr., refers to "the bands of Jeffersonian militia, formed in the various cities from Baltimore to Boston, armed and openly drilling, preparing to stand against the Federalist army."[90]

If John Adams had been elected for a second term in 1800, the American Civil War might have broken out sixty years ahead of time. Also, the pattern of activities of "Jeffersonian militia" in 1798–99 prefigured that of other anti-Federal militia active in a number of American states nearly two hundred years later.

X

In November 1798 the news reached America of the destruction of the French fleet by Nelson in the Battle of the Nile. Paradoxically, this major defeat of French military power was extremely beneficial to those whom the French regarded as the friends of France in America: the Republicans. The destruction of the French fleet suggested to the American public that France—whatever the intentions of its governors—could no longer pose a serious threat to America. The costly and otherwise burdensome measures of the Federalists henceforward appear as also *unnecessary*. This combination of events and conditions would lead to the election of Thomas Jefferson to the Presidency in 1800.

Jefferson never referred to the Battle of the Nile. It would be for him an unattractive topic, for it destroyed his hope for a French descent in Britain (of which he had still been dreaming as late as the spring of 1798). But he is confident, at the close of 1798, of a coming reaction in favor of the Republicans, under the impact of high Federalist taxation. He writes to John Taylor of Caroline (26 November 1798): "This disease of the imagination will pass over, because the patients are essentially republican. Indeed, the Doctor is now on his way to cure it, in the guise of a tax gatherer. But give time for the medicine to work, & for the repetition of stronger doses, which must be administered."[91]

Jefferson's last recorded references to the French Revolution—during the period of the continuing existence of a phenomenon of that name— occur in the first quarter of 1799. There are *two* such references. The first is ambivalent; but mainly negative in its implications. The second—and last of all—is radically negative, and startlingly novel.

The first is contained in a letter of 25 January 1799 to Elbridge Gerry, the member of the American negotiating team who was considered most sympathetic to France (and had therefore been vehemently attacked by the Federalists for alleged collusion with the Directory). To Gerry, Jefferson reaffirms his by now well-established commitment to American neutrality: "And I am not for linking ourselves by new treaties with the quarrels of Europe; entering that field of slaughter to preserve their balance, or joining in the confederacy of kings to war against the principles of liberty."[92]

After some general remarks about what these principles involve—in relation to religion, the press, science, etc.—Jefferson directly addresses his own relation to the French revolution.

> *To these I will add, that I was a sincere well-wisher to the success of the French revolution, and still wish it may end in the establishment of a free & well-ordered republic;* but I have not been insensible under the atrocious depredations they have committed on our commerce. The first object of my heart is my own country. In that is embarked my family, my fortune, & my own existence. I have not one farthing of interest, nor one fibre of attachment out of it, nor a single motive of preference of any one nation to another, but in proportion as they are more or less friendly to us.[93]

The opening words (which I have italicized) made Jefferson's position in January 1799 identical to that of Washington towards the French Revolution from late 1791 up to Washington's death in 1799.

The second and much more remarkable reference occurs in a reply to a letter from an old acquaintance, Thomas Lomax, on 12 March 1799. Jefferson is writing just after the receipt of a conciliatory message from Talleyrand which proved to be the beginning of the end of the quasi-war with France (dating from May 1798). Jefferson claims that America now realized "that France has sincerely wished peace and their seducers [the Federalists] have wished war." Then, as is often the case with him, Jefferson recalls another aspect of the matter (in this case the Directory's provocative and humiliating dealings with the representatives of the United States) and goes off on what might appear to be quite a different tack:

> The atrocious proceedings of France towards this country, had well nigh destroyed its liberties. *The Anglomen and monocrats had so artfully confounded the cause of France with that of freedom, that both went down in the same scale.* I sincerely join you in abjuring all political connection with every foreign power; and tho I cordially wish well to the progress of liberty in all nations, and would forever give it the weight of our countenance, yet they are not to be touched without contamination from their other bad principles. Commerce with all nations, alliance with none, should be our motto.[94]

That second sentence (italicized by me) is flabbergasting in the light of so much that had gone before, and that is recorded in this book. So it was *the Federalists* who had confounded the cause of France with that of freedom! This is an entirely new offense, on the part of the Federalists, and it is the reverse of their original one. In the heyday of his revolutionary fervor, in 1789–93, Jefferson had excommunicated Federalist leaders—John Adams and Alexander Hamilton—precisely for their *failure* to identify the cause of Revolutionary France with the cause of freedom. It was for this offense that these Americans had been stigmatized as "heretics" and "apostates." To fail to identify the cause of the French Revolution with the American Revolution was to apostatize from the latter.

But now, in early 1799, when the French Revolution itself is tottering to its end, Jefferson wishes to *separate* "the cause of France" from "the cause of freedom" in America. So he has the nerve to blame the Federalists for having "artfully confounded" the two.

That sentence provides, at any rate, a fine ironic curtain-line to the long and strange story of Thomas Jefferson's involvement with the French Revolution as recorded in his correspondence.

XI

As observed previously, luck was often on the side of Thomas Jefferson. And there is no better example of his luck than the fact of the demise of the French Revolution in the year before the Presidential election year of 1800.

On 18 Brumaire (9 November) 1799, there occurred the event which Edmund Burke had predicted, nine years before, as the inevitable conclusion of the French Revolution.

> It is known, that armies have hitherto yielded a very precarious and uncertain obedience to any senate, or popular authority; and they will least of all yield it to an assembly which is to have only a continuance of two years. The officers must totally lose the characteristic disposition of military men, if they see with perfect submission and due admiration, the dominion of pleaders; especially when they find, that they have a new court to pay to an endless succession of those pleaders, whose military policy, and the genius of whose command (if they should have any) must be as uncertain as their duration is transient. In the weakness of one kind of authority, and in the fluctuation of all, the officers of an army will remain for some time mutinous and full of faction, until some popular general, who understands the art of conciliating the soldiery, and who possesses the true spirit of command, shall draw the eyes of all men upon himself. Armies will obey him on his personal account. There is no other way of securing military obedience in this state of things. But the moment in which that event shall happen, the person who really commands the army is your master; the master (that is little) of your king, the master of your assembly, the master of your whole republic.[95]

After the *coup d'état* of 18th Brumaire, Napoleon Bonaparte, as Chief Consul, is sovereign ruler of France and most of continental Western Europe. This is the period of which Victor Hugo later wrote: *Et du Premier Consul déjà par maint endroit / Le front de l'Empereur brisait le masque étroit.*

The final sentence of the "Proclamation of the Consuls to the French People" (15 December 1799) is already in the terse and trenchant Napoleonic style: "Citizens, the Revolution is established upon the principles which began it: it is ended."[96]

As it happened, Bonaparte's proclamation occurred on the day after the death of George Washington. So the dates 14–15 December 1799 doubly mark the end of an epoch in the life of Thomas Jefferson.

Having declared the French Revolution at an end, Bonaparte also wanted to bring the "quasi-war" with America to an end. The great realist saw at once that there was no point in trying to push the Americans around, after the destruction of the French fleet in the Battle of the Nile. Peace negotiations led, on 3 October 1800, to the signature of a Franco-American Convention at Môrtefontaine, Joseph Bonaparte's seat, north of Paris. The great fete at Môrtefontaine, attended by the First Consul and 150 subordinate dignitaries, is said to have been "the most splendid occasion of its kind since the beginning of the French Revolution." It was in fact the last in a series of Arcadian Franco-American manifestations that had begun with the Apotheosis of Benjamin Franklin ten years before. The most recent example had been the presentation of James Monroe's credentials to the National Convention. Môrtefontaine . . . there is something appropriately elegiac about the name, a suitable place for a wake.

Those celebrations took place on the eve of the Presidential election in the United States. As it turned out, the Convention of Môrtefontaine did John Adams no good. What it did, however, was to put his successful rival, Thomas Jefferson, in an unprecedentedly strong situation as President, with regard to foreign affairs. The United States now had solid international agreements with both major belligerents. True, these agreements had both been secured (on the American side) by Federalist administrations. The Jay Treaty had been secured by Washington's second administration, on the teeth of bitter opposition from the Republicans. The Convention of Môrtefontaine had been achieved by John Adams personally in the teeth of bitter opposition from the Federalist side, which probably cost Adams his chance of a second term.

But no matter how achieved, the two treaties were now in being, and together they signified acceptance of American neutrality by both belligerents: a most agreeable Federalist legacy for the incoming Republican President. On the general significance for the United States of the settlement of 1800 (which effectively replaced the old Franco-American treaties of 1778) the authors of the *Age of Federalism* offer a judicious commentary:

> Quite possibly the greatest benefit of all from the Convention, it too a symbolic one, was that which accrued to the United States. And here the American negotiators, in burying the treaties of 1778 for practical purposes once and for all, had in effect handed to their Republican successors what amounted to a free gift. It was not the obligations of an alliance, simply in

itself, that had come to make these treaties such a burden. Few Americans, Republican or Federalist, had ever felt themselves bound by compulsions of that sort, even at the height of the enthusiasm in America for France's revolution in the delirious days of 1793. It was rather the ideological coercions surrounding the treaties, and the entire web of fraternal claims that connected them with America's own Revolution, that had come to play such havoc in the domestic politics of the United States. These coercions, which the Republicans had once joyfully accepted and which the Federalists had come more and more bitterly to resist, were now in large part removed. Still, the very poisonousness of American partisan politics prevented any real detachment in grasping the merits of the Convention of 1800. Most Federalists felt bound to find every kind of fault with an arrangement that appeared to make any palpable concessions to the detested French, while few Republicans could accord other than grudging approval to the work of any mission that had gone to France under Federalist auspices. Nor were the Republicans yet quite prepared to admit that their own ideological attachment to France, which had helped so much to bring their party into being and had once so fortified their claim to wide popular support, had by this time become a heavy embarrassment. They were now relieved from it, and without the additional burden of having to get rid of it for themselves, or even of having to say so.

Nobody appreciated this more richly than Thomas Jefferson, as he prepared to assume the presidential chair in 1801. Jefferson was now serenely free to announce, with no reference at all to the Convention of 1800, a policy of "peace, commerce, and honest friendship with all nations, entangling alliances with none."[97]

The last convulsions of the French Revolution, its demise, and the consequences of its demise had all helped to clear the way for Jefferson's election to the Presidency. In the last year of the French Revolution's existence Jefferson had begun to associate "the cause of France," no longer with hope for America, but with what was wrong with America. In his letter of 12 March 1799 Jefferson charged the Federalists with having "confounded the cause of France with that of freedom." As Bonaparte emerged as the heir of the French Revolution and its conquests, Jefferson's feelings about what France stood for in relation to America underwent a complete reversal from what they had been in 1789–93. France now stood, no longer for the regeneration of American freedom, but for the forces that were threatening American freedom.

XII

On 31 January 1800, Jefferson touches briefly and queasily on the coup of 18th Brumaire at the end of a letter to Bishop Madison: "I will say nothing to you on the late revolution of France, which is painfully interesting. Perhaps when we know more of the circumstances which gave rise to it, & direction it will take, Buonaparte, its chief organ, may stand in a better light than at present."[98]

Two days later, in a letter to Thomas Mann Randolph, Jefferson refers to the dictatorial ambitions which he (and many others) then attributed to Alexander Hamilton. "The enemies of our constitution are preparing a fearful operation, and the dissensions in this state are too likely to bring things to the situation they wish, when our Buonaparte, surrounded by his comrades in arms, may step in to give us political salvation in his way."[99] *Our Buonaparte* . . . This is the grisly end to the long affair. As the once beloved object, the French Revolution, lies dying, it is acquiring in the mind's eye of Thomas Jefferson the loathly lineaments of Alexander Hamilton.

SEVEN

A THEMATIC OVERVIEW
Liberty, Slavery, and the Cult
of the French Revolution

How is it that we hear the loudest yelps for liberty from the drivers of negros?
Samuel Johnson

Jefferson scholars, biographers, and editors have traditionally not attempted that Johnsonian question.

The nearest that Thomas Jefferson himself ever came to answering it is in a passage in a 1786 letter addressed to a French correspondent, Jean-Nicolas Démeunier, regarding "the slave law . . . passed in Virginia without the clause of emancipation." At the end of a long reply, Jefferson writes:

> What a stupendous, what an incomprehensible machine is man! Who can endure toil, famine, stripes, imprisonment or death itself in vindication of his own liberty, and the next moment be deaf to all those motives whose power supported him thro' his trial, and inflict on his fellow men a bondage, one hour of which is fraught with more misery than ages of that which he rose in rebellion to oppose. But we must await with patience the workings of an overruling providence, and hope that that is preparing the deliverance of these our suffering brethren. When the measure of their tears shall be full, when their groans shall have involved heaven itself in darkness, doubtless a god of justice will awaken to their distress, and by diffusing light and liberality among their oppressors, or at length by his exterminating thunder, manifest his attention to the things of this world, and that they are not left to the guidance of a blind fatality.[1]

In Jeffersonian rhetoric, pious ejaculations have a tendency to gush out in rather suspect contexts. Jefferson's own contribution to the law in question had been an attempt to increase repressive measures against free blacks and mothers of children of mixed race (below, p. 206).

The object of this chapter is to inquire into the relationship between the Cult of the French Revolution, on the one hand, and the interaction between the commitment to Liberty and the fact of slavery, in Jefferson's Virginia, on the other hand.

We have first to look at that Virginian interaction in itself before we can attempt to inquire into how the Cult of the French Revolution may relate to it.

I

The general tendency of mainstream Jeffersonian scholarship over many years had been to treat slavery and liberty as separable phenomena, and of unequal importance. Jefferson abhorred slavery, and put his abhorrence on record on several occasions, as in *Notes on the State of Virginia,* and as in the letter to Démeunier quoted above. Abhorrence of slavery and adoration of liberty are obviously perfectly consistent and compatible positions. So one can discuss Thomas Jefferson on Liberty, while leaving the matter of slavery to one side as irrelevant (since Jefferson's abhorrence of the same had been abundantly established). The *locus classicus* in this kind is Julian P. Boyd's introduction to the 1967 edition of John P. Foley's *Jefferson Cyclopedia* (of 1900). In that introduction Boyd says: "An accident of history may have thrust the role upon him, but it was the unwavering commitment that caused him to become the archetypal spokesman of liberty." Although Foley's *Cyclopedia* contains an abundance of entries under "Slavery" Boyd does not allude to that matter at all in his introduction.[2]

By the time Boyd penned that introduction, such an approach was already ceasing to be tenable. In the 1960s and 1970s a kind of revolution occurred in American scholarship with relation to the topic of liberty and slavery in Jeffersonian Virginia. I should now like to look at, and quote from, six major contributions to that revolution. These are in chronological order: Robert McColley, *Slaves and Jeffersonian Virginia* (Urbana, Ill., 1964); Winthrop Jordan, *White over Black* (Chapel Hill, N. C., 1968); William Cohen, "Thomas Jefferson and the Problem of Slavery" (*Journal of American History* LVI, December 1969); David Brion Davis, *Was Thomas Jefferson an Authentic Enemy of Slavery?* (Oxford, 1970); Edmund S. Morgan, "Slavery and Freedom: the American Paradox" (address delivered in Washington, D.C., 1972); and John Chester Miller, *The*

Wolf by the Ears: Thomas Jefferson and Slavery (New York, 1977). Let us now look at these *seriatim,* bearing in mind always that what we hope to explore, ultimately, is the relation of all this to the Cult of the French Revolution.

Robert McColley

Robert McColley appears to have been a pioneer in this particular matter. At least, I don't know of anything so incisive to have appeared on the subject before his book.[3] As far as relations between the fact of slavery and the ideal of freedom are concerned, the core of this book is chapter 6: "Gentlemen's Opinions on Race and Freedom." The opening paragraph of this chapter goes to the heart of the matter:

> The crowd of notable statesmen who represented Virginia in the early republic wrote and spoke against slavery with vigor and feeling. Their sentiments have often been cited as evidence that they were as antislavery as any Americans of their time, and that they were clear headed and secure in their belief that slavery would soon cease to exist. A close examination of the things they said about slavery, and where and when they said them, produces more complex conclusions. Virginians were most often defending slavery while denouncing it, for unlike southerners of later generations, they could command the sympathy of outsiders simply by showing the right attitudes.

In the immediately following passage, McColley ends by suggesting one form of link between the topic of slavery and the Cult of the French Revolution. (I shall come back to this). McColley:

> During the Revolutionary War, Virginians were obliged to cooperate as closely and amicably as possible with soldiers and statesmen from the northern states and from France, almost all of whom found slavery distasteful. Again, in the two decades following the drafting of the federal constitution, Virginians were pleased to collaborate with northerners in the formation of national parties, and whether they avowed Federalism or Republicanism, they were certain to meet many enemies of slavery. Further exposure to foes of slavery came from the enthusiastic support of the French Revolution given by Virginians, and from partisanship for France in her wars against Britain.

McColley goes on to establish some important distinctions:

> This is not to say that Virginians cynically adopted a mask of antislavery for the benefit of outsiders whose esteem they hoped to win. Rather, they

found themselves partners in the liberal vanguard of their times, and were properly embarrassed at a stigma from which their other partners were free. Accepting with pleasure, and sometimes with fervor, most of the assumptions of the Enlightenment, Virginia's leaders must necessarily denounce slavery as an evil institution. From their frequent statements in this vein, these statesmen have caused their constituents to enjoy the reputation of being antislavery, as if the statesmen were voicing the convictions of their society and class. But if one looks closely, it appears that attacks on slavery usually occurred in the relations of Virginia with the outside world. In private correspondence, in the Congress of the United States, and in foreign capitals, Virginians typically indicted slavery whenever the subject arose. But among the class of wealthy planters whom they chiefly represented not one Virginia statesman of the Jeffersonian era ever advanced a practical proposal for the elimination of slavery, or for the systematic amelioration of the Negro's condition, with the single exception of St. George Tucker, a jurist and pedagogue. Schemes were, indeed, discussed in private. But Tucker excepted, no politically prominent man came forward publicly to advocate the end of slavery. As there is practically no evidence to suggest that the dominant planters would have responded to such initiative, one must conclude that those leaders who genuinely hated slavery refrained from acting because they were convinced that their leadership would be rejected. Under a system of frequent elections, the Virginia statesman who came out publicly against slavery would very quickly be retired to private life.

The Virginia statesman saved himself from the charge of hypocrisy by acknowledging certain "truths" about Negroes, slavery, and society. He developed a set of logical propositions which made it natural and consistent for him to denounce slavery in principle, yet satisfy his constituents in practice that he would do nothing to injure their interests. Some of the axioms which were used to support these propositions were reasonable enough for the times. To entertain others must have required considerable mental effort.

One of the more dubious notions was that Virginians could not be held responsible for the existence of slavery among them, because it had been forced upon their ancestors by the tyranny of the English crown. The Virginia Constitution of 1776 mentioned how the King of England, "by an inhuman use of the negative," had prevented the colony from excluding slaves. Only the intervention of gentlemen from the Deep South kept Jefferson from including this count in his indictment of George III contained in the Declaration of Independence. But, of course, neither the Crown nor anybody else had ever forced a Virginian to buy a single slave. For over

twenty years before the Revolution the British government had prevented
Virginia from barring the further introduction of slaves, but this hardly represented either renunciation of slavery on the part of Virginia or a systematic policy of the Crown to force slavery into areas where it was not wanted.
By the time colonial Virginia tried to prevent slave importation, her leading
planters were faced with the problem of perennial overproduction, and of
course owned more than enough slaves, who were a large majority in the
Tidewater area. Also, given this problem of overproduction, the value of
slaves was likely to fall if slave traders were permitted to dump unlimited
quantities of their merchandise into a Virginia market which had a limited
capacity to absorb them. As a rule Virginians did not like to sell their slaves,
at least not in the open market. But neither were they happy when the market value of their slaves declined.

After considering such matters as the efforts of the ruling class of
colonial Virginia to control the size of their slave population, McColley
goes on:

> All of these complexities were kept out of mind, however, or at least out
> of public utterance, and Virginians after the Revolution stuck to their
> dogma that the evil of slavery dwelt among them because of the diabolical
> commercial policy of the Old Empire. Given this notion of inherited evil
> without inherited guilt, they often represented themselves as laboring under
> a burden. The wretched class of unfortunates residing among them, they
> claimed, depended for its mere survival on their stewardship and careful
> management.

The notion of "inherited evil without inherited guilt" is worth keeping in mind with reference to the Cult of the French Revolution.

From a general consideration of the position of Virginian landowners
as a class, McColley goes on to consider the specific case of Thomas Jefferson:

> In brief, the antislavery pronouncements of Virginia's statesmen were so
> rarely accompanied by any positive efforts against slavery as to cast doubt
> on their sincerity, and when initiative against slavery was proposed by oth-
> ers they normally resisted it. This makes still more doubtful the proposition
> that their constituents were agreeable to antislavery sentiments. The indi-
> rect evidence available to us on the position of the Virginia planters suggests
> that most of them were for all practical purposes proslavery. But even if the
> average planter held views on the Negro question identical to those of
> Thomas Jefferson, slavery would have remained fixed in Virginia, for the
> most liberal of all Virginia statesmen was himself unable to find a practical

means to dismantle the institution he freely acknowledged as a curse. He was effectively prevented from doing so because, on the one hand, he shared too many of the traditional southern ideas about the character and potentialities of the Negro, and, on the other hand, he was unwilling to risk the certain loss of political influence that outspoken opposition to slavery must have caused.

Jefferson attained an important station in public life at a fairly early age, and continued to command the serious attention of many Americans until his death in 1826. Over a period of six decades his hopes about slavery changed significantly, so that the possibility and the imminence of emancipation seemed much stronger to him at one time than at others. In the years just following the Declaration of Independence he worked out an elaborate law for the gradual emancipation and removal of the Negroes of Virginia but he, along with his colleagues in revising the laws, refrained from submitting this to the legislature. At the time Jefferson thought that the people of Virginia would very likely be more receptive to his scheme after the passage of years brought an increase in liberal and humanitarian sentiment. But the occasion never arose, and it seems clear that by the time of his presidency, Jefferson had entirely dismissed the notion of doing anything himself in behalf of emancipation. In 1891 Moncure D. Conway, a native Virginian who had suffered immense odium by being an abolitionist before the Civil War, ruminated in a private letter about Jefferson's reputed opposition to slavery. "Bancroft has given him a world-wide reputation," Conway wrote, "as having tried to pass an antislavery act in Virginia. Never did man achieve more fame for what he did not do."

McColley makes a number of other points, some of which are more fully developed in the other (slightly later) studies we are about to consider.

Winthrop Jordan

In Winthrop Jordan's seminal work, *White over Black: American Attitudes towards the Negro, 1550–1812*, chapter 12, "Thomas Jefferson: Self and Society," occupies more than fifty pages of the text. In the opening part of this chapter, Jordan identifies what he calls "Jefferson's central dilemma: he hated slavery but thought Negroes inferior to white men." Jordan quotes the famous passage from *Notes on the State of Virginia*, which established Jefferson's reputation as an enemy of slavery:

> There must doubtless be an unhappy influence on the manners of our people produced by the existence of slavery among us. The whole commerce between master and slave is a perpetual exercise of the most boister-

ous passions, the most unremitting despotism on the one part, and degrading submissions on the other. Our children see this, and learn to imitate it;
for man is an imitative animal. . . . The parent storms, the child looks on,
catches the lineaments of wrath, puts on the same airs in the circle of
smaller slaves, gives a loose to his worst passions, and thus nursed, educated, and daily exercised in tyranny, cannot but be stamped by it with
odious peculiarities. The man must be a prodigy who can retain his manners and morals undepraved by such circumstances. And with what execra-
tion should the statesman be loaded, who permitting one half the citizens
thus to trample on the rights of the other, transforms those into despots,
and these into enemies, destroys the morals of the one part, and the amor
patriae of the other. For if a slave can have a country in this world, it must
be any other in preference to that in which he is born to live and labour for
another: in which he must lock up the faculties of his nature, contribute as
far as depends on his individual endeavours to the evanishment of the human race, or entail his own miserable condition on the endless generations
proceeding from him. With the morals of the people, their industry also is
destroyed. For in the warm climate, no man will labour for himself who
can make another labour for him. This is so true, that of the proprietors of
slaves a very small proportion indeed are ever seen to labour. And can the
liberties of a nation be thought secure when we have removed their only
firm basis, a conviction in the minds of the people that these liberties are of
the gift of God? That they are not to be violated but with wrath?

Jordan comments: "While he recognized the condition of slaves as
'miserable', the weight of Jefferson's concern was reserved for the malevo-
lent effects of slavery upon white men."

The second section of Jordan's chapter 12 is headed "Jefferson: the
Assertion of Negro Inferiority." In this section Jordan writes:

His sensitive reaction to social "passions" and "prejudices" was height-
ened by dim recognition that they operated powerfully within himself,
though of course he never realized how deep-seated his anti-Negro feelings
were. On the surface of these thoughts lay genuine doubts concerning the
Negro's inherent fitness for freedom and recognition of the tensions inherent in racial slavery. He was firmly convinced, as he demonstrated in the
Notes on Virginia, that Negroes could never be incorporated into white
society on equal terms.

"Deep rooted prejudices entertained by the whites; ten thousand recollections, by the blacks, of the injuries they have sustained; new provoca-
tions; the real distinction which nature has made; and many other circumstances, will divide us into parties, and produce convulsions which will

probably never end but in the extermination of the one or the other race.—
To these objections, which are political, may be added others, which are
physical and moral."

The "real distinction which nature has made" was for Jefferson not only
physical but temperamental and mental. Negroes seemed to "require less
sleep," for "after hard labour through the day," they were "induced by the
slightest amusements to sit up till midnight, or later" though aware that
they must rise at "first dawn." They were "at least as brave" as whites,
and "more adventuresome." "But," he wrote, withdrawing even this mild
encomium, "this may perhaps proceed from a want of forethought, which
prevents their seeing a danger till it be present. When present, they do not
go through it with more coolness or steadiness than the whites." Negroes
were "more ardent," their griefs "transient." "In general," he concluded,
"their existence appears to participate more of sensation than reflection. To
this must be ascribed their disposition to sleep when abstracted from their
diversions, and unemployed in labour. An animal whose body is at rest, and
who does not reflect, must be disposed to sleep of course."

Within the confines of this logic there was no room for even a hint that
daily toil for another's benefit might have disposed slaves to frolic and to
sleep.

"Of far more serious import for the Negro's future," says Jordan,
"were Jefferson's remarks on mental capacity. More than any other single
person he framed the terms of the debate still carried on today."

"Comparing them by their faculties of memory, reason, and imagination, it appears to me, that in memory they are equal to the whites; in reason much inferior, as I think one could scarcely be found capable of tracing
and comprehending the investigations of Euclid; and that in imagination
they are dull, tasteless, and anomalous. It would be unfair to follow them
to Africa for this investigation. We will consider them here on the same
stage with the whites, and where the facts are not apocryphal on which a
judgment is to be formed. It will be right to make great allowances for the
difference of condition, of education, of conversation, of the sphere in
which they move. Many millions of them have been brought to, and born
in America. Most of them indeed have been confined to tillage, to their own
homes, and their own society: yet many have been so situated, they might
have availed themselves of the conversation of their masters; many have
been brought up to the handicraft arts, and from that circumstance have
always been associated with the whites. Some have been liberally educated,
and all have lived in countries where the arts and sciences are cultivated to
a considerable degree, and have had before their eyes samples of the best

works from abroad. . . . But never yet could I find that a black had uttered a thought above the level of plain narration; never see even an elementary trait of painting or sculpture."

Despite his stress on the necessity for "great allowances," Jordan goes on,

Jefferson seemed unable to push the logic of environmentalism very far; in fact he stopped at just the point where that logic made a case for Negro inferiority. He seemed incapable of complimenting Negroes without immediately adding qualifications. "In music," he continued, picking up a widespread popular belief, "they are more generally gifted than the whites with accurate ears for tune and time, and they have been found capable of imagining a small catch." Further ability was "yet to be proved."

Jordan:

Not content with a general assessment, Jefferson went on to disparage the widely known Negroes who had been puffed by the antislavery people as examples of the Negro's equal capacities. Those known to him were poets, and by speculating on the theoretical effects of slavery upon poetry he twisted the environmentalist logic into anti-Negro shape. "Misery is often the parent of the most affecting touches in poetry.—Among the blacks is misery enough, God knows, but no poetry. Love is the peculiar oestrum of the poet. Their love is ardent, but it kindles the sense only, not the imagination." He dismissed Phyllis Wheatley with the airy remark that she was "not . . . a poet. The compositions published under her name are below the dignity of criticism." Ignatius Sancho he treated with more respect but decided that Sancho's works did "more honour to the heart than the head" and substituted "sentiment for demonstration." Sancho was the best of his race, but among literary figures in England "we are compelled to enroll him at the bottom of the column," if, Jefferson added pointedly, he was in fact the real author of the material "published under his name." This higher criticism was surprising in a man who wrote twenty years later that "of all men living I am the last, who should undertake to decide as to the merits of poetry. In earlier life I was fond of it, and easily pleased."

Jefferson was thoroughly aware that the environmentalist argument could serve (and actually had) to make a case for Negro equality, and hence he went to great lengths to prove that the Negroes' lack of talent did not stem from their condition. He turned to the slavery of classical times and wandered happily and discursively among the Romans and the Greeks, arguing that ancient slavery was more harsh than America's yet produced slaves of talent and demonstrable achievement. Unaware that he might be inverting cause and effect he noted that some ancient slaves excelled "in science, insomuch as to be usually employed as tutors to their master's children." There had been slaves, then, who had demonstrated significant attainments; and those who had "were of the race of whites." As for Negroes, he concluded, "it is not their condition then, but nature, which has produced the distinction."

Jordan:

Having baldly stated his belief in innate inferiority, Jefferson immediately introduced his next subject by reopening the question he had just closed: "Whether further observation will or will not verify the conjecture, that nature has been less bountiful to them in the endowments of the head," increasingly aware of how far he had allowed himself to go. Genuine alarm underlay his admonition, towards the end of his passage on Negroes, that caution must be exercised "where our conclusion would degrade a whole race of men from the rank in the scale of beings which their Creator may perhaps have given them." But he extricated himself in highly satisfying fashion by dumping the whole problem in the broad lap of American science, thus permitting qualification of his previously stated position to the point of inconsistency. "The opinion, that they are inferior in the faculties of reason and imagination, must be hazarded with great diffidence. To justify a general conclusion, requires many observations, even where the subject may be submitted to the Anatomical knife, to Optical glasses, to analysis by fire, or by solvents. How much more then where it is a faculty, not a substance, we are examining; where it eludes the research of all the senses; where the conditions of its existence are various and variously combined; where the effects of those which are present or absent bid defiance to calculation."

Jordan:

Growing happier with his solution he thus labored the obvious fact that assessing mental ability was an immensely difficult task. With nearly audible relief he remodeled an anti-Negro diatribe into a scientific hypothesis, thus effectively depersonalizing a matter which was for him obviously of some personal importance. "To our reproach it must be said, that though for a century and a half we have had under our eyes the races of black and of red men, they have never yet been viewed by us as subjects of natural history. I advance it therefore as a suspicion only, that the blacks, whether originally a distinct race, or made distinct by time and circumstances, are inferior to the whites in the endowments both of body and mind. It is not against experience to suppose, that . . . [they] may possess different qualifications."

Jordan: "A 'suspicion only' of 'different qualifications' represented a rather different proposition from 'It is not their condition then, but nature, which has produced the distinction.'"

Jefferson's insinuations of the inferiority of blacks—it is mostly a matter of apparently reluctant insinuation, rather than of direct "assertion"—are also the theme of the two following sections of Jordan's chapter 12, "The Issue of Intellect" and "The Acclaim of Talented Negroes." Having established Jefferson's consistency in depreciating any example brought to his attention of black talent suggestive of possible equality with whites, Jordan goes on to consider the relation of all this, in Jefferson's mind and psyche, to the self-evident truth in the Declaration of Independence that "all men are created equal":

> Jefferson's confusion at times became monumental. On the one hand he had intellectually derived his belief in human equality from the existence of an orderly creation which had shaped every natural species each to its own mold; and on the other he possessed a larger unquestioning faith, strengthened by his political experience, which predisposed him toward equality. The problem of the Negro's intellect stripped these approaches of their apparent congruity. For he could not rid himself of the suspicion that the Negro was naturally inferior. If this were in fact the case, then it was axiomatic that the Creator had so created the Negro and no amount of education or freedom or any other tinkering could undo the facts of nature. Thus Jefferson suspected that the Creator might have in fact created men unequal; and he could not say this without giving his assertion exactly the same logical force as his famous statement to the contrary. His science-theology rammed squarely into his larger faith, and the result was intellectual wreckage.

Yet Jefferson made no intellectual effort to extricate himself from this wreckage. His curiosity, normally so active, is sluggish here. Jordan cites arguments of a Northern writer against the doctrine of innate black inferiority, who held:

> "that there is no more difference between them [blacks] and those whites who have had the same education, and have lived in the same habits, than there is among different persons of that class of whites. In this opinion I am inclined to acquiesce. It is neither birth nor colour, but education and habit, which form the human character."

On this Jordan comments:

> Though it is difficult to judge exactly what most Virginians or other south-
> erners would have thought of this statement, it is clear that only one man
> in the South felt compelled to take the opposite position publicly. Jefferson
> alone spoke forth, and this fact in itself suggests, at very least, strong feeling
> on his part, an uncommon need to discourse upon the subject. It was not
> that he alone felt need for scientific experiment. George Wythe, Jefferson's
> much-admired mentor, undertook to give both his own nephew and his
> mulatto servant boy classical educations as a comparative test of the Ne-
> gro's ability. On the other hand, Jefferson, who delighted in compiling the
> facts of the natural world, never attempted any such experiment despite
> ample opportunity. And the structure of his relevant passage in the *Notes,*
> where his appeal to science followed lengthy and very definite pronounce-
> ments on Negro inferiority, indicated clearly that his appeal to the highest
> court was not the starting point for his thoughts about Negroes but a safe
> refuge from them.

Perhaps the most important feature of Jordan's analysis is that it demonstrates that Jefferson was *exceptional* among his fellow Virginians not
in expressing abhorrence of slavery—which was a fairly routine rhetorical
exercise at this time among respectable Virginians, such as Patrick Henry
(above, pp. 71–72)—but in the persistence with which he harped on the
theme of innate black inferiority: a theme about which most Virginians
were tongue-tied, in public at least, in the late eighteenth and early nineteenth centuries. Jordan writes: "His derogation of the Negro revealed
the latent possibilities inherent in an accumulated popular tradition of
Negro inferiority; it constituted, for all its qualifications, the most intense,
extensive, and extreme formulation of anti-Negro 'thought' offered by
any American in the thirty years after the Revolution."

In this specific respect, Jefferson was a pioneer. The classic pro-
slavery position of the mid-nineteenth century, based on the dogmatic assertion of the innate inferiority of blacks, had been legitimized in advance
by those persistent and ostensibly reluctant lines from the sanctified pen
of Thomas Jefferson.

William Cohen
William Cohen's essay "Thomas Jefferson and the Problem of Slavery"[4]
is valuable principally for its analysis of Jefferson's position on free blacks
and escaped slaves, of Jefferson's solution of colonization, as well as for
Cohen's final summation of the contradictions in Jefferson's position on
race and slavery.

Cohen considers some 1776 legislative proposals of Jefferson's of which the most significant were those which introduced new restrictions and penalties applying to free blacks and to miscegenation, involving white women. Cohen writes:

> In November 1776, Jefferson was chosen as a member of a committee whose task was to revise, modernize and codify the statutes of Virginia. Among his assignments was the job of drawing up the legislation dealing with slaves. He later described this bill, which he completed in 1778, as a "mere digest" of the existing legislation on the subject, and to a certain extent this was true. The bill did contain a strengthened version of a law which prohibited the slave trade, and Jefferson was merely codifying previous laws when he included provisions barring Negroes from testifying against whites and forbidding slaves to possess arms or to leave the property of their masters without a pass. Jefferson's measure also included the usual penalty of whipping for such slave offenses as rioting, presenting seditious speeches, and running away, but here, too, he was copying earlier legislation.
>
> Nevertheless, the bill was more than a digest of earlier codes and it contained some significant additions which were designed to prevent the increase of the state's free Negro population. It was to be illegal for free Negroes to come into Virginia of their own accord or to remain there for more than one year after they were emancipated. A white woman having a child by a Negro would be required to leave the state within a year. The individual who violated these regulations would be placed "out of the protection of the laws." This would have left them subject to re-enslavement or even to murder at the whim of their neighbors and was, therefore, a most severe punishment.

As eventually passed by the Virginia legislature after the end of the war, in 1785, the revising act did not contain Jefferson's "significant additions." It would seem that Jefferson's abhorrence of the presence of free blacks, and of white women who gave birth to children of mixed race, was stronger than was normal among his contemporaries of his own class. Jefferson probably treated his own slaves somewhat better than other slaveowners did, but he seems to have been at least as harsh as other landowners in his treatment of slaves who escaped and were recaptured. Cohen writes:

> In his daily life there were few differences between Jefferson's behavior as an owner of men and that of Virginia plantation masters who opposed his antislavery speculations. His bondsmen were well fed and clothed, and

their work load was comparable to that of white freemen. In this regard their lot may have been easier than that of many other slaves in the state. Nevertheless, when he dealt with runaways, sales of slaves, breeding, flogging, and manumissions, his behavior did not differ appreciably from that of other enlightened slaveholders who deplored needless cruelty, but would use whatever means they felt necessary to protect their peculiar form of property.

During Jefferson's adult lifetime, more than forty of his Negroes attempted to escape. Thirty of these were mentioned by him in a letter to an Englishman, Dr. William Gordon, who had fought on the American side in the Revolution and returned to Great Britain in 1786. Jefferson described the depredations of Lord Cornwallis and his troops when they over-ran his estate in 1781 and added: "he carried off also about thirty slaves; had this been to give them their freedom, he would have done right, but it was to consign them to inevitable death from the smallpox and putrid fever then raging in his camp."

This account differs markedly from the cold facts recorded in his "Farm Book" when these events took place. In that document, which was not intended for the public eye, he listed the names of the slaves that he had lost and described what had befallen them. Next to eight entries in a group he wrote: "fled to the enemy and died". Another two slaves were said to have "joined the enemy and died"; while four more, "joined the enemy, returned and died". Beside three names he wrote laconically: "joined enemy"; and it is presumed that they managed to survive the war. One slave, Barnaby, was described as having "joined the enemy, but came back again and lived". Nowhere in this account is the term "carried off" seen, and Jefferson's later use of the phrase glosses over the fact that more than one seventh of his blacks chose to desert him.

Jefferson's statement that Cornwallis would have done right if he had taken the Negroes to free them is at variance with the Virginian's behavior both before and after 1781. In 1769 he placed an advertisement in the Virginia Gazette asking for the return of a runaway slave named Sandy. Throughout his life Jefferson hired slave catchers and asked his friends to keep an eye peeled for his thralls when they struck out for freedom. In early September 1805, Jame Hubbard, a stout Negro who worked in the plantation nail factory, ran away, but was soon apprehended and returned. About five years later he escaped again. A year passed before Jefferson learned that Hubbard was living in the area of Lexington and dispatched Isham Chisolm to retrieve the bondsman. It was too late, however; Hubbard had departed only a few days earlier for parts unknown. When Chisolm returned empty-handed, Jefferson offered him a bonus of twenty-five dollars to go after the man a second time. This time Hubbard was caught and brought back in irons, and Jefferson reported: "I had him severely flogged in the presence of his old companions . . ." He then added that he was convinced that Hubbard "will never again serve any man as a slave, the [sic] moment he is out of jail and his irons off he will be off himself". Before Jefferson could implement plans to have him sold out of the state, Hubbard disappeared again.[5]

In theory, Jefferson's "solution" to slavery consisted in "colonization": the deportation of all the freed blacks from the United States. Cohen: "The entire body of Jefferson's writings shows that he never seriously considered the possibility of any form of racial coexistence on the basis of equality and that, from at least 1778 until his death, he saw colonization as the only alternative to slavery."

Late in his life, however, Jefferson was beginning to admit the impracticability of this solution, at least in its widest sense, while reiterating his faith in an attenuated form of it. Cohen writes:

> In 1824 Jefferson argued that there were a million and a half slaves in the nation and that no one conceived it to be "practicable for us, or expedient for them" to send all the blacks away at once. He then went on to calculate:

>> Their estimated value as property, in the first place, (for actual property has been lawfully vested in that form, and who can lawfully take it from the possessors?) at an average of two hundred dollars each . . . would amount to six hundred millions of dollars which must be paid or lost by somebody. To this add the cost of their transportation by land and sea to Mesurado, a year's provision of food and clothes, implements of husbandry and of their trades, which will amount to three hundred millions more, and it is impossible to look at the question a second time.

> Since African colonization seemed an impossibility, Jefferson suggested a plan which entailed "emancipating the afterborn, leaving them, on due compensation, with their mothers, until their services are worth their maintenance, and putting them to industrious occupations until a proper age for deportation." The individuals who would be "freed" immediately after their birth would eventually be sent to Santo Domingo which, according to the newspapers, had recently offered to open its doors to such persons. In effect, Jefferson was proposing that the federal government buy all newborn slaves from their owners (at twelve dollars and fifty cents each) and that it pay for their "nurture with the mother [for] a few years." Beyond

this, the plan would not cost the government anything, for the young blacks would then work for their maintenance until deported. Santo Domingo had offered to bear the cost of passage.

Jefferson noted that a majority of Americans then living would live to see the black population reach six million and warned that "a million and a half are within their control; but six millions, . . . and one million of these fighting men, will say, 'we will not go'". The Virginia statesman concluded his proposal by urging that neither constitutional problems nor human sentiment ought to be allowed to stand in its way:

> I am aware that this subject involves some constitutional scruples. But a liberal construction, justified by the object, may go far, and an amendment of the constitution, the whole length necessary. The separation of infants from their mothers, too, would produce some scruples of humanity. But this would be straining at a gnat, and swallowing a camel.

Thus, only two and a half years before his death, Jefferson reiterated his long held belief that emancipation was imperative for the sake of the nation, but that it must be accompanied by colonization. Even here, however, his theory differed from his practice; and in this case his inconsistency would follow him beyond the grave for he did not offer to free his slaves on the condition that they leave the country. On the contrary, in his will he requested the Virginia legislature to grant special permission to the five slaves he manumitted to continue to live in the state.

In his conclusion, Cohen provides a succinct summation of the contradictions in Jefferson's position with regard to slavery and free blacks. Cohen writes:

> Jefferson was a man of many dimensions, and any explanation of his behavior must contain a myriad of seeming contradictions. He was a sincere and dedicated foe of the slave trade who bought and sold men whenever he found it personally necessary. He believed that all men were entitled to life and liberty regardless of their abilities, yet he tracked down those slaves who had the courage to take their rights by running away. He believed that slavery was morally and politically wrong, but still he wrote a slave code for his state and opposed a national attempt in 1819 to limit the further expansion of the institution. He believed that one hour of slavery was worse than ages of British oppression, yet he was able to discuss the matter of slave breeding in much the same terms that one would use when speaking of the propagation of dogs and horses.

David Brion Davis

David Brion Davis's 1970 Harmsworth Inaugural Lecture at Oxford followed by Edmund S. Morgan's presidential address of 1972 (below) appear to signify the beginning of acceptance by the academic establishment of the "revisionist" arguments of the writers cited above. Davis makes a point of central importance, not adverted to by the previous writers: "One can argue that Jefferson's anti-Negro prejudice actually contributed to his hostility towards slavery, since he never thought of emancipation except as a means of ridding the land of the despised and unwelcome race."

Davis is also good on Jefferson's anti-slavery rhetoric:

> In 1786, when Jefferson was in France and was contributing detailed information for an article on the United States [*sic*] in the *Encyclopédie méthodique,* he wrote a strained reply to the editor's question: Why had Virginia adopted a new slave law without provision for emancipation? [Jefferson had actually helped to draft the law in question, and had tried to make it even more restrictive.] Jefferson told of his planned amendment [gradual emancipation followed by deportation; never seriously pursued]. . . . He seemed anxious to avoid raising any question of political conflict over slavery. And here Jefferson began to experiment with the locutions which for the rest of his life would characterize his response to such questions. Since his replies became so standardized, it is not unfair to conflate a number of examples: there was not "a man on earth" who more "ardently desired" emancipation or who was more prepared to make "any sacrifice" to "relieve us from this heavy reproach, in any practicable way", but—and Jefferson's "hints" deserve underscoring—the public mind needed "ripening" and would not yet "bear the proposition".

In his conclusion, Davis finds "the most important" factor in Jefferson's overall position on slavery to have been "a continuing identification with the interests of a planter class." All in all, Davis's Oxford lecture constitutes a definitive negative to the question posed in its title.

Edmund S. Morgan

Edmund S. Morgan was professor of history at Yale University at the time, and his paper "Slavery and Freedom: the American Paradox" was delivered as the presidential address of the Organization of American Historians at Washington D.C. on 6 April 1972.

Early in his paper, Morgan identified what he saw as the challenge, to American historians:

The challenge, for a colonial historian at least, is to explain how a people could have developed the dedication to human liberty and dignity exhibited by the leaders of the American Revolution and at the same time have developed and maintained a system of labor that denied human liberty and dignity every hour of the day.

The paradox is evident at many levels if we care to see it. Think, for a moment, of the traditional American insistence on freedom of the seas. "Free ships make free goods" was the cardinal doctrine of American foreign policy in the Revolutionary era. But the goods for which the United States demanded freedom were produced in very large measure by slave labor. The irony is more than semantic. American reliance on slave labor must be viewed in the context of the American struggle for a separate and equal station among the nations of the earth. At the time the colonists announced their claim to that station they had neither the arms nor the ships to make the claim good. They desperately needed the assistance of other countries, especially France, and their single most valuable product with which to purchase assistance was tobacco, produced mainly by slave labor. So largely did that crop figure in American foreign relations that one historian has referred to the activities of France in supporting the Americans as "King Tobacco Diplomacy", a reminder that the position of the United States in the world depended not only in 1776 but during the span of a long lifetime thereafter on slave labor. To a very large degree it may be said that Americans bought their independence with slave labor.

The paradox is sharpened if we think of the state where most of the tobacco came from. Virginia at the time of the first United States census in 1790 had 40 percent of the slaves in the entire United States. And Virginia produced the most eloquent spokesmen for freedom and equality in the entire United States: George Washington, James Madison, and above all, Thomas Jefferson. They were all slaveholders and remained so throughout their lives. In recent years we have been shown in painful detail the contrast between Jefferson's pronouncements in favor of republican liberty and his complicity in denying the benefits of that liberty to blacks.

In a footnote to that last sentence, Morgan refers to the works of Cohen, Jordan, and Davis discussed above. Morgan does not refer to McColley's pioneering book of 1964, which seems to have been generally ignored by later writers on the subject.

The paradox referred to by Morgan is in fact far sharper in the case of Jefferson than in the case of the other two Virginians whom he names. George Washington was sparing in his use of eloquence, and deeply distrusted the fervor of Jefferson and the Jeffersonians in the cause of an absolute and deified Liberty, incarnate in the American and French Revolutions. In that cause, from 1790 on, Madison was little more than Jefferson's disciple. But it is true that Jefferson-on-Liberty was a distilled essence of a collective brew of discourse widely prevalent among Virginian slaveowners in the late eighteenth century.

Morgan discusses the particular case of Jefferson:

> Let us begin with Jefferson, this slaveholding spokesman of freedom. Could there have been anything in the kind of freedom he cherished that would have made him acquiesce, however reluctantly, in the slavery of so many Americans? The answer, I think, is yes. The freedom that Jefferson spoke for was not a gift to be conferred by governments, which he mistrusted at best. It was a freedom that sprang from the independence of the individual. The man who depended on another for his living could never be truly free. We may seek a clue to Jefferson's enigmatic posture toward slavery in his attitude toward those who enjoyed a seeming freedom without the independence needed to sustain it. For such persons Jefferson harbored a profound distrust, which found expression in two phobias that crop up from time to time in his writings.

Two phrases there are particularly interesting: "The man who depended on another for his living could never be truly free." How about the man who depended *on slaves* for his living? Did Jefferson feel, deep down, that there was something seriously wrong with his own freedom? And could uneasiness on that score have sought relief in the contemplation and adoration of an abstract, hypostatized, immaculate Liberty? Morgan does not consider such possibilities, and this is understandable, since no certain answers to those questions are available. Nonetheless, the questions are important, and I shall come back to them, later in this chapter and in the Epilogue.

Then, "passionate aversion to debt." As Morgan notes, "Jefferson himself was a debtor all his adult life." There is a parallel here to Jefferson's avowed passionate aversion to slavery. The two things which Jefferson held in passionate aversion were the twin conditions of his material existence, throughout his life. These are conditions of extreme psychological stress. I shall look at some of the possible implications later, in relation to the French Revolution.

Jefferson's second phobia, as identified by Morgan, "was his distrust of the landless urban workman who labored in manufactures." Morgan goes on, "In Jefferson's distrust of artificers we begin to get a glimpse of the limits—and limits not dictated by racism—that defined the republican vision of the eighteenth century."

In the long sections of his lecture that are devoted to debt and free labor, it seemed to me for a while that Morgan was diverting attention from the centrality of racism within the paradox he was investigating. But towards the end of the lecture, in showing the political advantages accruing to the rulers of Virginia from having slaves, rather than free laborers, to do the manual work, Morgan does address himself to the question of racism, and to some purpose.

> In Virginia neither badges nor philosophers were needed. It was not necessary to pretend or to prove that the enslaved were a different race; because they were. Anyone could tell black from white, even if black was actually brown or red. And as the number of poor white Virginians diminished, the vicious traits of character attributed by Englishmen to their poor could in Virginia increasingly appear to be the exclusive heritage of blacks. They were ungrateful, irresponsible, lazy and dishonest. "A Negro can't be honest," said Landon Carter and filled his diary with complaints of the congenital laziness and ingratitude of black men.
>
> Racism thus absorbed in Virginia the fear and contempt that men in England, whether Whig or Tory, monarchist or republican, felt for the inarticulate lower classes. Racism made it possible for white Virginians to develop a devotion to the equality that English republicans had declared to be the soul of liberty. There were too few free poor on hand to matter. And by lumping Indians, mulattoes, and Negroes in a single pariah class, Virginians had paved the way for a similar lumping of small and large planters in a single master class.
>
> Virginians knew that the members of this class were not in fact equal, either in property or in virtue, just as they knew that Negroes, mulattoes, and Indians were not one and the same. But the forces which dictated that Virginians see Negroes, mulattoes, and Indians as one also dictated that they see large and small planters as one. Racism became an essential, if unacknowledged, ingredient of the republican ideology that enabled Virginians to lead the nation.

John Chester Miller

John Chester Miller's *The Wolf by the Ears: Thomas Jefferson and Slavery,* the last in our series, is the longest (525 pages) and most comprehensive study of Jefferson and slavery. The title is taken from a late (1820) statement by Jefferson, and probably the most candid he ever made about slavery: "We have the wolf by the ears and we can neither hold him nor safely let him go."

Inevitably—since all these studies are based on a limited number of data—much of the ground covered by Miller had also been covered by his predecessors. What is most impressive in Miller's book to my mind is his intuitive capacity to penetrate through Jefferson's verbiage into Jefferson's mind. This is the kind of capacity that tends to be held in low esteem by academic historians, and indeed there are obvious reasons for a degree of skepticism concerning such a capacity. But where a writer has achieved such a degree of familiarity with Jefferson's statements on slavery and with their context as John Chester Miller came to possess, then I think his occasional intuitive diagnoses should command respect. One example of these follows:

> By expressing suspicions of the inferiority of blacks, Jefferson succeeded in preserving his inner equilibrium and made it possible to live temporarily with an institution which he constantly assured himself was in the course of eventual extinction.[6]

Another example:

> Basically, Jefferson feared blacks. . . . A highly impressionable man, Jefferson was particularly sensitive to the emanations of resentment and hatred he felt from the presence of large numbers of black slaves.[7]

If that diagnosis is correct, as I think likely, then the Paradiso of Monticello was floating just above an Inferno and a Purgatorio. But the Virginian Divine Comedy was unlike that of Dante in one basic respect. Dante's Paradiso is inviolable and invulnerable: Jefferson's Paradiso is under constant threat from his Inferno. (The significance of the Jeffersonian Purgatorio will be explored later.)[8]

The precarious inner balance of the potentially tragic Virginian version of the Divine Comedy is under growing threat from the North. As Miller points out (this time working, as Miller usually does, from a solid basis in Jefferson's explicit statements), Jefferson "regarded the growth of Northern cities as a political and economic threat to the South and to republicanism."[9]

This is true but an understatement. Jefferson regarded the growth of the Northern cities as not only a political and economic threat but also—and above all—as a *spiritual* threat. The Northern cities were the great centers of "heresy" and "apostasy." And by 1790, these spiritual evils were encroaching into Virginia itself, through the growing power of the new Federal Government, but also the growing power within that government of the heresiarch Alexander Hamilton, Secretary of the Treasury. It was not irrelevant that Hamilton was a known enemy of slavery, and actually a member of an abolitionist society (as also was that other heresiarch,

John Adams). The Virginians never challenged Hamilton or Adams over the issue of slavery. The last thing the Virginians wanted to do, circa 1790, was to precipitate a national debate over slavery. Slavery was their business, and nobody else's. But a threat to the institution of slavery was implicit in the growing power of the Northern cities and the Federal Government. The spiritual and the political and economic threats, and the threat to slavery, were all apprehended as one collective threat to the Virginia that Thomas Jefferson knew and loved, with a love tinged with guilt and anguish. The accursed wind from the North was fanning the flames of the potential Inferno under Monticello.

It was at this point, in 1790, that the Cult of the French Revolution begins to take its central place in the defense of a concept of Liberty that included the liberty to own slaves, and to feel bad about owning them. And also to assume that slavery, if let alone, would die out of its own accord. On that last assumption, Miller writes:[10]

> This sturdy conviction that slavery was doomed despite the considerable evidence that it was alive, well, and flourishing, accounts for Jefferson's ability to make with clear conscience his resounding pronouncements about the rights of man, the Laws of Nature, and the role of the United States as moral leader of the world. It is as though when Jefferson wrote and spoke about these high matters, he experienced a convenient defect of vision which prevented him from seeing black. Certainly he enunciated American principles and ideals quite as though slavery and black Americans did not exist. He apostrophized "the people" of the United States without betraying any recognition whatever of the fact that one fifth of the inhabitants of the Republic were enslaved. "I am not among those who fear the people," he said, ". . . the people being the only safe depository of power"; governments are republican only in proportion as they embody the will of the people, and execute it"; "educate and inform the whole mass of the people." "The people," in Jefferson's frame of reference, were clearly composed of free white Americans.
>
> Similarly, he left black Americans wholly out of consideration when he declared that "every man, and every body on earth possess the right of self-government; they receive it with their being from the hand of nature." And blacks were clearly nonexistent within his range of consciousness when he asserted that all governments derive their just powers from the consent of the governed and that the freedom and happiness of man were "the sole objects of all legitimate government." (The freedom and happiness of blacks were not even an incidental concern of the federal and state governments.) In America, he said in 1813, "everyone, by his property, or by his satisfac-

tory situation, is interested in the support of law and order" without mentioning that black slaves were included among that "property."

Even the affirmations of his faith in the republican experiment which seem to apply unequivocally to blacks were actually intended by Jefferson to refer to whites only. "Nothing is unchangeable," he said, "but the inherent and indivisible rights of man. . . . The earth is given as a common stock for men to labour and live on." If employment were not provided by landowners, he said, "the fundamental right to labour the earth returns to the unemployed." In the United States, it did not seem to him to be too soon to apply the principle that "as few as possible shall be without a little portion of land. The small land holders are the most precious part of a state." Even when he declared that he was resolved to "put it out of the power of the few to riot on the labours of the many" he meant by the "few" the merchants, speculators, and bankers of the North, and by the many he meant the white farmers and planters.

Nor, obviously, did Jefferson feel that the existence of slavery on American soil impugned the position of the United States as the Heaven-designated example to all the nations, or that the United States suffered by comparison with other countries that had already abolished slavery. Republican government, he declared, was "the only form of government that is not eternally at open or secret war with the rights of mankind"—and this despite the fact that the monarchical government of Great Britain had abolished slavery in 1772 by judicial decision.

Jefferson not only assumed that slavery had been placed in the course of ultimate extinguishment; he often spoke as though the event had already occurred, as if the United States had freed the slaves, removed them to another land, and made its peace with the Author of Nature. His proclivity for living in the future, reveling in the felicities that awaited mankind, sometimes obscured present realities for Jefferson. As a protective device, it had the effect of relieving him of the overpowering, paralyzing sense of guilt that a realistic contemplation of the existing state of affairs might have induced in a man less oriented toward the future; on the other hand, it tended to diminish the need for the kind of incessant, dedicated, and uncompromising action that had distinguished Jefferson's career as a revolutionary.

II

My chronological account, in the body of this book, of Thomas Jefferson's involvement with the French Revolution, necessarily stopped in 1800. But when we are considering the general pattern of Thomas Jefferson's attitudes to slavery—and also, not less important, to free blacks—

later developments of importance have to be considered. Some of these fall to be considered in the next section of this chapter (Saint Domingue/Haiti). In the present section I want to consider Jefferson's attitude to the proposed extension of slavery (in the 1820s) and to the education of free blacks (in 1817 and after).

First, the extension of slavery.

Jefferson's famous reference to "the firebell in the night" has been interpreted as a prophetic reference to the coming Civil War. And so it was. But what Jefferson was warning against, in the context, was not any danger arising from slavery itself, but a danger arising from *Northern interference* with slavery, including the extension of slavery. As Miller writes, "Ironically, the firebell that so alarmed Jefferson was occasioned by an effort in Congress to halt the spread of slavery into the territories and to prevent the admission of Missouri into the Union as a slave state." [11]

As Miller shows, in his chapter on "The Missouri Controversy," Jefferson defended the extension of slavery on the grounds that it would eventually cause slavery to fade away through the effects of "diffusion." This was an elegant variation on his old theory that slavery would somehow, sometime, die from natural causes. When opponents of the extension of slavery quoted that old tract of his, *Notes on the State of Virginia*, to contrary effect, Jefferson did not react. Nor did he abandon his theory that slavery was best combated by extending it indefinitely.

Jefferson's relation to slavery is a classical case of *Odi et amo*. He sincerely abhorred it, but he also cherished and championed it. His concept of liberty included not merely the liberty to own slaves, but also the liberty to extend slavery.

In Jefferson's relation to free blacks, however, there is no touch of *amo*; it is all *odi*. In his early writings on slavery and blacks, Jefferson had depicted himself as anxious to find out whether, indeed, some gifted blacks might demonstrate themselves to be the equals of whites. But when that Providence to which Jefferson so often appealed gave him a splendid opportunity to find out, in 1817, Jefferson flatly refused. The case of General Kosciusko's will is most instructive. Miller writes:

> In 1817, in his capacity as executor of the estate of his late friend General Thaddeus Kosciusko, the Polish hero of the War of American Independence, Jefferson discovered that he had been directed by the general's will to sell about seventeen thousand dollars in government securities and to devote the proceeds to the purchase, manumission, and education of young blacks. He refused to execute this project and as a result the bequest was

diverted to other purposes which had nothing to do with furthering the education of blacks.

Miller goes on to situate Jefferson's decision in the context of his greatest educational project, the foundation of the University of Virginia.

> By avoiding even the pretense of educating his own slaves and by refusing to execute the provisions of General Kosciusko's will, Jefferson was obeying the laws of the commonwealth of Virginia at a time when it was particularly important to him not to appear to be a lawbreaker. Had he had the temerity to make the education of blacks an integral part of his educational plan for Virginia he would have ensured its defeat and, equally certainly, forfeited his good name in the opinion of his fellow Virginians. To most Virginians a black who could read and write was a dangerous subversive who threatened the established order by the very fact that he was educated. They knew all too well that education developed in people of color the qualities of ambition, discontent, and independence. In this spirit the Virginia legislature enacted a law in 1819 denying readmission to the state to any free black who left the commonwealth in order to secure an education. This was the same legislative body which chartered the University of Virginia.[12]

Jefferson's University of Virginia was a place for the inculcation of Southern values, which now included the extension of slavery. Miller writes:

> At the University of Virginia, Jefferson resolved that Missourism and only Missourism, the true constitutional doctrine, would be taught. As James Madison said, Jefferson intended that the institution should be a "nursery of Republican patriots as well as genuine scholars."
>
> Of the three American-born professors (only two of whom were educated in the United States) appointed to teaching posts at the University of Virginia, all were politically sound according to the criteria laid down by Jefferson. The vigilance of the overseers of the University was rewarded: not a trace of political "heresy" could be detected in the tight-knit little "academic village" created at Charlottesville. If any professor had had the temerity to raise the standard of anti-Missourism on that campus he would have found that "the illimitable freedom of the human mind" did not extend *that* far.[13]

Miller goes on to consider the curriculum at Jefferson's University of Virginia:

Jefferson was far more greatly concerned with what books were read by the intellectual elite than with the reading matter which found its way into the hands of the common people. He believed that public opinion was made at the top—by the educated, the talented, the born leaders whom Nature had clearly designated as superiors. It was with the best interests of this "natural aristocracy" in mind that he compiled a list of good and bad books designed to serve as a guide to students at the University of Virginia.

Among the "good" books on Jefferson's agenda was John Taylor's *The Constitution Construed*. This volume, Jefferson declared, contained "the true political faith", all that anyone needed to know about the federal Constitution and how it was to be interpreted. Taylor carried strict construction to its logical conclusion and made states' rights the governing principle of the American Union. Of "life, liberty and property", he said that "the last is the chief hinge upon which social happiness depends".

Taylor had always differed from the sage of Monticello on the subject of slavery. He had characterized Jefferson's strictures on slavery in the *Notes on Virginia* as "mental fermentation and bubbles" which had had the effect of obscuring from the reader the fact that slaves were more frequently the object of benevolence than anger on the part of their masters, and that the ownership of Africans usually brought out the finest instincts in white men—witness George Washington, James Madison, James Monroe, and Thomas Jefferson himself, all sterling characters and all slaveowners. Taylor regarded slavery as a misfortune to agriculture—blacks were really not intelligent enough to perform even their menial tasks satisfactorily—but it was folly to think of emancipating them: if they remained in the commonwealth they would almost certainly try to slit their former masters' throats, and if they were deported, as Jefferson advocated, the South would gratuitously strip itself of its labor force, thereby condemning itself to colonial servitude to the North. Being irreplaceable and immovable, the slaves ought to be treated kindly by the masters and their labor utilized more efficiently in the new scientific agriculture advocated by Taylor. In any event, chattel slavery, as Taylor saw it, was infinitely preferable to the brutal exploitative system of wage slavery practiced in Great Britain and the Northern states.

This straightforward assessment of slavery's advantages and drawbacks was vastly more congenial to most Southerners than the caviling doomsday attitude Jefferson had adopted in the *Notes On Virginia*.

In short, the University founded by the Apostle of Liberty became, by Jefferson's own decision, a seminary for the inculcation of the dominant ideology of the antebellum South.

Saint-Domingue/Haiti, 1790–1812

Insistently from 1790 to 1793, and more tentatively thereafter, Thomas Jefferson associated the French Revolution with Liberty. As far as I can find, Jefferson never referred to the French Revolution as affecting slavery. Yet the implications of the French Revolution for the institution of slavery were tremendous, and terrifying from the point of view of the slaveowning society and culture of which Jefferson was firmly, though equivocally, part.

From 1790 to 1793 (the very period in which Jefferson was most enthusiastic about the French Revolution), that revolution was destroying a society that rested on precisely the same social and economic foundations—enslaved blacks—as did his own beloved Virginia. Jefferson's capacity for mental compartmentalization, and for not seeing anything he did not want to see, is nowhere else so well exemplified as by his capacity to ignore (or to avert his eyes from) what the holy cause of liberty was doing—to a society based, like his own Virginia, on slavery—in Saint-Domingue (aka, San Domingo), in 1790–93.

Saint-Domingue (later Haiti) was that part of the island of Hispaniola which was under French rule. This was sugar-producing territory and extremely profitable, when worked by slave labor. The free population of Saint-Domingue on the eve of the French Revolution (and for a limited time thereafter) consisted of three competing elements: *les grands blancs,* slaveowning whites; *les petits blancs,* whites without slaves; and *les gens de couleur,* people of mixed race, who would have been defined in the United States as "free Negroes." The great majority of the population consisted of black slaves. Some of these, in the nature of a slave-based society, must really have been *gens de couleur,* like the Hemingses, but slaves were slaves and the laws took no cognizance of color shadings among them. As in Virginia, slaves were property, not people, politically and socially speaking, and the political institutions under which they lived were no business of theirs. That was common ground between *les grands blancs, les petits blancs,* and *les gens de couleur,* and about all the common ground there was between them.

The French Revolutionaries did not intend to bring about any large or violent changes in France's most valuable possession, Saint-Domingue. As in so many other areas (La Vendée for example, and Ireland) what happened in Saint-Domingue was an altogether unforeseen and disconcerting series of consequences following from the fulminating assertion of large general principles, whose application, in particular circumstances, gave rise to vehement disputes, followed by violent conflict.

In the case of Saint-Domingue, the detonating factor was the doctrine of the Rights of Man, proclaimed by the National Assembly in August 1789, and reaching Saint-Domingue towards the end of the same year.

But to whom exactly, in Saint-Domingue, did the doctrine of the Rights of Man apply? Not to the slaves, obviously; *grands blancs, petits blancs,* and *gens de couleur* were all agreed in that much (at least initially; at a later stage the leaders of the *gens de couleur* tried to coopt the slaves, with disastrous results for themselves). The beneficiaries most favored by the National Assembly—the same National Assembly as had produced the Rights of Man—were the slaveowners, *les grands blancs.* Somewhat more plausibly, *les petits blancs* asserted their own claim, arrogating to themselves the potent revolutionary title *les Patriotes.* For a time it seemed as if a new white Rights-of-Man oligarchy might emerge, through the cooption of *les petits blancs.* But already changes were happening within the French Revolution which were to have a fateful impact on the course of events in Haiti. The early revolutionary leaders, headed by the Feuillant Barnave, had favored *les grands blancs* (or rather those of the slaveowners who would consent to wear the tricolor emblem of the Rights of Man). But already the faction who would replace the Feuillants, the Girondins, were sending out a different signal through the Parisian society Les Amis des Noirs, which they dominated (and which Jefferson had refused to join in the pre-revolutionary period). Les Amis des Noirs wanted the *gens de couleur* to revolt, which they did, in October 1790. The revolt of the slaves—far more formidable because of their numbers—began less than a year later, in August 1791. Saint-Domingue was now in the grip of multiple ethnic civil war, with all the accompanying horrors, resembling those of former Yugoslavia two hundred years later.

Thomas O. Ott, historian of the Haitian Revolution estimates the role of the French Revolution in detonating the great calamity:

> By 1789 Saint-Domingue was on the verge of a social upheaval. White disunity, exploitation of the *gens de couleur,* maltreatment of the slave, and the abolition movements all contributed to the explosive situation. Yet violence might never have erupted had it not been for the social shock waves of the French Revolution. Even then the whites might have survived had they not followed the road to revolution during the crucial years of 1789 to 1791.[14]

At an early stage in the calamity, in May 1791, Edmund Burke addressed himself to the question of the impact of the Rights of Man on the population of Saint-Domingue. This was on 6 May 1791 in the course of the great debate in the House of Commons which signalled the rupture between Burke and Charles James Fox over the French Revolution:

As soon as this system arrived among them [the French], Pandora's box, replete with every mortal evil, seemed to fly open, hell itself to yawn, and every demon of mischief to overspread the face of the earth. Blacks rose against whites [in Saint-Domingue], whites against blacks, and each against one another in murderous hostility; subordination was destroyed, the bonds of society torn asunder, and every man seemed to thirst for the blood of his neighbour.

> Black spirits and white
> Blue spirits and grey
> Mingle, mingle,
> mingle

All was toil and trouble, discord and blood, from the moment that this doctrine was promulgated among them; and he verily believed that wherever the rights of man were preached, such ever had been and ever would be the consequences.

France, who had generously sent them the precious gift of the rights of man, did not like this image of herself reflected in her child, and sent out a body of troops, well seasoned too with the rights of man, to restore order and obedience. These troops, as soon as they arrived, instructed as they are in the principle of government, felt themselves bound to become parties in the general rebellions and, like most of their brethren at home began asserting their rights by cutting off the head of their general. Ought this example to induce us to send to our colonies a cargo of the rights of man? As soon would he send them a bale of infected cotton from Marseilles.[15]

Burke hated slavery and opposed the seating of slaveowners in the House of Commons. As he wrote at the time (Annual Register, 1765, p. 37): "Common sense, nay self-preservation, seem to forbid, that those, who allow themselves an unlimited right over the liberties and lives of others, should have any share in making laws for those who have long renounced such unjust and cruel distinctions." In April 1791—the month before his speech on Saint-Domingue—Burke was in the minority which voted in favor of Wilberforce's motion for the abolition of the slave trade. Burke was not attacking the French Revolutionaries for abolishing slavery, which they were not in fact trying to do. (They did not declare slavery abolished until after the insurgent slaves had abolished it themselves in 1793–94; see below, p. 283.) Burke's point was that, by loudly proclaiming a set of ambiguous and highly emotive propositions—the Declaration of the Rights of Man—the French Revolutionaries were inadvertently precipitating interracial civil war in Saint-Domingue, causing hideous suffering to all categories of its inhabitants, whether free or slave, white, black, or racially mixed.

Burke's statement in the Commons was made three months in advance of the outbreak of the slave rebellion in Saint-Domingue, and Burke's remarks were generally felt, at times, to be wildly exaggerated. (Latter-day retrospective admirers of the French Revolution will still find them so.) Yet the subsequent course of events in Saint-Domingue, as in France itself, fully bore out what Burke was saying in 1791. In general, outsiders did not pay much attention to the confused and confusing events in Saint-Domingue up to the time—the summer of 1793—when the outcome of the revolutionary period brought an unaccustomed and frightening simplicity and clarity into the situation. The outcome was the total victory of the insurrectionary slaves, and the elimination—by death or flight—of the whole white population, along with most of *les gens de couleur.*

Thomas Jefferson was Secretary of State, in Washington's first administration, throughout the period of the civil disturbances in Haiti from the outbreak of the insurrection of the *gens de couleur* (October 1790) through the beginning of the slave revolt (August 1791) and the triumph of that revolt (June—July 1793). Divided on so much else, Washington's first administration was united on this one. A historian of American policy towards the Haitian Revolution writes: "Washington and his chief advisers, Thomas Jefferson and Alexander Hamilton, sought to suppress the Haitian rebellion because it posed multiple threats to American interests and they did not like slave revolts." [16]

In seeking to suppress the slave revolt in Saint-Domingue—ineffectively, by subsidies to the planters—Jefferson and his colleagues were not at variance with French Revolutionary policy, as expounded by Parisian leaders in the period. At no time, until after the total victory of the slaves, in the summer of 1793, did the French Revolution, as embodied in the National Assembly, treat the Rights of Man as a warrant for the emancipation of slaves. The French Revolutionary Proconsul Sonthonax did declare slavery abolished in Saint Domingue on 29 August 1793, but by that date the slaves of Saint-Domingue had abolished slavery themselves. The National Convention, in Paris, did not get around to abolishing slavery (throughout the French dominions, and the British ones also) until February 1794, and that also was the recognition of a *fait accompli,* rather than a positive policy. And by February 1794, Jefferson was no longer Secretary of State. There had been no direct conflict between American policy towards Saint-Domingue and French Revolutionary policy (as officially formulated in Paris). Jefferson was disturbed, towards the end of 1791, by the lukewarm attitude of the National Assembly towards the planters.[17] But the fate of the planters, in Saint-Domingue itself, was no longer an issue after the summer of 1793.

It *was*, however, an issue in the United States in the summer of 1793, to a greater degree than ever before, with the arrival of thousands of white refugees, bearing their horror stories, from Saint-Domingue, after the destruction of the white capital, Cap François, in June 1793. And in some quarters the French Revolutionary decrees abolishing slavery seems to have had an even greater impact than did the actual events of Saint-Domingue itself, or even the arrival of the refugees in the United States. About the impact of these events in South Carolina, Rachel N. Klein writes:

> Although representatives throughout the state were duly alarmed when the slaves emancipated themselves in 1791 [sic], not until the fall of 1793 after France [sic] had recognized the revolution in Saint-Domingue by issuing an emancipation decree, did coastal conservatives identify the French Revolution as a dangerous threat to slavery. France's general emancipation decree of February 1794 heightened those fears by proclaiming the liberation of slaves throughout the French [and British] colonies.[18]

(There is some confusion here about the dates and nature of the events in Saint-Domingue. What happened in 1791 was not a revolt of *slaves* but of free *gens de couleur*. The insurrection of the slaves triumphed in July 1793. The immediately subsequent declaration of the abolition of slavery in Saint-Domingue (29 August 1793) was by the French Proconsul on the spot, Sonthonax, who would not have had time to seek and obtain any instructions from his superiors in France. But the slight haziness about events in Saint-Domingue does not invalidate Klein's account of reactions in South Carolina).

The shock of the events of 1793, and of the French Revolutionary decrees emancipating slaves, cannot have been confined to "coastal conservatives in South Carolina." In the nature of the case, those events and decrees must have been profoundly troubling to *all* slaveowners. And they must have been particularly troubling for slaveowners who, like Jefferson, had been enthusiastic for the French Revolution. Yet, if the faith of Jefferson and his friends in the French Revolution had been shaken by these events and decrees, there is no overt sign of this in any of their recorded utterances in 1793, and very little thereafter (except for one letter of Jefferson's to Monroe on 17 July 1794 speaking of a danger of French excitement leading to slave insurrection). We may infer—as I do—that that faith has received a shock from the visible decline in fervor of references to the French Revolution from 1793 on, as compared with the earlier period, but there is hardly anything explicit to confirm the inference. Southerners who had been enthusiastic for the French Revolution since 1789–90—like Jefferson, Madison, and Monroe—did not reject it, on hearing what had happened in Saint-Domingue. They were able—in almost all their explicit utterances—to treat the French Revolution and the slave insurrection in Saint-Domingue as totally discrete phenomena. The French Revolution was admirable, the slave insurrection was abominable, and there was no connection between the two. (Except for those revolutionary decrees of emancipation, to which Jeffersonians did not refer.)

That at least was the official Republican position. Putting the thing at its most mundane level, the Republicans, including their slaveowning leaders, had too much political capital committed to the cause of the French Revolution to be able to reverse themselves in a hurry. On the contrary, they were all very careful to make the point that the demand— conveyed through Jefferson himself—for the recall of Citizen Genet did not involve any diminution of respect for the French Revolution itself. It was Genet alone who had been solely responsible for everything that had gone wrong in the relations between the United States and the French Republic. There even seems to have been a tendency to make Genet and his friends scapegoats for any pro-black symptoms on the side of the French Revolution. Eugene Perry Link writes of southern realization that "Brissot had founded the Société des Amis des Noirs and Genet was a member. The discovery of this fact did much to discredit the ambassador in the South."[19] And if the French Republic could not be held responsible for the actions of its own Minister Plenipotentiary in the United States, how could it be held responsible for a slave insurrection in Saint-Domingue? The slave insurrection, after all, had been directed not only against the planters but also against the authority of the French Republic itself. (And, if the Republican leaders had been obliged to discuss those French Revolutionary decrees, they could have pointed out, correctly, that the decrees in question were issued only *after* the slaves had themselves thrown off, by force, the authority of the French Republic.)

Yet, with the analytical part of his mind—which often suffered occultation where the French Revolution was concerned—Jefferson had to know that the French Revolution *did* bear a great deal of responsibility for the cataclysm in Saint-Domingue. As Secretary of State, Jefferson had had to follow the progress of events in an area which was of great concern to the United States, for economic and other reasons. He had seen *les grands blancs, les petits blancs,* and *les gens de couleur* dispute and eventually fight over the question of which groups were, and which were not, entitled to the benefits of the Declaration of the Rights of Man of August 1789. And then he had seen the news of the Declaration, and especially of the fight among the masters over the Declaration, percolate down to the slaves and there produce a volcanic explosion. No doubt, not all the slaves were directly interested in French Revolutionary ideas, but some undoubtedly were. Thomas O. Ott writes:

> The boundless nature of ideas also made the principles of the French Revolution dangerous in a slave society: how were the slaves to know that they were not included? It is significant that one Negro chief, after the slaves revolted, asked the whites in besieged Le Cap François, "Have you not sworn to maintain the French Constitution? . . . Have you forgotten that you have formally sworn to the Declaration of Rights . . . which says that men are born free and equal?"[20]

Had there been a successful slave revolution in Albemarle County, Virginia, one of its leaders could have put questions of identical purport to the master of Monticello and author of the Declaration of Independence.

There is no recorded statement of Jefferson's showing any awareness of the relevance of the diffusion of French Revolutionary ideas to slave insurrections. But he did become acutely aware that what had happened in Saint-Domingue—in the sense of the crude fact of a successful slave insurrection—could happen also in Virginia. For some time, Jefferson fought off that realization. As late as May 1793, before the fall of Cap François, Jefferson—still at that time under the French Revolutionary spell of Citizen Genet—had received with some complacency an ideology-saturated report from Genet about the situation in Saint-Domingue. Jefferson wrote: "The French minister Genet told me yesterday that matters appeared now to be tolerably well settled in St. Domingo; that the Patriotic party had taken possession of 600 aristocrats and monocrats, had sent 200 of them to France, & were sending 400 here; and that a coalition had taken place among the other inhabitants."

Jefferson even adds a callous and flippant reflection, ideologically oriented. "I wish we could distribute our 400 among the Indians, who would teach them lessons of liberty & equality."[21] The 400 represents the number of white refugees from Saint-Domingue in the United States in May; before the mass exodus of July.

As late as May 1793, Jefferson's writings show no signs of any empathy with his fellow slaveowners of Saint-Domingue. They were "aristocrats and monocrats," like John Adams and Alexander Hamilton, and so the loathly opposites to the liberty-loving slaveowners of Virginia. But by

July 1793, with the news of the fall of Cap François and its consequences, Jefferson's feelings towards the victims of the slave revolt have undergone a sea-change. He writes to James Monroe:

> The situation of the St. Domingo fugitives (aristocrats as they are) calls aloud for pity and charity. Never was so deep a tragedy presented to the feelings of man. I deny the power of the general government to apply money to such a purpose, but I deny it with a bleeding heart. It belongs to the State governments. Pray urge ours to be liberal. The Executive should hazard themselves more on such an occasion, & the Legislative when it meets ought to approve & extend it. It will have a great effect in doing away the impression of other disobligations towards France. —I become daily more and more convinced that all the West India Islands will remain in the hands of the people of colour, & a total expulsion of the whites sooner or later take place. It is high time we should foresee the bloody scenes which our children certainly, and possibly ourselves (south of Potomac), have to wade through, & try to avert them.[22]

Jefferson is by now no longer under the spell of Citizen Genet, and the spell of the French Revolution itself seems to be weakening, in that being an "aristocrat" no longer puts a person beyond the pale of pity and charity. In terms of the real French Revolution, then raging in France under Robespierre, as distinct from the French Revolution imagined by the Jeffersonians, Jefferson had become an *indulgent*: a capital offense in a France ruled by Robespierre's Committee of Public Safety, from the summer of 1793 to the summer of 1794.

The sole reference to Revolutionary France—here identified as simply "France"—in Jefferson's letter to Monroe is Jefferson's opinion that American benefactions towards French refugees will have "a great effect in doing away with the impression of other disobligations towards France." The "disobligations" are probably Genet-connected and certainly political. The theory that any French Revolutionary government, suffering from a feeling of political "disobligation," would be appeased or mollified by a display of American benevolence towards aristocratic French refugees is fantastic even above the norm of Jeffersonian musings about the French Revolution. And I suspect there is a reason for the increase in the fantasy level. Jefferson is trying, and finding it increasingly hard, to cling to the belief that the interests of Virginian slaveowning and the dissemination of French Revolutionary ideas are compatible. The course of events in Saint-Domingue made it hard to go on believing that. But the fantasy that pity for the aristocratic refugees would find favor in the eyes of revolutionary France provided temporary consolation for a sense of growing alienation.

Let me return for a moment to that metaphor from the *Divine Comedy*. Jefferson had feared that a wind from the Northern states of the Union was fanning the flames of a potential Inferno under Monticello. But the course of events in Haiti from 1789 to 1793 demonstrated that the wind from Revolutionary France had actually fanned the winds of a *real* inferno in Saint-Domingue: a hell on earth for the whites. And Virginia was within range of the sparks from Saint-Domingue. The principal threat to the slaveowning community was no longer coming from the North but from the South.

The slow decay of Jefferson's faith in the French Revolution, as recorded in his letters, dates from 1793. But the decay may not have been as gradual as the written record suggests. I suspect that the living faith actually died in the late summer of 1793. The later utterances, favorable to the French Revolution, all have lost the fire of real conviction, and some bear the traces of guilt at the loss of that fire. The death of that faith has to be ascribed to two causes: the mission of Citizen Genet, and the news from Saint-Domingue. But the two are parts of a single phenomenon: the French Revolution impinging on the New World. The French Revolution, not as a Platonic shadow in American minds, but in its habit as it lived and as long as it lived: fiery, imperious, uncontrollable, domineering, and potentially destructive, beyond all calculation. Anyone with anything to lose would want to keep their distance from *that* French Revolution. And the Virginia slaveowners had *everything* to lose, and most reason to avoid any close contact with the grim phenomenon they had admired from afar.

Genet himself ascribed his recall to (among other reasons) "the terror of the slave-owners." Genet's specific hypothesis is redundant; his own behavior was quite adequate to elicit a demand for his recall, on behalf of any government to which he might have been accredited. But when he writes of "the terror of the slave-owners," he is probably alluding to something he had experienced. It is by no means improbable that he noted a change in Jefferson's attitude towards the French Revolution after the news from Cap François.

In the matter of Citizen Genet, as in so much else, Jefferson was lucky as well as skillful. In the controversy over the *Rights of Man* Jefferson had managed to send a message across to Americans who were in love with the French Revolution. The message was that, although Jefferson was a member of a suspect administration, his own heart was in the right place. When Jefferson (however reluctantly and even guiltily) wrote the letter requesting the recall of Citizen Genet, he was sending a similar message to those Americans (especially Southerners) who were beginning to fall *out* of love with the French Revolution, in the second half of 1793. Jefferson's heart was still in the right place, only the right place had changed position.

The many Americans who were neither strong Federalists nor strong Republicans would not be impressed, henceforward, when Federalists denounced Jefferson as "a Jacobin." Was it not Jefferson who had sent Citizen Genet packing, and was not Genet the very personification of the French Revolution?

Jefferson himself always denied that this was the significance of the transaction in question, but the fact that it was seen in that light smoothed his path towards the Presidency.

III. "THE CONTAGION OF LIBERTY"

The intensity of Jefferson's feelings about what had happened in Saint-Domingue was to become apparent after the French Revolution was over. Between the end of 1793, and of his tenure as Secretary of State, and his entry into the functions of the Presidency in 1801, Jefferson had had no say in the formation of foreign policy. When he took office as President, he continued the basic policy of his predecessors—"no entangling alliances"—bitterly as he had challenged them and it in the past. Only in one respect did he reverse the policy of his immediate predecessor. This was over Saint-Domingue/Haiti.

John Adams's administration had favored the independence of Saint-Domingue and had helped its black rulers to resist the French. Under Jefferson, the United States encouraged the French—now under Bonaparte—in their efforts to crush the blacks and restore slavery. Early in Jefferson's first administration, the new President encouraged the French to invade Haiti. And in his second administration, after the failure of the French invasion, he imposed an embargo on an independent Haiti. The embargo symbolized American rejection of a state ruled by slaves who had freed themselves: no free blacks in the Western hemisphere.

In a remarkable 1993 essay, "The Power of Blackness: Thomas Jefferson and the Revolution in Saint-Domingue," Michael Zuckerman contends that what the Republicans were trying to do was "to establish a quarantine against the contagion of servile revolt."[23] Zuckerman goes on to rephrase the nature of the quarantine in question, defining it memorably as being designed for the confinement of "the contagion of liberty."

Zuckerman is in the interesting position of being a left-wing writer who vastly prefers the Federalists to the Republicans, in relation to Saint-Domingue. As he writes:

> In St. Domingue it was the Federalists who held far more closely to the faith of the founders and the Jeffersonian Republicans who tried far more tenaciously to betray and traduce the will of a people. It was the Federalists who were known to aid the oppressed in their effort at independence and the Republicans who resisted that effort. It was the Federalists who restored freedom and the Republicans who attempted the restoration of a colonial regime and, indeed, the reimposition of slavery itself.

Zuckerman continues: "Race was at the root of all these ironies. Race drove all these Jeffersonian retreats. Race overrode all other considerations for Jefferson wherever it was salient at all, and race was centrally salient in St. Domingue. [Jefferson] was the foremost racist of his era in America. And St. Domingue constituted the crisis in which all this became clear."

Jefferson's practical policy, as President, towards Saint-Domingue, cannot be easily reconciled with his (theoretical) commitment to "colonization" as the future for American blacks after (imaginary) emancipation. As Zuckerman puts it, "Even as he maintained his unyielding aversion . . . to the mixture of colour on the continent, he set himself intransigently against a separate black state on the islands. Even as he grew increasingly silent and depressed about the future of Africans in America, he moved malevolently against them in the Caribbean."

Zuckerman's conclusion is something to remember: "Even as he yearned to get rid of them, he refused to let them go."

Tim Matthewson, in a recent study, "Jefferson and Haiti," published in the *Journal of Southern History*, volume 61, challenges Zuckerman's interpretation. According to Matthewson, Zuckerman "produces no documentation to support his claim (p. 185) that Jefferson and the Republicans endorsed the French plan to restore slavery or his assertion (p. 188) that Jefferson was motivated by implacable malice towards the Haitians".[24] Yet Matthewson himself produces evidence tending to support Zuckerman's interpretation, on both points.

On the first point indeed, Matthewson goes further than Zuckerman did. Matthewson shows that it was Jefferson who actually proposed what took shape as Bonaparte's plan for the subjugation of Haiti (Saint-Domingue). Matthewson:

In July 1801, the French Charge d'Affairs, Louis A. Pichon used the occasion of his first interview with President Jefferson to enter into a full discussion of U.S. policy towards Saint-Domingue. President Jefferson told the Charge that the United States opposed the island's independence under black rule and wanted to see French authority restored, but he also reminded the young Frenchman that the United States had interests in the island. The French islands, like much of the rest of the Caribbean, were dependent on American merchants for provisions and the President informed Pichon that the trade was lucrative and could not be easily abandoned. Jefferson's words were encouraging to Pichon, and the President also proposed a concert with England [i.e. between France and England] against Toussaint [the Haitian leader]. As Pichon reported this conversation, the President proposed that "in order that this concert may be complete and effective you [France] should first make peace with England, then nothing will be easier than to furnish your army and fleet with everything, and to reduce Toussaint [the Haitian leader] to starvation."

Pichon reported that conversation to Talleyrand on 22 July 1801. But the green light from Jefferson was important to Bonaparte, and he adverted to it when, on October 1801, he gave his instructions to General Leclerc, head of the expedition whose mission was the subjugation of Haiti. Matthewson writes (p. 219): "On October 8, 1801, when French Consul, Bonaparte appointed [General] Leclerc to head the expedition, he seemed certain of Jefferson's support. Jefferson had promised that from the moment that the French army arrives, every measure shall be taken to starve Toussaint and to aid the army."

Leclerc's instructions were based on an optimistic interpretation of Pichon's conversation with Jefferson. The instructions ignore Jefferson's warning about American economic interests, and the lucrative trade with Haiti/Saint-Domingue.

The Leclerc expedition was a disastrous failure, owing mainly to the fierce resistance of the ex-slaves, to a climate inimical to newly arrived whites, and to the fact that the peace between France and Britain—recommended by Jefferson in July 1801, and concluded in April 1802—broke down during 1803. Matthewson (pp. 209–10) adduces a fourth factor: the "help" and "encouragement" allegedly provided by Jefferson to the Haitians in their resistance to the French. Actually Matthewson's narrative (from which his interpretations sometimes tend to stray) shows that Jefferson gave no help at all to either side. The only "encouragement" he gave was to the French, to attack the Haitians, but once they were in, he left them to their fate and refused their requests for American credits. Throughout the period of the Leclerc expedition, Jefferson pursued the policy adumbrated in the "economic" part of his conversation with Pichon. United States policy, under Jefferson's first administration, was governed by economic forces, and not by ideological ones. "Starving Toussaint" might be a laudable objective (racially speaking) and one to be recommended to the French, but if American merchants could make money by selling food and other goods to Toussaint's forces, why then so be it.

When I contemplate American policy towards Haiti under Jefferson's first administration, I am reminded of "Uncle Amos" in Edwin O'Connor's brilliant novel *The Last Hurrah*. Uncle Amos was a keen white supremacist, but not at all costs. He applied for membership in the Ku Klux Klan, but withdrew his application on finding that he would have to pay for his own sheet.

That is how it was in Jefferson's first term. In Jefferson's second term, however, with the French gone, and Haitian independence a *fait accompli,* Jefferson imposed an embargo on Haiti. (This is Zuckerman's "Even as he yearned to get rid of them, he refused to let them go.") At first sight, the anti-Haiti embargo of Jefferson's second term appears in direct contradiction to the economic considerations which dominated policy towards Haiti in his first term. The contradiction is probably more marked in theory than in reality. The embargo—very hard to enforce—may have been more symbolic than practical. What it did was to mark the rejection of the legitimacy of a state controlled by ex-slaves. Once that symbolic point was established and maintained, I suspect, actual trade relations with Haiti continued much as before, but clandestinely. Jefferson's abhorrence of the existence of such a state was real, but abhorrence would not be allowed to obstruct the reality of profitable (if clandestine) trade relations. Head and Heart again.

Matthewson's well-researched essay does not refute, but rather confirms, Zuckerman's view that Jefferson "endorsed the French plan to restore slavery." Matthewson shows that Jefferson endorsed the French plan to subjugate Haiti, and there is no doubt that, if the French had succeeded in that, slavery would have been restored. But Matthewson also shows that, having *endorsed* the French plan, Jefferson failed to *support* it. Matthewson's account therefore qualifies Zuckerman's in an important way, showing that Jefferson's policy towards Haiti was less ideology-driven than Zuckerman would suggest. Specifically, Matthewson shows that Zuckerman's contention that "race overrode all other considerations for Jefferson" is not tenable in relation to Haiti.

On the other hand, Matthewson's assertion that Zuckerman produces no documentation to support his claim—that Jefferson was "motivated by implacable malice towards the Haitians"—appears as somewhat disingenuous. Matthewson shows himself aware of considerable documentation of racist attitudes on Jefferson's part towards the Haitians. Thus Matthewson acknowledges (p. 27) that Jefferson's letters of the period contain "numerous references to his fears and racial phobia" and (p. 7) that he "occasionally disparaged the blacks," for example calling them "the Cannibals of the terrible republic" and comparing them to assassins.

It might reasonably be observed that it is not necessarily racist to "disparage" the behavior of people who (like the ex-slaves in Haiti) regularly engaged in massacres of men, women, and children. True, but the whites, in trying to repress the ex-slaves, *also* engaged in regular and indiscriminate massacres, and neither Jefferson nor other white commentators had anything to say about that. White mass-murderers were not described as "Cannibals"; black ones were.

Matthewson's challenge to Zuckerman on Jefferson and Haiti is strenuous, and in part successful. I cannot find, however, that any similar challenge has been mounted to the six studies of Jefferson's positions on slavery and race in the United States quoted earlier in this chapter. It seems that the case presented in those studies has won general acceptance and that Jefferson's credentials as an "authentic enemy of slavery" etc. have lapsed, as far as modern students of Jefferson are concerned. In this connection a 1993 collection of essays, *Jeffersonian Legacies,* is of some significance.[25]

Jeffersonian Legacies grew out of the University of Virginia's commemoration of the two hundredth anniversary in 1993 of the birth of its founder, Thomas Jefferson. Peter Onuf, the editor of *Jeffersonian Legacies,* describes the commemorative conference of 1992 as "revisionist in spirit." Certainly the three essays in *Jeffersonian Legacies* which are devoted to Jefferson and slavery are indeed revisionist, and daringly so, granted the occasion and the pious traditions of the University of Virginia, whose press is the publisher of *Jeffersonian Legacies.* The three essays are: "Those Who Labor for My Happiness: Thomas Jefferson and His Slaves," by Lucia C. Stanton; "Treason against the Hopes of the World," by Paul Finkelman; and "The Strange Career of Thomas Jefferson: Race and Slavery in American Memory 1945–1993," by Scot A. French and Edward L. Ayers.

Lucia Stanton's valuable and well-researched essay adds a good deal of detail to the picture of Jefferson's relations with his slaves that emerges from the studies previously considered. Her tone is non-judgmental but her details do not detract from the bleakness of the scene as already established. There is a paragraph for example, on Jefferson's overseers:

> Jefferson's views on physical punishment no doubt reduced whipping on his plantations to levels well below those of many of his neighbors. The whip was, however, by no means eliminated. From the 1780s Jefferson employed on the Monticello plantation over twenty overseers with diverse temperaments and management styles. Some were cruel, even by the standards of the day. William Page, "peevish and too ready to strike," spent four years in Jefferson's employ. When he later became overseer at John Wayles Eppes's neighboring Pantops, Eppes was unable to hire slaves in the neighborhood because of "the terror of Pages name". The "Tyrannical" William McGehee, overseer at the Tufton farm for two years, carried a gun "for fear of an attack from the negroes". One of Monticello's white house joiners deplored the cruelty of Gabriel Lilly, overseer there from 1801 to 1805. Lilly whipped Critta Hemings's seventeen-year-old son James three times in one day, when he was too ill to "raise his hand to his Head". Yet Jefferson considered it impossible to find "a man who fulfills my purposes better than Lilly and would have kept him longer had he not demanded a doubling of his salary." (Uncle Amos again . . .)

(Critta Hemings was the fourth child of John Wayles—Jefferson's father-in-law—by the slave woman Betty Hemings; see Appendix.)

Critta was Sally Hemings's elder sister. Critta's son, who was flogged by Gabriel Lilly, was a grandson of John Wayles. Apparently the protection that was accorded to John Wayles's "black" children—all of whom were house slaves—was not extended to the next generation.

Jefferson himself was aware of an ethical-financial dilemma of slaveowners in relation to the selection of overseers: "My first [concern] is that the labourers may be well treated, the second that they [overseers] may enable me to have that treatment continued by making as much [profit] as will admit it. The man [overseer] who can effect both objects is rarely to be found."[26]

As may be inferred from the title, Paul Finkelman's essay is more vehemently "anti-Jefferson" in its rhetoric than anything contained in the studies previously considered, but it does not seem to me that it adds anything of substance to what those studies have already quietly established.

The most original, and to me the most interesting, of these essays is the French-Ayers study of "The Strange Career of Thomas Jefferson." The career is the *posthumous* career, specifically in the second half of the twentieth century. This was, of course, a period of erosion of Jefferson's liberal reputation, in relation to slavery and race. French and Ayers detail the almost frantic efforts of certain pious Jeffersonians, headed by Dumas Malone, to stop the rot. After Fawn Brodie's *Thomas Jefferson: An Intimate History* (1974) had popularized the idea of a love affair between Jefferson and Sally Hemings, the discrediting of that idea came to seem, to these Jeffersonians, a matter of extreme importance. The weightiest evidence in favor of a liaison between Jefferson and Sally is the claim of Madison Hemings, who is known to be Sally's son, that his father was Thomas Jefferson (see Appendix). Madison Hemings, already copiously disparaged by Jeffersonians, had now to be comprehensively discredited. Dumas Malone and an assistant set about this task in an article in the *Journal of Southern History* (November 1985) with the aid of a slave/animal analogy with deep roots in slaveholding tradition. French and Ayers write (*Legacies*, p. 435):

> In a journal article entitled "A Note on Evidence," Malone and his research assistant, Steven Hochman, dismissed the Hemings memoir as a piece of propaganda. Malone wrote that the Hemings memoir "reminds us of the pedigree printed on the numerous stud-horse bills that can be seen posted around during the Spring season. No matter how scrubby the stock or whether the horse has any known pedigree, owners invented an exalted lineage for their property. Horses could not know what was claimed for them, but we have often thought if one of them could read and would happen to come across his pedigree . . . he would blush to the tips of his ears at the mendacity of his owner."

I invite the reader to compare the above passage with Madison Hemings's own statement, as set out in the Appendix. You may or may not agree with me that a comparison between Hemings's sober and dignified statement and the jeering malice of the above tirade redounds to the credit of the former slave, and not to that of the eminent scholar.

In the foreword to *Jeffersonian Legacies,* Peter Onuf says that the 1992 Conference at the University of Virginia (which gave rise to *Legacies*) was "structured around central themes: Jefferson and rights, education, the democratic tradition and race." There is a problem here. Conceptually, the other themes cannot be handled in isolation from race. Jefferson's position on race—once we have ascertained what it is—must (one would think) necessarily affect our assessment of Jefferson's position on rights, education, and the democratic tradition. But this is not what seems to be happening in the essays collected in *Jeffersonian Legacies.* The essays specifically devoted to race are indeed revisionist, and sometimes downright iconoclastic. But most of the other essays remain very much in the tone, and governed by the assumptions, of traditional Jeffersonian scholarship. Scholars considering "other" aspects of Jefferson seem to feel that changes in the assessment of his attitudes to slavery and race are not relevant to their particular field, which is somehow felt to be immune to racial problems and conflicts. In *Legacies* this attitude comes nearest to explicit formulation in Steven Conrad's essay entitled (aptly enough) "Putting Rights Talk in Its Place." Conrad says, "Setting aside, as I mean to here, the question of Jefferson's putative hypocrisy as a rights advocate, I turn to the theme of my essay . . ."

"The theme of my essay" turns out to have no blacks in it at all. With the magic words "setting aside" the whole tiresome subject of Jefferson and blacks is eliminated from the subject of Jefferson and rights. And other contributions to *Legacies* show signs of similar dispositions, though expressing them more cautiously than Conrad has.

It is as if, almost instinctively, a kind of strategy of damage limitation were emerging among certain Jefferson scholars, running roughly as follows: "Let the field of Jefferson, slavery and race be entirely abandoned to those who feel strongly about such matters. And then let the rest of us get on with our scholarly work very much as we used to do in the good old days without allowing all these vulgar modern considerations and controversies to obtrude on the tenor of our austere deliberations."

I have an idea that the authorities of the University of Virginia well understood what they were about when they allowed the 1993 Jefferson commemoration to take the particular turn it did. And Jefferson himself, a grandmaster of damage limitation, would have thoroughly approved.

IV

In purely political terms, it is not difficult to reconcile the Jeffersonian commitment to the Cult of the French Revolution (fervent from October 1789 to July 1793 and desultory thereafter) with the defense of the institution of slavery in Virginia and the rest of the South. Virginia felt threatened by the power of the Northern cities, and the real threat—although no more than an implicit one in the 1790s—was to the existence of slavery in the South, after it had disappeared from the North. Virginians did not, in public, explicitly acknowledge that what was felt to be threatened was slavery. To start a national debate on that topic would have been quite contrary to their interests. Yet they needed to defend what they felt to be the liberty of Virginia, and the distinguishing characteristic of Virginian liberty was the liberty of Virginian gentlemen to own slaves.

Slavery was protected by the Constitution, but it was a grudging protection, as far as many in the North were concerned. Some Northern writers were already addressing the South as from a superior moral height. This was intolerable, especially for high-spirited Virginian gentlemen. Yet to answer the Northerners, on their chosen topic of slavery, would be both difficult and risky. What was needed was a *general* topic, one which was, ostensibly, not sectional at all, but which would enable the South to take the high moral ground against the North, and win national support by so doing.

The political genius of Thomas Jefferson—working, I think, instinctively—identified that topic as the Cult of the French Revolution, presented as the legitimate culmination of the American one, together with which it constituted one single holy cause of "liberty." The Cult had the inherent property of putting the Northern leadership on the defensive, because it endangered their commercial and financial relations with Britain. Thus the Northerners could plausibly be represented as having defected—"apostatized" in the holy jargon of the Cult—from the American Revolution itself, by reason of their refusal to embrace the French one.

Thus the moral tables were turned. Southerners need no longer listen to Northerners lecturing them about slavery. The Virginians themselves would eliminate slavery in their own good time and in their own way, and how and when they chose to do it was entirely their own affair. The Northerners were talking about slavery only to divert attention from their own corruption, Anglomania, and monarchical inclinations—all evident from their refusal to accept the French Revolution, true heir to the American Revolution and touchstone of the sincerity of the commitment of any American to the principles laid down by Thomas Jefferson in the Declaration of Independence.

So let's not talk about slavery! Let's talk about the French Revolution!

The Cult certainly met a political need, and got the Republican Party off to a flying start. But it also met an emotional need, on the part of the Virginians, so that their commitment to it was heartfelt (up to the summer of 1793) and not just a matter of expediency. Basically the emotional need was the need to feel pure.

The Jacobins, guided by Robespierre and St. Just, divided the world into *les purs* and *les corrompus*. In this respect at least the Jeffersonians were true Jacobins. They were themselves *les purs*. Adams and Hamilton were *les corrompus par excellence*. (Washington, the Virginian who had declined into being an American, had to be watched.)

In a caste society, such as Jefferson's Virginia, the notions of purity and of contamination are of central importance, and heavily fraught. Ideas of moral purity, sexual purity, genetic purity are all there in shadowy interaction, and all threatened with contamination from the omnipresent pariah caste. One reaction to all that is the hysterical exaltation of the purity of Southern (white) womanhood. But the question of the purity of Southern (white) manhood remains in the shadows of silence.

It was easy enough for the *petit-bourgeois* Robespierre to feel confidently *pur* in every sense of the word. Hardly so easy for the Virginian aristocrat. Jefferson has told us himself, with eloquence, of some of the deleterious moral effects that slavery has on the slaveowners. But his picture is probably Bowdlerized.

In considering the themes of purity and contamination in a slaveowning culture, and the relevance of these themes to the politics of Thomas Jefferson, it is impossible to leave Sally Hemings altogether out of the picture. Orthodox Jeffersonians—once they were forced to recognize her existence at all—have sought to dismiss discussion of her as mere prurient tittle-tattle. This will not do. Whether Jefferson slept with her or not, and whether or not she bore his children, she remains an important figure in his life. She was his deceased wife's half-sister and she was a slave, and Jefferson chose to have her with him as his personal servant—if no more than that—for many years of his life. Granted the importance of the themes of purity and contamination within the slaveowning culture, that relationship cannot have failed to play an important part in the emotional life of Thomas Jefferson and, through that, in his political life also.

More generally, the slaveowners—in this period—acknowledged that slavery was morally wrong and also refused to give it up. A strong sense of guilt, even if repressed, is inseparable from such a situation. Those who feel guilty, while refusing to give up that about which they feel guilty, often take refuge in the thought that it is somebody else who is *really* guilty. This is what Freud calls "projection." In Jefferson's draft of the Declaration of Independence, there is a classic example of projection. This is the passage in which George III is blamed for the presence of slaves in America. George III (according to Jefferson's draft):

> waged cruel war against human nature itself, violating its most sacred rights of life and liberty in the persons of a distant people who never offended him.... This piratical warfare, the opprobrium of *infidel* powers, is the warfare of the *Christian* king of Great Britain. Determined to keep open a market where MEN should be bought and sold, he has prostituted his negative for suppressing every legislative attempt to prohibit or to restrain this execrable commerce.

On this passage, William Cohen writes:

> Jefferson made this onslaught despite the fact that his fortune was founded partly upon profits derived from the slave trade. His father-in-law had engaged in this commerce, and several of the bondsmen inherited by Jefferson bore African names. Moreover, the locations of the Negro quarters were indicated in his "Farm Book" by such appellations as Angola and Guinea.

One might add that the emphasis on the infamy of George III, in allowing the slaves to be sold, implies that there were no willing Virginian buyers, sharing in the infamy and in the loot. This is projection indeed, in one of its wildest forms.

The importance of the Cult of the French Revolution on the emotional side, within American politics, is that it enables projection to be carried out in a much more plausible and satisfactory fashion, by dumping the burden of Southern guilt, over slavery, onto the North, for defection from the ideals of the American Revolution, as revealed anew, and purified, in the French Revolution.

At the most exalted point of his commitment to the Cult, in January 1793, Jefferson had a vision of the French Revolution as a destroying and redeeming Angel, purifying and liberating humanity through the slaughter of millions.

It is worth looking again at that Adam and Eve letter, in the light of the matters under discussion in the present chapter. Jefferson wrote:

> My own affections have been deeply wounded by some of the martyrs of this cause but rather than it should have failed, I would have seen half the earth desolated. Were there but an Adam and Eve, left in every country, and left free, it would be better than it now is.

Let us leave common sense and common humanity behind for a moment and follow Thomas Jefferson into the wild vision which, however fleeting in its surfacing, was evidently generated by a powerful wish.

I think we can begin to see what the wish is, if we put a very simple question based on Jefferson's supposition. The question is: *What color are the American Adam and Eve?*

There can only be one answer to that, on Jeffersonian assumptions. Adam and Eve have to be white, because Adam and Eve are *free*. There is no room, in Jeffersonian America (or even in the Hemisphere), for free blacks. Adam and Eve are free and white, and therefore all their descendants are free and white. In terms of racist theology, it is a reversal of the Fall. Washed in the blood of the victims of the French Revolution, and other revolutions inspired by it, humanity is born again. Above all, *America,* and even higher above all, Virginia, is born again, washed clean at last from that deep blurred single stain, composed of blackness and of guilt. The French Revolution gives back to America its lost innocence.

A vision; no more and no less. But visions always tell us something. And this one tells us something about the sources of the power of the Cult of the French Revolution, in its heyday, over the emotional life, and the mind, of Thomas Jefferson.

Let us return, finally to our Dante metaphor. Paradiso is the Monticello of the whites. Inferno is the Monticello of the blacks. Purgatorio, salvifically interposed between the two, and making the whites worthy of Paradiso, by purging them from sin and guilt, is the Cult of the French Revolution.

EPILOGUE

THOMAS JEFFERSON AND THE IMPENDING SCHISM IN THE AMERICAN CIVIL RELIGION

In an address at Michigan State University on 5 May 1995, President Clinton warned right-wing paramilitaries not to attempt "to appropriate our sacred symbols for paranoid purposes."[1]

The President was speaking in the aftermath of the destruction, apparently by American right-wing fanatics, of the Federal building in Oklahoma City and its occupants on 19 April 1995. The aftermath of that ghastly act had brought media reports of widespread paramilitary conspiracies in several states—and notably around the militia groups in Michigan—for the organization of armed resistance to the Federal Government. The President was seeking to exclude such conspirators from what is called "the American civil religion."

There is quite a copious literature about the American civil religion and, while there are differences about the exact nature of this powerful but nebulous concept, there is also a broad consensus about its general nature.

The term "civil religion" was first used by Rousseau and refers to "the religious dimension of the polity." *American* civil religion has been summed up as "an institutionalized collection of sacred beliefs providing sources of cohesion and prophetic guidance through times of national crises."[2] Among the sacred beliefs, a cult of liberty has been important from very early on. Robert N. Bellah quotes a 1770 observer as noting that "the minds of the people are wrought up to as high a degree of enthusiasm by the word liberty as could have been expected had religion been the cause."[3]

In the American civil religion, liberty, nationalism, and faith are fused. As Norman Mailer put it: "In America the country was the religion. And all the other religions of the land were fed from that first religion."[4]

James H. Smylie declared, around the same time: "Civil religion is the way we have identified ourselves as God's people and under his providence, the way we have invoked divine sanction in the use of power and in the support of civil authority and the way in which we justify our national actions."[5]

Central to the American civil religion are two eighteenth-century documents: the Declaration of Independence and the Constitution. Around these documents, and linked with them in the religion, is a limited number of historical figures; for all Americans, the Founding Fathers; for most Americans, also Abraham Lincoln. In the pantheon of the American civil religion, however, two holy personages stand out with larger halos. As the authors of *Civil Religion and the Presidency* write:

> The Declaration of Independence, the Constitution, and later, Lincoln's Gettysburg Address became the scriptures of the new public faith. Just as the colonists saw their own church governments as vehicles of God's participation in history, so these public documents became the covenants which bound the people of the nation together in a political and religious union. A leadership imagery developed that parallelled the biblical covenant of Israel and led to the Founding Fathers mythology. Before long Washington had become the Moses-liberator figure, Jefferson the prophet.[6]

I. Jefferson the Prophet

There is no difficulty in seeing Jefferson as the prophet of the American civil religion if you think of him *only* as the author of its most sacred document, the Declaration of Independence, and leave it at that. But there is great difficulty in fitting the historic Jefferson, with all we know of him, into the civil religion of modern America—as generally and semi-officially expounded—at all, let alone seeing him as the prophet of the same.

Thomas Jefferson was indeed, in his day, a prophet of American civil religion. Indeed if his original draft of the Declaration of Independence had been accepted, the Declaration would have been more explicitly linked to the American civil religion than it is in its present form. Where the Declaration, as we now have it, opens its second paragraph with the words, "We hold these truths to be self-evident," Jefferson's original draft had had "We hold these truths to be sacred and undeniable." The drafting of the Declaration had been entrusted by Congress to a committee of five, of which the leading members were Jefferson, John Adams, and Benjamin Franklin. Although Rousseau's phrase "civil religion" does not seem to have been in circulation in America at this time—when it would have been suspect in the eyes of churchmen—Jefferson (whether through Rousseau or not) was a "civil religion" person, in his habitual use of language. Adams objected strongly to the mixing up of politics and religion. Franklin was more consistently secular than Jefferson in his style. Carl Lotus Becker notes, on the change in the manuscript to "self-evident": "It is not clear that this change was made by Jefferson. The hand-writing of 'self-evident' resembles Franklin's."[7] The change was an improvement, functionally speaking, for a revolutionary manifesto. Anyone who rejects a "self-evident truth" is, by definition, either a fool or a knave. And that is precisely what the Founders wanted to say about anyone who opposed the Declaration. Jefferson himself appreciated the polemical force of this word, and often used it later.

The Jefferson of the early 1790s, the champion of the French Revolution, was an ardent believer in, and prophet of, civil religion in the sense adumbrated by Rousseau. That is, he sought to animate an apparently secular and political idea—that of liberty—by breathing into it the kind of emotions and dispositions with which religion had been invested in the Ages of Faith. Of this religion Thomas Jefferson was more than a prophet, he was a Pope. As author of the Declaration of Independence he possessed the *Magisterium* of liberty. He could define heresy and excommunicate heretics. To fail to acknowledge (for example) that the French Revolution was an integral part of the holy cause of liberty along with the American Revolution was heresy, and the heretic had to be driven from public life.

John Adams, classed as a heresiarch within this system, naturally resisted the Jeffersonian civil religion: "John Adams argued in his 'Dissertation on the Canon and the Feudal Law' that the linking of the religious and civil authority was a wicked one, subject to the worst kind of abuses."[8]

Thomas Jefferson ardently preached and energetically practiced his own version of civil religion. But is that civil religion compatible with the *American* civil religion as we know it today? Let us see.

In investigating that question we have to begin by asking another question: What kind of American was Thomas Jefferson?

He was a good American in the general sense; he held America and Americans to be vastly superior to Europe and Europeans, morally and socially speaking. But he was not an American nationalist, politically speaking. He was not an "America firster." He was a "Virginia firster."

He continued to speak of Virginia as "my country" even when he was representing the United States abroad. Nor was this an isolated trick of speech. The United States was not an object that engaged his emotions; Virginia was. The Declaration of Independence was for him a sacred document, part of the civil religion of liberty. The Constitution of the United States was not; it was a political document, just about acceptable, and no more, for pragmatic reasons, and remaining acceptable only as long as the Federal Government respected what Virginians regarded as the limits of its authority. Federal institutions, including the Presidency, were workaday things, not invested with the spiritual aura of the civil religion. Virginia remained the holy land of Liberty.

In his will Jefferson did not mention the fact that he had been twice President of the United States as among the significant events of his career. He did mention—as well as his authorship of the Declaration of Independence—his foundation of the University of Virginia. In terms of that old dialogue between Head and Heart, the Heart was always with Virginia, and only the Head with the United States.

In political life, as in his personal emotional life, Jefferson's Head usually prevailed over his Heart; as in the case of the recall of Citizen Genet. But this was not always the case. When Virginia appeared to be threatened by an excess of Federal Government, in 1798, under President John Adams, Jefferson encouraged Virginians to resist. Virginians, and other Southerners, of later generations, in challenging what they perceived as the excessive claims of the Federal Government were, to that extent, in the Jefferson tradition.

In the 1830s, John C. Calhoun, the great propagator of the States Rights ideology in the antebellum South, claimed Jefferson's authority for his "Nullification" doctrine: that states could treat as null and void Federal laws they regarded as intruding on the proper sphere of the states. Calhoun invoked as precedents the Virginia and Kentucky resolutions rejecting the Alien and Sedition Laws passed by Congress in 1798. Calhoun noted that the Kentucky resolutions were "now known to have emanated from the pen of Mr. Jefferson."[9]

Jefferson's authority was important to the leaders of the antebellum South, in the 1830s, as validating the philosophy of Nullification: a philosophy that had within it the germs of the eventual Secession. But by the 1840s the Nullification philosophy had come to be regarded by Southerners, as axiomatic—"self-evident truths," indeed—so Jefferson's validation was now surplus to requirements. And Jefferson was by this time becoming deeply unpopular with the more ardent defenders of Southern institutions. The reason was that the hated abolitionist press, from the

1830s on, had been making copious use of Jefferson's "anti-slavery" writings, mainly from *Notes on the State of Virginia*. Back in the late eighteenth century, the Virginian slaveowners who were Jefferson's contemporaries hadn't taken Jeffersonian "anti-slavery" seriously. They knew Jefferson personally, and knew he meant no harm. And many of them were in the habit of saying the same sorts of things themselves, in appropriate company.

By the mid-nineteenth century, however, Southerners *had* to take Jefferson's anti-slavery writings seriously because *Northerners* were taking them seriously, and using them against the South. Taking the Declaration of Independence in conjunction with Jefferson's "anti-slavery" utterances—well publicized in the North for more than two decades—Northerners, on the eve of the Civil War, were able to read anti-slavery intentions into the Declaration of Independence itself, and thus enlist both the Declaration and its author on their own side in the coming war. In a letter of April 1859, Lincoln wrote:

> All honour to Jefferson—to the man who, in the concrete pressure of a struggle for national independence by a single people had the coolness, forecast, and capacity to introduce into a merely revolutionary document, an abstract truth, and so to embalm it there, that today, and in all coming days, it shall be a rebuke and a stumbling block to the very harbingers of re-appearing tyranny and oppression.[10]

This letter was really a campaign manifesto, Merrill D. Peterson writes, "Lincoln's letter circulated freely during the presidential campaign of 1860. It was a masterpiece, the *Cincinnati Daily Gazette* declared, 'the most pointed and most forcible political letter ever written . . . a platform in itself.'"[11]

After the Civil War, that accolade from the martyred President secured a continuing place for Jefferson in the pantheon of the American civil religion. The Jeffersonian vessel had survived the rapids of the Civil War, and remained holy in the eyes of large numbers of Americans, both among the victors and the vanquished. In his posthumous reputation, as in his political career, luck was on Jefferson's side.

Still, there were always some begrudgers, and there were many more in the North than in the South. In the North, after the Civil War, Hamilton, not Jefferson, was at the center of the civil religion. In the South—more firmly than before the Civil War—it was Jefferson who was at the center. That is to say that the sectional and regional alignment, as between North and South, was again for a time essentially what it had been in the late eighteenth century. The reasons for the popularity of Jefferson in the postwar South are of great importance in relation to Jefferson's position in the American civil religion in the late twentieth century, and will be considered in sections of this Epilogue (below, II and III).

In the first half of the twentieth century, the most important phase affecting the posthumous reputation and civil-religious status of Thomas Jefferson was the New Deal. As Merrill D. Peterson puts it: "The Roosevelt administration built a great national temple to Jefferson's memory." The temple is the Jefferson Memorial in Washington, dedicated by President Franklin Delano Roosevelt on the two hundredth anniversary of Jefferson's birth, 13 April 1943. According to an official brochure: "Inscriptions at the memorial were selected by the Thomas Jefferson Memorial Commission and were taken from a wide variety of his writings on freedom, slavery, education and government." The section of the inscriptions that deals with freedom and slavery runs as follows:

> God who gave us life gave us liberty. Can the liberties of a nation be secure when we have removed a conviction that these liberties are the gift of God? Indeed I tremble for my country when I reflect that God is just, that his justice cannot sleep forever. Commerce between master and slave is despotism. Nothing is more certainly written in the book of fate than that these people are to be free.

All of this passage, except for the last sentence, is taken from *Notes on the State of Virginia*. The last sentence is taken from Jefferson's *Autobiography*. That sentence, as isolated in the Memorial inscription, deceives the public as to Jefferson's meaning. For the original passage in the *Autobiography* continues: "*Nor is it less certain that the two races, equally free, cannot live in the same government. Native habit, opinion has drawn indelible lines of distinction between them.*" (Emphasis added.)

In short, these people are to be free, and then deported. Jefferson's teaching on that matter is quite clear and often repeated.

Those who edited that inscription on behalf of the Jefferson Memorial Commission must have known what they were doing when they wrenched that resounding sentence from the *Autobiography* out of the context which so drastically qualifies its meaning. The distortion, by suppression, has to be deliberate.

In that inscription on the Jefferson Memorial in Washington, D.C. the liberal-Jeffersonian lie about Jefferson's position on liberty and slavery assumes, literally, monumental proportions.

The quarter-century following the dedication of the Memorial saw Jefferson's reputation, especially as a liberal, at its height. John F. Kennedy, and his liberal intellectual entourage, strongly contributed to the general and almost universal acceptance of the Jefferson Memorial. By the mid–1960s Jefferson's towering position, within the American civil religion, appeared assured for all time.

Merrill D. Peterson's invaluable work *The Jefferson Image in the American Mind* was published in 1960. By now, a successor volume, covering the last decades of the twentieth century, is badly needed. In particular, a detailed study of the impact of the civil rights movement, and ensuing changes, on Jefferson's image in the American mind, needs to be made. In default of such source material, I propose to "cut to the chase," as the filmmakers say, and consider factors affecting the place of Thomas Jefferson in the American civil religion, as these appear to me today (1995). The two major factors, in my opinion, are challenges to the authority of the Federal Government and the race issue. These factors have been linked in earlier momentous phases of American history: in 1798, when Virginia and Kentucky were threatening revolt against Federal authority; in the period before the Civil War, during and after the Civil War itself, and in the civil rights crisis of the 1960s. They are still linked today, and they raise serious questions about the place of Thomas Jefferson in the civil religion of modern America. Let me begin with the challenge to the authority of the Federal Government.

The President's full name—William Jefferson Clinton—attests his family's allegiance to a Jeffersonian tradition, probably through FDR. As President-elect, Clinton attested his personal commitment to that tradition by a symbolic gesture: in the week of his inauguration, Clinton retraced Jefferson's trip—as President-elect—from Monticello to Washington (in December 1800). And the White House staff underlined the significance of this gesture by letting the press know that the new President-elect, at this solemn moment in his life, was reading an advance copy of a new biography of Thomas Jefferson.[12]

When, therefore, Clinton warned the right-wing paramilitaries not to attempt "to appropriate our sacred symbols for paranoid purposes," we may assume that the heritage of Thomas Jefferson was associated in his mind with the defense of the sacred symbols. But Jefferson is an unreliable ally in this particular matter. Jefferson in his middle years—and even before the French Revolution—was in the grip of a fanatical cult of Liberty, seen as an absolute, to which it would be blasphemous to assign limits. In this period—roughly 1787 to 1793—Jefferson was intoxicated with what Edmund Burke called "the wild *gas* of liberty." That phrase occurs in the book with the confutation of which Jefferson, as Secretary of State, managed to associate himself publicly in April 1791, greatly to his own political advantage at the time. The passage in *Reflections on the Revolution in France* in which Burke uses this phrase is worth quoting here:

> When I see the spirit of liberty in action, I see a strong principle at work; and this, for a while, is all I can possibly know of it. The wild *gas,* the fixed air is plainly broke loose: but we ought to suspend our judgement until the first effervescence is a little subsided, till the liquor is cleared, and until we see something deeper than the agitation of a troubled and frothy surface. I must be tolerably sure, before I venture publicly to congratulate men upon a blessing, that they have really received one. Flattery corrupts both the receiver and the giver; and adulation is not of more service to the people than to kings. I should therefore suspend my congratulations on the new liberty of France, until I was informed how it had been combined with government; with public force; with the discipline and obedience of armies; with the collection of an effective and well-distributed revenue; with morality and religion; with the solidity of property; with peace and order; with civil and social manners. All these (in their way) are good things too; and, without them, liberty is not a benefit whilst it lasts, and is not likely to continue long. The effect of liberty to individuals is, that they may do what they please: We ought to see what it will please them to do, before we risque congratulations, which may be soon turned into complaints.[13]

In America, the holy cause of liberty became "combined with Government," in the manner stipulated by Burke, through the enactment and acceptance of the American Constitution. Washington, Adams, and Hamilton were all spiritually Burkeans; so was Madison, while he worked with Hamilton on the *Federalist Papers,* and before he fell under the Jeffersonian spell, from 1790 on. (These Founders were Burkeans, *not* in that they got their ideas from Burke, but in that the principles on which they worked were identical with those enunciated by Burke in the passage where he refers to the matters with which liberty has to be "combined.")

In resisting the enterprise of the right-wing paramilitaries—who are also libertarian extremists—President Clinton has most of the Founders on his side, and the Constitution itself. But Jefferson is different. The liberty that Jefferson adores is not a liberty "combined" with all those tedious Burkean things, as in the Constitution, but a wild liberty, absolute, untrammeled, universal, the liberty of a great revolutionary manifesto: the Declaration of Independence. The other Founding Fathers saw the Declaration as embodying generalities which would need, at a later stage, to be combined with and confined by practical considerations. But Jefferson saw the principles of the Declaration as transcendent truths of which he himself, as author of the Declaration, was also the destined and authoritative interpreter.

Even before the French Revolution—and even before the American Constitution—Jefferson had approved the keeping of the spirit of armed rebellion alive in America and elsewhere. In the context of Shays's Rebellion in Massachusetts in 1767, Jefferson wrote: "God forbid we should be 20 years without such a rebellion. . . . The tree of liberty must be refreshed from time to time with the blood of patriots and tyrants. It is its natural manure."

That is something very like a Jeffersonian charter for the most militant section of the modern American militias, is it not? If President Clinton is relying on the authority of Thomas Jefferson to keep those sacred symbols out of the clutches of paranoid paramilitaries, the President can be refuted out of the mouth of the very authority he invokes.

Jefferson's enthusiasm for what later came to be called "permanent revolution" antedates the French Revolution. But the advent of the French Revolution fortified and exalted that enthusiasm. In propagating the cause of the French Revolution in America, and incorporating it with the American Revolution, into a single holy cause of freedom, one of the things Jefferson is doing is emancipating the cause of freedom from the limits set to it in America by the American Constitution. The holy cause is now universal and transcends the limits of any merely local legislation. You can't tell the French Revolution that it is in breach of the American Constitution, so the Cult of the French Revolution clips the wings of the American Constitution. There are indeed *no* limits that can be assigned to the holy cause of freedom; neither geographical boundaries, nor limits assigned by conventional ideas of morality and compassion. In the "Adam and Eve" letter to William Short, the Secretary of State instructs that squeamish diplomatist (and defector from the ideals of his patron Jefferson) to stop complaining about French Revolutionary atrocities and accept that there is no limit (except the sparing of two persons per nation) to the slaughter that may legitimately be perpetrated in the holy cause of freedom. And the letter to Short is not a case—as Jeffersonian apologists like to imply—of an isolated flash of hyperbole. The letter to Short is a follow-up to the *Notes on a Conversation with George Washington*, in which Jefferson records that faith in the French Revolution has been his "polar star" and his belief that Washington is a belated convert to that faith (converted by the victories of French Revolutionary armies). In his letter to Short, Jefferson is setting out the merciless, and almost limitless, exigencies of polar faith.

Those in the culture of the modern American militias who see themselves as at war, or on the verge of war, with the Federal Government are fanatical believers in liberty as Jefferson was. In the letter to Short, what Jefferson is saying is that there is no limit to the slaughters that may legitimately be perpetrated in the cause of liberty. We cannot even say categorically that Jefferson would have condemned the bombing of the Federal building in Oklahoma City and the destruction of its occupants. If he believed that that action was *not* perpetrated in the cause of liberty, he *would* have condemned it, and demanded the punishment of its perpetrators (as he did in relation to the bloody deeds of certain persons classified by him as *banditti,* in the early phases of the French Revolution). But if he had accepted that the deed *was* perpetrated in the cause of liberty—as its perpetrators and their admirers appear sincerely to believe that it was—then he would have condoned that act. This is not just an inference from the general principle laid down in the letter to Short. It is an inference from Jefferson's abiding faith in the French Revolution throughout its most sanguinary phases (1792–94). Jefferson condoned the September Massacres of 1792, atrocities on a far greater scale, numerically, than the 1995 massacre in Oklahoma City. After September, as before, the French Revolution remained Jefferson's polar star. The Adam and Eve letter was written after the news of the massacre of several thousand helpless people by the Paris mobs had reached America. Philip Freneau, Jefferson's protégé—an employee at the Department of State—explicitly defended the September Massacres in the *National Gazette,* at that date the principal organ of Jefferson's Republican Party, and under Jefferson's direct and active patronage in Philadelphia.

It is true that Jefferson later—and retrospectively—condemned "the atrocities of Robespierre." But that was in 1795, and Robespierre (who did not order the massacres of September 1792) was not only dead, but anathema to the new masters of the French Revolution. While Robespierre was alive, and the Terror was actually raging, Jefferson had no comment to offer on French Revolutionary atrocities. When Madison informed Jefferson, in a letter, of the massacre of the Brissotins (Girondins) in May–June 1793, Jefferson, in a longish letter in reply to Madison, makes no reference to that transaction. Presumably all such matters are still covered by the "Adam and Eve" doctrine of six months earlier.

It is true that there was a pragmatist in Jefferson as well as a visionary fanatic, and the pragmatist acquired the upper hand over the visionary in the late 1790s. Of this phenomenon Robert N. Bellah, the leading authority on the American civil religion, writes as follows, somewhat misleadingly.

Early in the history of the new nation there had been a deep revulsion against the excesses of the French Revolution and a tendency to contrast it with the moderate and humane character of the American Revolution. Such a contrast was stated most vigorously by the early Federalists and was in some form or other accepted by Jeffersonian Democracy as well.[14]

In reality the deep revulsion against the excesses of the French Revolution (while they were happening) was exclusively a Federalist affair. The Republicans, headed by Jefferson himself, stoutly defended the French Revolution throughout the period when the reports of the said excesses were reaching America. If possible, anything horrible in the reports from Paris was ascribed by Republicans to the manipulation of the news by the British (as in Jefferson's letter to Tom Paine of October 1789. In private, the esoteric doctrine of the Republican leaders—as revealed by Jefferson to William Short—was that what the Federalists called excesses were really taking place, but were entirely justifiable, however drastic, because undertaken in the cause of liberty.

The Republicans, headed by Jefferson, began to detach themselves from the cause of the French Revolution after 1793, and especially from 1795 on. But this was not because Jefferson and the rest of them were belatedly experiencing some form of revulsion against excesses which they had systematically condoned (often by denying their existence) at the time of their perpetration. The detachment of the Republicans from the French Revolution was the result of a growing perception in 1794–95, that the enthusiasm for the French Revolution, among the American people, was cooling. It was cooling not because of those excesses—which were at their worst during the period when Americans (other than Federalists) were most enthusiastic about the French Revolution—but because of developments in the United States itself and in a neighboring territory, Saint-Domingue (Haiti), and because of Washington's influence.

Those developments included Citizen Genet's interferences in the affairs of the United States and the simultaneous victory of the black slaves in Saint-Domingue and ensuing massacre and dispersion of the whites. The exact nature of the connection between the black insurrection and the French Revolution remains open to argument. But it would have been hard for the slaveowners to remain enthusiastic for the French Revolution after February 1794 when the French National Convention, then dominated by Robespierre, decreed the emancipation of all slaves, both in the dominions of the French Republic and of Great Britain (which had included, up to 1783, the American colonies).

The emancipating Act of February 1794 was probably not the least of "the atrocities of Robespierre" in the eyes of Virginia slaveowners, including Thomas Jefferson.

After these events—and especially after Washington's withering stigmatization of the Republican and Democratic Societies in December 1794—Jefferson and his colleagues realized that the cause of the French Revolution, formerly a major political asset to them in the United States, had now become a liability. So they cut their losses. They never repudiated the French Revolution—still cherished by many of their rank-and-file—but it was as if this part of their political stock-in-trade had been removed from the front window. You could still get it, but only if you asked for it; as some of Jefferson's correspondents did.

In this matter, by the time Jefferson became President, the pragmatist had prevailed over the visionary, Head over Heart.

Yet when we are talking about the American civil religion and its sacred symbols, the visionary in Jefferson, the champion of the French Revolution, remains disturbingly—and subversively—alive and relevant. Jefferson does not fit into the modern American civil religion *as officially and semi-officially expounded*. That version of the ACR involves, as James Smylie puts it, "divine sanction in the use of power and in the support of civil authority."[15] That is not what the *Jeffersonian* civil religion is about. But other versions of the ACR are extant in modern America, even if official America, and the textbooks written for it, take no cognizance of their existence.

In religion—in both its supernatural and political forms, and in America as well as in the Orient—the spirit bloweth where it listeth. The places and communities where it listeth to blow are seldom congenial either to urban sophisticates or to official establishments. At present the regions of America in which a revolutionary version of the American civil religion is most active are principally the wilder parts of the American Middle West and Northwest, from Oklahoma out to the State of Washington.

Out there, there are tens of thousands of Americans ready to fight the Federal Government in the cause of liberty. In Burkean terms, these people are intoxicated with "the wild *gas* of liberty." In Jeffersonian terms, they are people who are prepared to refresh the tree of liberty with its "natural manure," their own blood and that of those they identify as tyrants, including the agents of the Federal Government.

Some people seem to feel that since the militia rebels are "right-wing" they cannot be Jeffersonians. But the Tree of Liberty is a mystical, abstract, absolute entity knowing nothing of mundane political distinctions.

It accepts its natural manure, the blood of patriots and tyrants. Which are the patriots and which the tyrants makes no difference to the quality of the manure or the health of the bloodthirsty organism that feeds on it.

As far as I know, the present revolutionaries in and around the militia movement have not made much use of Jefferson personally, though they do of course claim descent from the American Revolution and from the Declaration of Independence. Many of them would probably be put off Jefferson by the respect so long accorded him by urban intellectuals and (as far as the so-called "Christian right" is concerned) by his reputation for Godlessness. But if this movement prospers—as I fear it may in the coming century—then it will develop its own intellectuals, its own ideologies, and its own press, and these are certain to seek and find legitimation for *their* revolution—including its excesses—in the writings of Thomas Jefferson. Jeffersonian liberty is an absolute, not confined by specific ideological content, and revolutionaries of any stripe, whether right or left, have equal entitlement to his blessing, provided they are prepared to kill and die for whatever version of liberty they happen to believe in.

In Jefferson's own time, the defense of liberty included the defense of slavery (in practice, though not in theory) so that Jeffersonian liberty is not so liberal that it cannot accommodate libertarians of the white right.

Interpolation (February–March 1996): The opening sections of this Epilogue (above) were written in the summer of 1995. I was not then aware of any evidence of a specific link between any modern right-wing extremists and the Jeffersonian tradition. I have subsequently become aware of significant evidence to that effect. I am letting the above sections stand, exactly in the form they originally went to the publisher, but I now wish to add the following:

It is now known that the two prime suspects in the Oklahoma City bombing both claim Jeffersonian inspiration. In a profile of the second man charged with the bombing, Terry Lynn Nichols, Serge F. Kovaleski (*Washington Post,* 3 July 1995) wrote: "[Nichols] read the works of Thomas Jefferson and Thomas Paine and was particularly impressed by Jefferson's maxim "The tree of liberty must be refreshed from time to time with the blood of patriots and tyrants."

CNN, on 31 January 1996, broadcast a news item about Timothy McVeigh headlined: "McVeigh's Shirt Expected To Be Key Evidence." In the course of a discussion of the shirt, the following remarks were made:

Susan Candiotti, CNN Correspondent: "Sources tell CNN when Tim McVeigh was arrested driving away from Oklahoma City on the day of the bombing he was wearing a T-shirt emblazoned with words of rebellion and bloodshed. McVeigh's shirt bore this quotation, 'The tree of liberty must be refreshed from time to time with the blood of patriots and tyrants.' The words were written by Thomas Jefferson shortly after the American Revolution when some people felt threatened by the new federal government." (The words were actually written in February 1787, before the federal government came into existence, and they were about a rebellion against the State of Massachusetts. See above, chapter 2.)

Dr. Steven Hochman (identified as "Jefferson scholar"): "What Jefferson is saying is that it is a fact that in order to preserve freedom, you're going to have a situation where there is violence, as a wake-up call you might say, to the leaders." (We have encountered this Dr. Hochman before. He was Dumas Malone's research assistant, and co-author, along with Malone, of a contribution to the *Journal of Southern History* ridiculing the claims of Madison Hemings. See above, chapter 7.)

Susan Candiotti: "At the jail in Perry, Oklahoma, where McVeigh was first taken, the FBI asked for the clothing he was wearing but described the T-shirt in a way that kept the wording secret until now. CNN has been told the words are visible in McVeigh's mug shot taken at the jail. The FBI seized the only copy of that mug shot and will not release it. McVeigh's lawyer brushed aside any concern over the T-shirt slogan when we asked him how incriminating is this?"

Stephen Jones (McVeigh's lawyer): "Well, if Thomas Jefferson said it, I shouldn't think it would be incriminating at all"

II. Race and the American Civil Religion

It is difficult, in a general way, to fit Thomas Jefferson into the American civil religion in its official version (ACROV). But once the criterion of race is introduced, it becomes logically *impossible* to fit Jefferson into ACROV. Of course, what is logically impossible can be politically—and pedagogically—sustained for quite a long time. But I don't think this can be indefinitely maintained in the case of Jefferson. Too much scholarly work has been coming out, in that area (see above, chapter 7), that would need to be suppressed, for the cult of Jefferson to remain fully acceptable within ACROV, into the Third Millennium, now fast approaching. Barring a white racist revolution, that is.

Modern America is, and has been for more than a quarter of a century, a post-racist society: post-racist juridically and institutionally and in the ethos of all its establishments: political, social, financial, academic, scientific, and—not least significant—in the field of sport. The American civil religion, if it is to be a bonding force through the coming century, must be unequivocally multiracial. I am not sure that this is yet altogether so. The civil religion has been implicitly or explicitly a religion of white people for most of its history. I am not sure how far it has, by now, lived down that past. But obviously it must do so, in the coming century, if it is to remain a civil religion for the American people as a whole. There are—as in other Western countries—powerful racist undercurrents still around. But for both reasons, *because* this is officially a post-racist society, *and* because the racist undercurrents are still there, Thomas Jefferson is becoming a most unsuitable and embarrassing figure in the pantheon of the American civil religion in the late twentieth century and into the next. For Thomas Jefferson was demonstrably a racist, and a particularly aggressive and vindictive one at that (see chapter 7).

I don't mean by this that Jefferson was a racist because he owned slaves. A person might own slaves, in the conditions of the eighteenth century, without being a racist. The person might simply have inherited slaves, and not quite know what to do about it. I believe Washington, who manumitted all his slaves by his will, was in that category. (Jefferson manumitted none of his, except for the young Hemingses, who were probably his own children [see Appendix].) I am not aware of any utterances of Washington's that could reasonably be classed as racist. Washington did not, as Jefferson did (in Query XIV of *Notes on the State of Virginia*), go on about such topics as the supposed preference of black males for white women, as compared with the supposed preference of orangutans for black women (*Notes on the State of Virginia*, Query XIV). Nor does Washington display, as Jefferson does (most obsessively in Query XIV), the classical racist itch to identify black characteristics that may be interpreted as indicative of genetic inferiority.

It is precisely Jefferson's status as the oracle of Liberty, within the American civil religion, that is becoming unsustainable in a post-racist America. Consider the implications of the story of Jame Hubbard (chapter 7, pp. 267–68). Hubbard's sole offense was to claim liberty for himself, and to try to win it. For that offense, Jefferson had him "severely flogged in the presence of his companions." For many Americans today— I would hope for most Americans, and most other people—the hero of Liberty, in that story, is not the famous Thomas Jefferson but the otherwise unknown Jame Hubbard. And that perception has ominous implications for the future status of Thomas Jefferson in the civil religion of a post-racist and increasingly multiracial America.

The factor, however, that is bound eventually to eliminate a personal cult of Thomas Jefferson from the civil religion of a multiracial America is not his record in relation to slaves and slavery, but the policy laid down by him in relation to "free Negroes." Jefferson's vision of the future

America—after the hypothetical abolition of slavery by the slaveowners themselves—is a lily-white one. All the ex-slaves are to be deported to Africa. In the meantime, free blacks have to be eliminated from Virginia. Jefferson's proposals for their elimination were too draconian to be stomached even by his fellow slaveowners (above, chapter 7). His proposed (and rejected) amendments to the Virginian legal code included a recommendation for the penalization of what Virginian slaveowners called "miscegenation": by which they always mean sexual intercourse between black men and white women, never between white men and black women, an event of frequent but unmentionable occurrence. Jefferson made provision for the case of a white woman who might bear a mulatto child. Both the mother and her child were to leave Virginia, immediately after the birth. In the event of their failure to do so, mother and child were declared to be "beyond the protection of the law." In the circumstances, that proposition was a license for lynching: for the physical destruction of mother and child by any Virginian who might care to do the job. Volunteers would not be lacking.

Jefferson's white contemporaries refused to accept that sinister recommendation. But later generations of Southerners were to act in its spirit. It is no coincidence that Jefferson was much more popular in the South *after* the Civil War than he had been before the war. Before the war the issue had been slavery, and Jefferson had been a bit unsound on that, by the standards prevailing in the South in the immediate antebellum period. After the war, however, the question of the hour, for white Southerners, was the status of free blacks. And on *that*, Thomas Jefferson was absolutely sound.

It is true that white Southerners, after the war, were in no position to achieve Jefferson's ideal solution: the deportation of all the emancipated blacks. But the white Southerners could and did act in the spirit of Jefferson's major premise in this matter: they could ensure that there would be no *free* blacks in the Southern states. The blacks could be free technically—that is, no longer slaves under Federal law—but in reality there would be no free blacks on Southern soil. Any black who attempted to achieve real freedom was, at best, treated as Jefferson had treated James Hubbard for *his* attempt to achieve freedom. More drastic penalties than flogging, however, were available against persons perceived as guilty of serious racial misconduct. Such people were "beyond the protection of the law." That is, they could be lynched, with perfect impunity for the lynchers. And they were, regularly and in large numbers, after the end of the Reconstruction period and through the first two decades of the twentieth century.

For all this, the enforcers of white supremacy claimed, and with justice, a mandate in Thomas Jefferson's well-known doctrine that there was no place for free blacks in American society.[16] If blacks were emancipated and yet remained in America and in the South, then they had to be brought under restraint, in such ways as would insure that there were *really* no free blacks, at least on Southern soil. The Ku Klux Klan saw to that.

III. LIBERAL JEFFERSONIANS

Liberal Jeffersonians will no doubt be outraged at my suggestion that the Ku Klux Klan was ideologically descended from Thomas Jefferson. I hope liberal Jeffersonians *are* outraged and I propose to go on outraging them. I intend, if possible, to outrage them out of existence: not out of physical existence of course, but out of existence as the confused and confusing school of thought they actually constitute. For "liberal Jeffersonian" is a contradiction in terms. It is so at least if you think that "liberal racist" is a contradiction in terms. And modern American liberals can hardly contest that last point.

In the 1970s and 1980s, American liberals were greatly exercised about *apartheid* in South Africa and busy tracking down any person who might conceivably have given any kind of aid or comfort to that iniquitous system. In that connection, how about Thomas Jefferson? The Jeffersonian doctrine of No Free Blacks in America is a doctrine of apartheid for America.

Someone should write a thesis on "The Influence of Thomas Jefferson on Hendrik Verwoerd."

In the Jeffersonian liberal tradition, there has always been a strong element of unconscious or subconscious racism. Thus, in the late nineteenth century, Henry George regarded Jefferson as a radical who had "allied himself absolutely, unreservedly, actively permanently with the wronged masses."[17]

By far the most wronged masses in America, at the time George wrote that, were the blacks of the Southern states. And Jefferson's only contribution to those blacks was the doctrine that they had no place in America *as free people.* Jefferson's white Southern disciples were busy enforcing that doctrine, by floggings and lynchings, while Henry George was writing about Jefferson's "unreserved" alliance with "the wronged masses."

What is surprising about Jeffersonian liberalism is that it has managed (so far) to survive *both* the comprehensive discredit of racism among the educated and in official America in the second half of the twentieth century *and* the scholarly work that demonstrates that Jefferson was a racist (above, chapter 7). Thus as late as 1984—that is well after the publication of all the studies quoted in chapter 7—we find Richard Matthews writing in *The Radical Politics of Thomas Jefferson: A Revisionist View* (Lawrence, University Press of Kansas, 1984): "Jefferson not only presents a radical critique of American market society but also presents an image of—if not a road-map to—a consciously made, legitimately democratic American future." A legitimately democratic American future without any blacks in it.

I believe that in the next century, as blacks and Hispanics and Asians acquire increasing influence in American society, the Jeffersonian liberal tradition, which is already intellectually untenable, will become socially and politically untenable as well. I also believe that the American civil religion, official version (ACROV), will have to be reformed in a manner that will downgrade and eventually exclude Thomas Jefferson. Finally, I believe that Jefferson will, nonetheless, continue to be a power in America in the area where the mystical side of Jefferson really belongs: among the radical, violent anti-Federal libertarian fanatics: the very same paranoid conspirators against whose grasp President Clinton is rightly resolved to defend "our sacred symbols."

The Impending Schism

As the twenty-first century advances, there will be changes within the American civil religion (official version)—ACROV—to correspond to great changes in the society itself. The multiracial character of the society will be increasingly realized, as significant numbers of blacks, Hispanics, and Asians move up the economic ladder. Women, of all races, will also be moving up, and in many cases even faster and higher than the general rate of ascent of non-white people.

In these circumstances, ACROV will be needed more than ever, as a bonding force for a more and more visibly diverse society and polity. But within ACROV, the cult of the Founding Fathers will be affected. The present assaults on the campuses on the authority, in every field, of "dead white males" are often absurd, but they have their implications for the future, and in particular for the cult of the Founding Fathers, within ACROV.

In the new circumstances, the emphasis is likely to be increasingly on *documents,* rather than personalities, as the core of ACROV. Of the two main documents, the Constitution presents no problems for the new societal coalition, in which women and non-white people exercise increasing authority. The Constitution, as it now stands, is the work, not just of

Founding Fathers, but of many kinds of people, over many generations. Both abolitionists and feminists—overlapping categories in the nineteenth century—played their part in bringing the Constitution into the shape in which we have it today. The Constitution will be amended—an Equal Rights Amendment would appear to be inevitable, if present trends continue—during the first half of the coming century. The Constitution—amended and amendable—will be at the center of ACROV.

The Declaration of Independence is another matter; ACROV without the Declaration is unthinkable. The Declaration is the primary assertion of American nationalism, and the primary function of the American civil religion is to invest American nationalism with the aura of the sacred. Without the Declaration, then, there is no American civil religion.

Yet there are problems about the Declaration, in its relation to a society no longer exclusively dominated by whites. There are problems about the wording, and problems about the authorship. It is accepted that the words "all men are created equal" do not, in their literal meaning, apply to women, and were not intended by the Founding Fathers (collectively) to apply to slaves. Yet it is also accepted that the expectations aroused by this formula have been a force which eventually changed the meaning of the formula, to include women and people of all races.

The wording, in itself, offers no basic difficulty. The trouble is in the relation of the wording to the perceived authorship. In ACROV, as we know it in the twentieth century, Jefferson has the sacred status which belongs to the author of the most sacred document: the Declaration of Independence. And nothing is more certain than that Thomas Jefferson did not intend that black people should be free, in America. Freedom and blackness were incompatible in America: free blacks were to be banished back to Africa. The sublime principles of the Declaration did not apply to them. They are for whites only.

For many years, Jefferson's real views, concerning the future of blacks in America, were hidden by a fog of soothing obfuscation best exemplified by the relevant inscription in the Jefferson Memorial. People were told that Thomas Jefferson was against slavery, and his words to that effect were quoted frequently. But people were *not* told that, for Jefferson, black people had no future in America at all, *except as slaves*. Once they ceased to be slaves, they were to be sent packing. Nor would other non-whites be welcome. Jefferson's bright vision of the future of America is a monoracial one: whites only.

It follows that there can be no room for a cult of Thomas Jefferson in the civil religion of an effectively *multiracial* America, that is, an America in which non-white Americans have a significant and increasing say. Once the facts are known, Jefferson is of necessity an abhorrent figure, to people who would not be in America at all—or not free there—if Jefferson could have had his way.

Those people don't need Jefferson. But they *do* need the Declaration. The words "all men are created equal," taken in their literal meaning (without Jeffersonian implied reservations), are an important part of their American title deeds. Racists hold that blacks are genetically inferior; that is, that they were *not* created equal. Against that doctrine, it is important to be able to invoke the authority of the most sacred of American documents.

In these circumstances, in which the Declaration is needed, and Jefferson is not needed, I would expect to see a change in the perceived relation between Jefferson and the Declaration. There is an element of exaggeration in the present official perception of that relation, and that exaggeration will come under attack in the increasingly multiracial climate of the coming century.

The crucial question is: Was Thomas Jefferson the author of the Declaration of Independence?

Many Americans will answer that question with an indignant "*Of course* he was!" Yet there is really no "of course" about it. The Declaration was certainly not the sole and unaided work of Thomas Jefferson. The document did not spring fully formed from his head, like Athena from the forehead of Zeus. The work of preparing a Declaration—to justify the independence that Congress had actually proclaimed two days before—was entrusted by Congress, not to Jefferson alone, but to a committee which also included John Adams and Benjamin Franklin, figures of no less status than Jefferson in the America of 1776. Adams and Franklin would probably have had considerable input into discussions preceding the actual drafting of the document. Jefferson's draft was reviewed and corrected by the committee, before being laid before Congress, whose consensus it was designed to reflect. And Congress itself made further changes in the draft already amended by the committee. Carl Lotus Becker writes:

> Congress discussed his draft for three successive days. What uncomplimentary remarks the members may have made is not known; but it is known that in the end certain paragraphs were greatly changed and others omitted altogether. These 'depredations'—so he speaks of them—Jefferson did not enjoy: but we may easily console ourselves for his discomfiture since it moved the humane Franklin to tell him a story. Writing in 1818, Jefferson says: "I was sitting by Dr. Franklin, who perceived that I was not insensible

to these mutilations. I have made it a rule, said he, whenever in my power, to avoid becoming the draughtsman of papers to be reviewed by a public body." [18]

Franklin's story follows, and though it is amusing, it is not relevant here. What is relevant is the word "draughtsman" and it is evident that it was in that role, and not the more exalted role of "author," that Jefferson's colleagues envisaged him, in relation to the collective elaboration of the Declaration of Independence.

In the (official) American civil religion, as it evolves under the conditions of the coming century, the Declaration will be increasingly seen as a collective document. The Founding Fathers themselves will have declined in importance, in comparison with the sacred documents, but the *collective* authority of the Founding Fathers will still be found to be vastly more acceptable than the idea of the personal authorship of Thomas Jefferson. George Washington owned slaves, but he was not, as Jefferson was, committed to the elimination of free blacks from America. On the contrary, in manumitting all his slaves in his will, without stipulating that they be immediately deported to Africa, Washington was implicitly asserting that free blacks *do* have a future in America.

With the Declaration increasingly perceived as a collective document, Jefferson may be increasingly cast in the prosaic and subordinate role of a draughtsman. Jefferson's demotion from the sacred status of "author" of the Declaration would effectively put an end to the official cult of Jefferson within the American civil religion. Jefferson should be out of ACROV, I would guess, before the middle of the coming century. (Unless there is a racist counter-revolution by then, which seems highly unlikely, though not quite impossible.)

Jefferson should be out of ACROV. But he is likely to be at the center of an alternative, and powerful, version of American civil religion.

It is safe to predict that the liberal-Jeffersonian tradition will become extinct fairly early in the coming century. The huge contradiction within that tradition, with regard to race, renders it unfit to survive in a multiracial society. But the inevitable rejection of Jefferson by liberals, in multiracial America, will draw increasingly favorable attention to Jefferson on the far right. The very reasons why liberals will have to reject him are compelling reasons for the far right to adopt him. Or rather *re*-adopt him, for he was a hero to Southern white supremacists after the Civil War (above, chapter 7).

Doctrinally, Jefferson is far more suitable as a patron saint of white supremacists than of modern American liberals. The twin themes of State

Rights and No Free Blacks in America fit the positions of the far-right militia movements like a glove.

Rhetorically and emotionally also, the mystical Jefferson—the Jefferson of the Tree of Liberty and of the French Revolution—meets the needs of the modern far right. Jefferson's Liberty, a powerfully emotive concept, unanalyzed and without intellectual content, is the kind of Liberty which the militias love: what Burke calls "the wild *gas* of liberty."

The Jefferson who admired Shays's rebels, and hoped they would find imitators in later generations, and who inspired the Virginian and Kentucky resolutions of 1798, is providing those now resisting the Federal Government with clear warrant for their cause, and for the use of armed force should the incursions of the Federal Government make that necessary.

Finally, the Jefferson who made a cult of the French Revolution provides aid and comfort, not just to the far right in government, but to the most ferocious of its militant extremists. In the paroxysm of his enthusiasm for the French Revolution, in January 1793, Jefferson laid down the principle that there are (virtually) no limits to the slaughter that may be legitimately perpetrated in the name of Liberty. So that anyone in modern America, who is planning any act of mass destruction, may invoke the sanction of "the author of the Declaration of Independence," provided only that the act is deemed to be perpetrated in the holy cause of liberty.

For these and other reasons, I believe that at some time in the coming century the cult of Jefferson may, as it were, split off from its present home in ACROV, and find a new home on the wilder shores of American freedom. There may then be a new version of American civil religion, challenging the present orthodox version. Ironically—in terms of Jefferson's own civil-religious vocabulary—the new version would be seen, from the viewpoint of ACROV, as a heresy within the American civil religion. Schism would be a more appropriate term.

The schismatics could lay claim, and on more than plausible grounds, to the special protection of the most powerful prophet of the old united civil religion. The neo-Jeffersonian schism would be bitterly divisive, not only on religious but on racial lines. It would strengthen the tendencies that are already making for more attempted secessions, more inter-racial violence.

There might well be matter here for a new civil war, aimed at repealing the results of the last one. Only the next one would not be confined to the South nor—if it gains ground generally—would it be content with secession. It would aim at the enforcement, throughout America, of the Jeffersonian principle: No Free Blacks in America.

I believe that the orthodox multiracial version of the American civil religion must eventually prevail—at whatever cost—against the neo-Jeffersonian racist schism. That the orthodox version should prevail is vital not only for America, but for the future of non-racial democracy, and of Enlightenment values generally, in those parts of the world where these are now dominant and also in those parts where people are struggling to bring them into effective being.

IV. AMERICAN CIVIL RELIGION AND THE FUTURE OF THE ENLIGHTENMENT

In a book of mine published early this year,[19] I argued that the American civil religion may—somewhat paradoxically—be the major force working for the preservation of the Enlightenment, and with it democracy, in the world. There are two related points here: First, that Enlightenment and democracy are unlikely to survive in the rest of the world if they go down in America. Second, that democracy and the Enlightenment in America find a source of emotional sustenance in the American civil religion that has no equivalent in the other democracies of the world.

The central paradox is that the sacred documents of the American civil religion are Enlightenment documents, or rather documents which combine nationalism with Enlightenment, while the civil religion invests that combination with a sacred aura.

The word "combination" is a crucial one. I refer the reader here to the passage from Burke's *Reflections,* which I quoted earlier. The Declaration represents what Burke called "the spirit of liberty in action." The Constitution spells out how that spirit is to be "combined with Government" and all the other matters listed by Burke. Thus, what would otherwise be "the wild *gas* of liberty" is canalized and put to rational and constructive ends.

The Constitution is an *Enlightenment* document and it is also a *sacred* document. The emotional force of nationalism—that wild *gas*—is harnessed into the sustenance of democratic institutions. That is the unique strength of American democracy. Democracy in other countries depends—to a much greater extent than people in those countries are aware—on the example and perceived success of American democracy. And hardly anyone in any of those countries realizes how much the success of democracy in America depends on the American civil religion.

When I wrote *On The Eve of the Millennium* I did not see, as I now do, that the American civil religion is on the verge of schism. I did not see that because I had not yet realized—as I now do on the evidence presented in chapter 7—that Thomas Jefferson was a determined and implacable racist: No Free Blacks. The civil religion of a multiracial society cannot indefinitely accept a racist as a prophet. It might be better if it could: the pragmatic acceptance of an anomaly might be the best thing available, socially speaking. But religion—supernatural or civil—does not work like that. A sincerely felt religion requires veneration for its prophets. And how can a multiracial society revere the man who ordered the flogging of Jame Hubbard, and who sought to withdraw the protection of the law from a white woman giving birth to a mulatto child and from her baby? That cannot be, I think. Above all, how long can a multiracial society tolerate the continuing cult of a prophet who found the very existence of such a society unacceptable? Not very long, I think.

The elimination of the cult of Jefferson from the American multiracial civil religion seems to me to be inevitable at some point in the course of the coming century. But that means schism. The cult of Jefferson would continue, outside the mainstream, as a *white* cult, at the very center of a whites-only version of the American civil religion. This schism in the present American civil religion could well make the present white racist reaction turn into something much more formidable. President Clinton rightly tries to keep "our sacred symbols" out of the hands of white racists who see themselves as at war with the Federal Government. But there is one of the sacred symbols which cannot long be kept out of their hands, because Thomas Jefferson belongs wholly on the white racist side, and not at all on the pro-Federal and multiracial side.

The schism which I believe to be impending in the American civil religion would be an event of global significance. On the outcome of the civil racial strife around that schism would depend the future of the Enlightenment tradition and democracy, not just in America, but in the whole world.

I believe the multiracial version of the American civil religion—without Jefferson—will eventually prevail over the white racist version—with Jefferson. The multiracial version should ultimately prevail because most white Americans as well as all non-whites within the civil religion can be expected to hold to it. I think.

But the implications of a schism in the American civil religion are potentially so far-reaching that they defy all prediction. The schism involves the release of a spellbinding and anarchic racist prophet within Jefferson, from the prison of obfuscation, which his liberal admirers constructed for him and in which they held him so long. In his dimly lit liberal cell, the manic prophet was incommunicado. Through his liberal biographers, his wilder utterances reached the world only in sedative, soothing, and muffled paraphrase or through oblique and obscure references.[20]

But now the time of obfuscation and occultation is drawing to an end. A drama is about to manifest itself.

What *I think* is that a multiracial version of the American civil religion must prevail against the racist challenge. But what *I feel* is awe and foreboding at the potential consequences in the coming century, for the world as well as for America, of the impending schism in the American civil religion and of the concomitant emergence of Thomas Jefferson—the mystic, implacable Jefferson of the French Revolution—as prophet and patron of the fanatical racist far right in America.

APPENDIX

---•◆•---

MADISON HEMINGS'S STORY

M adison Hemings was undoubtedly a slave of Thomas Jefferson's
and a son of another of Jefferson's slaves, Sally Hemings. The Hemingses had been the property of John Wayles, Thomas Jefferson's father-
in-law, who died on 23 May 1773, in the year in which Sally was born.
Jefferson and his wife "received land and 135 slaves from the Wayles estate, including all eleven members of the Hemings family."[1]

Concerning the kinship between Jefferson's wife and Sally Hemings,
Virginius Dabney writes:

> Sally and the other Hemingses at Monticello apparently were descen-
> dants of John Wayles, a native-born Englishman who came to Virginia, and
> Elizabeth or Betty Hemings, a "bright mulatto" who was his slave. Betty
> was the daughter of Captain Hemings, an English seafaring man who
> stopped off in Virginia, and a "full-blooded African" woman, Madison
> Hemings said in his Pike County Republican interview. Whether this is cor-
> rect is uncertain. In any event, Jefferson's Farm Book says Betty was born
> about 1735. Apparently her mother was a slave on the plantation of Francis
> Eppes IV at Bermuda Hundred. In 1746 Betty was deeded to John Wayles
> as part of his marriage dowry when he wed Martha Eppes. Wayles took
> her as his concubine in 1761 after the death of his third wife, according to
> common report. Isaac Jefferson, the former Monticello slave, declared in
> 1847, "Folks said that these Hemingses was old Mr. Wayles' children."
> Madison Hemings confirmed this in 1873, and it apparently was true. The
> six children, in order of birth, were Robert, James, Thenia, Critta, Peter
> and Sally, the youngest, who was born in 1773.
> John Wayles, be it noted, was not only the reputed father of these chil-

dren; he was also the father of Mrs. Thomas Jefferson, née Martha Wayles, John Wayles's daughter by his first wife, Martha Eppes. Hence Sally Hemings and her brothers and sisters were seemingly the half-brothers and sisters of Martha Jefferson. It is doubtful whether Mrs. Jefferson knew that her father supposedly sired these individuals [sic], but Thomas Jefferson almost certainly did know. This would seem to explain why the Hemingses were given preferred positions at Monticello. All were house servants, and none was required to labor in the fields.[2]

Madison Hemings was born in 1805. He was living in Pee Pee Township, Ohio, after the Civil War, and he told his story to a local paper, the *Pike County Republican,* which published it on 13 March 1873. Madison told the paper:

Maria [Jefferson] was left at home, but was afterwards ordered to accompany him to France. She was three years or so younger than Martha. My mother accompanied her as her body servant. When Mr. Jefferson went to France Martha was a young woman grown, my mother was about her age and Maria was just budding into womanhood. Their stay (my mother and Maria's) was about eighteen months. But during that time my mother became Mr. Jefferson's concubine and when he was called home she was "enceinte" by him. . . . Soon after their arrival she gave birth to a child, of whom Thomas Jefferson was the father. It lived but a short time. She gave birth to four others, and Jefferson was the father of all of them. Their names were Beverley, Harriet, Madison (myself) and Eston—three sons and one daughter. . . . As to myself I was named Madison by the wife of James Madison, who was afterwards President of the United States. . . . I was born in my father's seat of Monticello in Albemarle County, Va near Charlottesville on the 19th. day of January, 1805. I was almost 21 years of age when my father died on the 4th. of July 1826. . . . About his home he was the quietest of men. . . . His general temperament was smooth and even: he was very undemonstrative. He was uniformly kind to all about him. He was not in the habit of showing fatherly affection to us children. We were the only children of his by a slave woman. He was affectionate towards his white grandchildren of whom he had fourteen, twelve of whom lived to manhood and womanhood. . . . My brothers, sisters and myself were used alike. They were put to some mechanical trade at the age of fourteen. Till then we were permitted to study at the "great house" and only required to do such light work as going on errands. . . . We were free from the dread of having to be slaves all our life long and were measurably happy. We were always permitted to be with our mother, who was well used. It was her duty all her life which I can remember, to the time of our father's death to take care of his chamber and wardrobe, look after us children and do such light work as sewing etc. Provision was made in the will of our father that we should be free when we arrive at the age of 21 years.[3]

The *Pike County Republican* was published in Waverly, Ohio. The local Democratic paper, also published in Waverly, was called *The Waverly Watchman. The Watchman* replied promptly to what Virginius Dabney carefully calls "the contentions attributed to Madison Hemings." The editor of *The Watchman,* John A. Jones, wrote, on 18 March 1873:

> We have no doubt but that there are at least fifty Negros in this county who lay claim to illustrious parentage. . . . The children of Jefferson and Madison, Calhoun and Clay far outnumber Washington's body servants when Barnum was in the height of his prosperity. They are not to be blamed for making these assertions. It sounds much better for the mother to tell her offspring that "master" [is] their father than to acknowledge to them that some other hand, without a name, had raised her in the dignity of mother. . . . This is a well-known fact to those who have been reared in those states where slavery existed, and with them no attention whatever is paid to the rumors. . . . The fact that Hemings claims to be a natural son of Jefferson does not convince the world of his truthfulness.[4]

The force of the claim "no attention whatever is paid to the rumors" is somewhat weakened by the acknowledged facts concerning the Wayles-Hemings relationship and the parentage of Sally Hemings.

The editor of *The Pike County Republican,* S. F. Wetmore, did not give in easily. By the end of the year, he had discovered another Monticello slave, Israel Jefferson, who lived in Brush Fork of Pee Pee Creek, Pebble Township, Ohio. As Virginius Dabney puts it, still carefully:

> Israel submitted to an interview and was quoted as confirming Madison Hemings's claim that his mother was Thomas Jefferson's concubine, and that the author of the Declaration of Independence was the father of her children. "I can conscientiously confirm his [Madison's] statement as any other fact which I believe from circumstances but do not positively know," Israel is quoted as saying.[5]

"Quoted as" is there to protect the Jeffersonian hypothesis that the story may have been an abolitionist plot. For Julian P. Boyd and Dumas Malone, this was not just a hypothesis but a self-evident fact: "Julian Boyd says that Hemings's statement 'was obviously prompted by someone . . . shaped and perhaps even written and embellished by the prompter'. And Dumas Malone, calling attention to the atmosphere of the time, assigns it a place 'in the tradition of political enmity and abolitionist propaganda'."

Readers will make up their own minds. To me the reported words of the two ex-slaves sound like their own words, and seem to me to possess that quality prized by Albert Camus: "the reserve that benefits a good witness."

At this stage there is no more than a difference of opinion; Madison Hemings may or may not have been what he claims to have been: the son of Sally Hemings and Thomas Jefferson. Madison's maternal origin is not in doubt. What is in dispute is whether or not Madison Hemings was the son of Thomas Jefferson. But there is an experimental way in which this dispute may perhaps eventually be resolved. I have consulted an eminent American geneticist as to whether comparison of DNA specimens from the remains of Thomas Jefferson could or could not establish whether or not Thomas was the father of Madison. The geneticist whom I consulted went to the trouble of consulting a number of his colleagues, in other universities, and in other branches of the relevant discipline. The answer is that, in the present state of genetic science, such a comparison would be most unlikely to decide the matter. But genetic science is making such rapid progress that comparisons which are not practicable now may become practicable. So the time may come when Madison Hemings's story can be put to the decisive test. In the meantime, it would be prudent for historians and biographers to refrain from dogmatic statements concerning that story since the time may come when one of the alternative hypotheses will be confirmed, and the other refuted by scientific evidence. In the present state of knowledge, it is prudent to suspend judgment on this matter.

NOTES

PRELUDE

1. John Adams's Diary for 29 April 1778 in *The Works of John Adams,* ed. Charles Francis Adams (Boston, 1851), Vol. 3, p. 147.

2. *The Writings of Benjamin Franklin,* ed. Albert Henry Smith (London and New York, 1907), Vol. 10, pp. 49–53.

3. Franklin, *Writings,* Vol. 10, pp. 68–69.

4. Franklin, *Writings,* Vol. 10, p. 72.

5. Quoted in Charles Francis Adams, *Life of John Adams; Works of John Adams* (Boston, 1851), Vol. 1, p. 453.

6. Hamilton to Edward Carrington, 26 May 1792; *The Papers of Alexander Hamilton,* 27 vols., eds. Harold C. Syrett and Jacob E. Cooke (New York and London, 1962), Vol. 6, pp. 426–45.

7. See Claude-Anne Lopez's entertaining work, *Franklin and the Ladies of Paris* (New Haven and London, 1966). Lopez has two chapters on Madame H and her circle, "Notre Dame d'Auteuil" and "L'Académie d'Auteuil."

ONE

1. Dumas Malone, *Jefferson and His Time* (6 vols., Boston, 1948–81), Vol. 2, p. 132. Like all who have studied any aspect of Jefferson, in the second half of the twentieth century, I am much indebted to Dumas Malone's work. As is almost certain to happen with any good biographer, Malone feels affection as well as admiration for his subject. On several critical points, in connection with Jefferson's relation to France and the French Revolution, I have found Malone's interpretations often too indulgent, and have offered what I consider more parsimonious ones. Readers will make up their own minds, in each separate instance as to who seems to be more nearly right.

2. The Princeton Edition of *The Papers of Thomas Jefferson,* the first twenty of the twenty-four volumes of which so far published were edited by Julian P. Boyd, Vol. 7, p. 441. After first mention in each chapter, this monumental edition is cited as *JP,* Boyd.

3. *JP*, Boyd, Vol. 7, p. 538. In a footnote to this eerie letter, Boyd comments:

The very understanding letter from Mrs. Eppes of 13 Oct. 1784, transmitting news of Lucy's death, did not arrive until 6 May 1785, but since
Lafayette conveyed Currie's letter to TJ, since he had been in Virginia subsequent to Lucy's death, and since he was unfailingly tactful, it is to be hoped
that he broke the news to TJ and thus spared him the pain of discovering it
in an almost casual comment intermingled with "baloons . . . The Politic
business, &c. &c."

The Currie letter is noted in Jefferson's "Summary Journal of Letters" (SJL) as
"received 26 Jan. 1785."

4. *JP*, Boyd, Vol. 9, p. 560.

5. Ibid., pp. 560–61.

6. Dumas Malone, *Jefferson and His Time,* Vol. 2, pp. 134–35.

7. To Francis Eppes, 26 May 1787; *JP*, Boyd, Vol. 11, p. 379.

8. Malone, *Jefferson and His Time,* Vol. 2, p. 135.

9. Merrill D. Peterson, *Thomas Jefferson and the New Nation: A Biography*
(New York, 1970), p. 355.

10. Peterson, *Thomas Jefferson,* p. 707.

11. Interview published in the *Pike County Republican* (Ohio), 13 March
1873: reproduced in Judith P. Justus, *Down from the Mountain: The Oral History
of the Hemings Family* (Perrysburg, Ohio: 1990) as Addendum No. 1 (pp.
137–41).

12. Andrew Burstein, "The Problem of Jefferson's Biography" (*Virginia Quarterly Review* 70, no. 3 (1994), pp 403–20) refers to some recent work—including
Willard Sterne Randall's *Thomas Jefferson: A Life* (1993)—as "designed for the
voyeuristic public of the 1980's and 1990's . . . far from adequate treatments
[serving] only to give the popular audience what it wants—simple formulas and,
where possible, titillating copy."

13. Malone, *Jefferson and His Time,* Vol. 2, p. 135.

14. AA to TJ, 27 and 28 June, 1787; *JP*, Boyd, Vol. 11, pp. 501–3.

15. In her entertaining novel *Sally Hemings,* Barbara Chase-Riboud has a
brief and life-like dialogue between John and Abigail Adams about Sally, their
puzzling guest in London in June 1787.

16. Malone, *Jefferson and His Time,* Vol. 2, pp. 136–37.

17. Ibid., p. 207.

18. To John Adams, 25 May 1785; *JP*, Boyd, Vol. 8, pp. 163–64.

19. To James Monroe, 17 June 1785; *JP*, Boyd, Vol. 8, p. 233.

20. To Eliza House Trist, 18 August 1785; *JP*, Boyd, Vol. 8, p. 404.

21. To Walker Maury, 19 August 1785; *JP*, Boyd, Vol. 8, pp. 409–10. The
nephew in question was Jack Eppes, who later married Polly Jefferson. See above,
p. 19.

22. *JP*, Boyd, Vol. 5, p. 231n. Boyd's source is the *Virginia Council Journals,*
ii.343.

23. See *JP*, Boyd,, Vol. 9, pp. 29–31; 42, 45n, 291–92, 643; Vol. 10, pp.
145–48.

24. *JP*, Boyd, Vol. 10, p. 505. In a footnote, Boyd comments: "Lafayette's
letter of 2 Nov. has not been found and is not recorded in SJL [Jefferson's "Sum-

mary Journal of Letters" written and received], but its import is as clear as TJ's resentment of the implications."

25. To Lafayette, 11 April, 1787; *JP*, Boyd, Vol. 11, pp. 283–85.

26. *JP*, Boyd, Vol. 11, p. 95. Nearly three years before, Madison, writing to Jefferson, had offered a similar but more polished and definitive assessment of Lafayette:

> In a word, I take *him to be as amiable a man* as *his vanity will admit,* and as *sincere an American as any Frenchman can be;* one *whose past services* gratitude obliges *us to acknowledge* and *whose future friendship* prudence *requires us to cultivate.* (Madison to Jefferson, 17 Oct. 1784 [*JP*, Boyd, Vol. 7, p. 446])

The two Virginians appear to have seen their French ally in much the same light.

27. Malone, *Jefferson and His Time*, Vol. 2, p. 45.

28. In his *Mémoires*, published posthumously in 1821, Morellet devotes a full chapter (XV) to Benjamin Franklin, but doesn't mention his successor, Thomas Jefferson, at all.

29. See *Index to the Papers of Thomas Jefferson*, Vols. 7–12, compiled by E. S. Sherwood (Princeton, 1958). After Jefferson's return to the United States in late 1789, he wrote formal letters of thanks to a number of French acquaintances, including Condorcet and La Rochefoucauld.

30. *JP*, Boyd, Vol. 10, pp. 261–63; 623.

31. *JP*, Boyd, Vol. 12, pp. 577–78.

32. *Thomas Jefferson at the Court of Versailles:* A Dissertation Presented to the Graduate Faculty of the University of Virginia, 1966, p. 58. Earlier in this dissertation Pulley wrote:

> Unfortunately for the historian, Jefferson evidently saw Du Pont, Condorcet, La Rochefoucauld, and Lafayette so frequently in person that he seldom found it necessary to correspond with them. Thus one is left with the knowledge that they collaborated on certain projects, discussed liberal reforms, and quite clearly were in close contact during the eventful meeting of the Estates General, but there is almost no way of proving precisely what transpired among them. (*TJCV*, p. 38, n. 75)

I infer that Pulley was disconcerted to find that there is no written evidence, from Jefferson himself, of the "friendship" claimed (by Malone and others) as having existed between Jefferson and some of his Parisian contemporaries.

33. Malone, *Jefferson and His Time*, Vol. 2, p. 6.

34. Folder "William Short" in the Jefferson Research Center at Monticello (courtesy of the Director, Douglas Wilson).

35. Introduction to the 1967 edition of John P. Foley's *The Jefferson Cyclopedia* (two vols., 1900).

Two

1. *New Cambridge Modern History, Volume VIII, The American and French Revolutions, 1763–93,* ed. A. Goodwin, chapter XXI, "The Breakdown of the

Old Regime in France," by D. Dakin, pp. 592–617. This quotation is from the final paragraph of "The Breakdown."

2. *The Papers of Thomas Jefferson,* ed. Julian P. Boyd, Vol. 10, p. 203.

3. See Prelude.

4. *JP,* Boyd, Vol. 11, p. 48.

5. *JP,* Boyd, Vol. 11, p. 48.

6. *JP,* Boyd, Vol. 11, p. 174.

7. See Julian P. Boyd's long footnote to this letter (*JP,* Vol. 11, p. 175). Boyd says Abigail "bristled in disagreement" at Jefferson's earlier "pro-Shays" letter. Jefferson could not, in my opinion, have ignored such signals, coming from a dear and greatly respected friend had he not been in the grip of an emotion so strong as to generate uncharacteristic and inappropriate behavior.

8. To William Stephens Smith, 13 Nov. 1787; *JP,* Boyd, Vol. 12, p. 356.

9. *JP,* Boyd, Vol. 11, p. 174.

10. To Lafayette, 28 February 1787; *JP,* Boyd, Vol. 11, p. 186.

11. *JP,* Boyd, Vol. 11, p. 186; in the letter of 28 February 1787, already quoted from.

12. Lafayette to Hamilton, 12 April 1787; *The Papers of Alexander Hamilton,* 27 vols., eds. Harold C. Syrett and Jacob E. Cooke (New York and London, 1962), Vol. 4, p. 432.

13. Quoted in Louis Gottschalk, *Lafayette between the American and the French Revolution (1783–1789)* (University of Chicago Press, 1950), p. 314. Gottschalk thinks that Lafayette may have been influenced in reaching this conclusion by a letter on the sad condition of the peasantry written to him by Thomas Jefferson that "inveterate defender of the downtrodden" in the previous month (April). Perhaps. I think it more likely that Lafayette was thinking more of the impact those words would make on Parisians in the early summer of 1787.

14. Gottschalk, *Lafayette between the American and the French Revolution,* pp. 314–15.

15. *JP,* Boyd, Vol. 11, p. 692. Crèvecoeur as "J. Hector St. John" was the most famous of all eighteenth-century publicists of American immigration in his *Letters of an American Farmer* (1782). He was, at the time of Jefferson's letter to him, French Consul in New York (to 1790).

16. Dispatch to John Jay, 6 August 1787; *JP,* Boyd, Vol. 11, pp. 698–99.

17. R. R. Palmer, "The Dubious Democrat: Thomas Jefferson in Bourbon France"; *Political Science Quarterly* LXXII (Sept. 1957), pp. 394–95.

18. Jefferson to Jay, 19 November 1788; *JP,* Boyd, Vol. 14, p. 215. Jefferson gives family and business reasons for this application, and no doubt these were valid. But the visit would also give him an opportunity to catch up on political developments, both Virginian and national.

19. TJ to John Adams, 30 August 1787; *JP,* Boyd, Vol. 12, p. 68.

20. TJ to David Humphreys, 14 August 1787; *JP,* Boyd, Vol. 12, p. 33. Humphreys was a former revolutionary soldier, later a farmer and politician and a diplomatist. He was always a particularly warm admirer of George Washington and later became (by no coincidence) a political enemy of Thomas Jefferson's.

21. TJ to John Adams, 13 November 1787; *JP,* Boyd, Vol. 12, pp. 350–51.

22. TJ to George Washington, 14 August 1787; *JP,* Boyd, Vol. 12, p. 36.

23. Even *before* the Convention indeed, Jefferson's long letter to Washington

of 14 November 1786 (*JP*, Boyd, Vol. 10, pp. 531–33) reflects his fears about the setting up in America of a hereditary military aristocracy, of which Washington would, in the nature of the case, have been the monarchical or quasi-monarchical apex (although Jefferson does not make that point explicitly).

24. TJ to George Washington, 14 August 1787; *JP*, Boyd, Vol. 12, p. 38.

25. See below, chapters 3 to 6.

26. TJ to James Madison, 18 November 1788; *JP*, Boyd, Vol. 14, pp. 188–89. See also *The Republic of Letters: The Correspondence between Thomas Jefferson and James Madison 1776–1826*, ed. J. M. Smith (New York, 1995), Vol. 1, p. 524.

27. TJ to John Brown Cutting, 23 August 1788; *JP*, Boyd, Vol. 13, pp. 538–39.

28. TJ to James Madison, 18 November 1788; *JP*, Boyd, Vol. 14, p. 188.

29. TJ to George Washington, 4 December 1788; *JP*, Boyd, Vol. 14, p. 330.

30. Bailyn, essay "Thomas Jefferson," in *Faces of Revolution: Personalities and Themes in the Struggle for American Independence* (New York, 1992), pp. 22–41.

31. Below, chapter 4.

32. TJ to Richard Price, 8 January 1789; *JP*, Boyd, Vol. 14, p. 423.

33. TJ to Thomas Lee Shippen, 11 March 1789; *JP*, Boyd, Vol. 14, p. 639.

34. TJ to David Humphreys, 18 March 1789; *JP*, Boyd, Vol. 14, pp. 678–79. This seems to be an exercise in fence-mending. Humphreys was best known as a confidant of Washington's and would be expected to pass these observations on.

35. TJ to John Jay, 9 May 1789; *JP*, Boyd, Vol. 15, pp. 110–11. On the previous day, Jefferson had written in a similar strain to William Carmichael:

> We have had in this city a very considerable riot in which about 100 people have been probably killed. It was the most unprovoked and is therefore justly the most unpitied catastrophe of that kind I ever knew. Nor did the wretches know what they wanted, except to do mischief. It seems to have had no particular connection with the great national questions now in agitation. (TJ to William Carmichael; *JP*, Boyd, Vol. 15, p. 104)

36. TJ to William Carmichael, 8 May 1789; *JP*, Boyd, Vol. 15, pp. 104–5.

37. TJ to James Madison, 11 May 1789; *JP*, Boyd, Vol. 15, pp. 121–22.

38. See TJ to Lafayette, 6 May 1789; *JP*, Boyd, Vol. 15, pp. 97–98.

39. The *abbés* who figure frequently in Thomas Jefferson's letters were technically "lower clergy," but in practice hangers-on of the liberal free-thinking aristocracy.

40. TJ to John Trumbull, 29 June 1789; *JP*, Boyd, Vol. 15, p. 224.

41. TJ to Thomas Paine, 11 July 1789; *JP*, Boyd, Vol. 15, pp. 266–69.

42. Patrick Thierry, "*De la Révolution Américaine à la Révolution Française: Paine, Burke et les Droits de l'Homme* (Paris, 1986), p. 483.

43. TJ to Thomas Paine, 13 July 1789; *JP*, Boyd, Vol. 15, p. 273.

44. TJ to Thomas Paine, 17 July 1789; *JP*, Boyd, Vol. 15, p. 279.

45. TJ to Richard Price, 17 July 1789; *JP*, Boyd, Vol. 15, p. 280.

46. TJ to John Jay, 19 July 1789; *JP*, Boyd, Vol. 15, p. 288.

47. TJ to James Madison, 22 July 1789; *JP*, Boyd, Vol. 15, p. 300. The efficacy of mob violence in teaching "obnoxious" characters "to keep out of it's way" is

also noted in Jefferson's correspondence of this period (to John Jay, 23 July 1789; to Thomas Paine, same day; *JP*, Boyd, Vol. 15, pp. 301–2). A few days later, Jefferson writes to an English aristocratic acquaintance, Lord Wycombe, in a more soothing and humanitarian strain:

> I am in hopes the tumults are now at an end, and that the business of their constitution will be brought forward in a few days. While this prepares for them lasting advantages, it will have also the temporary one of diverting them from the bloody objects which have lately occupied their minds. (Letter of 25 July 1789; *JP*, Boyd, Vol. 15, p. 307)

48. TJ to Thomas Paine, 13 September 1789; *JP*, Boyd, Vol. 15, p. 424.

49. Conor Cruise O'Brien, *The Great Melody* (Chicago, 1992), p. 388.

50. Ibid., p 388.

51. Ibid., pp. 388–89.

52. Dumas Malone, *Jefferson and His Time*, (6 vols., Boston, 1948–81), Vol. 2, p. 180.

53. Note also the "lions, tygers and mammouts" passage (above, p. 48) and his praise for the National Assembly for its "resolution to set fire to the four corners of the kingdom and to perish with it themselves rather than to relinquish an iota from their plan of a total change of government" (above, p. 60).

54. See Macaulay's review of *Mémoires de Bertrand Barère* (ed. Hippolyte Carnot; Paris 1843) in Macaulay's *Miscellaneous Writings and Speeches* (London 1889), pp. 285–340. The "tree of liberty" quote is on p. 301. I am indebted for this reference to Owen Dudley Edwards.

55. TJ to Thomas Paine, 14 October 1789; *JP*, Boyd, Vol. 15, p. 522.

THREE

1. Letter of 15 December 1789; *The Papers of Thomas Jefferson*, ed. Julian P. Boyd, Vol. 16, p. 34–35.

2. Merrill D. Peterson, *Thomas Jefferson and the New Nation: A Biography* (New York, 1970), p. 391. Jefferson added in the same letter: "The ground I have already passed over enables me to see my way into that which is before me." This is rather funny, when contrasted with the recorded extent of Jefferson's capacity "to see his way into that which is before him" in the French politics of 1787–89. See above, chapter 2.

3. Letter of 15 December 1789; *JP*, Boyd, Vol. 16, p. 35.

4. Letter of 21 January 1790; *JP*, Boyd, Vol. 16, pp. 116–18.

5. David K. McCarrell, *The Formation of the Jeffersonian Party in Virginia* (unpublished Ph.D. thesis; Duke University, 1937), pp. 32–33.

6. John P. Kaminski and G.aspare J. Saladino, eds., *Documentary History of the Ratification of the Constitution*, vol. 10 [3], pp. 1476–77.

7. Kaminski and Saladino, eds., *The Documentary History of the Ratification of the Constitution*, Vols. 8–10, Ratification of the Constitution by the States: Virginia (Madison: State Historical Society of Wisconsin, 1988–1993), Vol. 1, p. 371; Vol. 3, p. 1483. I am indebted for these important references to Mr. Jeffrey Young.

8. Bernard Bailyn, ed., *The Debate on the Constitution: Federalist and Anti-federalist Speeches, Articles and Letters during the Struggle over Ratification, Part Two . . . Debates in the States Ratifying Conventions, Virginia June 22-27, 1788* (New York, 1993), pp. 706-8, "George Mason and James Madison debate the Slave-Trade Clause."

9. C. H. Ambler, *Sectionalism in Virginia from 1776 to 1861* (first published, 1910; reissued in New York, 1964), p. 59. Risjord also refers to "the predominantly Antifederalist Piedmont" (*Chesapeake Politics, 1781-1800* (New York, 1978), p. 326).

10. McCarrell, *Jeffersonian Party*, pp. 43-44.

11. Risjord, *Chesapeake Politics*, p. 316.

12. Ibid., pp. 86-87.

13. Alexander Donald to TJ, 24 November, 1788; *JP*, Boyd, Vol. 14, pp. 280-82.

14. Quoted in McCarrell, *Jeffersonian Party*, p. 54.

15. McCarrell, *Jeffersonian Party*, p. 54; Harry Ammon, *The Republican Party in Virginia, 1789 to 1824* (unpublished Ph.D. thesis; University of Virginia, 1948), p. 88.

16. Letter of 23 May 1789; *JP*, Boyd, Vol. 15, pp. 147-48.

17. Letter of 29 July 1789; *JP*, Boyd, Vol. 15, pp. 315-16.

18. Harry Ammon, "The Formation of the Republican Party in Virginia, 1789-1796," in *Journal of Southern History* XIX (August 1953), pp. 283-310.

19. The case of George Washington is irrelevant here. Washington—like Grant and Eisenhower later—was propelled to the Presidency by military glory. Jefferson, like almost all the other Presidents, had to find his way to the top by a political route.

20. See the Editorial Note "Jefferson's Alliance in 1790 with Freneau; *Gazette of the United States*," in *JP*, Boyd, Vol. 16, pp. 237-47.

21. See the chapter "The French Revolution in America" in Stanley Elkins and Eric McKitrick, *The Age of Federalism: "The Early American Republic, 1788-1800"* (New York, 1993).

22. *The Works of John Adams*, ed. Charles Francis Adams (Boston, 1851), pp. 220-399.

23. 10 August 1790; *The Writings of George Washington from the Original Manuscript Sources, 1745-1799*, 39 vols., ed. John C. Fitzpatrick (Washington, D.C., 1939), Vol. 31, p. 83.

24. Extract from the Speech of Edmund Burke, 9 February 1790; *JP*, Boyd, Vol. 16, p. 260.

25. Editorial Note; *JP*, Boyd, Vol. 16, p. 244.

26. Editorial Note; *JP*, Boyd, Vol. 16, p. 245.

27. Rachel N. Klein, *Unification of a Slave State: The Rise of the Planter Class in the South Carolina Backcountry, 1760-1808* (Chapel Hill, 1990). Chapter entitled "The French Revolution in South Carolina," p. 203.

28. Klein, *Unification of a Slave State*, p. 204.

29. Editorial Note; *JP*, Boyd, Vol. 16, p. 245. Washington's signature of the assumption bill may have influenced the *timing* of Hamilton's move over the *Gazette*, as Boyd appears to imply. Once that signature was affixed, Hamilton was

no longer in need of Jefferson's support within the Cabinet, and could afford to take Jefferson on; though not to the extent of not letting him win on the situation of the National capital.

30. Elkins and McKitrick, *Age of Federalism,* p. 381.

31. Edited by Harold C. Syrett and Jacob E. Cooke (New York and London, 1962).

32. Hamilton to Lafayette, 6 October 1789, in *The Papers of Alexander Hamilton,* ed. Syrett and Cooke, Vol. 5, June 1788–Nov. 1789, p. 425. As it happens, this letter was written on the day when the Paris mob forcibly translated the French royal family to Paris, having abducted them from Versailles.

33. Burke to Lord Charlemont, 9 August 1789; Burke's *Correspondence,* 10 vols., ed. Copeland (Cambridge and Chicago, 1968–78), Vol. 6, p. 10.

34. AH to GW, 15 September 1790; *The Papers of Alexander Hamilton* (ed. Syrett and Cooke), Vol. 7, p. 51. From the sequel, it looks as if Hamilton's words—supported by the new line of the *Gazette*—did not fall on stony ground.

35. Louis Martin Sears, *George Washington and the French Revolution* (Detroit, 1960), p. 81.

36. TJ to William Short, 27 April 1790; *JP,* Boyd, vol. 16, pp. 387–89.

37. TJ to Benjamin Rush, 4 October 1803; The Writings of Thomas Jefferson, 20 vols., ed. Andrew A. Lipscomb (Washington, D.C., 1903), Vol. 10, pp. 420–22.

38. Franklin himself had reservations about the French Revolution, as we saw in the Prelude. But these were not known either to the French or the American public.

39. *JP,* Boyd, Vol. 19, p. 79.

40. *JP,* Boyd, Vol. 19, p. 80.

41. *General Advertiser,* 4 October 1790; quoted in *JP,* Boyd, Vol. 19, p. 81, n. 6.

42. *JP,* Boyd, Vol. 19, pp. 106–7.

43. *JP,* Boyd, Vol. 19, p. 83.

44. *JP,* Boyd, Vol. 19, p. 83, quoting Maclay, *Journal,* ed. Maclay, p. 350. Maclay was quite a pungent diarist, but curiously timorous for a Senator. However his timidity may be indicative of the minatory atmosphere in the Senate as a whole, in this period, regarding the French Revolution.

45. John J. Beckley Papers, University of Virginia Collection 2764-a.

46. *JP,* Boyd, Vol. 19, pp. 84–85. The notion that Washington might have been "affronting" the unfortunate "monarch of France" at the end of 1790 by snubbing the National Assembly and/or the Paris Commune, shows a surprising unfamiliarity on the part of Jefferson's distinguished editor with the workings of the revolution by which Jefferson set such store. Louis XVI at this time considered himself to be—and actually was—a prisoner of the National Assembly, from which he tried to escape in June 1791, and was recaptured (below, p. 117). The Paris Commune played a major part in the King's deposition (August 1792) and in the processes that led to his execution in January 1793.

47. *JP,* Boyd, Vol. 19, pp. 89–90.

48. *JP,* Boyd, Vol. 19, p. 84.

49. *JP,* Boyd, Vol. 19, p. 86.

50. I would surmise—it is no more than a surmise—that the main reason why Washington kept Jefferson in this Cabinet up to late 1793 (when Jefferson left of his own accord) was that Jefferson would be even more dangerous outside than inside. This is a phenomenon of frequent occurrence in politics. One of Washington's twentieth-century successors, Lyndon Baines Johnson, embodied it in an earthy metaphor about a tent (in connection with the retention in office of J. Edgar Hoover).

51. *JP*, Boyd, Vol. 19, p. 79.

52. TJ to BV, 11 May 1791; *JP*, Boyd, Vol. 20, p. 391.

53. Peterson, *Thomas Jefferson*, p. 439.

54. TJ to Jonathan B. Smith, 26 April 1791; *JP*, Boyd, Vol. 20, p. 290.

55. Boyd writes this comment in the course of an Editorial Note: "*Rights of Man*: The Contest of Burke and Paine in America." *JP*, Vol. 20, pp. 268–90. Volume 20 was the last volume of the *Jefferson Papers* to be edited by Boyd, who died shortly after completing it. Boyd, at this stage of his labors was, for the first time, beginning to entertain doubts about his subject's veracity, and signs of these are discernible in the passage beginning: "There is no reason to doubt . . ."

56. *JP*, Boyd, Vol. 20, between pp. 384 and 385. (The publisher's preface is reproduced in facsimile in *JP*, 20. Curiously the version quoted in Boyd's Editorial Note (p. 272) omits the crucial sentence which *explicitly* identifies "the Secretary of State" as the author of the Extract.

57. *JP*, Boyd, Vol. 20, p. 274.

58. TJ to GW, 8 May 1791; *JP*, Boyd, Vol. 20, pp. 291–92. In a letter to Madison on the following day, and in one to his son-in-law, Thomas Mann Randolph, Jr., two months later, Jefferson offers similar explanations: the motive for writing in this strain is explained in the same way in all three letters: "to take off [a little of] the dryness of the note."

59. *JP*, Boyd, Vol. 20, p. 276.

60. *JP*, Boyd, Vol. 20, p. 289.

61. *JP*, Boyd, Vol. 20, pp. 280–81.

62. *JP*, Boyd, Vol. 20, p. 302.

63. Adams to Jefferson, 29 July 1791; *JP*, Boyd, Vol. 20, pp. 305.

64. TJ to JA, 30 August 1791; *JP*, Boyd, Vol. 20, p. 311.

65. Merrill D. Peterson, *Adams and Jefferson: A Revolutionary Dialogue* (Athens, Ga., 1976), p. 59. Peterson's reference to "mendacity" is interesting, in view of his acceptance in *Thomas Jefferson and the New Nation* (1970) of Jefferson's own version of his letter to Smith, that he had been "unwillingly thrust upon the public stage" (above, p. 103). It seems that Peterson, like Boyd, had finally wearied of Jeffersonian disclaimers.

66. TJ to TP, 29 July 1791. *JP*, Boyd, Vol. 20, pp. 308–10. This is the same day on which John Adams wrote to Jefferson, giving "full credit to your relation of the matter."

67. *JP*, Boyd, Vol. 20, p. 286.

68. JM to TJ, 25 July 1791; *JP*, Boyd, Vol. 20, p. 304.

69. See Philip M. Marsh, "John Beckley, Mystery Man of the Early Jeffersonians," *Pennsylvania Magazine of History and Biography* 72 (January 1948), pp. 54–69. Marsh describes Beckley as (variously): "Implacable enemy of Hamilton

... and the administrations of Washington and Adams, a passionate lover of France and later of Britain, gatherer and distributor of extensive secret information ... undercover political strategist of his time ... go-between for Jefferson and his friends ... party watchdog." Unfortunately Marsh does not allude to the affair of the *Rights of Man*. As Marsh himself says: Beckley "covered his tracks too well."

70. *The Papers of Alexander Hamilton* (ed. Syrett and Cooke), Vol. 14, p. 467.

71. Peterson, *Thomas Jefferson*, p. 575.

Four

1. GM to TJ, 10 January 1791; *The Papers of Thomas Jefferson*, ed. Julian P. Boyd, Vol. 18, pp. 482–85.

2. TJ to GM, 4 February 1791; *JP*, Boyd, Vol. 19, pp. 241–42.

3. Quoted in Meade Minnigerode, *Jefferson, Friend of France* (New York, 1928), p. 153.

4. Ibid., p. 154.

5. WS to TJ, 11 March, 1791; *JP*, Boyd, Vol. 19, p. 532.

6. WS to TJ, 25 April 1791; *JP*, Boyd, Vol. 20, pp. 256–62.

7. *JP*, Boyd, Vol. 20, p. 266n.

8. *Parliamentary History* (GB), XXIX, 249.

9. *JP*, Boyd, Vol. 20, pp. 561–62.

10. Dispatch of 26 June 1791; *JP*, Boyd, Vol. 20, pp. 573–79.

11. *JP*, Boyd, Vol. 20, pp. 584–88. Short developed this analysis in later dispatches.

12. *JP*, ed. Cullen, Vol. 22, pp. 125–26 (Charles T. Cullen succeeded to the Editorship of the Princeton edition of the Jefferson papers after Boyd's death).

13. TJ to Condorcet, 30 August 1791; *JP*, Cullen, Vol. 22, pp. 98–99.

14. Irving Brant, *James Madison*, 6 vols. (Indianapolis, 1941–61). Vol. 3: *James Madison, Father of the Constitution*, chap. 29, "The French Revolution," p. 372.

15. The description "sinecure" is used by Julian P. Boyd, whose account is in the Editorial Note: "Jefferson, Freneau and the Founding of the *National Gazette*" (*JP*, Boyd, Vol. 20, pp. 718–53).

16. Samuel E. Forman, "The Political Activities of Philip Freneau"; in *Johns Hopkins University Studies in Historical and Political Science* (Baltimore, Sept.–Oct., 1902), pp. 48–49.

17. "T. L." in *Gazette of the United States*, 25 July 1792.

18. TJ to GW, 9 September 1792; JP, Catanzariti, Vol. 24, pp. 351–60.

19. Frank Mott, *Jefferson and the Press* (Baton Rouge, La., 1943), p. 18. Of his general subject matter, Mott observes: "Bold though [Jefferson] was in his enunciation of his basic doctrines of society and government, his participation in practical politics led him to veiled and disguised procedures. The philosopher was impelled to learn the less admirable arts of the politician" (p. 23).

20. Forman, "The Political Activities of Philip Freneau," pp. 65–66.

21. *JP*, Boyd, Vol. 20, p. 744.

22. Ibid., p. 737.

23. Forman, "Political Activities of Philip Freneau," p. 70.

24. Mott, *Jefferson and the Press*, pp. 24–26.

25. *JP*, Cullen, Vol. 22, p. xxxviii.

26. TJ to GM, 23 January 1792; *JP*, Cullen, Vol. 23, pp. 55–57.

27. *JP*, Cullen, Vol. 23, p. 221n.

28. *JP*, Cullen, Vol. 23, pp. 221–22.

29. *JP*, Cullen, Vol. 23, pp. 260–61.

30. TJ to Sir John Sinclair, 24 August 1791; *JP*, Cullen, Vol. 22, pp. 72–73.

31. GM to TJ, 6 April 1792; *JP*, Cullen, Vol. 23, pp. 382–83.

32. WS to TJ, 15 May 1792; *JP*, Cullen, Vol. 23, p. 508.

33. TJ to GW, 23 May 1792; *JP*, Cullen, Vol. 23, pp. 535–40.

34. *JP*, Cullen, Vol. 23, p. 540n.

35. TJ to Lafayette, 16 June 1792; *JP*, ed. John Catanzariti, Vol. 24, p. 85.

36. TJ to JM, 29 June 1792; *JP*, Catanzariti, Vol. 24, pp. 133–34.

37. WS to TJ, 29 June 1792; *JP*, Catanzariti, Vol. 24, pp. 137–38.

38. Morris to Washington, 4 February 1792; in *A Diary of the French Revolution by Gouverneur Morris,* ed. B. C. Davenport (Boston, 1933; Vol. 2, pp. 349–58.

39. Morris's description of that trio as "Chiefs of the old Jacobins" requires some explanation. Morris's reports on the French Revolution, though of considerable historical interest, are far from being as good as Short's. One of Morris's weaknesses as a commentator was a tendency to show off his knowledge of the *history* of the French Revolution, which he had lived through in Paris (while on private business), since February 1789. He brings reminiscences of 1789 into his interpretation of 1792. And this in itself is a major source of distortion. In 1792, French people were not pondering the politics of 1789. And no French person, in 1792, could think of that trio as *any* kind of Jacobins. If they had attempted to address the *Club des Jacobins,* they would have been lynched.

40. GM to TJ; *JP*, Catanzariti, Vol. 24, p. 301.

41. *JP*, Catanzariti, Vol. 24, pp. 301–5.

42. *JP*, Catanzariti, Vol. 24, p. 305n.

43. GM to TJ, 22 August 1792; *JP*, Catanzariti, Vol. 24, pp. 313–15.

44. *JP*, Catanzariti, Vol. 24, pp. 322–25.

45. *JP*, Catanzariti, Vol. 24, pp. 364–65.

46. *National Gazette,* 7 November 1792.

47. Library of Congress, Pinckney Family Papers, LC iii 3. I am indebted for this reference (and for much else) to Mr. Jeffrey Young (see Acknowledgments).

48. *JP*, Catanzariti, Vol. 24, pp. 762–74.

49. *JP*, Catanzariti, Vol. 24, pp. 793–94.

50. TJ to John Trumbull, 1 June 1789; *JP*, Boyd, Vol. 15, p. 164.

51. *JP*, Catanzariti, Vol. 25, pp. 14–16. Concerning this letter Dumas Malone observes: "This private letter contains as fervid comments as Jefferson ever made on the French Revolution and it has been widely quoted by later writers for just that reason" (Vol. 3, p. 48). Malone himself refrains from quoting any part of it. A little earlier he had referred to Jefferson's "personal distaste for disorder and violence" (3:39).

52. Short's reply was from the Aranjuez in Spain and is dated 5 April 1793; *JP*, Catanzariti, Vol. 25, pp. 494–509. In the last pages (508–9), Short briefly defends his dispatches, and denies the conversations attributed to him (by Washington, if you believe Jefferson).

53. *JP*, Cullen, Vol. 22, p. 174.

54. TJ to WS, 23 March 1793; *JP*, Catanzariti, Vol. 25, p. 436.

55. I am told this is an unsound version of Catholic teaching. All the same I believe it to be a prevalent one among Catholics who (like members of other faiths) believe a lot of things that would be regarded as unsound by their own theologians (who in any case are often not unanimous).

56. *JP*, Catanzariti, Vol. 25, p. xxxix.

57. Catanzariti, who also edited Vol. 24 of *JP* in which *Notes of a Conversation with George Washington* appeared, had nothing to say about the crucial passage in *Notes* in that volume either. (He does annotate the *Notes,* but the annotations are of a purely technical character.) It is hard to understand how an editor who undertakes to discuss Jefferson's attitude to the French Revolution can ignore these *Notes.* But some editors seem to be so busy editing that they don't have time to read the stuff that is being edited. This was not true of Julian P. Boyd. I am not so sure about his two successors, to date.

58. *JP*, Catanzariti, Vol. 24, p. 305n.

59. James Roger Sharp, *American Politics in the Early Republic: The New Nation in Crisis* (New Haven, 1993), p. 73.

FIVE

1. Quoted in *Annual Report of the American Historical Association for the Year 1903*, Vol. 2. *Seventh Report of Historical Manuscripts Commission: Correspondence of the French Ministers to the United States, 1791–1797*, p. 194. This valuable collection will be cited henceforth as *AHA* (1903).

2. *AHA* (1903), pp. 43–44.

3. *AHA* (1903), p. 195.

4. TJ to JM, 28 April 1793; *The Republic of Letters: The Correspondence between Thomas Jefferson and James Madison 1776–1826*, ed. J. M. Smith (New York, 1995), Vol. 2, pp. 769–770.

5. JM to TJ, 29 May 1793; *Republic of Letters*, Vol. 2, pp. 777–78.

6. Harry Ammon, *The Genet Mission* (New York, 1973), p. 44.

7. This is not exactly how the Republican press in America depicted Hamilton. But it is exactly how the message of that press would have to be decoded by French Revolutionaries; minds without any shades of gray.

8. Ammon, *Genet Mission*, p. 25.

9. "Notes on the Reception of Edmond Charles Genet"; *JP*, Catanzariti, Vol. 25, pp. 469–70.

10. Ammon, *Genet Mission*, p. 47.

11. TJ to JM, 28 April 1793: in *The Republic of Letters*, Vol. 2, pp. 769–70.

12. Alexander DeConde, *Entangling Alliances* (Durham, N. C., 1958), pp. 196–97.

13. TJ to James Monroe, 5 May 1793; *Republic of Letters*, Vol. 2, p. 771.

14. TJ to GH, 15 May 1793; in *The Writings of Thomas Jefferson*, collected

and edited by Paul Leicester Ford, Vol. 6, 1792–1794 (New York, 1895), pp. 252–54.

15. *WJ*, ed. Ford, Vol. 6, pp. 254–57. *Grange* was in fact restored, but Genet did not desist from his other unwelcome maritime activities.

16. *WJ*, Ford, Vol. 6, pp. 260–61.

17. TJ to JWE, 23 May 1793; *WP*, Ford, Vol. 6, pp. 263–64.

18. TJ to Genet, 5 June 1793; *WJ*, Ford, Vol. 6, pp. 282–83.

19. *WJ*, Ford, Vol. 6, p. 323.

20. TJ to JM, 5 July 1793; *Republic of Letters*, Vol. 2, p. 792.

21. *Writings of Thomas Jefferson* (ed. Ford), I, pp. 235–37.

22. Ammon, *Genet Mission*, pp. 84–85.

23. Bemis, *American Secretaries of State and Their Diplomacy* (New York, 1958), Vol. 2, "Thomas Jefferson," pp. 81–82.

24. DeConde, *Entangling Alliances*, p. 248.

25. Ibid., p. 85.

26. Maude Howlett Woodfin, *Citizen Genet and His Mission* (Ph.D. thesis, University of Chicago, 1925), p. 424.

27. Woodfin, *Citizen Genet*, p. 348.

28. Ammon, *Genet Mission*, pp. 86–87.

29. *WJ*, Ford, Vol. 1, pp. 253–54.

30. TJ to JM, 18 August 1793; *WJ*, Ford, Vol. 6, pp. 393–95.

31. Meade Minnigerode, *Jefferson, Friend of France* (New York, 1928), p. 236.

32. TJ to JM, 25 August 1793; *WJ*, Ford, Vol. 6, pp. 397–98.

33. *AHA* (1903), pp. 238–41.

34. Ammon, *Genet Mission*, p. 118.

35. *WJ*, Ford, Vol. 1, pp. 237–43. The document dated July 10, 1793, is in the form of a memorandum but we know that it had gone to Washington. Paul Leicester Ford notes: "Jefferson's rough draft of this paper was retained by him in the Anas, but as it is abbreviated to an extent that renders it almost unintelligible I have printed it here from the fair copy given to Washington."

36. TJ to JM, 1 September 1793; *WP*, Ford, Vol. 6, p. 402.

37. Minnigerode, *Jefferson, Friend of France*, pp. 324–25.

38. Ammon, *Genet Mission*, p. 119; Minnigerode, *Jefferson, Friend of France*, pp. 323–24. Minnigerode's version is fuller. The letter does not appear in Ford's *Writings of Thomas Jefferson* (or if it does, I haven't been able to find it, in that weirdly organized compilation).

39. Minnigerode, *Jefferson, Friend of France*, p. 325.

40. Ibid., p. 332.

41. See the chapter "The War of the Resolutions" in Ammon, *Genet Mission*, pp. 132–46.

42. Ammon, *Genet Mission*, p. 154.

SIX

1. Douglas S. Freeman et al., *George Washington: A Biography*, 7 vols. (New York, 1948–57). Vol. 7: *First in Peace*, by John A. Carroll and Mary W. Ashworth, p. 154, n. 50.

2. Adet to the French Minister for Foreign Affairs, 21 March 1796; in *Annual Report of the American Historial Assocation* (1903), pp. 850–51.

3. These instructions (of 15 November 1793) are set out in *AHA* (1903), pp. 288–94. The instructions are, formally, from the Provisional Executive Council, but they are marked, "Seen and approved by the Committee of Public Safety," which is what counted in this period.

4. Fauchet et al. to Minister for Foreign Affairs, 21 March 1794; in *AHA* (1903), pp. 306–17.

5. Madison to Jefferson, 2 March 1794; in J. M. Smith (ed.) *The Republic of Letters: The Correspondence between Thomas Jefferson and James Madison* (New York, 1995), Vol. 2, p. 833.

6. TJ to JM, 3 April 1794; *Republic of Letters*, Vol. 2, p. 840.

7. W. P. Cresson, *James Monroe* (Chapel Hill, 1946), p. 123.

8. Fauchet to Minister for Foreign Affairs, 4 June 1794, *AHA* (1903), p. 373.

9. *Moreau de St. Méry's American Journey* [1793–1798], trans. and ed. Kenneth and Anna Roberts (New York, 1947). Genet was, at this time, no longer Minister but was present as Governor Clinton's son-in-law.

10. *Moreau de St. Méry's American Journey*, p. 144.

11. TJ to T. Coxe, 1 May 1794; *The Writings of Thomas Jefferson*, collected and edited by Paul Leicester Ford (New York, 1895), Vol. 6, pp. 507–8.

12. *George Washington*, Vol. 7, pp. 170–71.

13. *George Washington*, Vol. 7, p. 171.

14. Wherever Washington appeared to do anything clever, Jefferson supposed that Hamilton was behind it. But it was the *combination* Washington-Hamilton that was formidable. After Hamilton had ceased to be under Washington's "aegis" (as he himself put it) by leaving his Cabinet, Hamilton committed some frightful mistakes. It looks as if Hamilton had some very good ideas, and some very bad ones. Washington was able to sort them out, keeping the good ones and throwing away the bad.

15. *Republic of Letters*, Vol. 2, p. 827.

16. Cresson, *Monroe*, p. 129.

17. Cresson, *Monroe*, p. 130.

18. Cresson, *Monroe*, p. 130.

19. Cresson, *Monroe*, pp. 130–31.

20. Cresson, *Monroe*, p. 132.

21. The authors (Stanley Elkins and Eric McKitrick) of *The Age of Federalism* (New York, 1993; p. 506) call it "a tremendous ritual of reinterpretation."

22. Cresson, *Monroe*, pp. 132–33.

23. *Republic of Letters*, Vol. 2, p. 850.

24. Lance Banning, *The Jefferson Persuasion: Evolution of Party Ideology* (Ithaca, N.Y., 4th printing, 1994), p. 228.

25. GW to JJ, 1 November 1794; *George Washington*, Vol. 7, p. 215.

26. Elkins and McKitrick, *The Age of Federalism* p. 475–76. William Miller in his article "The Democratic Societies and the Whiskey Rebellion" (*Pennsylvania Magazine of History of Biography* LXII, July 1938, pp. 324–49) finds "no indication that the [Republican and Democratic] Societies ever specifically recommended disobedience to or violent demonstration against any law of Congress."

Miller, however, does not reject the view that the Societies represented "a general tendency towards rebellion that was first crystallized in the insurrection in Western Pennsylvania."

27. *George Washington*, Vol. 7, pp. 219–20.

28. Ibid., p. 222.

29. *Republic of Letters*, Vol. 2, p. 861.

30. Quoted in *Republic of Letters*, Vol. 2, pp. 862–63.

31. *Republic of Letters*, Vol. 2, p. 862, n. 8.

32. TJ to Madison, 28 Dec. 1794; *Republic of Letters*, Vol. 2, pp. 866–67.

33. Madison to TJ, 26 January 1795; *Republic of Letters*, Vol. 2, p. 870.

34. TJ to W. B. Giles, 27 April 1795; *WJ*, Ford, Vol. 7, pp. 11–12.

35. Above pp. 67–68, 143–48.

36. TJ to Démeunier, 29 April 1795; *WJ*, Ford, Vol. 7, pp. 12–15.

37. TJ to Tench Coxe, 1 June 1795; *WJ*, Ford, Vol. 7, pp. 22–23.

38. Randolph to Monroe, 31 May 1795; quoted in *George Washington*, Vol. 7, p. 246, n. 34.

39. Adet's instructions are set out in *AHA* (1903), pp. 721–30. They are dated 23 October 1794, and are probably more cautious than they would have been if drafted in, say, April 1795, after the intervening victories of French armies.

40. Full text in *AHA* (1903), pp. 734–39.

41. Adet to the Representatives of the People, 3 July 1795, *AHA* (1903), pp. 741–44.

42. Ibid.

43. Adet to Citizen Representatives, 6 July 1795, *AHA* (1903), pp. 744–45. This incident and the accompanying riot were widely recorded in the press at the time. Washington's biographers refer to "these disgraceful proceedings," (*George Washington*, Vol. 7, p. 259).

44. GW to AH, 29 July 1795; *George Washington*, Vol. 7, p. 273.

45. James D. Tagg, "Benjamin Franklin Bache's Attack on George Washington"; in *Pennsylvanian Magazine of History and Biography* 99 (1976): 191.

46. Tagg, "Bache's Attack, etc.," p. 195.

47. Quoted, with much more in the same vein, in *AHA* (1903), pp. 776–79.

48. Dumas Malone, *Jefferson and the Ordeal of Liberty*, Vol. 3, *Jefferson and His Time* (Boston: Little, Brown and Company, 1962) pp. 249–50.

49. Elkins and McKitrick, *The Age of Federalism*, p. 508.

50. Cresson, *James Monroe*, pp. 145–46.

51. Malone, *Jefferson and His Time*, Vol. 3, pp. 274–75.

52. *WJ*, Ford, Vol. 7, p. 56.

53. *AHA* (1903), pp. 881–83.

54. Noble E. Cunningham, Jr., *The Jeffersonian Republicans: The Formation of Party Organization, 1789–1801* (Chapel Hill, 1957), p. 100.

55. *AHA* (1903), pp. 896–97.

56. *WJ*, Ford, Vol. 7, pp. 72–79.

57. Malone, *Jefferson and His Time*, Vol. 3, p. 268.

58. *WJ*, Ford, Vol. 7, p. 77.

59. Madison to TJ, 9 May 1796; *Republic of Letters*, Vol. 2, p. 937.

60. Madison to TJ, 22 May 1796; *Republic of Letters*, Vol. 2, pp. 938–39.

61. TJ to Monroe; *WJ*, Ford, Vol. 7, pp. 79–81.
62. Malone, *Jefferson and His Time*, Vol. 3, pp. 269–71.
63. Cresson, *James Monroe*, p. 147.
64. *AHA* (1903), pp. 930–43.
65. *George Washington*, Vol. 7, p. 406.
66. Malone, *Jefferson and His Time*, Vol. 3, p. 276.
67. *AHA* (1903), pp. 947–49.
68. *Jefferson and His Time*, Vol. 3, p. 286.
69. *AHA* (1903), pp. 968–72.
70. *Republic of Letters*, Vol. 2, p. 948.
71. TJ to JM, 17 December 1796.
72. *AHA* (1903), pp. 982–83.
73. Turner's note on Adet's dispatch of 31 December (*AHA* [1903], p. 983).
74. *WJ*, Ford, Vol. 7, pp. 128–29.
75. Instructions for Létombe; *AHA* (1903), pp. 1010–16.
76. *AHA* (1903), pp. 1028–31; dispatch of 7 June 1799.
77. Ibid., pp. 1028–31.
78. Ibid.
79. *WJ*, Ford, Vol. 7, pp. 149–50.
80. TJ to ER, 24 June 1797; *WJ*, Ford, Vol. 7, pp. 152–55.
81. To Edmund Randolph, 27 June 1797; *WJ*, Ford, Vol. 7, pp. 155–56.
82. To Peregrine Fitzhugh, 23 February 1798; to James Madison, 21 March 1798; to James Monroe, 21 March 1798; *WJ*, Ford, Vol. 7, pp. 208–11 and 218–22.
83. *WJ*, Ford, Vol. 7, pp. 210–11.
84. Elkins and McKitrick, *The Age of Federalism*, p. 574.
85. *WJ*, Ford, Vol. 7, pp. 234–36.
86. Ibid., pp. 236–38.
87. Elkins and McKitrick, *Age of Federalism*, p. 595.
88. *WJ*, Ford, Vol. 7, p. 265.
89. TJ to S. T. Mason, 11 October 1798; *WJ*, Ford, Vol. 7, pp. 282–83.
90. Howe, "Republican Thought," etc; in *American Quarterly* XIX (Summer 1987), pp. 147–65.
91. *WJ*, Ford, Vol. 7, pp. 309–12.
92. Ibid., p. 328.
93. Ibid., p. 329.
94. TJ to Thomas Lomax, 12 March 1799; *WJ*, Ford, Vol. 7, pp. 373–74.
95. Burke, *Reflections on the Revolution in France* (1790): Penguin Classics ed., p. 342.
96. John Hall Stewart, *A Documentary Survey of the French Revolution* (New York, 1951), p. 780. This Proclamation is the final document in this collection.
97. Elkins and McKitrick, *The Age of Federalism*, pp. 689–90.
98. *WJ*, Ford, Vol. 7, pp. 419–21.
99. TJ to T. M. Randolph, 2 February 1800; *WJ*, Ford, Vol. 7, pp. 421–44.

SEVEN

1. TJ to JND, 26 June, 1786; *The Papers of Thomas Jefferson,* ed. Julian P. Boyd, Vol. 10, pp. 61–63.

2. Boyd himself, towards the end of his Herculean editorial labors on Jefferson's *Papers* had abandoned the uncritical approach manifest in that Introduction (see above, pp. 120–21).

3. McColley, *Slaves and Jeffersonian Virginia* (Urbana, Ill., 1964).

4. *Journal of American History* LVI (December 1969), pp. 503–26.

5. In a footnote to this paragraph, Cohen cites his sources: T. Jefferson to Bradley, Oct. 6, 1805, T. Jefferson to Reuben Perry, April 16, 1812.

6. *Wolf* (New York, 1977), p. 52.

7. Ibid., p. 64.

8. In some ways *The Ring* would be a closer parallel than the *Divine Comedy.* We can imagine Jefferson as being unbearably moved by Götterdämmerung. But Richard Wagner was only thirteen years old when Thomas Jefferson died. Better stick to Dante, whose work Jefferson knew.

9. *Wolf,* p. 85.

10. Ibid., pp. 96–97.

11. Ibid., p. 200.

12. Ibid., pp. 256–57.

13. Ibid., p. 260.

14. Thomas O. Ott, *Haitian Revolution* (University of Tennessee Press, 1973), p. 21.

15. Quoted in Conor Cruise O'Brien's *The Great Melody* (Chicago, 1992), pp. 418–19.

16. Timothy M. Matthewson, "George Washington's Policy Towards the French Revolution"; in *Diplomatic History* 3, no. 3 (Summer 1979), pp. 321–36; quotation on page 322.

17. Ibid.

18. Rachel N. Klein, *Unification of a Slave State* (Chapel Hill, 1990). Chapter, "The French Revolution in South Carolina," p. 211.

19. Eugene Perry Link, *Democratic Republican Societies 1790–1800* (New York, 1942), p. 186.

20. Ott, *Haitian Revolution,* p. 41.

21. Letter to Martha Jefferson Randolph, 26 May 1793: *WJ,* Ford, Vol. 6, pp. 267–68.

22. TJ to Monroe, July 1793: *WJ,* Ford, pp. 346–50.

23. In *Almost Chosen People: Oblique Biographies in the American Grain* (Berkeley, Calif., 1993).

24. "Jefferson and Haiti," by Tim Matthewson in *Journal of Southern History* LXI, no. 2 (May 1995).

25. *Jeffersonian Legacies,* ed. Peter Onuf (University of Virginia Press, 1993).

26. Edwin Morris Betts, ed., *Thomas Jefferson's Farm Book with Commentary and Relevant Extracts from Other Writings* (Charlottesville, Va., 1953), pp. 12–13.

Epilogue

1. Reported in *New York Times,* 6 May 1995.

2. Gail Gehrig, *American Civil Religion: An Assessment* (Storrs, Conn., 1981) p. 2. Gehrig is summarizing a model proposed in 1960 by Robert N. Bellah, perhaps the most influential modern writer on this subject.

3. Bellah, *The Broken Covenant: American Civil Religion in Times of Trial* (New York, 1975). By this time, Bellah was pessimistic about his subject: "Today the American civil religion is an empty and broken shell" (*Broken Covenant,* p. 142). Twenty years later, however, the American civil religion is palpably still there, and a force in the land. Soon, perhaps, to be more than *one* force.

4. Norman Mailer, "Evil in the Room," in *Life,* Vol. 13–14, 1972. Like Bellah, around the same time, Mailer was pessimistic about the future of American civil religion. Both writers were reflecting the mood of national despondency in the immediate wake of the lost war in Vietnam. The Reagan years saw the recovery of the American civil religion.

5. Smylie, "The President as Prophet, Priest, King," in *Civil Religion in America: Manifest Destiny and Historical Judgement: A Symposium,* ed. Harry F. Booth et al., presented as part of the two hundredth anniversary celebration of Dickinson College, Carlisle, Pennsylvania (April 12–14, 1973).

6. Richard V. Pierard and Robert D. Lunder, *Civil Religion and the Presidency* (Grand Rapids, Mich., 1988).

7. Carl Lotus Becker, *The Declaration of Independence: A Study in the History of Political Ideas* (New York ed., 1922 and 1940), p. 142, n. 1.

8. Smylie, "The President as Prophet, Priest, King," already cited. Smylie is not a believer in the identification suggested in his title, which had been proposed by other writers on the American civil religion.

9. *The Works of John C. Calhoun* (New York, 1854), pp. 352–59.

10. Quoted in Merrill D. Peterson, *The Jefferson Image in the American Mind* (New York, 1960), p. 162.

11. Ibid., p. 163.

12. See Joseph J. Ellis, "American Sphinx: The Contradictions of Thomas Jefferson," in *Civilization* (November/December 1994), p. 38. I am indebted for this reference to Mr. Darin Waters of North Carolina.

13. *Reflections,* Penguin Classics ed., pp. 89–91.

14. Bellah, *Broken Covenant,* p. 123.

15. Smylie, "The President . . . ," p. 93.

16. Merrill D. Peterson says that the Georgian Populist leader Tom Watson, in the early twentieth century, "through his magazine *The Jeffersonian* transmuted his class hatred into sectional and racial hatred of the most vicious sort" (*The Jefferson Image,* p. 258).

17. Quoted in Peterson, *Jefferson Image,* p. 258.

18. Becker, *Declaration of Independence,* p. 208.

19. *On the Eve of the Millennium* (Free Press, New York, 1996).

20. Consider Dumas Malone's handling of the "Adam and Eve letter" (above, chapter 4, n. 51).

APPENDIX

1. John A. Bear, Jr., *The Hemings Family of Monticello* (Ivy, Va., 1980), p. 3.

2. Dabney, *The Jefferson Scandals: A Rebuttal* (New York, 1983), pp. 26–27. Rebutting scandals, in relation to eighteenth-century Virginia, can be a tricky business.

3. The *Pike County Republican* story is reproduced in full as Addenda No. 1 in Judith P. Justus, *Down from the Mountain: The Overt History of the Hemings family* (Perrysburg, Ohio, 1990), pp. 137–41.

4. Dabney, *Jefferson Scandals,* p. 49.

5. Ibid., p. 49.

SOURCES

B y far the most important source for this book consists of the writings of Thomas Jefferson himself. I have relied mainly on the Princeton Edition of *The Papers of Thomas Jefferson* (edited by Julian P. Boyd and others), twenty-four volumes of which had appeared at the time when I was writing. For the period not yet covered by the Princeton Edition—that is, from the summer of 1793 on—I have used the early-twentieth-century edition of Paul Leicester Ford, *The Works of Thomas Jefferson,* in twelve volumes (New York, 1904–5 [Federal Edition).

It is appropriate to acknowledge here my deep indebtedness to the scholarly work of Julian P. Boyd, who edited the first twenty volumes of the Princeton Edition, and in particular to his superb Editorial Notes, which illuminate various complex episodes in which Jefferson was involved. Three of these shed much light on Jefferson and the French Revolution (See *TLA,* pp. 88–112, 119–21). I have ventured, in some instances, to take issue with Boyd's *interpretation* of certain issues, for reasons set out in my book (*TLA,* pp. 95–100). But it is characteristic of Boyd's integrity as a scholar that he himself supplies much of the material on which a challenge to certain of his interpretations can be based (*TLA,* pp. 100–101).

Next to Jefferson's own writings, the most important primary source for this particular monograph consists of the dispatches of French diplomatic representatives in the United States during the period of the French Revolution: principally, Louis Guillaume Otto, Jean-Baptiste Ternant, Charles-Edmond Genet, Pierre Antoine Joseph Fauchet, Pierre-Auguste Adet, and Philippe Joseph Létombe. Most of these despatches, in the original French, are collected in *Annual Report of the American Historical*

Association for the Year 1903, volume 2: *Seventh Report of Historical Manuscripts Commission: Correspondence of the French Ministers to the United States, 1791–1797.* This collection also contains Instructions issued by various French Revolutionary authorities to their Ministers in the United States. (Including one nominee who was never in fact accredited as Minister: Michelange Mangourit). These dispatches are often instructive with regard to Jefferson and the French Revolution. They are also often quite entertaining.

Other important primary sources used are the collected papers of Benjamin Franklin, Alexander Hamilton, James Madison, James Monroe, and George Washington, and Gouverneur Morris's *Diary of the French Revolution.* Editions used are cited in the footnotes to the chapters.

A minor but interesting primary source is Moreau de St. Méry, *American Journey* (1783–88; see chap. 6, n. 9).

Secondary works of which I have been able to make use are identified in the text and cited in the footnotes. It will be noted that the works used make up only a small proportion of the enormous literature about Thomas Jefferson. The reason for this is that the topic of Jefferson and the French Revolution is not one that has engaged the attention of Jefferson scholars to any great extent or in any great depth. Some of these scholars—as it seems to me—have been less interested in investigating Jefferson's relation to the French Revolution than in playing it down or covering it up (see chapter 4). For Dumas Malone's six-volume biography, and my use of it and reservations about it, see the Foreword and the notes to chapter 1, and the text and notes of *TLA* passim.

Secondary works which I have found particularly useful are listed below. I am listing here authors only and general subject matter. Full titles of works will be found in the notes to the individual chapters.

Prelude: Claude-Anne Lopez, on Franklin and the ladies of Paris.

Chapter 1: Judith Poss Pulley, on Thomas Jefferson at the Court of Versailles (unpublished dissertation).

Chapter 2: Louis Gottschalk on Lafayette; R. R. Palmer on Jefferson in Bourbon France; Bernard Bailyn, essay on Thomas Jefferson; Patrick Thierry, on Paine, Burke, and the *Rights of Man.*

Chapter 3: C. H. Ambler, David McConnell, Harry Ammon, Noble E. Cunningham, and Norman K. Risjord on Virginian politics; Stanley Elkins and Eric McKittrick, *The French Revolution in America,* in *The Age of Federalism;* Louis Martin Sears, on George Washington and the French Revolution; Merrill D. Peterson, *Thomas Jefferson and the New*

Nation and *Adams and Jefferson: A Revolutionary Dialogue*; Philip M. Marsh on John Beckley.

Chapter 4: Meade Minnigerode, on Jefferson and Genet (also quoted in chapter 5). Rachel Klein on South Carolina and the French Revolution; Samuel E. Forman on Freneau; Frank Mott on Jefferson and the press.

Chapter 5: Harry Ammon and Maude Woodfin on Genet; Alexander de Conde on entangling alliances; Samuel Flagg Bemis on Jefferson as Secretary of State.

Chapter 6: William Miller on the Democratic Societies and the Whiskey Rebellion; James D. Tagg on B. F. Bache and George Washington.

Chapter 7: Robert McColley, Winthrop Jordan, William Cohen, David Brion Davis, Edmund S. Morgan, and John Chester Miller on Jefferson and slavery; Thomas Ott, Alfred N. Hunt, Michael Zuckerman, and Tim Matthewson on Haiti. The University of Virginia Press collection *Jefferson Legacies* (edited by Peter Onuf).

Epilogue: Gail Gehrig, Robert N. Bellah, Norman Mailer, James H. Smylie, Richard V. Pierard, and Robert D. Lunder on the American civil religion; Carl Lotus Becker on the Declaration of Independence; Merrill D. Peterson on the Jefferson Image; Joseph J. Ellis on Jefferson's contradictions.

Appendix: Virginius Dabney on Jefferson scandals; John A. Bear, Jr., and Judith P. Justus on the Hemings family.

My use of secondary sources is more copious in chapter 7 and the Epilogue than in the main body of the book (Prelude and first six chapters). Chapter 7 and the Epilogue are dealing with topics which are related to, but not part of, my basic subject matter: Jefferson and the French Revolution. They are also dealing with periods both before and after the period I had set out to study: that of the French Revolution. For my purposes, in these two sections of my book, recourse to a number of secondary sources seemed advisable. But for the main body of the book, dealing directly with Thomas Jefferson and the French Revolution, I have relied mainly on the primary sources referred to in the opening paragraphs of this note, and cited in the footnotes to the first six chapters.

INDEX